SHOGUN

THE LIFE AND TIMES OF TOKUGAWA IEYASU: JAPAN'S GREATEST RULER

A.L. SADLER

New Foreword by ALEXANDER BENNETT
Foreword by STEPHEN TURNBULL

TUTTLE Publishing

Tokyo | Rutland, Vermont | Singapore

"Books to Span the East and West"

Tuttle Publishing was founded in 1832 in the small New England town of Rutland, Vermont [USA]. Our core values remain as strong today as they were then—to publish best-in-class books which bring people together one page at a time. In 1948, we established a publishing office in Japan—and Tuttle is now a leader in publishing English-language books about the arts, languages and cultures of Asia. The world has become a much smaller place today and Asia's economic and cultural influence has grown. Yet the need for meaningful dialogue and information about this diverse region has never been greater. Over the past seven decades, Tuttle has published thousands of books on subjects ranging from martial arts and paper crafts to language learning and literature—and our talented authors, illustrators, designers and photographers have won many prestigious awards. We welcome you to explore the wealth of information available on Asia at www.tuttlepublishing.com.

Published by Tuttle Publishing, an imprint of Periplus Editions (HK) Ltd.

www.tuttlepublishing.com

Copyright © 1937 *by George Allen & Unwin Ltd*

First edition, 1937, by George Allen & Unwin Ltd., London

First Tuttle edition, 1978
This edition 2022

LCCN 2022931885

ISBN: 978-4-8053-1717-4

25 24 23 22
10 9 8 7 6 5 4 3 2 1   2204VP

Printed in Malaysia

Distributed by
North America, Latin America & Europe
Tuttle Publishing
364 Innovation Drive, North Clarendon
VT 05759-9436 U.S.A.
Tel: 1 (802) 773-8930
Fax: 1 (802) 773-6993
info@tuttlepublishing.com
www.tuttlepublishing.com

Japan
Tuttle Publishing
Yaekari Building 3rd Floor
5-4-12 Osaki Shinagawa-ku
Tokyo 141 0032
Tel: (81) 03 5437-0171
Fax: (81) 03 5437-0755
sales@tuttle.co.jp; www.tuttle.co.jp

Asia Pacific
Berkeley Books Pte. Ltd.
3 Kallang Sector #04-01
Singapore 349278
Tel: (65) 6741-2178
Fax: (65) 6741-2179
inquiries@periplus.com.sg
www.tuttlepublishing.com

TUTTLE PUBLISHING® is a registered trademark of Tuttle Publishing, a division of Periplus Editions (HK) Ltd.

CONTENTS

LIST OF ILLUSTRATIONS

PLATES

MAPS

A wise mind will never condemn a man for the extraordinary acts to which he has been forced to save his country. When the safety of the country is at stake there must be no thought for justice or injustice, pity or cruelty, glory or shame. The sole inspiration must proceed from the demands of circumstances.   MACHIAVELLI

NEW FOREWORD

by Alexander Bennett

When I first read this book as an undergraduate studying Japanese history in the early 1990s, plenty of first-rate work had been published on this principal character of Japanese history by then. Sadler's 1937 book could always be found in the bibliographies, a testament to the author's pioneering prowess in the field of Japanese studies.

Arthur Lindsay Sadler was born in London on November 19, 1882. A talented student of languages, he graduated from St. John's College, Oxford, with a Bachelor of Arts in 1908 followed by a master's degree in 1911. Upon graduation, he immediately embarked on a lifechanging journey to Japan, where he was to reside until 1921. For most of his sojourn in Japan he taught English and Latin at the Sixth Higher School in Okayama Prefecture. He married Eva Botan Seymore in 1916 (who was of Japanese and English parentage), and in 1918 he moved to Tokyo to teach at the prestigious Peer's College (Gakushūin University).

Sadler proactively immersed himself in the culture while in Japan. In addition to the language, in which he reached a phenomenally high level of proficiency, he also tried his hand at various cultural pursuits, such as the tea ceremony and kendo. It seems, however, that his main interest was in architecture. In the preface to one of his books, *A Short History of Japanese Architecture* (now published by Tuttle as *Japanese Architecture: A Short History*, 2016) Sadler writes that instead of going to the "Near East" for continued research—as counselled to do by the esteemed Orientalist Dr. C. J. Ball—it was his attraction to Japanese buildings and gardens that took him to Japan. He adds, "And these houses and gardens were certainly no disappointment, but a source of continual pleasure all the time I stayed there—a diversion I regret I have missed since leaving Japan...."

He remained until 1921, after which he left Japan's shores to take up a position as the Chair of Oriental Studies at the University of Sydney in Australia. This post was offered to him following the death of his predecessor, James Murdoch, by the recommendations of none other than the British High Commissioner in Tokyo and the Viceroy of India themselves. As an aside, Murdoch had written the three-volume *A History of Japan*, the first comprehensive history of the country in English, so Sadler had big shoes to fill with his new appointment.

Although Murdoch had been involved in advising the Australian government's Defence Department vis-à-vis Asia, Sadler seemed to have little interest in international politics. He followed his predecessor by teaching Japanese concurrently for a few years at the Royal Military College, but devoted himself mainly to developing lecture content and courses to educate the very small but growing number of students wishing to specialise in Japanese language and culture, as well as "Oriental" history in general.

One of his star students, Joyce Ackroyd, was to become a prominent figure in Japanese studies in Australia. She published a paper on her mentor in which she described him in endearing and eloquent terms.*

> "Professor Sadler was already a legend when I first entered Sydney University in 1936. A large stocky man, he wore an unfashionable broad-brimmed hat with a turned-up rim, English tweeds, and pince-nez that emphasised his quizzical, slightly snobbish air. He exuded the unmistakable aura of the conservative English gentleman." (Ackroyd, p. 49)

Sadler was a prolific writer and published many books of significance throughout his career. The one you have in your hands is *The Maker of Modern Japan: The Life of Tokugawa Ieyasu* (1937). Others include *A Short History of Japanese Architecture* (1941) and *A Short History of Japan* (1946). Among his important translations are *The Heike Monogatari* (1918–21), Okakura Kakuzo's *The Book of Tea: A Japanese Harmony of Art, Culture and the Simple Life* (1932), and my personal favorite, Daidoji Yūzan's classic book on the way of the warrior *Budo Shoshinshū*, which was translated as *The Beginner's Book of Bushido* (1941). There are also publications on other diverse subjects, from Japanese flower arranging to Ise Shrine pilgrimages. Not limited to Japanese, he also translated Sun Tzu's classic treatise on strategy *The Art of War* from Chinese to English.

Although he is referred to now as a Japanologist, Sadler was a different kind of scholar to the specialists of today. In Ackroyd's words again,

> "... unlike today's specialised scholars who are piling assiduously sourced scrap on painfully acquired scrap, he absorbed immense quantities of information by extensive reading of original texts, and from the depth and breadth of his thoroughly internalised knowledge he wrote fascinatingly on Chinese strategy, Japanese architecture, the tea ceremony, Shinto ritual, feudal magnates, the

---

* Elaine McKay & Joyce Ackroyd (1986), "Professor A.L. Sadler", *Asian Studies Association of Australia. Review*, 10:1, pp. 49-53

Emperor Meiji, and scores of other topics, and translated medieval Japanese war-tales and diaries, Noh plays, Confucian texts, modern short stories, and much else." (Ibid. p. 52)

Clearly Sadler was a scholar of varied interests, and he was a protean pioneer who conveyed many aspects of Japanese culture and history to the West. The timing of his publications coincided with an age of urgency to understand Japan and its people. A review of this book published in 1942 sums this sentiment up well.*

"Biographical studies of outstanding figures of Japanese history in Western languages are still very few in number and will continue to be so for years to come. Consequently, an addition which reduces this gap is most desirable. Since the outbreak of war in the Pacific last December, Japanese studies have been receiving greater attention and emphasis than ever before for the very practical reason that for a nation at war, knowing the enemy is one of the first prerequisites to the winning of the war. If we are to properly appraise and understand the forces at work in Japan today, we must go back into her history to find the roots which go deeply into the past."

As for the life and achievements of Tokugawa Ieyasu, countless theses and books have been written on the subject in recent decades. Sadler's book became the standard reference on the subject for many years. Inevitably, however, there are assumptions in this book about Ieyasu's feats that have since been invalidated, or at least are hotly debated. The original title, "The Maker of Modern Japan," for example, is certainly not true in a historiographical sense. Modern Japan designates the post-Meiji period. The publisher has retitled the book as *Shogun: The Life and Times of Tokugawa Ieyasu, Japan's Greatest Ruler*, a much better alternative.

In writing the book, Sadler relied on works by respected Japanese scholars such as Tsuda Sōkichi and Ōmori Kingorō, and heavily on the primary source *Mikawa Go Fudo-ki*. Historical documents and works by Japanese scholars that Sadler referenced typically contain discrepancies, lack references, and distinctions between fact and fiction often lack clarity.

Primary sources are often trusted at face value simply because they were written close to when events described within took place (give or take a century or two!). It should come as no surprise that chroniclers of old were just as prone to disseminating mis- or disinformation as any

* Yanaga Chitoshi, *The Far Eastern Quarterly*, Vol. 1, No. 4 (August, 1942), pp. 401-403.

questionable media outlet today. The *Mikawa Go Fudo-ki*, for example, is very much a pro-Tokugawa text that tends to embellish the clan's greatness and play down any inconvenient truths.

Therefore, establishing the veracity of any given primary source is a perennial duty for historians and is a task that is chipped away at by revisiting and questioning the work of previous generations of scholars. In this sense, Sadler should not be criticized too harshly for any shortcomings in his book. It was a trailblazing contribution to the field, and it provided a starting point for future students of Japan over many decades.

As such, his work is widely regarded as a classic, but that is not to say that it is now irrelevant—far from it. His depiction of Tokugawa Ieyasu makes for fascinating reading. It is a biography that certainly does not give undue reverence to its subject. Instead, he offers a vivid description of both the brilliance and foibles of this giant in Japanese history. It remains a captivating launchpad for understanding the brilliance of Ieyasu and the beginnings of early-modern Japan, and will continue to do so for generations to come.

Alexander Bennett

FOREWORD
by Stephen Turnbull

I first became acquainted with Sadler's *The Maker of Modern Japan: The Life of Shogun Tokugawa Ieyasu*, in Manchester Central Reference Library in 1971. Reference books, particularly ones long out of print, had to be ordered from a catalog and were then brought to one's desk and stamped with the day's date. It says a lot about the level of interest in Japanese history in the early 1970s that the previous date stamp on this book was 1941.

Since then the passage of time has led to this once neglected work becoming regarded as a classic. Its topic is the life of Tokugawa Ieyasu, and although few nowadays would choose as a title "the Maker of Modern Japan" to describe the first Tokugawa Shogun, Sadler's vivid picture of the man who established his family's hegemony is proof enough of his contextual greatness. Yet Sadler's account is no hagiography. Ieyasu's ruthlessness in dealing with his own family and his youthful recklessness on the battlefield, which on at least two occasions came near to robbing Japan of its most successful contemporary leader, are related at length. Above all, Sadler illustrates Ieyasu's political strengths and his diplomatic skills, particularly in dealing with Hideyoshi and his heir.

The weaknesses in the work are those demanded by modern scholarship. The book is uncritical in its use of its restricted sources and almost totally lacking in references. Sadler's account of Nobunaga's victory at Nagashino using arquebusiers divided into three sections, firing in rotation, as "the machine gun and wire entanglements of his day" has become the accepted view of the famous battle, and the notorious final scene depicting the battle in Akira Kurosawa's film *Kagemusha* makes the action look as though the bullets were delivered by machine guns. The reality of the situation is somewhat less dramatic. *Mikawa Go Fudo-ki* (Sadler's source) says that 3,000 arquebusiers were deployed. The more reliable *Shinchō-kōki* has 1,000. Nor need we necessarily conclude from the observation that different squads of arquebusiers fired alternate volleys that this was an early application of the system of rotating volleys. Such a scheme, associated in particular with the military innovations of Maurice of Nassau, required the front rank to discharge their pieces then move to the rear to allow the second rank to do the same, a maneuver known as the counter-march. Yet even the Dutch were to discover that a minimum of six ranks, and preferably ten, were required to keep up a constant fire.

At Nagashino Nobunaga did not possess the resources to mimic machine guns. Many of the arquebusiers he arranged behind the palisades were not his own troops but had been supplied by allies and subordinates a few days before the battle took place. There was therefore no time to drill them in the counter-march. Alternate volleys were certainly delivered, but should be understood as a response to the successive waves of attack launched by the Takeda cavalry under the iron discipline of the five bugyō whom Nobunaga had placed in command of the squads. *Shinchō-kōki* records each of the five attacks, naming the Takeda generals who advanced to the beat of drums and were met by gunfire. *Mikawa Go Fudoki* breaks the action down further, noting that 300 arquebusiers in the sector held by the Okubo brothers faced a charge by 3,000 men under Yamagata Masakage. Interestingly, this is precisely the situation illustrated on the contemporary painted screen of the Battle of Nagashino owned by the Tokugawa Art Museum in Nagoya. Horses are shown falling dead and throwing their riders, classic images of a broken cavalry charge. Yet the Battle of Nagashino still had several hours to run, and from this point onwards the spears and swords of the samurai came into their own. Protected by the long spears of other foot soldiers, whose contribution to the battle was in no way inferior to their arquebus-firing colleagues, Nobunaga's armies fought the Takeda on a battlefield of their own choosing, and Katsuyori was decisively defeated by a skilled general who used a combination of arms to its best advantage.

So has *The Maker of Modern Japan*, renamed for this edition *Shogun: The Life of Tokugawa Ieyasu*, stood the test of time? With the limitations of a lack of comparative sources, and its uncritical acceptance of *Mikawa Go Fudoki*, it still provides a valuable and inspirational starting point for any student of the topic. Sadler's use of language, though florid, conveys a sense of the violence and grandeur of the age. His presentation of the historian Tokutomi's comment on the military prowess of Sasa Narimasa as being akin to a "dried sardine gnashing its teeth," or his reflection on Ieyasu's avoidance of venereal disease, which carried off "to the White Jade Pavilion" (one of Sadler's favorite phrases) so many of his rivals, as "even the spirochete were on his side," sets his subject well in its context. The image of Ieyasu drawing a sword on his deathbed completes a picture of the man who was the maker of Early Modern Japan at the very least, and as the creator of the Tokugawa state, an influence that in so many ways stretches to our modern age.

Stephen Turnbull
Visiting Professor of Japanese Studies
Akita International University

PREFACE

It hardly seems necessary to begin with the usual apology for producing another book on a Japanese subject in this case because Tokugawa Ieyasu is unquestionably one of the greatest men the world has yet seen, while not only is the type of government of which he developed the most perfect example yet known finding increasing favor in the West, but the empire he did so much to build up is becoming of ever greater international significance year by year. In these circumstances it may be convenient for students of Oriental affairs as well as for others interested in the lives of dominating personalities to have access to some of the outstanding facts of his life and character as they are usually presented to his own countrymen. Possibly lack of material available in European languages, leading to the very free use of the imagination, is the partial cause of the great want of accuracy in statements concerning Japanese history in many books that treat of it, and if this volume is of assistance in diminishing this tendency it may not be entirely useless. The fact that Tokugawa Ieyasu is less known to the average well-read person than his contemporary Akbar may be to some extent due to the lack of any account of his life in any European tongue. And that given here is rather introductory than exhaustive, and contains more material from Japanese sources than quotations from the European documents bearing on him and his period.

Had there existed in Japanese a good modern biography of Ieyasu of convenient length it might have been more profitable to translate it, but no suitable one is available. The most interesting treatment of his life by a modern writer is that in the great work of Tokutomi Soho, *History of the Japanese People in Modern Times,* which begins about the time of the birth of Ieyasu and continues the story down to the present day. To it I am greatly indebted, and I have availed myself freely of its monumental learning and critical judgment. No doubt a biography of this kind is somewhat repelling on account of its unfamiliar atmosphere and strange names. As a reviewer recently observed of another work on a Japanese theme, it unfortunately had so many Japanese names in it. But this is now a world in which it may be advisable to get used to them, for unquestionably people of the land of Nippon will always have Japanese names. In fact, unlike ourselves and our European neighbors their names are entirely Japanese, and very rarely, indeed, drawn from any foreign source, except where the exigencies of the script makes the pronunciation Sinico-Japanese. It may be of assistance to repeat that the vowels are as in Italian and the consonants as in English. When Ieyasu's name was written in our script in his own day in his letter to King James "Minnamoto no Yei ye yass," it was nearer to the actual sound than is the ordinary way of representing it now, for final *u* is practically silent in Japanese, and would be quite correct if the second syllable were omitted altogether. I have followed Brinkley in using the spelling with a single *y* as being the more concise.

In recent years the names of Tokugawa and Matsudaira have no doubt become more widely known outside their homeland owing to two very eminent bearers of them, Tokugawa Iemasa, now Japanese Ambassador at Istambul, seventeenth heir to Ieyasu in the main house, and Matsudaira Tsuneo, Ambassador at the Court of St. James, of the branch house of the lords of Aizu, descended from his grandson Masayuki, scholar and philosopher as well as feudal lord, both of whom have carried on the distinguished tradition of their family as diplomatic representatives both in Europe and America.

All names are in the normal Japanese order, surname first and given name second. In this period, as up to 1870, peasants and artisans had no surname, but might acquire one by becoming military men, for it was only after the days of Ieyasu that the samurai became a fixed caste, and in the sixteenth century as in the twentieth not only a baton but a halo were within the reach of any man of genius.

This book is not peppered with references, for they would be quite useless except to those who read Japanese historical texts, and for them the list of sources at the end will, I think, be sufficient. I wish to thank Miss Githa Conolly, B.A., for assistance in the preparation of the manuscript.

A. L. S.

The Tokugawa crest of three hollyhock leaves (Aoi-no-Go-mon), only used by the Shogun and the descendants of the sons of Ieyasu (Go-Kamon) and in a modified form by the various Matsudaira families, is said to have been adopted by Hirotada, the father of Ieyasu, because cakes were served to him on three of these leaves by one of the Honda houses when he returned after a victory. The Hondas have for their cognizance the same group of three hollyhock leaves but elevated on the stalk. Hence perhaps the punning story that Ieyasu admired the Honda crest, and when that warrior naturally asked him to take it as his own he replied, "O ha-bakari" ("The leaves only"), an expression which, divided differently "o habakari," means "by your leave." And the hollyhock which bows its head to the sun is regarded as a symbol of the loyal retainer who dutifully obeys his lord.

INTRODUCTION

IN the course of Japanese medieval and modern history there have been five great military administrators who by common consent stand out above the rest, numerous though the type has always been. Of these, two lived in the twelfth century, Taira Kiyomori and Minamoto Yoritomo, the latter the founder of the institution of the Shogunate or Hereditary Military Dictatorship, while the other three, Oda Nobunaga, Toyotomi Hideyoshi, and Tokugawa Ieyasu, were contemporary in the sixteenth. The last of these, with whose life this book deals, may well be described as the perfecter of the system inaugurated by Yoritomo, for after his death in 1616 it continued to be carried on according to his plans by his descendants till 1868, when the administration of the Empire ceased to be a Tokugawa family affair, but became entrusted to officials chosen from all the people by examination and selection.

And not only did Tokugawa Ieyasu found a dynasty of rulers and organize a system of government, but he rounded off his achievement by contriving before his death to arrange for his deification afterwards, and to set in train the re-orientation of the religion of the country so that he would take the premier place in it.

As the Great Gongen, a Shinto-Buddhist reincarnation, he played an imposing divine part, and there is no town in Japan where his shrine in this capacity is not to be found, while his headquarters is the world-famous resort of Nikko, in the province of Shimozuke, where embowered in giant cryptomerias stands that perfectly situated and gorgeous mausoleum of which the late Lord Curzon observed that "no sovereigns, not even the Pharaohs of Egypt, had more glorious and worthy sepulchres." And with it, too, commenced a new style of architecture to be perpetuated in the hardly less resplendent shrines of his successors, the lords of Edo, whose two groups of mausolea are with the mighty castle they tenanted in life, still the glory of the modern capital of Tokyo.

And this man, who rose to be undisputed Lord of the Empire and who for nearly three hundred years was the tutelary deity of his successors, who continued this dominion and of all who owed allegiance to them, was in a sense a self-made phenomenon. Born in a time of national strife in the family of a noble of small territory though ancient birth, and surrounded by ambitious, energetic, and unscrupulous rivals, he had to make his reputations as a first-class fighting man, and so become welcomed as an ally by Oda Nobunaga, then well on his way toward grasping the supreme power himself. Calm, capable, and entirely fearless, and with a conscientious objection to revealing any brilliance, Ieyasu grew stronger and stronger, and when Nobunaga was assassinated—a not uncommon fate in those times—and Hideyoshi, the talented foot-soldier who had risen to be his Chief of Staff, stepped into his place as Dictator, by a combination of diplomatic and military skill he still contrived to gain ground and increase his influence. He was a man who could put his eldest son to death to keep political faith with Nobunaga, and swallow his pride to do quite a menial service to disarm the jealousy of the upstart Hideyoshi. And when this undoubted genius died at the comparatively early age of sixty-two, Ieyasu deliberately brought all opposition to a head and crushed it in a decisive battle, after which he was able to make himself Shogun, a thing neither of his predecessors had been able to do since they did not come of the proper family. For it had become just as strong a convention that the Shogun could only be of the Minamoto clan as it was that the Kampaku, the Mayor of the Palace, must be of the lineage of the great Kamatari, the founder of the Fujiwara house.

The remaining fifteen years of his life he devoted to organizing the country, making laws for it, and arranging for its education in the system of Confucian ethics he considered most suitable to ensure its stability and exterminating the remaining heirs of Hideyoshi. He also found time to encourage trade with Europe, and to acquire some knowledge of the politics of the Occident, playing off the Protestant powers of Holland and England against Catholic Spain and Portugal, and above all to educate his son Hidetada to continue his work by retiring from the office of Shogun and letting him carry it on for more than twelve years under his supervision. From the Englishman, Will Adams, he extracted information on maritime affairs and politics, while he had a Jesuit secretary to act as *advocatus diaboli*. And all the while he was never too busy to listen to lectures on his favorite Confucian studies, or to superintend the collection and publication of books that dealt with them or with military matters, history, or economics. So keen, indeed, was he on publishing that he was engrossed in it right up to the very last days of his life. His interest in finance was no less, and he supervised in its minutest details the expenditure of his large household.

Moreover, between the age of eighteen and sixty-three he contrived to beget from judiciously chosen consorts some twelve or more children, nine of them sons, a very necessary provision for the family system on which his government depended, and for want of which his rival Hideyoshi had been so severely handicapped.

All these things accomplished, he died peaceably and reasonably contentedly in his bed at the age of seventy-five, characteristically occupied to the last in superintending the printing of a political textbook and arranging the details of his coming deification. Himself a rationalist like most of the intelligent of his country, he saw that there was a need of gods for the new era, and stepped in to supply the deficiency. Religion he evidently thought good as a solace for the worker and for those not advanced enough to practice ethics for its own sake, but under secular government supervision so that the priest, whom he regarded as a non-producer like the actor and the courtesan, might not get too much control. And in this he was not in any way peculiar, for if it be a sign of efficiency in an aristocracy that it keeps its priests in order, that of Japan has seldom been found wanting. When one considers Henry VIII of England chaffering with the Pope about his divorce and then petulantly repudiating him and his pretensions here is indeed a contrast, for it is difficult to think of these Japanese autocrats consulting anyone, especially a Buddhist priest, about domestic matters of such a kind. When Hideyoshi went to the Daigo fête at the Buddhist temple of that name he took all his six or seven consorts with him in state, and the abbots and archbishops were highly honored to be allowed to be humble members of the party. So none kept his clerics more in their place than Ieyasu, or used them more efficiently. It was their business to carry out his orders and to assist his Government in various ways, and if they did so they were allowed to live in peace and carry on their aesthetic and ceremonial business at a moderate profit. But any attempt to usurp the power of the military authorities was put down with an iron hand, as we see in the case of the quelling of the Monto sect. This is the sect that has so often been likened to institutional Christianity in the West and is much like it in that it relies on the help of an external savior and the repetition of formula in a way quite contrary to the "self-help" doctrine of the earlier Buddhism. It was and still is skilful and assiduous in propaganda, and financially well organized, and its easy salvation is attractive to those too tired or too lazy to think. At the present day it does not hesitate to imitate Christian hymns or other advertising methods to increase its influence, and has easily the largest number of temples. It was the most dangerous menace that Ieyasu had to encounter apart from the rival nobles. It long defied Nobunaga, and needed the subtlety of Hideyoshi to draw its fangs and use it. Ieyasu defeated it militarily, and divided and weakened its ruling family, for though popular in its appeal this sect is the appendage of a noble house and has that very Japanese institution a hereditary Buddhist Pope, or rather, after Ieyasu had dealt with it, a pair of them. And impotent enough they remained during the Tokugawa era, but it must not be forgotten that it is this Amida sect that during the same period came to dominate quite absolutely the whole land of Tibet.

Ieyasu had as it were a long-lived Wolsey and two Cromwells in the persons of Tenkai and the two Hondas, none of whom he had any reason to suspect or remove. All three outlived him, the former not dying till 1644, by which time he had been able to establish the shrines of Nikko, of which he was Warden and Abbot, and also the Kwaneiji of Ueno, the Tokugawa temple that corresponded to Hieizan by the capital. So he had ample time to arrange all details of the complete deification of Ieyasu, which was his life's work.

Ieyasu never put anyone to death from personal motives of any kind, so that his friends and retainers had the greatest confidence in him and were certain of consideration if they served him well. And he was far too shrewd to be taken in by slander and so approachable that he heard all sides of a case. On the other hand, he never spared any of his own family or relations if their conduct endangered the family solidarity and supremacy.

Taking all in all, it was he who made the system under which Japan as we know it was forged into shape. The material was there, and the institutions and the culture, but they were not effectively harmonized and made to interpenetrate and blend until about the middle of the seventeenth century.

The sixteenth century was one that produced great autocrats everywhere. It was the age of Henry VIII and Elizabeth, Francis I, Akbar, Ivan the Terrible, and Suleyman the Magnificent, and a time in which even the Pope was a militarist, but among them all, with the possible exception of Akbar, there was probably none who blended the qualities of first-class military commander and strategist and equally consummate statesman and administrator as did Tokugawa Ieyasu.

It seems likely that the year of his birth, 1542, in which year Akbar and Mary Queen of Scots also saw the light, was that in which the first Europeans reached Japan, and though the early contacts with them were dealt with by his predecessors Nobunaga and Hideyoshi, yet it was Ieyasu and his son and grandson, acting on the principles he laid down, who finally disposed of the problems they created.

The Portuguese and Spaniards who came first, and between whom the New World had been divided by a Papal Bull, may have expected to find in Japan a people similar to those they encountered in India and South America, where their superior armaments, added to their fanatic fervor and gold-seeking enthusiasm, carried all before them. But though, like other unknown lands, Japan had since Marco Polo's day been reputed an El Dorado, when these missionaries and conquistadores arrived there they were confronted by a people not only their superior in military qualities but distinctly their equals in most other things as well. Therefore from first to last they found themselves chiefly used as conveyers of any information on technical or scientific matters that these island people had not yet acquired, while their attempts to implant their religious ideas and customs were adroitly evaded, for none have ever shown themselves more skilful than the Japanese in licking off the bait of knowledge and leaving the hook of fanaticism standing naked.

And these Western ecclesiastics there as elsewhere were by comparison like dogs chained by the leg. The chain may be short and they will be correspondingly fierce, or it may be long and they will be more amiable and free in their maneuvers, but it is always there, and their limitations are as obvious as their mental activity is circumscribed. But Ieyasu, like Nobunaga and Hideyoshi, was trained in the atmosphere of Zen philosophy with slight regard for written texts or the literal value of words, so that his far wider horizon of thought would have inspired him with little respect for their emphatically enunciated dogmas even if he had had much admiration for them in other directions. It is even conceivable that he may have wondered why they did not keep a globe at the Vatican, for then might have been avoided the clashing of Portuguese and Spanish interests which took place when these nationals met face to face in Japan, after having started off in opposite directions from Europe.

And speaking of the relations between the Pope and his Church and the Tokugawas, it is interesting to note that it was the action of Pepin, Mayor of the Palace to the Merovingians, that made the Pope a temporal sovereign, and that the giving of the Papal States to the head of the Roman Church was the reward for the decision of the Pontiff that it was correct for Pepin to assume the nominal title of King and dethrone the Merovingian sovereign since he already possessed the actual power. It was just this that the Japanese Shogun never thought of doing, for to him the Mikado was more like the deity than his representative, and the European kings never thought of abolishing the Papacy. Japanese have always objected to the God in the skies owing to the tendency to arrogance of his representatives and interpreters on earth, and so the Government has always had a Commissioner for Religions, whose function it is to keep all non-national superstitions in their proper place. They may perhaps be allowed to be to some extent an opiate for the people but not for the rulers.

The popular view of Ieyasu as shown in the well-known picture of him sitting eating the rice-cake that Nobunaga and Hideyoshi between them have made depicts him as a fortunate figure into whose mouth the ripe fruit of other men's labor fell. And lucky he sometimes was, but rather more one who made his own luck. For without his assistance neither Nobunaga nor Hideyoshi would have been able to overcome their enemies so quickly, and if he had thrown in his lot with these powerful opponents the outcome would certainly have been different. He was favored to some extent by fortune, however, for by the victory of Nobunaga he was rid of the menace of Imagawa, while by the treachery of Akechi Mitsuhide he was relieved of the pressure of Nobunaga. Takeda Shingen and Uesugi Kenshin were considerate enough to expend most of their efforts fighting each other, and then to die when their deaths were most convenient for him, while the not too long life of Hideyoshi delivered into his expectant grasp all the fruit of what the genius of the Taiko had achieved, and the death at a comparatively early age of the great lords who might have supported Hideyori out of loyalty to his father made it comparatively easy for him to extirpate the house of Toyotomi.

And after Hideyoshi's death it is obvious that Ieyasu was his natural successor. The Taiko's desperate efforts to ensure the succession for his son Hideyori were bound to be unsuccessful, but he seems to have been so blinded by parental feeling as not to see it. Even had Ieyasu been a self-sacrificing saint and tried to hand over the country to Hideyori, it would not have been easy in view of the factions and jealousies that would probably have been quite beyond such a youth and his mother to overcome. And Ieyasu was by temperament no such altruist. Had he been he would have indeed been unique in his age when even the Buddhist clergy were acquisitive.

But the way in which he snatched the Empire from the youthful Hideyori has not gone to improve his reputation with posterity, and on the other hand it has tended to idealize the house of Toyotomi. Some consider that his house would have come to the top anyhow, without such methods, and if so his unscrupulous action was an unnecessary blot on his reputation. But this want of scruple was part of the man and of the period, and it is not to be wondered at that he should wish to see his family firmly established as lords of a peaceful realm before he died. And this he did see, and so died happy and contented. No historical figure seems to have had a more peaceful parting. Could he have been sure of living till ninety like his son Tadateru, he might have chosen to act differently, but though he is described as one who "waited for the cuckoo to sing" instead of killing it if it didn't like Nobunaga, or coaxing it to do so like Hideyoshi, there came a time when even he could not afford to wait, and that though patience was the quality he set most store by.

But in the earlier period especially a considerable element in his success was the capacity to put up with anything when convinced that it was good. With all his reputation for rectitude he was infinitely adaptable, for this rectitude of his was a quality that always accommodated itself to the needs of the time and occasion. And there is almost no example of his being swayed by his emotions. So though his natural inflexibility seemed almost superhuman, yet at times he could, if he thought it advisable, be just as consistently pliant and yielding. And in accordance with his maxim of realizing one's limitations he never trusted to one string but always took care to have an ally. When he fought Nobunaga it was Imagawa and when he opposed Takeda it was Nobunaga, and when he faced Hideyoshi he was supported by Hojo. And the most unsleeping vigilance and ceaseless energy underlay his success in these schemes. For the foundations of the Tokugawa supremacy rested more on this diplomatic skill than on any force of arms. When others were confident of their ground Ieyasu was always suspicious and alert, so that while shaking hands with Hideyoshi he was meditating a closer alliance with Hojo, though at the same time none was more convinced than this "First Warrior of the Coastland" that his supple diplomacy needed the support of a well-prepared and efficient striking force backed by the most resolute and fearless determination.

The unfavorable view taken of his character by some of his countrymen is exemplified by such a writer as Oike, who is the champion of Ishida as a patriot, and expresses surprise and regret that fate singled out to be the unifier of the Empire one whose ways were not in accordance with the loftiest ideals known to the Chinese classical writers. "Ieyasu," says he, "bereft of all compassion and good faith, stirred up a revolt and took advantage of a widow and an orphan to seize the supreme power and to steal a large territory for himself in so doing. And not only did he live to a green old age, but he handed down his dominion to his descendants, who continued to hold it for nearly three centuries, and though when they were able to do so no longer they handed it over to the rightful sovereign, they still enjoy wealth, dignity, and honor. And this in spite of the words of the sages that providence favors only the virtuous. Truly if we think virtue ought to be rewarded and crookedness to be punished, it is difficult to write history with any sympathy for an old thief like this who does things that few could bear to do, and carries it off quite shamelessly." But this judgment seems slightly exaggerated, for Ieyasu did not do anything in the unscrupulous way that his neighbors, Oda, Takeda, Saito, Fukushima, Uesugi, and others had not done or would not do, while compared with such a character as Matsunaga Hisahide is represented to have been by his contemporaries he was distinctly on the righteous side. But the virtues desirable in the ordinary farmer or bourgeois are hardly of much use to a military dictator, and the fact was that the time was ripe for the centralization of the administration towards which much had been accomplished by Nobunaga and Hideyoshi, and that Ieyasu was there to carry on the work. And it is open to question whether, as this commentator asserts, he could have done it as effectively, his environment being what it was, if he had been less tenacious or disingenuous. And, after all, Yodo was only one of several widows, and not the main one at that, while it is by no means absolutely certain that Hideyori was Hideyoshi's orphan. Ieyasu may have been a less lovable personality than Hideyoshi, though circumstances allowed him to be more kindly than Nobunaga, but probably he would compare quite favorably with the autocrats of his period in other countries. Superstition and fear and disease-bred inferiority feeling did not make him put to death his consorts and best counselors as they did Henry VIII and Suleyman the Magnificent; neither did sentimentalism lead him to spare rebellious children after the manner of Akbar.

His success was the result of his great self-control, lack of blind egoism, and shrewd rational insight into human nature allied with a powerful physique and a mind absolutely devoid of fear of anything either seen or unseen, a combination not often found even in autocrats. His was an extraordinarily well-balanced and cautious mind, everlastingly curious and critical and impartial, overlooking nothing that might be useful, and never taking for granted the superiority of its own conclusions.

He was a very perfect specimen of a type that Japanese nationality and training tends to produce, and if some of his qualities are attributed to a compensation for the hardships of his youth, it must not be forgotten that these were only relative and that on the other hand he was a fully fledged general long before he was twenty, with very wide scope for initiative and responsibility. Had he not been born with great powers he could hardly have been able to take advantage of the opportunities offered to him, and though no doubt many were tired of war and inclined to wish for unification and peace, there were not a few who would have liked to be the one to impose it, several of them figures of conspicuous ability.

In an endocrine study of Napoleon, Berman remarks: "His intellect was mathematical, logical and rational, and remarkable for a prodigious memory. Such an intellect is the product of an extraordinary anti-pitui-

tary. That he never permitted feeling to interfere with the dictates of his
judgment, a quality that rendered him the most unscrupulous careerist
in history, must be put down to an insufficiency of post-pituitary....All
women were to him *filles de joie*. Sexual rather than social attractions
in women appealed to him. He was never in love, never possessed of
permanent affection or tenderness for any woman."[*] This description
is to a certain extent not inapplicable to Ieyasu, and the two have bull-
necked corpulence in common as well, another postpituitary quality,
found, it seems, in very many of these born supermen.

Since there may be some to whom the position and functions of
the Shogun in Japan are not very well known, a short explanation may
not be out of place. The word Shogun means "general" or "army commander," since "sho" means "lead" and "gun" "army." And it is still
in use in that sense in a generic way, though the more ordinary word
is "Taisho" or "Great Leader," to distinguish it from the Middle and
Lesser leaders, the Lieutenant- and Major-Generals. Probably the words
Marshal or Constable conveyed much the same meaning in Europe,
though Imperator is exactly the translation of Shogun, and just as this
officer, when he came to command more than the army, gave Europe
a new word for its sovereigns, so also the expression "Shogun" came to
mean no ordinary general. In ancient days in Japan the Emishi or Ainu,
the people who correspond to the Picts and Scots and Welsh of England, were a similar menace. In very early times the Mikado or Sumera
Mikoto, the August Sovereign himself, or one of his sons in his stead,
used to go forth and chastise them, but later on they thought it better
to send a professional soldier to do it, giving him a Sword of Commission as a symbol to be kept until the task was accomplished, when it was
returned to the Throne.

The best known of these "Barbarian-Quelling Great Generals" was
one Tamura Maro, whom the Mikado Kwammu ordered to subdue
the Emishi of Mutsu at the end of the eighth century, and he, like all
the early Shoguns, gave up his authority and surrendered his sword of
commission when this campaign was ended.

It was not until the twelfth century, when the two rival clans of the
military class, the Taira and Minamoto, whose official business it was
to fight the battles of the Government, espoused the cause of two opposing branches of the Imperial House and fought each other that the
leader of the victorious clan, Minamoto Yoritomo, proceeded to cause
himself to receive from the Sovereign a perpetual commission, and one
that specified him as chief of the military governors and tax administra-

---

[*] *The Glands Regulating Personality.*

tors, whom he proceeded to place in all the provinces of the Empire. He thus became Lord High Constable and Lord Chancellor, and Chancellor of the Exchequer, controlling the military, legislative, and financial branches of the Government, and leaving nothing at all for the Kambaku and other Ministers and Court officials to do but to supervise and perform ritual and ceremonial functions and to confer titles.

The Kambaku was an official who might be said to be inside the Imperial Court what the Shogun was outside it. When the Sovereign himself administered a Chief Minister was necessary, and he was naturally the chief of the most powerful courtier family, this being since the seventh century the Fujiwara. That he should be Regent when the Mikado was a minor was inevitable, and so rose the device of keeping him one, but to make assurance doubly sure, in course of time the office of Sessho-Kambaku, or Regent for a Mikado whether minor or adult, was instituted, and continued until 1868, though the Shogunate rendered it merely a title. Below it there was also the Dajo-daijin, or President of the Council of State, a title also granted to many Shoguns as an honor.

And as the office of Kambaku and of Minister of the Left and Right and so on in the Imperial Court had long been hereditary in the Fujiwara family even as the sovereignty and the Three Sacred Treasures had been in the Imperial family, so did the function of Shogun become in the Minamoto family. But the hereditary principle did not necessarily include primogeniture, about which there was no particular bigotry, since seniority qualified by adoption and plurality of consorts supplied all that was needed.

Immediately after Yoritomo a curious modification took place, for as no males were left in his direct line owing to mutual assassination, the family of his wife, who was a Hōjō, carried on the administration under the title of Regent, and did so most ably, while Imperial Princes were elected Shogun. An Imperial Prince would count as a kind of super-Minamoto, because this name was given to younger sons of Emperors when they became subjects and undertook administrative or military work in the provinces or on the frontiers. The difference therefore between the Court nobility, who were largely similarly descended, and these military families was one of function and locality rather than of blood, and we find in the time of Yoritomo a branch of the Fujiwara that lived and administered in the province of Mutsu in the north that was as hard and energetic as any Taira or Minamoto. Since the Taira were exterminated both on land and sea by Yoritomo, they cease to be a factor in affairs until the sixteenth century, when the clan is heard of again in the person of Oda Nobunaga, who was, or was alleged to be, of that house. Hideyoshi, too, who belonged to no clan, seems to have borrowed it from his lord, as was the way of the time, for he is addressed by the Emperor of China as Taira Hideyoshi. So neither Nobunaga nor Hideyoshi could become Shogun, masters of the Empire though they were, the former being styled Vice-Shogun and the latter Kambaku, for Court conventions were more easily flouted than military ones, since the indignation of courtiers could have no practical consequences.

The rule of the Hōjō Regents was a good one on the whole, and lasted for more than a century before it fell owing to the feebleness of the last of them, and there ensued a short restoration of power to the Throne under the Mikado Go-Daigo, an able and energetic sovereign, which only continued for three years, but quite long enough to convince the warrior class that the accession to power under it of Court Nobles and Ecclesiastics and other civilians was neither profitable nor pleasant. This restoration was brought about by the loyalist soldiers Kusunoki Masashige and Nitta Yoshisada, assisted at first by Ashikaga Takauji but afterwards opposed by him when he realized that it would not be in his own interests.

Ashikaga and Nitta were both branches of the Minamoto, and it was Takauji, a fearless and unscrupulous intriguer, who set up the next dynasty of Shoguns, while Yoshisada and Masashige were killed.

The Sovereign Go-Daigo said to Nitta Yoshisada, "I profoundly praise your loyal services. My wish is to pacify the country with the aid of your family, but Heaven has not yet vouchsafed its aid. Therefore I make peace for the moment and bide my time....." That night Yoshisada prayed at the shrine of Hiyoshi, "Look down on my loyalty and help me to perform my journey safely so that I may raise an army to destroy the insurgents. If that is not to be, let one of my descendants achieve my aim." Two hundred and six years later there was born in Mikawa of the stock of Yoshisada one of the greatest generals, and altogether the greatest ruler that Japan has ever produced, Minamoto Ieyasu. Heaven answered Yoshisada's prayer tardily but signally.[*]

And Ieyasu did more than pray for victory. He seems to have acted on the Japanese maxim "Work is better than prayer," to a greater extent than his eminent ancestor. On one occasion certainly he is said to have prayed for victory at Atsuta shrine, and to have told his men that the deity had informed him that he would win if the coins that he was bidden to throw down should come up heads. This happened sure enough, for Ieyasu had ensured it by sticking together a number of coins head outward "for the benefit of his superstitious soldiers." But whether there then existed any coins that could have been so stuck together, or whether this method of decision was then known, is doubtful, and more likely the story is merely a later tribute to the cunning of the old Gongen of the type likely to be told by public storytellers.

---

[*] Brinkley: *History of Japan*.

But Takauji could not make his capital at Kamakura in the east as Yoritomo had done because the struggle between the two branches of the Imperial House still continued, for Go-Daigo escaped from Kyoto and made his Court in the hills of Yoshino, therefore called the Southern Court. So he made his headquarters in the Muromachi district of Kyoto so that he could protect the Northern Mikado there, who was his nominee. In Kamakura he placed a Governor to look after his interests.

As the struggle between the rival Courts went on for the next sixty years, or rather the attempts of the Southern, which was the more legitimate, to get back to Kyoto, there really existed during this period a Shogunate with Mikado and Shogun complete, the former in this case being made by the latter, and a proper Imperial Court with a Mikado, a retired Mikado who ruled, and an Imperial Prince who commanded the army as in ancient times.

The result of all this was that the Ashikaga Shogunate was always in a state of divided resources, and when there was added the habit of family discord and residence in the most luxurious city of the Empire it is not to be wondered at that it had no hold on the country lords, who soon became practically independent, while the Shoguns, if capable at all, were only so as aesthetes.

And this aestheticism was expensive, and further impoverished everyone, while the offices of Chief Minister and Governor and so on became hereditary again in certain families, who quarreled incessantly about property and precedence. Shoguns like Yoshimitsu, the third of the line, 1367–1408, may be compared in some ways to Charles II of England, elegant and entertaining people who did much for art but were quite irresponsible in other things, and who even came to adopt the same policy of dependence on a foreign country, China, for financial advantage.

The authority of the early Ashikaga Shoguns hardly extended beyond the capital except in the days of the sixth, Yoshinori, who was soon assassinated by one of his ministers, but that of the later ones did not embrace even this, for Kyoto was fought over and destroyed by these families of ministers in their rivalry with one another, quite heedless of the wishes of Mikado or Shogun alike. Of these Shoguns five out of the fifteen were exiled, and two, Yoshinori and Yoshiteru, were assassinated, and this last brings us to Yoshiaki, who was set up again by Nobunaga and with whom the dynasty ended.

Thus this Ashikaga period of two centuries, with its fifteen Shoguns, had been one of great confusion, continuous wars, and indiscriminate treachery, so that it was no wonder that everyone was tired of the lack of any central government and ready to welcome any strong ruler.

Therefore the acts of Nobunaga, Hideyoshi, and Ieyasu can hardly be correctly estimated apart from a realization of these things, and if Nobunaga, for instance, be condemned as an exterminator, it is very clear that there were many who could be dealt with in no other way, so that as a result his successors did not need to be so drastic, and while Ieyasu's methods often appear crooked this was only so from the perspective of the vastly improved standards brought about by his family's good government. For the virtues of loyalty and filial piety that are so outstanding after the beginning of the Tokugawa period were little known or practiced in the age of land-filching and office-grabbing that preceded it, and it is not surprising that the famous word "Bushido" is first found in a work belonging to the early part of the sixteenth century.

The actual administration of the Ashikaga was much the same in detail as that of the Hōjōs, the difference being that the officials who had only been overseers of territory became practically hereditary possessors of it for want of any to prevent them.

As to the relations between the Shoguns and the Mikados who lived in the same capital, they were those of great cordiality bordering at times perhaps on familiarity, and they entertained each other frequently as long as they had any money to do so. During the later years of the period both Courts were dependent on the bounty of the great military houses, and palace and mansion alike were destroyed.

How very different was the Tokugawa Shogunate, even in its most decadent period, may be seen from a vivid glimpse of the relations between the Shogun and the people in the days of Iesada, the thirteenth of the line who ruled from 1853 to 1858.

This is given in a story entitled *Go-narisaki Go-yo no Ie,* which may be freely rendered "The House where the Shogun Rested," which runs thus. It was the custom for the Shogun to go forth once a year with his hawks and bring down a crane, which was immediately sent by express messenger to the Court at Kyoto. There it was divided into halves, and one of these presented to the Mikado, while the other was returned equally expeditiously to Edo to be used in the crane soup, which was always served at the banquet given by the Shogun to the great lords at the New Year festival. And incidentally, since there were so many of these lords the portion of each was so microscopic that in the days of Iemitsu the third Shogun that outspoken old Councilor Okubo Hikozaemon was heard to observe quite audibly, "Crane soup? Well, I've got plenty of this sort of crane in my back yard," whereat, being challenged by His Highness to produce them, he appeared at the Castle next day with a big bundle of vegetables under his arm.

However, on the occasion when he went forth to bring down this very necessary crane the Shogun used to proceed through the city on foot, quite simply attired in a falconer's costume consisting of a cotton jacket and pantaloons with straw sandals on his feet, and attended by a comparatively modest suite of some seventy or eighty officers, a survival of the simplicity of the Divine Founder of his house. And it was the only day in the year on which he was exposed to anything like fatigue or discomfort, for Shoguns were not what they once had been. Still his route through the city was cleared and guarded, and the gates into the side streets were shut and no spectators allowed on the route, as, proceeded by forerunners who fanned away imaginary effluvia with large white fans, Tokugawa Iesada walked through the ward of Asakusa in a dignified manner toward the outskirts of the city. Suddenly, feeling somewhat unwell, for he was a delicate young man, His Highness abruptly left the procession and sat himself down in the front of the nearest house, which happened to be the shop of a certain silk merchant called Joshu-ya. To say that everyone was thunderstruck was to understate the situation considerably. It was, says the narrator, as if the sun had incontinently set in someone's dustbin. Since the days of the Deified First Shogun two hundred and fifty years before, such a thing had never been. In his days it certainly had been, for Ieyasu is said to have sat down in a much less reputable shop-front than that of a silk merchant on at least one occasion. However, one of Iesada's suite retained sufficient self-possession to call for something for his lord to sit upon, and a new mat was produced by a shop assistant and laid down for him, whereupon another official called out, "Now then, mine host, some hot water," and this, too, the master of the establishment soon brought in the first cup that came to hand, hardly knowing what he did. And as he contemplated the mighty Lord of the Empire before whom the greatest Daimyos crouched in humble attitude sitting on his mat and drinking hot water out of an ordinary cup, his confusion was understandable. Though literally he did not contemplate it, for he and all his put their faces as close to the ground as they could and kept them there.

After sitting there half an hour or so to rest the Shogun was sufficiently recovered to resume his journey. But scarcely had he departed before an officer of the ward rushed in to impress upon the master of the shop that the mat on which His Highness had sat must not be lightly treated, so after due consideration a shelf was put up on the same level as, and next to, the God-shelf, and on this the mat and the cup were elevated out of reach of the touch of the common herd.

Moreover, the next day another official called and summoned Joshu-ya to appear before the chief of the ward. This he did in some

SAKAI SAEMON-NO-JO TADATSUGU

trepidation, fearing that he might be liable to punishment for something that he had unwittingly done amiss, and he was greatly relieved and gratified when the dignitary pronounced, "It was most praiseworthy of you to officiate as you did at the Place where His Highness rested," and presented him with an honorarium of five kwan-mon, quite a modest sum of copper money, and a large paper lantern on which was inscribed in big black characters, "O Nari-saki Go-yo no Ie," "August Place where His Highness rested."

But such an honor, like most others of its kind, seemed likely to result in a financial loss to Joshu-ya, for all his friends and neighbors and many others who could properly be said to be neither forthwith presented themselves at his shop to congratulate him and also as a matter of course to drink his health and otherwise refresh themselves, it is unnecessary to say at his expense. It is true that the people of his ward brought him the ceremonial presents usual at such times, but in return he was in duty bound to give them a fine feast, so that in one way or another these disbursements ate and also drank rather a large hole in his reserve funds.

And when all this was over at length he was not allowed to rest entirely in peace, for the officials made a point of calling on him quite often to make sure that proper respect was being paid to the mat and the cup, this latter being now carefully bestowed in a box of paullownia wood specially made for it. These things would in due time be handed down in his family as an heirloom of extreme value, but at present Joshu-ya felt rather in the position of one "with whom the devil has put out his son to nurse."

Not so long after this event Tokugawa Iesada went, perhaps not so unexpectedly, to become "a Guest in the White Jade Pavilion," and Iemochi, the last but one of the line, announced his succession in 1858. He, too, died suddenly after eight years' tenure of the Shogunate while on his way to Kyoto, so suddenly, in fact, that many thought it suspicious though probably it was natural enough, for these later day Generalissimos had become somewhat enervated and delicate from having nothing but ceremonial duties to perform and little contact with anyone but the lady attendants of the Inner Palace.

But just about this time a fire broke out in Edo as often happened, and what is more in Asakusa where Joshu-ya lived, and before long the flames were roaring uncomfortably near his shop. He had little time to do more than put out the precious mat and cup into the fireproof storehouse first of all, and then send off the women of his household to take refuge at his branch shop in the center of the city, before an officer of the ward made his appearance again as he was trying to save a few other

things and ordered him to hang out the lantern he had been given by
the authorities and which it had not so far occurred to him to use. What
was his surprise to see soon afterwards none other than one of the two
Lords Commissioners of Edo, His Excellency Yamaguchi Tsuruga-no-
kami, come hurrying up the street and take his seat on the camp-stool
of command exactly opposite his shop. And in no time some twenty or
thirty of his men had surrounded the house and issued orders to the fire-
men, who at once crowded round and got upon the roof and attacked
the neighboring houses with all their might, pulling them down and
chasing away the sparks so that soon there was a clearing round Joshu-
ya's premises that the flames could not cross. And so effective was this
concentration that though all the rest of the block was burned out the
fire passed over this officially protected spot and left it quite unscathed.

And the sight of this shop standing alone and unharmed under the
protection of the lantern of authority in the midst of the great space
swept clear by the flames made the people gasp at the mighty power
of the Shogunate as it also proved to Joshu-ya that entertaining His
Highness had indeed been profitable after all. And those who know the
Japan of these days will probably reflect that however much things may
appear to have changed, in reality there is little difference. And with a
government so well ordered it was as easy to transfer it as it is to shift
a well-strapped package from one pair of shoulders to another, as the
Chinese philosopher Chuang Tz' puts it.

And indeed the Shogun living a life apart in the great fortress that
Ieyasu had built for him and surrounded by ladies-in-waiting, officials,
greater and lesser daimyos, and samurai was one of the most imposing
rulers to be found in any land, and quite comparable to the occupant
of the Dragon Throne in the Forbidden City of Peking. While he lived
he was the Mighty Lord of Edo and Master of the Empire, and when
he died he passed, under a sonorous posthumous title by which he was
henceforth known, to be enshrined in a mausoleum as elaborate and gorgeous as that of the Divine Ieyasu, and only inferior in size and position.
His name and his crest were naturally forbidden to all other houses, and
to this day none but a member of the family has ever assumed them,
while the original name of Matsudaira is limited to cadets of his house.

And so great was the reverence for the Founder himself that before
his name in the histories or elsewhere a space was left blank in the line
or the phrase "katajikenaku mo," "with reverence be it spoken," was
used as a prefix. And he was always spoken of by one of his honorific
divine titles, Gongen Sama or Tosho-ko or Shinkun, Honored Incar-
nation of God and Buddha, Prince Orient Luminary, or Divine Lord,
while beside his great shrine in Nikko there were three more important

ones at Edo, in Shiba and Ueno, and within the Castle precincts.

This sacrosanct position enjoyed by the Shoguns, and especially by the first one, might be expected to result in the suppression of anything unfavorable to the dynasty and the magnifying of all its virtues as well as the ascription of some that were non-existent. No doubt to some extent this is the case, though since Japanese have probably never conceived anything like our Victorian taboos this does not apply to individual characteristics as much as to the idea of the supremacy of the Shogunate in general. And even this censorship did not prevent the circulation of literature that led to the Shinto Revival and that quickening of the feeling of reverence for the Imperial House that brought about the Restoration of Meiji. After that sentiment went to the other extreme, and the tendency of critics has been to depreciate everything connected with the Tokugawa house and to extol the virtues of Hideyoshi and even of Nobunaga, though nobody has much that is favorable to say on behalf of the Ashikagas, and Takauji their founder is still held up to execration as a Judas-Cromwell.

And monographs have been published quite recently on Ishida Mitsunari, justifying him as a loyal servant and altruistic defender of the house of Toyotomi and a fine character generally, while there is an elaborate life of Hideyoshi also appearing in many volumes by the popular writer, Yada Soun, but no considerable work on Ieyasu has been issued since the Restoration.

CHAPTER 1

THE PEDIGREE OF THE TOKUGAWAS

THE Tokugawa family traces its descent from Hachimantaro Yoshiie of the Seiwa Genji line. He had a son Yoshikuni who, for some reason or other, went down to Ashikaga in Shimotsuke and there set up a house and brought a large tract of land under cultivation. His elder son Yoshishige took the name of Nitta, and his younger Yoshiyasu kept that of Ashikaga. And the son of Yoshishige took the name of Tokugawa, and also it seems of Serata. This branch, however, for a long time did not prosper at all, for excess of loyalty made the Nitta family cleave to the fortunes of the Southern Emperors at Yoshino in the period of the divided Monarchy of the North and South Period, as it is sometimes called. It was the Ashikaga, who took the other side, who were successful, and started a new line of Shoguns. Meanwhile, the family of Nitta or Tokugawa was nearly exterminated, and those who survived had to live in retirement. But after a while Arichika and Chikauji (d. 1407?), father and son, appear in the province of Mikawa, having become priests of the Shōmyoji at Ohama in that country. Now in Mikawa there lived a powerful personage named Gorozaemon, of the village of Sakai, who fortunately had only a daughter, and so had to look round for an adoptive husband for her. His eye was taken by the fine bearing and evident strength and ability of Chikauji, and he suggested that he might apply for the position. This seemed good to Chikauji, and he left the temple and its possible ascetism and married the maiden. She proceeded to bear him a son and then to die. But the fortune of Chikauji did not desert him, for there was yet another wealthy and influential landowner in that district, also with one daughter, and his name was Tarozaemon Nobushige, of the village of Matsudaira, a name that was destined to be borne by a very large proportion of all the feudal nobles in the land. By him, too, was Chikauji sought out, and nothing loath he bestowed himself on the family as son-in-law. He gave his possessions in the village of Sakai to the son he had there, whose name was Tadahiro, and who became the ancestor of the house of Sajai, whose fortunes were so bound up with that of Tokugawa. He himself now became Matsudaira Chikauji, and here another son, Yasuchika (1369), was born, and the family flourished, and evidently profited greatly by the troublous times, for by the time of his son Nobumitsu they are to be found in possession of one-third of all Mikawa. The son of Nobumitsu was Chikatada, and his son Nagachika was so exceedingly long-lived that he was still a hale old man of eighty and more in the days of Hirotada, father of Ieyasu. Nagachika had two sons, Nobutada and Nobusada, the latter, it seems, no great credit to the family, and the cause of a considerable amount of strife in it. Kiyoyasu, the son of Nobutada, was a fine soldier, and his friendship was solicited by both Takeda Nobutora, father of the great Kenshin, and also by Oda Nobuo Mitsu, uncle of the more famous Nobunaga. Oda later made secret overtures to the effect that if Kiyoyasu attacked his province he would be on his side, his intention being to oust his elder brother Nobuhide, the head of the clan. So Kiyoyasu set out against this province. But his wicked uncle Nobusada, seeing an opportunity, sent to Nobuhide to say that he was about to take the castle of Anjo, the headquarters of Kiyoyasu, from which he had set out. When Kiyoyasu heard of this he was naturally very troubled at the possibility of his base being taken behind his back, and he was rendered more so by another rumor started by someone that his most faithful retainer Abe Sadayoshi was also in league with his uncle. Abe Sadayoshi was very indignant when he heard this slander, and called his son Yashichi, telling him that it was false, and would be proved so if proper examination was made. But if this was not done, and he was put to death on suspicion, he impressed on him the need of his continuing to serve their lord faithfully as if nothing had happened. Just after this Sadayoshi's horse began to be restless and kick out, and there was some confusion, and Kiyoyasu came out and gave orders to catch it and tie it up. Hearing the noise, Yashichi at once concluded that his father was being arrested and was in danger, and without more ado rushed out on the spur of the moment without any reflection and cut Kiyoyasu down. He was at once killed himself, but that did not save Kiyoyasu, who was only twenty-five. But he was not without an heir, his son Hirotada being ten years old.

Like the Afghans in *Kim*, the warriors of these days begot their man as well as shot him by the time they were fifteen. The army of Kiyoyasu had to retire immediately he was killed, and it was Abe Sadayoshi who took charge of his son, for the charge of treason seems to have been quickly shown to be false, and he was trusted as before. But he thought it wise to leave the province, for he feared the evil uncle Nobusada, who was trying to become the chief of the house, and who was at present in a strong position. He went therefore with the boy to the house of his aunt, the younger sister of Kiyoyasu, who was married to one Tojo Mochihiro of Ise. Here he was welcomed and their anxieties were at an end, but unfortunately it only lasted for a time, for Mochihiro died not long afterwards, and his son Yoshiyasu held different views on clan policy, thinking it would be more profitable for him to make alliance with the house of Oda. So Sadayoshi decided not to stay, and went back again to Suruga province, where he sought the protection of the powerful lord Imagawa Yoshimoto. This suited Imagawa very well, and he assented, and so assisted him to go back to his chief city of Okazaki in Mikawa. His uncle Nobusada was not pleased at Hirotada's return, but he could not object, for the Imagawa were too strong to resist, and so now the clan was only semi-independent under their control.

CHAPTER 2

TAKECHIYO

In Tembun 10 (1541) Hirotada came to terms with his neighbor Mizuno Tadamasa, Lord of Kariya in Mikawa, and married his daughter Dai-no-kata. So in December of the next year (1542) the son was born to him who was afterwards to become famous as Ieyasu, and given the temporary name of Takechiyo.* Hirotada and his wife were stepbrother and sister, for Kiyoyasu's second wife was the former consort of Mizuno and mother of Dai-nokata. Hirotada was seventeen and his wife fifteen when their son was born. It was a world of strife that the infant Takechiyo entered, for four months before his birth took place the fierce battle of Azukizaka, when Imagawa advanced into Owari and Oda Nobuhide and his younger brother Tsuda Nobumitsu met him and repulsed him after a desperate conflict, in which the Seven Spears of Azukizaka distinguished themselves on the side of Oda. Hirotada was with Imagawa on this occasion. Again, two days before Takechiyo's birth Oda Nobuhide attacked the stronghold of Ueno at night and burst through the outer defenses, and the commander Naito Kiyonaga had all he could do to drive him out again.

The dissatisfaction of Hirotada's uncle Matsudaira Nobutaka arose from his castle being seized behind his back by Okubo Tadakazu and Naito Jinzo acting on a plan of Abe Sadayoshi, who thought he was becoming too strong, he having been meanwhile enticed away to receive congratulations from Yoshimoto on his valor. When he came back and found his castle gone he not unnaturally felt aggrieved, and complained to Hirotada, but as he got no satisfaction he went over to the side of Nobuhide. That leader immediately again started to attack Okazaki from several directions. A month before this (July 12, 1543) Takechiyo's grandfather Mizuno Tadamasa had died, and his son Nobumoto succeeded. But he was not satisfied with his treatment by Yoshimoto, so he went over to Oda with his two strongholds of Kariya and Ogawa. Hirotada therefore considered himself in duty bound to break with him and send back his wife. He was only then nineteen years old, and the two were, it would seem, quite happy together. But his loyalty to

---

* Takechiyo = "A thousand ages like the bamboo."

his suzerain came before personal considerations. So she left her small son, aged two, and went to the house of Sakai Uta-no-kami Masachika, who was to give her an escort to take her to Kariya. So with twenty horsemen the girl of seventeen returned to her family, very reluctantly leaving her husband and son, and not particularly looking forward to meeting her brother. When they got to within 18 cho of Kariya she told the escort to go back, for her brother was famous for his quick temper and ferocity, and would certainly attack them if he saw them, and if that happened and they were killed, as they certainly would be with so small a force, it would place another barrier between the two families, whereas she hoped that in time they would again be reconciled and her brother and her son would be on friendly terms. The officers of the escort saw the force of this, and in Takechiyo's interest assented, and calling up some countrymen of the Mizuno territory handed over the lady's litter to them. They then started to return, but lingered a while, wondering how she would fare, when sure enough Tadamoto appeared with several hundred horsemen, whereupon they thought it best to hurry and quickly disappeared into their own territory. So Mizuno had to content himself with the tamer adventure of seeing his sister safe home.

The lady does not seem to have borne any grudge against her husband's family for this, and from what is known of her appears to have been magnanimous in temper as well as of vigorous physique, for she soon after married Hisamatsu Sado-no-kami Toshimatsu and by him had seven more children.* From her, in all probability, Ieyasu inherited much of his character.

Hirotada soon married a second wife, the daughter of Toda Danjo-no-Shohitsu Yasumitsu, Lord of Tawara, and had several concubines as well, so that he had four children besides Takechiyo.† Ieyasu became afterwards on very good terms with these half-brothers, and the family flourished in consequence. He saw something of his mother occasionally too, and always showed the greatest reverence for her, and when she died at the age of seventy-five he had her buried in the Jodo temple of Sokeiji, in Edo, and changed its name to Denzu-in, her posthumous title.

Nobuhide now incited Matsudaira Tadamoto, lord of Kamiwada,

---

* Three sons, Katsumoto, Yoshikatsu, and Sadakatsu, three daughters married respectively to Matsud-aira Izu-no-kami Nobukazu, Matsudaira Tamba-no-kami Yasunga, and Matsudaira Gemba-no-kami Iekiyo, and a fourth who died in infancy.

† A brother, Iemoto, afterwards known as Shoko-in who became a cripple at thirteen and died at fifty-six, then a sister Tako-hime who married first Matsudaira Tadamasa, Lord of Sakurai, then his younger brother, Tadayoshi, and then Hoshina Tadamitsu. Another girl was Ichiba, first married to Arakawa Kai-no-kami Yorimochi, and afterwards to Tsutsui Kii-no-kami Masayuki. The other was Yada-Hime, married to Nagasawa Genshichiro Yasutada.

to attack Okazaki, and Hirotada in great irritation sent one Kakehi Shigetada to go and ostensibly offer to surrender it. Tadamoto was just thinking how nice it was to be thus welcomed by the retainers of that place, who evidently preferred him to their lord, when suddenly he was fatally stabbed by Shigetada, who had come for no other purpose, and as soon as it was successfully accomplished managed to escape and hurry back to Hirotada, who was overjoyed at his success. And this was to have some effect on the fortunes of Takechiyo, for when Nobuhide heard of it he was as angry as Hirotada had been pleased, and at once gathered as great a force as he could, and marched on Okazaki. This was a very dangerous situation for Hirotada, and he called on Imagawa for help. Yoshimoto was willing enough to assist, but thought he might as well take advantage of the situation to get a greater hold over Hirotada, so he bargained for Takechiyo as hostage. He did well, for he got him, though he would probably have had to support Hirotada anyhow to prevent the victorious Nobuhide becoming his next-door neighbor.

Takechiyo was in his sixth year, and it is hardly likely he was old enough to understand the position, or care much about going to a distant town, though his father was pained at parting from his only son, and the veteran vassals felt it a blow to their prestige. So he set off with an escort of fifty men and a train of twenty-seven companions of about his own age, and servants. But when they came near Tawara in Atsumi district of Mikawa, that Toda Yasumitsu who had been turned out of his stronghold waited for them at Shiomizaka with his brother Goro, seized and ran off with Takechiyo, quickly put him on board ship and brought him to Oda Nobuhide at the fortress of Kowatari in Owari.

He was put in charge of Kato-no-kami Nobumori at Atsuta, and Nobuhide wrote to his father suggesting that he hand over Okazaki at once if he did not wish his small son to be put to death. Hirotada replied at once that if Takechiyo were killed it would hardly be the worse for Okazaki, since he was being sent as a hostage to Imagawa at Suruga, and that ally would understand that it was no fault of his that he did not reach his destination, but would rather have greater faith in him when he saw that he could sacrifice his son to the welfare of the clan. Nobuhide was struck with admiration at these sentiments and did Takechiyo no harm, but ordered Kato to take him to the temple of Manshoji at Nagoya, and there keep him safely but carefully. And there he stayed three years. Not uncomfortable as far as his living conditions went, for Kato was kind to him, and Kono Ujiyoshi sent him small birds to amuse him. Moreover, his mother, now the wife of Hisamatsu Toshimatsu, was at Akoya, not far off, and though she could not come herself she sent retainers to take him presents of clothes and delicacies of fruit and fish, and to keep her well informed about him. One of the Okazaki retainers, Kaneda Yozaemon, risked his life trying to break through and get his young lord back, lost it, but only in vain, and had his body exposed on the Mita bridge at Atsuta.

Meanwhile Hirotada did not relax his efforts to win back Anjo, and led an army against it, but Nobuhide brought up a larger force so that he was attacked on both sides and extricated himself with some difficulty, himself fighting in the van and exposing himself so recklessly that Honda Tadatoyo had to drag him away almost forcibly, and sacrifice his own life that his lord might not be overpowered. For this his family was granted the badge of a horse that his lord used on his own fan.

Neither was Hirotada safe at home, for one of his retainers, Iwamatsu Hachiya the One-eyed, attempted to assassinate him. He slipped in to where Hirotada was sleeping and thrust at him, but missed and only grazed his leg. Hirotada sprang up sword in hand, while One-eyed Hachiya fled. He ran straight into the arms of Uemitsu Shimpachiro, who was on his way into the house, and the pair grappled and both fell into the moat. Matsudaira Nobutaka also ran with a spear handy, but Uemitsu had by this time settled his opponent and was suitably rewarded.

Now a certain Tada Yasumitsu, Hirotada's uncle-in-law, had gone over to Oda in the belief that he was stronger, and Imagawa Yoshimoto immediately attacked him with Sakai Tadatsugu, one of the Okazaki commanders, and took his castles of Imahashi and Tawara. Meanwhile Imagawa sent a force to join the Mikawa troops, led by his uncle Sessai Choro, a Zen monk general, who had long and successfully commanded his armies. Together they inflicted a defeat on Nobuhide, and in the course of the fighting the rebel uncle Matsudaira Nobutaka was killed. Then, just as Hirotada seemed likely to get some peace he died, probably of consumption, in 1549. He was only twenty-four years old. He is described as a fine character as that was then understood, kind to his men, loyal and unyielding, an intrepid soldier, and a good tactician. He had ruled his clan well, though for years his health had been failing. He was laid in the ancestral temple of Daijuji, and received the Kaimyo Zui-un-inden Ojo-dokan Dai-Koji: "Great Enlightened Recluse, adaptable in rule and firm in principle, in the Temple of Favoring Clouds." About the same time Oda Nobuhide also died of an epidemic at the age of forty-two.

Thereupon Sessai led the Imagawa men against his eldest son Nobuhiro, who had succeeded for a while, soon to make way for the famous Nobunaga, the second son, who, by driving out his elder brother and killing his younger one, served his own interests without outraging the ethics of the time, which demanded respect for seniority. Nobuhiro was besieged in his castle of Anjo and eventually cut off and isolated in the main defense, whereupon word was sent to Nobunaga that the attack would be pressed home until he had to commit suicide unless it was agreed to exchange him for Takechiyo. To this Nobunaga consented, with the result that the small boy of eight was handed over to Imagawa. For the first time he was able to return to his ancestral home at Okazaki, though only for about a month to perform the memorial services for his late father and to meet the officials of the clan. Then he was sent off to Sumpu, the capital of Imagawa, that he might be under his eye and away from his own clan, which was henceforth to be governed by relays of officers of the Imagawa house and in their interest.

As a hostage at Sumpu, Takechiyo was, of course, well treated and allotted appropriate and dignified surroundings. The records are not unanimous about his entourage, but it seems likely that he had two elder guardians, Sakai Masachika and Naito Masatsugu, aged respectively twenty-seven and twenty, and seven pages of about his own age or a few years older. Among these were Amano Yasukage, thirteen; Sakakibara Tadamasa, nine; Abe Mototsugu, nine; Ishikawa Kazumasa and Torii Mototada, thirteen; all afterwards to become eminent officials and leaders of the Tokugawa house. Torii Mototada, who was perhaps his best friend in life, was the son of the Chief Councilor of Okazaki, Torii Tadayoshi, a veteran well over seventy, who used to visit his young lord whenever he could find time, and whom Takechiyo was accustomed to address affectionately as grandfather.

Takechiyo was put in the charge of one Kyushima Tosa, and his residence was in Miyagasaki-cho. His left-hand neighbor was another hostage, Hojo Ujinori, fourth of the seven sons of Hojo Ujiyasu, lord of Odawara, the temperature of whose feelings for Imagawa varied, as was the manner of the time, according as his advantage dictated. With Ujinori, who was apparently about the same age, Takechiyo was quite friendly, but this could not be said to be the case with his right-hand neighbor, one Haramiishi Mondo, a retainer of Imagawa, who resented him, possibly not without reason, because he flew his hawks over his land and trespassed on it, and trampled it down, so that Mondo exclaimed: "I've had about enough of the boy from Okazaki," and treated him with discourtesy. This Takechiyo did not forget, and when later in life, after the battle of Takatenjin, where he was fighting on the side of Takeda, Mondo fell into his hands, he had him relieved of his head at once, while a certain Okawachi, who had been kind to him during this period, was well treated and his life spared.

Some accounts say that he lived in the house of his grandmother from the age of eight to sixteen, and was brought up by her. She was the

mother of Dai-no-Kata, and daughter of Okawachi Mototsuna, lord of
Terazu in Mikawa, a descendant of the famous Gensammi Yorimasa,
and she had retired and become a nun with the title of Keyo-in. She
is described as having gone with her nephew to reside at Sumpu, and
perhaps Takechiyo's house was within her grounds. He learnt writing
at the Zen Temple of Rinzaiji under the warrior-priest Sessai, and the
room he used there is still to be seen, but it does not seem that he
was particularly studious, and what evidently interested him most was
hawking, the hobby he loved almost from the cradle to the grave, and
other outdoor exercises. There are not many details of his life during
this period, and only a few anecdotes, the best known of which is
probably the one that related how he was carried on the shoulder of
a retainer to see one of the stone-throwing contests that seem to have
been often held on the river-bed of the Anegawa. One side was three
hundred strong, and the other only half the number. The boy backed
the smaller party, which won. He considered that their knowledge of
their inferiority would stimulate them to greater efforts, and also that
the few were more manageable. Though this may not have shown any
profound wisdom or precocity, observes Tokutomi, it was a proof that
he had some independence of mind even at this early age. A second
incident also points to the same quality. At the age of nine Takechiyo
was present at the New Year reception in the Imagawa mansion, a most
stately and ceremonial function, when all the vassals and allies came to
congratulate Yoshimoto on his continued prosperous existence. One
sitting near observed the boy, and remarked to his neighbor that he was
the grandson of Kiyoyasu. The other was not so sure, and two or three
were discussing it when the subject of their surmises got up and made
his way unconcernedly through the assembled notables to the edge of
the verandah of the hall of audience, where he proceeded to assume
the attitude of the famous manikin who is the oldest citizen of Brus-
sels. In quite a natural and unflurried manner he finished his business
and returned to his place, while those who saw it looked at each other
in surprise at his nonchalance. "Yes, you're right. He's the grandson of
Kiyoyasu," said the objector. And all his life long he possessed an almost inhuman composure. Without any affectation he did just what he
wanted in his own way. It was presumedly not long after this that, finding fault with his page Torii Mototada, son of the veteran Councilor
Torii Tadayoshi, who had charge of the clan finance and administration, for clumsiness in handling a shrike that he was using in hawking,
he flung him down with some force on the verandah. When this came
to the ears of Tadayoshi he was very pleased, and said he was sorry he
could not live to see the boy become head of the clan, for such dras-

tic treatment of his son when he was quite in the power of the father showed an intrepid character that would make him a fearless leader.

It is also related that one day he went for a walk to the Zen monastery of Daishoji and noticed twenty or so fowls in the courtyard. He asked the abbot to give him one, and he replied that he would be pleased to let him have the lot. "They've grown up with us you see, and so we keep them, but they do a great deal of damage to the kitchen garden," he explained. "What an extraordinary monk this is!" remarked Takechiyo with a grin, "he doesn't seem to know how to eat eggs."

Another story ascribed to his eighth year is one to the effect that he was presented by a Shinto priest of the Atsuta shrine with a dusky ouzel to amuse him. The retainers brought it to him and praised its rarity, but the boy Takechiyo replied: "It may be a rare bird, perhaps, but for a certain reason I don't care for it. You had better take it back." Which they did to the considerable surprise of the donor. Then Takechiyo deigned to explain his reason. "Apparently this bird has no song of its own, so it shows its defect by imitating those of other birds. Birds have their characteristic notes. The bush-warbler does not imitate the cuckoo, and the skylark does not mimic the stork. So it is with people. They are valued for their natural character. People with this easy facility for doing all sorts of things never do anything great. Beings without ability of their own who merely assume qualities, even if they are only birds or animals, are no fit companions for a future leader of men." But Yamaji Aizan is of the opinion that this is a reflection back of views that Ieyasu did actually express much later in life. Incidentally it explains the low place assigned to actors in Japan.

CHAPTER 3

MATSUDAIRA MOTONOBU. MOTOYASU. THE BATTLE OF OKE-HAZAMA

So he continued to live an active but uneventful life at Sumpu till he was fifteen, when the Gempuku or Coming-of-age ceremony was held for him under the auspices of Yoshimoto, who was his "Eboshioya" or "Hat-father," investing him with this sign of maturity, and giving him the adult name of Matsudaira Jirosaburo Motonobu, which contained one of the syllables of his own, for now he put away the infant style of Takechiyo. Sekiguchi Gyobushoyu Chikanaga, Yoshimoto's brother-in-law, and soon to become Motonobu's father-in-law, assisted at this ceremony as "Hair-arranger."

The Imagawa mansion was a miniature reproduction of the Court of his relative the Ashikaga Shogun at Kyoto, conducted with all the stately grace of the household of a great Court noble. And Yoshimoto's wife was indeed the daughter of such an one, for her father was the Dainagon Naka-no-mikado Nobutane. And there was no lack of her many relatives and connections to set the fashion as it should be in all things, though not, of course, to pay for it. This part was left to Yoshimoto, to the detriment of his revenues and the discomfort of his hard-pressed peasants. There poetry and painting and tea-ceremony and flower-viewing were all important, and beauty spots near Sumpu were even called by the names of the famous scenes round the capital.

So, with his income of some hundred thousand koku and great name and fine taste, there was none more distinguished than this long-bodied short-legged little lame man, with the long hair and blackened teeth of a courtier. And he was a fine tutor for Motoyasu in what not to do or be. For though not deficient in either courage or ability, he was no natural soldier like Nobunaga or Kuroda Josui, who in stature and disability he somewhat resembled. As long as his uncle the Zen monk Sessai led his army things went well, but after he died in 1555 Yoshimoto had to take charge himself, and there was a difference.*

Soon afterwards Motonobu asked for and received permission to

---

* Sessai had been trained at the Kenninji, and then become abbot of the Myōshinji in the capital, but had returned to his province, where he acted as abbot of the Rinzaiji at Sumpu.

ARMOR WORN BY IEYASU AT THE PROVISIONING OF
OTAKA, 1560

return to Okazaki to pay his respects to the tomb of his father and to receive the homage of his senior retainers. Here he showed his tact by declining to disturb Yoshimoto's Governor, who was living in the main castle, and wished to vacate it for him. "A young man," he objected, "should always give way to his elders." Yoshimoto was, of course, suitably impressed when this was reported to him. "He is indeed a young man of discrimination," he remarked, "his father would have been pleased with him had he lived."

Torii Tadayoshi, the senior councilor, now eighty years old, took him to the strong room of the castle and showed him the rice and money he had stored there on the quiet, pointing out to him that with such resources one could keep many good retainers and so enlarge one's territory. "I keep these coins in packages of ten kwan piled up, and in that position they are safe enough, but if you store them horizontally they may easily break away and roll off and be lost." Motonobu never forgot this advice, and often referred to it in after-life, and was ever vigilant, as were few of his class, to check any capricious movements of his cash.

And if these ten years had been difficult for Takechiyo, they had been more uncomfortable for his retainers, since they had been almost entirely at the disposal of Imagawa, and he had been a hard ruler. Their revenues were taken and spent by him, and little was left for them to live on but the actual land that some of them had. The highest of them fared badly, and the poorer could hardly keep body and soul together by working hard on the farms like the ordinary peasant.

What their condition was appears from one of the reminiscences of their young lord. When he returned to Okazaki he was out hawking one day, and it was the season of planting out the young rice. A certain retainer of his named Kondo was working among the farmers when he saw his lord coming, and immediately he smeared his face all over with the mud of the rice field. But his master recognized him and called out his name, so he washed off the mud again and presented himself, putting back into his belt the sword that he had laid down on the dyke-path. He had only a single garment and a bit of rope for a girdle, and looked anything but impressive as he crawled out of the muddy field very ill at ease. "If I were not the owner of this land," observed Motonobu, "I could not sympathize with you as I ought, but if you hadn't a real love for a soldier's life you couldn't put up with these scanty stipends that force you to do work like this. It is indeed pathetic, but one must go with the times, and now it is necessary for all of us without exception to school ourselves to rough and unpleasant tasks. It is certainly nothing to be ashamed of. Still, you remember the saying: 'brought up in poverty, dies in comfort.' It may encourage you when you feel resentful."* Noticing the tears in his eyes, Kondo and the rest were also affected, and much moved by their master's consideration. And this was not all, for they had to be polite and even flattering, as far as such country samurai were able, to the Imagawa officials, and tolerate contemptuous treatment from them lest their young lord should suffer. Moreover, they had to bear all the brunt of the fighting with Oda, because Yoshimoto not only wanted to spare his own men, but deliberately set out to weaken the Mikawa clan so that he might get it more completely into his own hands. Many of the Matsudaira family were killed and wounded in these battles, but the clan did not become disheartened. On the contrary, their former factions were obliterated, and this loss and hardship united them in a great fervor of devotion for their chief, and forged them into the seasoned warriors who made the name of Mikawa so famous in the country for all time.

Anyhow, they thought, it was better to have some independence under even such an exacting ally as Imagawa than to be delivered over completely into the hands of the house of Oda. And that was the alternative. So the enthusiasm with which they welcomed back their vigorous young lord was mixed with a great confidence in the future. He did not stay long at Okazaki, however, and in the spring of the next year was back again at Sumpu, where he was then married to the daughter of Sekiguchi Chikanaga, described as lord of the castle of Mochibune, income 27,000 koku, and married to Yoshimoto's younger sister, or, according to some, his aunt. It was a union for family advance, as are most in Japan, whether of high or low, the advantage being that of the house of Imagawa in this case, of course.

And he changed his name once more, as well as his state, for now he assumed the title of Matsudaira Kurando Motoyasu, after his grandfather Kiyoyasu, whom he admired as afterwards his own grandson was to admire him. As a wedding present one of the Mikawa retainers offered a fine warhorse called Arashikage or Chestnut Blast. It was evidently worth having, for Motoyasu immediately presented it to the Shogun Ashikaga Yoshiteru, thus making his name known in high places, and receiving in return an autograph letter and a dagger.

The next year, 1558, at the age of seventeen he fought his first battle. Yoshimoto suggested it as was his way: "Western Mikawa has always been your territory," said he, "and now Suzuki Shigeteru, lord of the castle of Terabe, has deserted us and gone over to Oda Nobunaga with it. How awful!" So Motoyasu took himself back to Okazaki, got

---

* Ieyasu advised his Mikawa retainers to marry women who could weave cotton cloth, so that if they could not get enough rice when the men were away on campaign they could sell the material and so get along till they came back.

his men together, and went out against Terabe and attacked it. Immediately he proved himself a cool though enthusiastic commander. Personally he led the attack, and they burnt the outer defenses of the stronghold, after which they turned their attention to several subsidiary posts that lay near. But the main castle was not so easily taken, and, observing that one might be easily put in an awkward position if taken in the rear by a party sent out from one of these flanking forts if they were not destroyed, he managed to set fire to the main castle and then retired without more ado. As he expected, Nobunaga, hearing of the attack fairly quickly, sent out a force to take him in the rear, but Motoyasu was ready for them, and swinging his men round attacked and drove them off with considerable loss. He then returned and was congratulated by Yoshimoto on a fine piece of work and presented with the sword he was then wearing, as well as 300 kwan of land, his own land naturally, not Yoshimoto's.

Emboldened by this, the Okazaki retainers petitioned Yoshimoto to allow their lord to return to them permanently, but that did not suit the Imagawa plan, which was just then contemplating a serious move against Oda and Kyoto. So nothing came of it. However, they had some cause to rejoice for the next year, 1559, his first son was born, taking in turn the hereditary youthful name of Takechiyo, afterwards Nobuyasu. He thus achieved Paternity just one year later in his life than his own father had done, since he had been born when Hirotada was seventeen. But on the other hand he was to have some half a century of premeditated creative activity before him. And the same year also he put another achievement to his credit. This was a not very extensive but very well planned military operation known as the Provisioning of Otaka. Otaka was a frontier fort that had been one of a chain constructed by Nobunaga to guard his domains, but which had been treacherously surrendered to Imagawa by a commander whom he had influenced. He had placed in command there one Udono Nagamochi with orders to hold it stoutly against Oda. Nobunaga in great anger at being deceived, though he need not have worried for it was a common enough thing in those days, bade the commanders of the flanking posts make every effort to prevent any provisions being taken into it, and as it was situated in a salient that projected into Nobunaga's territory this was not difficult, and very soon the garrison was hard put to it to get enough to eat. Its relief was an operation the Imagawa generals were not enthusiastic about, for escorting baggage animals is neither very glorious nor spectacular. "Matsudaira Kurando is young it is true, but his knowledge and intelligence are beyond the ordinary," suggested Yoshimoto, "Moreover, he has many very meritorious veterans under him, so how about asking him to get these provisions into Otaka?" Motoyasu immediately consented. "That's the sort of duty I like," he replied. "And I shall be equally ready to undertake at any time these difficult jobs that other leaders don't care for."

Now there were five frontier forts near each other, Otaka, Washizu, Marune, Terabe, and Umezu, and against the last two of these Ieyasu directed vigorous attacks to be made by about a thousand of his men at midnight, while he himself with another eight hundred, disposed so as to enclose the pack animals that carried the provisions, made his way quietly to a spot just about a mile away from Otaka, soon the attackers penetrated the works of the two castles and set fire to whatever they could, making at the same time as great a noise as possible. Seeing and hearing this the men of the next two forts of Washizu and Marune immediately sent out most of their garrisons to the assistance of Terabe and Umezu. Then, taking advantage of the noise and confusion that inevitably followed the night attacks and fires, Ieyasu led his men in three columns with the twelve hundred pack animals safe in the middle right into Otaka under the eyes of the troops left behind in Marune and Washizu, who could only look on and do nothing, for they were far too few to attack with any chance of success.

This success was very pleasing to Yoshimoto, who was not slow in providing more opportunities for such a capable leader and his hard-fighting forces. So Motoyasu spent the rest of the year in operations on this frontier, and also against his uncle Mizuno Nobumoto, on the whole profitable ones, and planned with a view to preparing for the decisive move against Owari and the capital that Yoshimoto proposed to make the next year. In the July of the next year, therefore, with all the forces of Mikawa, Totomi, and Suruga, Yoshimoto marched out of his capital of Sumpu, leaving his son Ujizane, who preferred the tearoom to the battlefield, to look after affairs at home. It seems probable that the total number of his levies was about twenty-five thousand men.

These he pushed on through Mikawa to the frontier, where his two castles of Narumi on the Tokaido road and Otaka south of it, stood facing the five forts that Nobunaga had built right opposite and around them. These had to be reduced before any further advance could be made on Nobunaga's capital of Kiyosu. Again Motoyasu, with his Mikawa veterans, was given one of them to reduce, and after a stiff fight, in which he lost more than one captain, he stormed and burnt the fort of Marune. This he did by a skilful co-ordination of his forces. First, he made a sharp attack which was repulsed with some loss, whereupon the commander suddenly opened the gates and sallied out with his men to strike before the attackers had rallied. But Motoyasu was ready for this, and brought a concentrated fire of matchlocks and archers to bear on the enemy, which not only stopped them, but deprived them of their commander, who fell struck by a bullet. Immediately the Mikawa samurai counter-attacked and drove the others back, following on their heels and bursting with them into the fort before the gates could be closed, when they set fire to the place and overcame all resistance. For this deed Motoyasu was again commended and given the honor of commanding in Otaka, and bidden to rest his men and animals there. Meanwhile the other fort of Washizu had also been taken by the Imagawa men, and it looked as though the road to Nobunaga's province lay open. Certainly Nobunaga, who had but small domains, and whose army was correspondingly small, for he could probably not muster more than five or six thousand men, ought to have been nervous. It does not appear that he was, however. He was only twenty-seven, which for these days was a good age for a leader. Yoshimoto was forty-five. The two wardens of Washizu and Marune had sent urgent messages to him that they could not hold out more than a day or two, but when these reached him in the evening he did not seem much interested, but went on discussing other affairs with his councilors till late in the night, when he dismissed them without any special orders. So they went, one of them observing that even a mirror of wisdom got clouded when its luck was out.

But Nobunaga was up with the daylight next morning, and the first thing he did was to chant a snatch of the No "Atsumori," which runs: "Man's life is fifty years. In the Universe what is it but dream and illusion? Is there any who is born and does not die?" And he blew on a conch for his armor, had breakfast after putting it on, then helmeted himself and started. He had only six companions and a couple of hundred men when he set out from Kiyosu, but as he advanced his force swelled to over two thousand. Some say that on the way to battle Nobunaga wrote a prayer for victory, which he gave to a retainer to deposit at the great Shinto Shrine of Atsuta, and the text of the prayer is given. It abuses Yoshimoto as a bandit and a tyrant and annexer of other people's territory. Also, very significantly, as a destroyer of Shinto shrines. Nobunaga may not have been unconscious of the humor of this, but it was a convention and looked well. Certainly his demeanor as he rode off was as unlike that of the conventional general as possible, for he is described as leaving the shrine precincts sitting sideways in the saddle, with his hands on the front and back pommels, swinging himself round on the back one and humming an air with such entire want of ceremony that the Shinto priests stood looking after him in astonishment and remarking: "He doesn't look a bit as if he was just going into a fight."

By this time Washizu and Marune had fallen, and all he saw of them was clouds of smoke. Not at all upset, he made a detour and sent out scouts to see where Yoshimoto was. They reported that he had camped at a place called Dengaku-hazama to rest his men and celebrate his successes. Since he was rather contemptuous of Nobunaga's army, and his men were feasting and drinking to further triumphs, they did not keep a very vigilant watch, so Nobunaga judged it a good opportunity for a sudden attack.

Yoshimoto kept his usual state in the field. Garbed in a surcoat of red brocade and armor with a white breastplate, and girt with a war-sword by Samonji and a dagger by Matsukura Go, he sat viewing the heads ceremoniously, calling for some Noh choruses to be chanted the while, and declaring that neither God nor Devil dare meet his armies. And all the Shinto and Buddhist priests and monks of the neighborhood came out bringing fish and liquor to entertain his men.

Meanwhile Nobunaga very ostentatiously took up a position right opposite to Yoshimoto's camp at a place called Zenshoji, just close to Narumi on the Tokaido, and there displayed his banners and insignia, and rigged up quite an imposing array with dummy troops, after which he took three thousand men and made a rapid march with them so as to get round the hills and drop down suddenly on Yoshimoto when least expected. As it happened, the weather favored him, for it was a stifling hot day, and about noon, as his men drew near their objective the hill behind Yoshimoto's camp, the sky suddenly clouded and blackened, and there was a violent storm of rain which made the men there huddle together at the same time that it screened their enemy's movements. And with its ceasing Nobunaga's force rushed down the slope on to them in a headlong charge, and the sudden impact found them quite unprepared and threw them into complete confusion. In all directions they stampeded and left Yoshimoto quite unprotected. And so little did he realize what had happened that he thought it was only a quarrel among his own men, and shouted out an order to one who came running up and who he took for one of his own retainers. But it was one of Nobunaga's men who saw who it was, and without more ado aimed a spear-thrust at him. Then Yoshimoto understood, but it was too late, for though he at once drew his sword and cut through the shaft of the spear with an answering blow, continuing the sweep so that it gashed into his assailant's knee, before he could do any more a second enemy came up and cut off his head. Aesthete though he was, he died a soldier's death, and at the loss of their leader his army immediately melted away with more than two thousand five hundred casualties.

This battle, known as Oke-hazama from the name of the nearest hamlet to Yoshimoto's camp, was one of the decisive actions of Japanese history, in that it placed Nobunaga in the front rank of military leaders, and placed the acquisition of supreme power within his grasp.

Now, when the news of Imagawa's defeat and death was brought to Matsudaira Motoyasu, he was urged to withdraw his forces at once, but for the time he refused, "because if the news should be false and Yoshimoto still be alive, it would not look at all well. Then came a messenger from uncle Mizuno Nobumoto of Kariya, pressing him to retire while there was time, for in the opinion of that relative if the report was reliable Nobunaga would certainly strike at him without delay. So with his usual caution he sent a runner to the battlefield to make sure and having done so, drew off his troops not without difficulty to Mikawa, for the roads were beset by bandits and unfriendly troops. Here he took up his quarters in the Daijuji temple, outside Okazaki, for the Imagawa officers were still in the castle and he did not wish to appear too precipitate in grasping even what was really his own. "Still, if castles were being given away, he might as well take one."

The Imagawa men were not long in deciding to retire to their headquarters, and then Motoyasu moved in. This was on the twenty-third of the fifth month of 1560, when he was nineteen years old.

So Nobunaga's victory, though profitable enough for himself since it placed him at once among the first powers of the Empire was equally so for Motoyasu, in that it gave him the first firm step forward from which he never looked back. It was the first installment of his proverbial good fortune.

Motoyasu was quite uncertain when Nobunaga might not appear before his capital, but he did not wait quietly there without doing anything, but pushed out tentatively into the Owari territory and took a couple of strong positions till he came on Oda Gemba in Kutsukake, and there halted.

However, in the spring of the next year, 1561, Nobunaga made overtures to him through Takigawa Kazumasu, who approached his chief retainer Ishikawa Kazumasa. The wives, and children of the great retainers, as well as those of Motoyasu for that matter, were still in Suruga and so hostages, while in addition it naturally went against the grain to abandon the ancient ally of their clan. But these were mainly sentimental considerations, and as such not to be taken too seriously. The fact was that Imagawa Ujizane was neither wise nor strong, while Nobunaga was both, and evidently the coming man. And the interests of the clan must be considered before everything. Imagawa Ujizane is described as "devoted to Japanese verse and football, and even more

given up to drink and dalliance, and without any ideas about retriev-
ing his position." With all his father's defects in such an age, he had
little of his energy.

At the discussion with his councilors of their plans for the future
Sakai Tadatsugu gave excellent reasons for joining Nobunaga and forsaking Imagawa. Ujizane was incompetent and cared nothing for war
or avenging his father. All he did was to indulge in artistic activities and
dissipation. He openly declared that he preferred a retainer who had a
good eye for a work of art to one who knew a good strategic position
when he saw it. Moreover, Mikawa was indebted for nothing to the
Imagawas, for Yoshimoto had taken every advantage of their clan when
he could, had worn down their forces in the van in his incessant wars,
and starved their families at home. He had intended their destruction,
and now it would be well to bring about that of his house in return, or
rather not to hinder it, for under one like Ujizane it would fall of itself.
The only problem was the hostages. This certainly was a difficulty, and
it was voiced so vigorously by one Sakai Shōgen, lord of Ueno, that the
councilors suspected his loyalty and wanted to have him killed. This
Motoyasu opposed, for he did not think it necessary. Shōgen was, after
all, only ultraconservative in his views. And it is notable that those
views were apparently those of Shōgen's chief councilor, one Honda
Masanobu, afterwards the chief Tokugawa adviser, and also to be heard
of later on again on the conservative side when he took the part of the
Monto monks in Mikawa.

Sure enough Ujizane did put to death eleven of the hostages given
by several of the small clans, who now proceeded to leave him and go
over to the rising power of Mikawa.

As for Nobunaga, he meant to go up to the capital, but it would be
less easy for him if he had an enemy on his rear, and so also the Okazaki men would feel safer if they had an ally against people like Takeda
Shingen, their rather too exuberant neighbor. So Motoyasu decided he
would risk it, though many of his councilors were against it. "A flaw in
our ancestral bow and arrow," they grumbled in their whiskers. Thus
Motoyasu became the ally of Nobunaga, and went up to his castle of
Kiyosu to pay his respects with considerable ceremony, Nobunaga going out to meet him and escorting him personally from the outer ward
of the castle to the inner apartment. The people of the place crowded
round clamorously as he entered the city, and this irritated his page
Honda Heihachiro, then aged seventeen. "Stop that rude noise," he
shouted. "Don't you see it is the Lord Motoyasu of Mikawa who has
arrived?" Evidently the populace of those times was not as subservient
to dignitaries as it afterwards became. It is true that one of Motoyasu's

men, Uemura Shinrokuro, a real "Mikawa Bushi," insisted on following his master everywhere, carrying his sword, and that he persisted even when some complained of this very obvious precaution. But when Nobunaga heard of it he only commended his soldierly conduct, and ordered that none should obstruct him. Moreover, when he presented swords to Motoyasu, as was usual on these occasions, a long one by Nagamitsu and a short one by Yoshimitsu, both famous smiths of Bizen, he gave Uemura one by Yukimitsu. So everything went off happily, and he came home again, to find that Imagawa Ujizane had sent to know his intentions. At once he sent an envoy to Suruga to explain that it was just a gesture to protect himself for a while, in fact that it was very necessary in both their interests, and Ujizane's suspicions were allayed, for he was anything but a deep thinker.

In all this Motoyasu revealed the attitude to which he ever afterwards adhered through life. He wielded two weapons of reasonableness and force. And when he could use the former he did, for he gained his point with less expenditure and effort. But he knew this would be useless unless backed by force, and none had it readier at all times than he. Tokutomi observes that "his militarism was diplomatic, and his diplomacy was militaristic." Nobody in the Empire valued armaments more or took more care of them. He took so much care of them that he never used them rashly, and unless driven to it by unavoidable necessity. Others in this age, of course, used these two methods also. But perhaps none made so few failures as he did, and that owing to his extraordinary patience and self control.

Now while these things were going on Shingen and Kenshin were so busy with one of their periodic battles at Kawanakashima that they had no time to take notice. And so this pair of cunning schemers was outwitted, and Motoyasu and Nobunaga made their arrangements while their backs were turned. And that this alliance between them lasted for twenty-two years, all the days of Nobunaga, was certainly a tribute to the practical spirit of the principals and their insight into the situation, for both benefited by it greatly, Motoyasu by no means least. And it was unique, for since the Kamakura period, that is for two hundred and fifty years, no feudal chiefs had trusted each other and worked together for so long. And since Nobunaga was a person by no means easy to get on with, as others found to their undoing, it says much for the Mikawa lord that he had the necessary adroitness. That he did not do it without sacrifice is evident from the case of his son Nobuyasu, but where policy was concerned Motoyasu had no emotions, only calculations.

This alliance set Nobunaga free to devote some attention to his unpleasant neighbor and father-in-law Saito Toshimasa, commonly known as Dosa, Lord of Mino. So far it had been difficult to do anything with him, and he had been a thorn in the side of the house of Oda for some time. That was why they had taken his daughter into their house. But this they regarded as merely a temporary expedient, and now Nobunaga felt safe enough to use force instead of diplomacy.

Saito Toshimasa disliked his eldest son Yoshitatsu, who was a big fellow six feet five high, but a leper, and preferred his two younger ones. He himself was harsh and cruel by nature, given to burning and boiling people who displeased him, and putting them to death in unpleasant ways. So when the eldest son enticed the two others and slew them, he naturally turned his hand against him, and a battle ensued between father and son, in which the father came off worst and was killed. This was Nobunaga's opportunity. He would punish this malignant parricide. Full of righteous indignation of the Confucian order, he exclaimed: "It is my duty to take the head of this leper and avenge my father-in-law." His indignation was quite Gladstonian in its opportuneness. But Yoshitatsu was strong as well as malignant, and not easily overcome, and Nobunaga did not prevail. However, Yoshitatsu died, presumably from his disease, this year at the age of thirty-five, leaving his son Tatsuoki to carry on the campaign. Nobunaga moved his headquarters to Komaki Hill, about eighty meters high, and to the south of Kiyosu, which dominated all the surrounding plain, afterwards to become famous as one of Ieyasu's great battlefields, and in 1564, with the skilled assistance of Hideyoshi, who now for the first time makes his appearance as his assistant, he overcame Tatsuoki and annexed his province. This is the end of his family, and it was perhaps no loss, for it was of less antiquity, if anything than respectability, since Toshimasa, who had assumed both his names, was born in obscurity, became a priest and then an oil dealer, eventually gaining his territory by various treacherous tricks and homicides.

CHAPTER 4

IEYASU QUELLS THE MONTO SECT

IN the sixteenth century in Japan one of the greatest powers was the Monto sect of Buddhists. One Japanese historian remarks that though strife between the secular and religious powers is a characteristic of Christian kingdoms, yet those who say that it has never existed in Japan must be ignorant of the history of that country. This is true enough, for in Japan the great monasteries have always tended to accumulate possessions owing to the freedom from taxation and control by the civil governors that they enjoyed, and the right they had of affording refuge to those who wished to escape from the oppression of the competitive world outside. These rights needed guarding in a land like Japan, where the military were not much inclined to be frightened by the ghostly terrors with which the monks tried to threaten them, and so the soldier monk consequently eventuated. Since the temples had so much property there would be no lack of volunteers for the honor of guarding it, and the great groups of temples like Hieizan and Nara (Tendai and Ritsu sects), and later the Amida and Nichiren sects, not to speak of the Shingon of Koya and Negoro, not only resisted the military government, but fought viciously among themselves, in all cases for loaves and fishes, or fish and saké rather, and not for any particular belief in the efficacy of their doctrines, except perhaps in the case of Nichiren, the only really bigoted sect, with a bible and drums complete. The Monto sect was particularly popular because it made no great demands on its believers either ethically or intellectually, while its priests were permitted to marry and hand down their temples and eat fish and live just like any layman. So great did the power of this sect become that in about 1529 it is said to have plotted to put Shōnyo Shonin, Lord Abbot of the Hongwanji, on the throne, and his military commander Shimotsuma into the place of the Shogun, though it did not succeed any better than the famous usurping monk Dōkyo in the eighth century.

The three great leaders of this sect were Shinran (1174–1268), Kakunyo, died 1356 *aet.* eighty-two, and Rennyo (1415–1499), eighth generation from Shinran. He became a monk of the Hongwanji at Kyoto at the age of sixteen, and soon made such a reputation for holiness and eloquence that the monks of Hieizan got jealous, and persecuted him so that he had to run away. He went like the founder to the northwest to Echigo (for Shinran had been banished there too because of the rivalry between the other sects). He was soon back again as head of the Hongwanji, who gave him money to repair his temple, and so again excited the wrath of the Hieizan bonzes, who regarded such favors as their monopoly, so that they set fire to the Hongwanji, and Rennyo with difficulty escaped with his life. He went back to Echizen, and here, too, he had trouble, for his branch temple was destroyed by rivals of another branch of the same sect, of which there were then nine. He returned to Kyoto and died there aged eighty-five. From him descends the house of Otani of the East and West Hongwanji. He was posthumously created Daishi in 1883. "At twenty-nine he was washing his baby's clothes himself, and at thirty-five he was selling oil to keep himself alive, and reading the sacred books by the light of the moon. At thirty-eight he had only one meal a day, but amid all his want he preached incessantly, traveling all over the East and North, having no time even to warm a seat." He was very eloquent and a master of the vernacular tongue, which he not only used but wrote, compiling a Jodo Scripture in simple style that all could understand (Go-Bunsho). He was in all ways adaptable and adroit in his manner, and did nothing unreasonable or fanatical, but yet was always ready to press the advantage of belonging to his sect whenever he could see or make an opportunity. He was a fine organizer, and a very optimistic, cheery, and indefatigable worker, who never gave way to difficulties. Owing to him his sect of the Hongwanji became the most powerful of all the branches, whereas till his day it had been the weakest. Nor did he lack descendants to carry on his work, for he had twenty-eight children, fifteen daughters, the youngest born when he was eighty-two, and thirteen sons, the last born when he was eighty-four. It may be regarded by some hypercritical moderns as a shortcoming that he was no monogamist, but that was by no means the opinion of his contemporaries.

With such advantages it is no wonder that this sect became powerful, and took advantage of the impotence of Emperor and Shogun to strengthen itself at their expense. It is not strange that it became so strong, but that it did not become stronger. It was this sect that a little later took possession of Tibet, and rules it still through Lama incarnations of Kwannon and Amida. Anyhow by 1488 these monks had taken the whole province of Kaga and dispossessed the Governor Togashi, and its chief city Kanazawa was their headquarters in the sixteenth century. But especially was their power great through their control of Osaka, the greatest trading center of the country, where they made a strong place then called Ishiyama, in the center of the converging river systems that meet there, and make it a position extremely easy to defend on the one hand, and equally easy to provision on the other. Just such another strong place they had at Nagashima, near Kuwana, in Ise province, with the sea in front and a confluence of rivers round it, while not far off was another at Tomita in Owari. In Mikawa, the home of Ieyasu, there were three powerful temples of this sect, Toro, Harisaki, and Sasaki, all acknowledging, like the others, no authority but that of the chief of the Hongwanji, and collecting money and soldiers to enforce their will. It was not remarkable therefore that there should be a collision between these monks and the feudal lords. This arose over a question of requisitioning supplies for the soldiers. When the monks refused to comply with the request of the generals of Ieyasu to allow them to enter the temple premises, they thought they saw an opportunity to get possession of the province as they had managed to do of others like Kaga, and hoped to take advantage of the dislike of some of the old leaders of the clan for the new policy of making alliance with the Oda and turning away from the Imagawa. They had therefore some strong supporters among the military men, especially one Honda Masanobu, who was to become a very prominent figure as counselor of Ieyasu in the future, and who was at this time one of the chief leaders of the ecclesiastical party. The danger to Ieyasu was that while he was occupied with reducing this insurrection he might be attacked by Imagawa Ujizane, as well as by the sympathizers with the Ikkoshu, who occupied castles only a few miles from his capital. Fortunately his frontier castles were loyal and Imagawa luxurious and incompetent. When the monks showed their contempt for him by ill-treating the relatives of his officers, one of Ieyasu's commanders, Sakai Uta-no-kami, issued a formal reproof to them, bidding them reflect on the more sanctified side of their profession. It runs as follows:

"Sakai Uta-no-kami to the Ikko Bonzes, on account of their breaking into the house of Suganuma Tojuro when he was absent on duty and beating the inmates and leaving them half-dead:

1. The conduct of Bonzes should be restrained and gentle, and their motives should be merciful and kind. It is the business of the clergy to help the laity. But the Bonzes of the Joguji have waved the banner of self-will and embraced the policy of violence, and beaten innocent women and children. Is this according to the rule of their order?
2. Beating women and children is simply retaliation. Retaliation is one of the deadly sins of the Buddhist Canon.
3. Breaking into houses and taking property is robbery. Cases of it should be respectfully reported to the authorities. What right have you to take the law into your own hands without judicial permission? That is not

proper behavior for clerics. Your own meditations will convince you of this. And when one considers the matter the Ikko sect, contrary to the Buddhist precepts, permits indulgence in women and flesh eating, thus defiling the Buddhas and polluting the Deities. This is not only disregard of the Three Sacred Things, but disobedience to the laws of the Imperial Court and of the Military Officials. It is the cause of armed conflicts and the loss of life. Without question this is a Sect that must be strictly prohibited. The Jōgūji is a temple named after the Imperial Prince Jōgu.* It ought therefore to be more holy than others. Instead of that it takes its place with rebels and behaves lawlessly in defiance of its princely patron's teachings. Shaving the head and wearing priestly robes is only to put on the outward signs of sanctity, like a bat that pretends to be a bird. Violence and covetousness and arrogance and discontent are the ways of the devil."

However, in the rebellion that he thus had to face in his own province Ieyasu proved too much for the Monto sectaries, principally because the majority of the military leaders were on his side, and those against him were old and less influential, and so the comparatively larger numbers of the other side, chiefly made up of farmers, who have always been far more susceptible to the propaganda of the Amida sect than any other class, did not in this case prevail. And this in spite of the fact that they wore in their helmets tablets written by the priests to stimulate their courage, inscribed with the legend: "He who advances is sure of Heaven; but he who retreats of eternal damnation." It is noticeable that the introduction of firearms through the Portuguese made it easier to get some sort of an army of comparatively untrained farmers, though the matchlock did not prove such a great asset as they may have hoped, since it was not very convenient to use when the weather was wet, as it often is in Japan, and its range was possibly not greater, and its accuracy not as great, as the bow and arrow. It is here that there is some difference between conditions in Japan and Europe, for in Japan the samurai was an archer, either horse or foot, and did not trust so much to his armor as the European knights did, neither did he advance in the massed charging formation that would be more vulnerable to gun fire. In this trouble the youthful gallantry and enthusiasm of Ieyasu were more inspiring to his side than the hopes of Heaven and fear of Hell were to the other, so that by 1564 the revolt was put down and the province re-united, on condition that those who took part in it should not be affected either in life or property, and that the temples should be as they were originally. These terms, put forward by the Monto side, were agreed to by Ieyasu, but he immediately gave orders for the tem-

---

* Jogu = Shotoku Taishi.

TOYOTOMI HIDEYORI

ples to be pulled down, and when the monks remonstrated with him for breaking his promise, he explained that by "as they originally were" he understood the bare site of the ground before they were built on it. We shall see that this was not the last time Ieyasu employed a piece of sharp dealing of this kind to make a military operation decisive. In some provinces, such as Echigo (Uesugi) and Izu (Hojo), these Monto monks were prohibited from entering.

The following details that describe his share in the fighting show how loyalty and military spirit very largely paralyzed even those arms that were raised against their lord.

Mizuno Tojuro was accompanying our Lord this day (Battle of Adzuki-zaka against the Ikkoshu in 1563, Ieyasu *aet.* 22), and noticing one Hachiya Hannojo retiring, he called out to him to come back and fight. Hachiya turned and shouted that it would be ridiculous for him to fight such a white-shinned warrior, but Ieyasu rode at him all the same, whereat he dropped his spear point and retired. Seeing this, Matsudaira Kinsuke reproached him also in a loud voice for cowardice, whereupon Hachiya turned once more: "It is because I can't bear to fight my Lord that I turn my back," he said. "Not because I am afraid of fellows like you," and he charged at him, ran him through, and went to take his head. But Ieyasu rode at him again, shouting: "Get out, you dirty beast," whereat he would not face him, and turned and fled. He rode at Kakehi Sukedayu also, and he too turned and made his way to the rear, though he had just wounded one of Ieyasu's leaders in the ear, and was pressing on to do him some more vital damage. An arrow shot by Kondo Shinichiro struck his reins as he held them, but just missed his body. In a great rage he dashed on the enemy by himself, and they did not await his onset, but fled in all directions. He caught up with Namikiri Magoshichiro, and urged on his horse with his stirrups, while he dealt him two blows with his spear in the back. But they did not go deep, as he was whipping up his horse, and he got off with a slight wound.

Again, as Ieyasu was pressing on a bullet hit his armor, but did not penetrate, and he took no heed, bent on showing the foe that he would not retreat. Ishikawa Jurozaemon came against him flourishing his spear, when Naito Masanari, who was beside him, called out: "Ishikawa is my maternal uncle, but my lord comes first," and he shot an arrow that pierced him through both legs, and he fell. Tsuchiya Chokichi was of the Monto faction, but when he saw his lord hard pressed, he shouted to his companions: "Our lord is in a critical position with his small band. I won't lift a spear against him, even though I go to the most unpleasant kind of hells," and he turned against his own party and fought fiercely with them till he fell dead. Now when Ieyasu returned to Okazaki and loosened the strings of his armor two bullets fell out of his shirt.

Later in life, referring to this fight, when Kato Kiyomasa was once boasting of having overcome and killed a certain captain, Ieyasu seemed little impressed, and observed: "When I was fighting a hard battle with the Ikko rebels in my youth, and the enemy were drawing their bows at me, I merely turned and glared in rage at them, and they dropped their weapons and fled."

He also later laughed at Namikiri Magoshichiro, who had returned to his allegiance and become his retainer once more, for his wounds in the back, which Namikiri denied, pretending to have forgotten the incident, and when Ieyasu pressed him he said it was somebody else to whom he owed any wounds he might have. Then Ieyasu described their position carefully, and challenged him to strip and prove him wrong. He also told him that it was very improper for warriors to tell lies. As he still denied it, Ieyasu laughed the louder and exclaimed: "Ah, then you ran away from somebody else as well evidently. But my spear had blood on it all right."

And another fact is noticeable in this campaign, and that is that Ieyasu managed to get assistance from his own sect of the Jōdō, another branch of the Monto type of Buddhism, but of different political habits, so that his ancestral temple of the Daijuji sent a thousand men, both priestly and lay, to fight for him, and also one of the previously described banners inscribed with reward and imprecation. As a reward for this, perhaps, he afterwards ordered some of his former retainers who came back to him when the revolt was over to give up Monto and join Jōdō. Which they did. There must have been many after this who were shepherded into this Jōdō sect by him. He thought it best that his men should all be in the same compartment of the "Pure Land"—should there turn out to be one. Meanwhile they did not assist the power of the Hongwanji on earth, and Ieyasu had not done with the Hongwanji either.

In 1565 Nobunaga made his headquarters at the capital city of the Saito, which he renamed Gifu. He then married his younger sister to Asai Nagamasa, the powerful lord of Omi, his neighbor, and a daughter he had adopted to Takeda Katsuyori, the son of the redoubtable Takeda Shingen, who menaced him on the other side. Having thus protected his flanks by matrimony, he marched into the capital with little difficulty when he was invited to do so by the Emperor, and there proceeded to assist Ashikaga Yoshiaki to become Shogun vice his elder brother Yoshiteru, who had been put to death by Matsunaga Hisahide, after that malignant and eccentric aesthete had murdered his master, Miyoshi Chokei. Nobunaga made the Emperor a grant of money, and restored some of the Imperial territories that had been lost. And Hideyoshi became Governor of Kyoto. And there was peace for a while. But not for long.

Somewhere about this period, when the weather had been very frosty, Nobunaga sent Ieyasu a present of a basket of peaches, which elicited a characteristic comment. His retainers crowded round admiring them and praising their excellence and rarity. But Ieyasu said nothing. They thought it rather odd, and noticing this, and never backward in giving good advice, he delivered himself thus: "Yes, this fruit may be a rare delicacy, but Nobunaga's territory is far larger than mine, so the things we can fancy must be in proportion. If people like me take to wanting rare things there will be only loss and no advantage. It would only mean planting good rice land with useless trees, and giving the men more work. In the same way, keeping fancy animals means wasting good money in getting and then in looking after them, while a taste for curios means frittering away your mentality on worthless playthings. And not only that, but it is to impair the military capacity of the fief, because there will be less money to pay good retainers. So people who have any sense won't bother about rarities. Of course great lords like Nobunaga have the means to do as they like, but I have more pressing needs to spend my money on." And with a laugh he gave the fruit away to his retainers. When Takeda Shingen heard the story he commented: "Ieyasu cherishes great hopes for the future, and so he takes great care of his health. He won't eat anything out of season." Shingen was no simple Mikawa samurai.

Ieyasu always ate wheat porridge in the hot weather in the Mikawa days. So when an attendant once brought him a bowl of fine rice with a thin covering of wheat on the top he was distinctly irritated. "I suppose you think I eat it from stinginess," he objected, "but you don't understand my motive at all. The land is not in a peaceful state just now, and everything is disturbed. The people cannot eat or sleep in peace, so why should I alone live in luxury? I have to save as much as I can so that military necessities are not neglected. If I fare delicately it must come out of the people's pocket."

When the Yahagi bridge at Okazaki was washed away by a flood Ieyasu gave orders for it to be rebuilt. But his councilors raised objections. They pointed out that it would cost a lot of money, and if there were no bridge the river would be a splendid defense against a sudden attack on the city. In fact, its being washed away was really providential, so why not have a bridge of boats instead. "I don't agree at all," replied Ieyasu. "This is one of the famous bridges of the Empire, celebrated in our national histories, and sung of in the Noh dramas. If I do as you advise it will hinder the traffic on the Tokaido highway, and my name will be handed down to future generations as the lord who would not rebuild an ancient landmark because he grudged the expense, and was fearful of an attack by his neighbors. Moreover, you know the saying that a place is better defended by the spirit of its men than by any help of God or advantage of geography. That applies to dangers both within and without. Attacks don't only come from outside." So the bridge was rebuilt without delay. But his successors were not so solicitous about the convenience of traffic on the Tokaido highway. Quite the contrary in fact, for their view was that easy communications brought more rascals to Edo.

CHAPTER 5

TOKUGAWA IEYASU,
LORD OF MIKAWA AND TŌTŌMI

IEYASU'S wife and son were still hostages at Suruga with the wives and children of his other retainers, and the problem was how to get them back. Ishikawa Kazumasa, Councilor of Ieyasu, insisted on going to Suruga to keep his young master company anyhow, and to die with him when he was put to death, for, he declared, it would not be seemly that he should die unaccompanied by any retainer. So naturally at great risk he went. Then, early in 1562, Ieyasu suddenly attacked Udono Nagateru in his fort of Kaminojo, took it, killed Nagateru, and seized his two children. These he offered to exchange for his wife and son, and Ujizane, shortsighted as usual, accepted. So Ishikawa was spared to bring back the child Takechiyo and his mother to Okazaki in triumph. But when they were safe the Mikawa men were not long in showing their neighbors that they took no account of them, and then Ujizane seems to have realized that he had been done and flew into a temper. He ordered Sekiguchi Chikanaga, Ieyasu's father-in-law, to commit suicide, and he also had impaled the twelve other women and children held as hostages. But it was too late, and this had no effect except to irritate the Mikawa men further, and also to deepen the estrangement between Ieyasu and his wife.

A month or two after this Motoyasu changed his name once more to Ieyasu, the one by which he is usually known. The reason for his assumption of the syllable *Ie* which became the characteristic one of his line, for the name of most of the Shoguns begin with it, was that a certain learned priest recommended it as particularly auspicious since the greatness of the Minamoto family began with Yoshiie. Ieyasu highly approved of the suggestion, which was, he said, no doubt put into the priest's mind by the God Hachiman, and acted on it forthwith. At least so says the Mikawa Go-Fudoki. Yoshiie was, it may be remembered, known as Hachimantaro, the War-God's eldest son. Ieyasu's name was now free from any association with the Imagawa house, and so reflected his intentions for the future.

In May 1564, after settling the Monto monks in March, Ieyasu carried out another smart piece of field work in relieving one of his frontier forts that was threatened by a very large force of the Imagawa men, who, with the assistance of Takeda Nobutora, surrounded it, and would have reduced it, no doubt, if he had not at once gone to its assistance. Gathering a small force he moved rapidly against the Imagawa troops, but they were not sufficiently well led or at any rate were irresolute, so that with little difficulty he penetrated their lines, stopped in the fort of Ichinomiya till the next morning, and then evacuated the place, escorting the relieved garrison back safely to Okazaki. Already it seems his known capacity and decisive movements were able to paralyse the initiative of even a very superior army.

A few weeks after he was back again assaulting Yoshida, or Toyohashi as it is now called, the town opposite Ichinomiya, which though part of Mikawa was still held by Ujizane. He was not successful in taking it, but managed to arrange for its cession to him on condition that he became reconciled with the Imagawa house and gave suitable hostages. His younger stepbrother, Matsudaira Yasutoshi, and O Fu, the daughter of Sakai Tadatsugu, being considered suitable by both sides, they were sent and the agreement concluded, this Sakai Tadatsugu being then appointed commandant of Yoshida castle. As the few other strong places in this southeastern corner of Mikawa then proceeded to attach themselves also to Ieyasu, he was now for the first time able to call himself lord of the whole province. He was also to have a rest from fighting for some three years or so, and had time to look to the internal administration of his domain.

The next year, 1565, he appointed three Bugyo or Commissioners to take charge of the affairs of the province. These were, of course, under the authority of himself and his chief hereditary councilors, Ishikawa, Honda, Sakai, and Sakakibara, who formed the ruling oligarchy of the clan. These three were Koriki Yozaemon Kiyonaga, Honda Sakuzaemon Shigetsugu, and Amano Saburobei Yasukage. Evidently Ieyasu thought it well to appoint officers whose characters would supplement each other, since the people nicknamed them Buddha Koriki, Devil Sakuza, and Neither-one-nor-the-other Amano Saburobei. Of the three Devil Sakuza is the most striking, as it is perhaps to be expected, for neither the amiable nor the neutral are so prolific of anecdote as the severe and downright. Honda Shigetsugu was the extremely consistent Mikawa warrior, with all his good points and deficiencies. The former benefited his master while the latter mostly recoiled on himself to a greater degree than they might had his master been less astute and far-sighted. He had his kindly side, too, for he is said to have carefully written out his orders in the simple syllabary so that no one might be in ignorance of them. And, moreover, to have written under them equally simply that there might be no mistake: "And Sakuza will give it to any-one who disobeys." A letter that he wrote home has been recorded as of the admirable conciseness that becomes a soldier. It runs: "Just one word. Beware of fire. Don't make O Sen cry, and keep the horse in good condition." (Hito fude Mosu. Hi no Yojin. O Sen nakasu na. Uma Koyase.) O Sen was his daughter.

The next complication in Ieyasu's life was Takeda Harunobu, lord of Kai and Shinano, and as much of their vicinity as he could get, whose house had held a fief in these mountain provinces since the twelfth century. He was reckoned to be among the first two or three soldiers of the time, and a wise and progressive administrator as well. He was now about fifty-five years old, and so in his prime. He had, when about thirty, shaved his head and become a Zen monk, taking the name of Archbishop Shingen, for he was fond of learning and meditation, but he did not become less acquisitive on that account or any milder in his methods. Just now he had put to death his eldest son, Yoshinobu, and sent back this son's wife to Imagawa Ujizane, whose daughter she was. He also told one of his chief councilors, who did not agree with the policy thereby inaugurated, to commit suicide. This was the way he picked his quarrel with Ujizane, who up to the present had been his ally. But now, seeing that the house of Imagawa was on the decline, he was anxious to accelerate the process and get as much of his territory as he could. Seeing also how formidable an adversary Ieyasu had proved himself, and that he was allied with Nobunaga, and con-sidering his own need to guard against the threat of his powerful and actively hostile neighbor, Uesugi Kenshin, another philosophical mili-tarist, Shingen decided to suggest that an agreement be entered into between himself and Ieyasu to attack Ujizane and share his territory.*

He seems first to have suggested to Ujizane that if given Tōtōmi he would attack Ieyasu and pay him back for forsaking the Imagawa alliance. But Ujizane refused, probably because he did not trust Shin-gen, whereupon Shingen made advances to Ieyasu. As his subsequent conduct showed he did not necessarily mean the arrangement to last forever, as probably Ieyasu was quite aware, but it suited them both for the time, and so it was decided that Ieyasu should take Tōtōmi while Takeda appropriated Suruga.

Meanwhile Nobunaga engaged his son Nobutada to Shingen's daughter, and married his daughter to Nobuyasu, Ieyasu's eldest son. Shingen's monastic commitments were not such as to ensure his celi-

---

* It was on this occasion that Ujizane, who held the sea-coast, cut off Shingen's supply of salt, and thus gave Uesugi the opportunity of offering to send a supply of this necessary commodity from his own province to that of his enemy. This chivalrous act of Kenshin has become proverbial.

bacy it will be seen, though those of his neighbor, Kenshin, were. But Kenshin happened to be of more ascetic temperament. No great difficulty was experienced by either Shingen or Ieyasu in getting possession of these provinces. Ujizane's men did not even await the onset of Takeda's well-trained troops. They made off and left him, and he fled and took refuge with the commander of the castle of Kakegawa, the largest town well across the river Oi in the next province of Tōtōmi. Shingen then entered and burnt his capital of Sumpu. But this roused Hōjō, Ujizane's ally, and he at once attacked him and gave him a beating, partly on account of his greater force at sea, for he had three hundred ships. Shingen was defeated at Okitsu, and four hundred heads were taken by Hōjō, and as his provisions then gave out he was forced to return disappointed to Kai.

Ieyasu meanwhile had moved in to Tōtōmi and besieged Imagawa Ujizane in Kakegawa. Reminding him of their former relations, he suggested that if he came out and surrendered the place and also the province to him, he would assist Hōjō and Uesugi against Takeda so that the province of Suruga might be restored to the Imagawa house. This seemed eminently practical to Ujizane, and he agreed and was escorted by Icyasu's men to Hōjō who wished to restore his capital to him, but since Shingen had burnt it he thought it would be more comfortable to go elsewhere, and retired to Izu. Afterwards he went to Kyoto, where he seems to have shone at football, but not to have impressed Nobunaga with his capacity as a lord of provinces. For when more than ten years later Ieyasu was given Suruga he suggested to Nobunaga that he would share the province with Ujizane, to whom he had always been well disposed. But Nobunaga would not hear of it. Ujizane was a fellow providence did not favor, he observed. So Ujizane never became a territorial magnate again, but his fate was not an unhappy one considering his tastes. Eventually he went to Edo when Ieyasu was established there, and there he died only a year before Ieyasu himself, at the age of seventy-seven. And his descendants became masters of ceremonies to the Shogun, so they were provided with a good income and a dignified occupation.

But Shingen was not disconcerted by his experience with Hōjō, and six months later, about July 1569, was back again in Suruga, and not only so but made another incursion into Hōjō's territory, managed to lure him out of his impregnable fortress of Odawara and inflicted a reverse on his troops. Then once again he took the capital and province of Suruga. He tried also to stir up trouble for Ieyasu in Tōtōmi by inciting a dependant to attack him, but without success, and after a protest by Ieyasu the affair was smoothed over, and the peace between them kept for a little while longer.

It may have been about this time that Shingen tried to get Ieyasu put out of the way by assassination. He escaped, we are told, by his assiduity to his devotions. For Shingen sent a young man who entered his household and won his confidence, and thinking Ieyasu would fall asleep and remain so after a drinking party, he went to his bedroom and stabbed through the bed quite systematically. But Ieyasu was not there, for it was his custom to get up early and pray before Buddha, and a little drink had not made him depart from it. When he found out what had happened he did not punish the youth, but sent him back to Shingen, observing that he was clearly a very loyal retainer.

In December of the same year Matsudaira Ieyasu obtained permission from the Emperor through the Shogun Yoshiaki and the ex-Kambaku Konoe Sakihisa to assume or resume the surname of Tokugawa, which had originally been borne by Minamoto Yoshisue, the great-grandson of the redoubtable Hachimantaro Yoshiie. The change served to reaffirm his connection with this time-honored line, and at the same time to distinguish his house from the many other collateral Matsudaira families. The supposition that he did it to emphasize his conviction that the time was approaching when his branch, the house of Nitta, which Yoshisue's father, Yoshishige, founded, would supersede the house of Ashikaga in the Shogunate rather exceeds the possibilities of the situation since he was only the lord of two provinces. But as he must have been already convinced of his capacity, and was by no means lacking in ambition, his foresight probably led him to be ready for any eventuality.

In the beginning of the year 1570 he transferred his capital to a site in the province of Tōtōmi, then known as Hikuma, which he fortified and re-named Hamamatsu, leaving his castle of Okazaki in charge of his eldest son, Nobuyasu. His mother seems to have stayed there with him, for her violent temper and eccentricity made it uncomfortable for her to live with her husband. She had a residence at Okazaki called Tsukiyama, and so is usually known as the Lady Tsukiyama. This move to Hamamatsu was contrary to Nobunaga's wishes, for he thought it would make the co-operation of their forces less easy than if Ieyasu stayed at Okazaki, and thus weaken his position *vis-à-vis* Takeda. But Ieyasu was not nervous, and preferred to disregard Nobunaga's views and take the risk.

But he was not left undisturbed in Hamamatsu for long. Nobunaga found that he had need of his services owing to a new and formidable menace. Up till now he had been on good terms with the Shogun Yoshiaki, as might be expected, seeing that Yoshiaki owed his security and prosperity to him, but when he got accustomed to the services of his new protector and Vice-Shogun he began to think his attentions irksome and resent his obvious superiority and power. Yoshiaki had by nature the habit of intrigue, and in fact it was the only weapon he had ever had the chance to wield. So, unable to curb his inclination to indulge it any longer, he started to show Nobunaga what he could do by arranging a combination to bring him down.

He therefore invited Takeda Shingen, with Asai Nagamasa, and Asakura Yoshikage, lords of Omi and Echizen respectively, to attack him from all sides. And this was the more serious because the position of these two latter menaced his communications with his home province. With Asakura Nobunaga was not on friendly terms, because this lord, formerly Nobunaga's equal, for they had both been vassals of Shiba, resented his assumption of authority and refused to fall in with his suggestion that he should come up to the capital and acknowledge it. But Asai was married to Nobunaga's sister, and was regarded by him as an ally. Now, as soon as Nobunaga discovered what was brewing, he acted decisively as usual, but without exactly advertising his intention.

CHAPTER 6

THE RETREAT FROM ECHIZEN AND BATTLE OF THE ANEGAWA

On the third day of the third month of 1570 Nobunaga went to the Jorakuji in Omi to hold a wrestling tournament to entertain Ieyasu. Ieyasu, however, did not arrive in time, but went up to Kyoto, ostensibly for sightseeing. Nobunaga was holding a Noh performance in the capital on the occasion of the banquet to the Shogun, congratulating him on the completion of his palace, which was attended by the great lords and Court nobles. Actually under cover of these festivities he was making preparations to strike a blow at Asakura of Echizen, chief of the party hostile to him, which was aided and abetted by the Shogun.

So with Ieyasu he set out and marched by the Hokurikudo to Tsuruga, and in a couple of days took the two forts of Tezutsuyama and Kamigasaki. He was just about to attack Asakura's capital, Ichijogatani, when he heard that Asai of Omi had turned against him. Asai was his younger sister's husband, and though he had long been connected with Asakura there was no reason to think he would not remain neutral. But he had evidently been persuaded by the Shogun to break definitely with Nobunaga, and the latter was now in a very awkward position, for he could be cut off from his base and attacked on both sides.

At a council of his allies, both Ieyasu and Matsunaga Hisahide advised retreat, which they thought would be safe if executed speedily and at once, for they did not rate Asai's capacity very high. So Nobunaga started off first with part of the forces, according to some accounts so hastily that he did not stop even to say farewell to Ieyasu. Fortunately Matsunaga had a friend who was lord of the castle of Kuchigi in Omi, and they went to him and asked for a guide to the by-roads that ran through that part to Ohara and Kyoto. Matsunaga went fully prepared to kill him if he refused, but there was no need, for he consented and thus they were able to avoid the high roads and bring their force safely back to the capital. To Ieyasu and Hideyoshi were left the task of keeping Asakura back and managing the retreat of the rearguard. Since the whole army was some hundred and ten thousand men, this was not easy, and at one time Hideyoshi, with less than a thousand men, was hard pressed by Asakura, whereon he asked Ieyasu for assistance. This was readily given, and the Mikawa men charged the enemy vigorously as usual and drove them back, Ieyasu himself taking a matchlock and making good practice. Thinking it better to keep his men away from the others to avoid confusion on the road, he made a detour by Ohama in Wakasa, and so back by Mount Kurama. Hideyoshi did not forget this help, for he specially thanked Ieyasu for it when he came up to the capital after Komaki.

After this adventure Nobunaga asked Ieyasu to go home and get his forces ready for another attack, while he went out again against Rokkaku, a friend of Asai. On this occasion he narrowly escaped being shot by a priest, who fired at him, but the two bullets did not pierce his coat. Then he went to Gifu, and once more led his men against Asai, before whose headquarters at Odani he appeared on the nineteenth of the sixth month. This he menaced by attacking Yokoyama Castle on the left bank of the Anegawa to the southeast. Here he awaited Ieyasu, who soon arrived with some five thousand men. Asakura sent about ten thousand to join the force of somewhat less that Asai put in the field. The allied forces of Asai and Asakura now drew up on the other side of the river with the intention of attacking Nobunaga at dawn on the next day, but he meant to forestall them and take the offensive himself. Ieyasu had been ordered to engage Asai's army of some eight thousand with the six thousand under his command, a thousand of these being the force of Inaba Ittetsu, another ally, but immediately before the bat-tle Nobunaga changed his mind and determined to oppose Asai, against whom he felt particular resentment, himself.

Ieyasu consented at once, though his commanders objected that it might throw his army into confusion, since orders had already been issued about their positions. "To confront a great force is a fine thing," observed Ieyasu, phlegmatic as ever.

Nobunaga had twenty-three thousand under him, but their quality was not that of the Mikawa bushi,

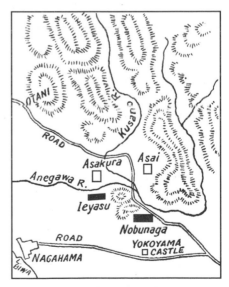

BATTLE OF THE ANEGAWA, 1570

led by the various Matsudaira chiefs, nine in all, and especially were
the levies of Omi doubtful for they had a wholesome respect for Asai.
So they were placed under Hideyoshi, who never minded what troublesome task he was assigned. Nobunaga arranged his army thirteen
ranks deep, so that the shock might be effectively withstood. And this
precaution proved by no means unnecessary. So at four in the morning
the battle began, both armies attacking across the shallow stream of the
Anegawa, that was only about three feet deep, and a hard fight ended
in a signal victory for Nobunaga with a toll of three thousand one
hundred and seventy heads, a large proportion taken by the Tokugawa
force. For the victory was very largely owing to the splendid fighting
quality of the Mikawa men and their fine handling by Ieyasu. Sakai and
Ishikawa commanded his van, and Sakakibara and Honda the second
division. They attacked and held Asakura's large force in spite of strenuous resistance, and while doing so noticed that Asai had broken deeply
into Nobunaga's ranks and even menaced that commander himself,
for one Endo Kizaemon had determined to seek him out and take his
head, and was only prevented when quite close by Takenaka Kyusaku,
who had already many heads to his credit, springing upon him and
cutting him down in the nick of time. Ieyasu had ordered Sakakibara
and Honda to cut across the river and take the enemy in the flank,
which they did successfully, making him give ground and throwing his
men into disorder. Then, seeing Nobunaga in need of help, he threw
part of his troops on to Asai's flank, while Inaba Ittetsu, who had held
his men in reserve up to this, fell on his right, while at the same time
a body of the men besieging Yokoyama Castle hurried away and supported him. This was a real feudal battle judging by the account in the
Mikawa Fudoki, which gives a vivid picture of the bands of retainers
fighting in groups, the lopping of heads by sword and bill, the confused
mingling of the armies, the clouds of black smoke and dust, and above
all the streams of perspiration that bathed the combatants, for it was
the hottest season of the year. How Ieyasu was attired on this occasion
we are not informed, though it is related that he was well splashed with
blood "when about the middle of the fray someone, I know not whom,
of Asakura's men mingled with his guard and made a sudden onslaught
on him, whereupon Amano Saburobei and Kato Kiemon Masatsugu
sprang upon him and slew him." But Nobunaga wore no armor, only
"a white summer dress with a black surcoat over it with a Paullownia
crest in silver, and a black war hat."

Nobunaga showed his gratitude to Ieyasu after the victory, which
was mainly won by his assistance, by presenting him with a sword by
Nagamitsu, which was formerly an heirloom of the Shogun Yoshiteru,

and an arrowhead that had belonged to Minamoto Tametomo, as well as by describing him as "one whose merit this day is beyond description, for it has no equal till now, and is unlikely to be excelled in future, who is the sheet-anchor of our house, and the great builder of the portal of martial valour."

CHAPTER 7

MIKATA-GA-HARA

IEYASU therefore returned to his provinces with a military reputation greatly enhanced by these operations, but he found plenty there to tax his resources, for it was not long before Takeda Shingen was again active. He sent a detachment up the Tenryu river in ships to attack Kakegawa, a strong place not so far from Hamamatsu, while two other divisions of his troops marched south from Shinano and menaced Okazaki in one direction and Yoshida in the other. Nobunaga advised Ieyasu to retire from Hamamatsu on Yoshida, leaving only a garrison there to impede the enemy, but retirement without very good reason was not a maneuver that appealed to him, so all he did was to send to Uesugi Kenshin suggesting an alliance against their common foe.

Unfortunately Hojo Ujiyasu had died at the end of the year 1570, and his son Ujimasa who succeeded him was proceeding to desert Uesugi and ally himself with Takeda, so that Shingen had little to fear on the east and could concentrate his forces without anxiety on his western frontiers. Moreover, Asai and Asakura, making common cause with the Tendai monks of Hieizan, were again threatening Nobunaga, who also had the equally troublesome Monto sect in their strong place at Osaka to deal with. Shingen adroitly represented also to the Hongwanji monks in control of the provinces of Echizen and Noto that he was assisting their brethren in Osaka who were being besieged by Nobunaga by creating a diversion behind him, and therefore they might make themselves useful in their turn by also attacking Uesugi in his rear. He also notified that particularly treacherous character, Matsunaga Hisahide, that there was an opportunity for him to regain power in the capital if he turned against Nobunaga, which, of course, he promptly did. It was a situation that needed all the capacity of Nobunaga and his brilliant assistant Hideyoshi to cope with. Yet all the same, with neither Nobunaga nor Ieyasu was Shingen openly at war. He was only in that condition which may be called an absence of peace.

Nobunaga eased the situation a little perhaps by striking out at the nearest and possibly the most hated foe within reach. This was the Tendai Buddhist monasteries on Mount Hiei. Nobunaga had less reason than usual to love the priests of Buddha just now, for they were

most cordially supporting his enemies with all their forces, from motives of self-protection no doubt, since they realized that they would
be his next objective—for he greatly coveted the great and impregnable
fortress of Ishiyama at Osaka, and resented the power they wielded
round the capital. He was attacking Miyoshi of Settsu on the outskirts
of Osaka when the Shingon monks of Nēgoro and Saiga brought up
three thousand matchlockmen against him, and immediately after this
the Monto monks of Ishiyama began hostilities also. Hearing he was
thus embarrassed, Asai and Asakura again took the field with the intention of breaking through into the capital, and in November 1570 they
marched round by Otsu, though when Nobunaga's generals led back
an army against them they did not meet it but ascended Hieizan and
combined with the monks there. Nobunaga immediately sent word
to these temples that if they assisted his enemies he would certainly
march against them and burn the Komponchu-do and the twenty-one
shrines of the Sanno Gongen, while if they were on his side he would
make it worth their while. But they remained hostile, though Asai and
Asakura did not manage to turn their help to any account, for probably
owing to lack of supplies when the winter snow closed the roads to the
north, or possibly because Nobunaga persuaded the Shogun to arrange
it for his own advantage, they agreed to make peace and go home.
Then Nobunaga again began operations round Osaka with the Monto
monks, but in August he suddenly returned to the capital and threw his
forces round Hieizan so as to close the sacred mountain in on all sides.
When they saw that he intended to destroy the place both Emperor
and Shogun as well as some of his own generals asked him to desist.
But he took no notice of them, and on October 20, 1571, attacked and
set fire to all the monasteries so that they were completely destroyed
and nothing at all remained, while the monks without exception, with
many fair ladies and children, who had little excuse for existing there,
were brought before Nobunaga and put to death to the number of
several thousands. Not even some reputable priests and scholars were
spared, and the destruction of records and works of art was regrettable.
But as the Record of Nobunaga observes: "Quite unabashed by the
disapproval of the world, and without regard for the Buddhist precepts
they had retired from it to observe, they were given up to the enjoy-
ment of fish and birds and women, while their palms were ever open
to take a bribe," and as, in addition, they had been for four centuries
more of a menace to the Imperial capital than the protection against
bad influences that their founder intended, and with no respect even
for the word of the Emperor himself, their drastic removal was not very
regrettable. And there was at least one note of unfeigned approval, for

the Jesuit fathers wrote: "On the Feast of St. Michael, 1571, God punished this great enemy." But, like many Japanese actions that foreigners approve, it was not done for their benefit. Hieizan never gave anyone any further trouble.

Meanwhile Ieyasu had been able to give no assistance to Nobunaga in his difficulties because of the menace of Takeda Shingen on the other side of him. In fact he was giving all he could by preventing that warrior from coming in also to join in the fights round the capital, for Takeda had now made an alliance with Hojo and was more free to move westward. At the same time he made friends with Satomi and Satake, two lords on the other side of Hojo, so that if by any chance he should be treacherous they might attack him from the rear. One result of this alliance was that Hojo drove out Imagawa Ujizane, and he went and took refuge with Ieyasu in Hamamatsu, where he was quite kindly received for the sake of old times.

Shingen's plan was to keep the peace with Nobunaga until he had overwhelmed Ieyasu, when the way would be open for him to march on to the capital. There, too, he had arranged that he should at least not be hindered. Among other things, Archbishop Shingen was brother-in-law to Lord Abbot Kennyo Kosa, of the Hongwanji, for both had married daughters of the Court noble, Sanjo Kimiyori, and by use of this connection he had obtained a promise that the monks of this sect in Kaga, Noto, and Echizen, which region they largely controlled, should rise and restrain his chronic adversary Kenshin, while Matsunaga Hisahide might be trusted to forward his interests in Kyoto as well. Nobunaga also did not wish to appear as an open enemy of Shingen. It was much more convenient for him to remain a covert one, and the question was how to keep up the fiction if his ally Ieyasu was actually engaged in war, or what could hardly pass as anything else, with him. So he again advised Ieyasu to retire to Okazaki for a while, and so avoid a clash. But this did not suit the temper of Ieyasu at all. "I hardly think the time opportune," he replied to Nobunaga. "A man who would retire like that," he said to his councilors, "has no business to call himself a warrior." Meanwhile Nobunaga was busy making an agreement with Uesugi Kenshin behind Shingen's back, so that Kenshin could be ready to stultify his pre-arranged plan by keeping well on his guard against the monks and being ready to descend on Shingen's rear when a suitable occasion offered.

So Takeda Shingen was the first to make a decisive move, for in October of 1572 he left his capital of Ko-fu, taking advantage of the season when the snow would keep Uesugi at home. He had with him twenty thousand men of his own and a couple of thousand of Hojo's, and marched to Tōtōmi while his general, Yamagata, took five thousand to make a diversion in eastern Mikawa.

They advanced without much difficulty through the province, and a force of three thousand under Okubo Tadayo and Honda Tadakatsu, who were sent out to make a reconnaissance, had some difficulty in getting back again, and only managed it through the adroit way Honda managed the retreat. Yamagata had meanwhile taken Yoshida and marched west and joined the main army, which had also taken Ieyasu's stronghold of Futamata on the road to Hamamatsu. At this juncture three thousand of Nobunaga's men under the three leaders, Sakuma Nobumori, Hiraide Norihide, and Takigawa Kazumasa, came into Hamamatsu in response to Ieyasu's request for help. A council was then held, and all were against making any attack, as were Nobunaga's generals, who brought advice from him to stand on the defensive. But Ieyasu would not listen to them. "To let an enemy come marching up to your castle without shooting an arrow at him is not to be a man," was his comment, as he gave orders to his generals to lead out their men. They amounted to some thousands in all, counting Nobunaga's detachment. They proceeded to a plain called Mikata-ga-hara on the road north and about three-quarters of a mile from the city of Hamamatsu, where Ieyasu had determined to stop Shingen. For it seems not to have been Shingen's intention to fight Ieyasu or assault Hamamatsu if he could help it, for he wished to spare his troops for his main purpose, the subduing of Nobunaga. Therefore he would have marched past and through into Mikawa had it been possible. And that would have added considerably to Nobunaga's difficulties.

So Ieyasu drew up his men in what is called "stork's wing" formation, in line with the main body, which he himself commanded, a little in rear of the flanks. On his right was Nobunaga's contingent under Sakuma, Hiraide, and Takigawa, a Mikawa corps under Sakai Tadatsugu on the extreme flank of it, and on the left wing four more bodies of troops commanded by Ogasa-

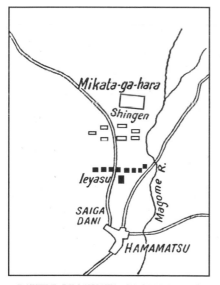

BATTLE OF MIKATA-GA-HARA, 1572

wara Nagayoshi, Matsudaira Ietada, Honda Tadakatsu, and Ishikawa Kazumasa. Ieyasu's inspector of the forces, Torii Motohiro, again advised him, after viewing the size of the Takeda forces, that it would be wiser not to provoke a combat, but if he did not to assault on the front, but to wait till the enemy had marched past and then attack on his rear. His master was usually so careful, he commented. How was it that he was now so rash? Ieyasu replied sarcastically that if Torii was thus possessed by the Spirit of Timidity he was no good to him. Takeda's advanced troops were arranged in echelon and were hardly inferior in numbers to the whole of the Tokugawa side, while behind them was the main body under Shingen, with some fifteen thousand more. What followed was what might have been expected. Takeda's men attacked the two wings of the Tokugawa force with great vigor and precision in close order on the latter opening fire on them. The Mikawa men on the left threw them back in disorder, but on the right Nobunaga's men, who had no heart for the fight, gave way and were overwhelmed. Takigawa and Sakuma lost their heads and bolted, and though Hiraide stood firm under this disadvantage and fought valiantly with his men, it was not long before he was killed and his division scattered. Takeda's two attacking divisions then retired, and in their place two fresh ones moved up and continued the battle.

Sakai Tadatsugu thus left in the air though he fought with the greatest tenacity, was forced back on the main body, and Shingen now ordered a fresh company to work round and assault the Tokugawa left in the rear. The fight had begun about four o'clock in the afternoon, and snow had been falling steadily all the while. It was now almost twilight, and Shingen, seeing the enemy reel back in all directions before the attacks of his fresh divisions and of the others who were now supporting them again after a short rest, gave the signal for a general attack. This the Mikawa men, now wearied from the continued fighting and with no reserves, could no longer resist, and they abandoned their positions and retreated as best they could. Ieyasu ordered Okubo Tadayo to plant his standard slightly to the rear of the upland of Sai-ga-dani, where the action had been fought, as a rallying point for his scattered troops. But seeing Mizuno Masashige heavily engaged with two divisions of the enemy who were menacing his flanks, he turned back again to aid him. The Takeda men were now swarming up all round to cut them off, and sweeping them with a hot fire of arrows and bullets, and it looked as though Ieyasu and his staff would not succeed in extricating themselves. But news of their plight had reached Hamamatsu, and just as they were almost surrounded Natsume Jurozaemon Masayoshi, captain of its garrison, rode out to his master's aid with twenty-four men.

"Get back immediately with our lord to the castle," he called out to those about Ieyasu, "We are going to hold back the enemy and die in his place." "Why should we let you sacrifice yourself?" replied Ieyasu. "I will stand with you, and we will fall together." "Leaders like our lord must think of the future of their house; it is not their business to fight like common soldiers," burst out Natsume in great excitement, and without more ado he caught at Ieyasu's bridle, pulled the horse round, and brought down the haft of his spear with a whack on its rump, calling out at the same time to his squire to ride hard with him to Hamamatsu. Ieyasu's charger was a spirited one, and soon outdistanced most of the enemy. With five men only he reached the castle safely. On the way, however, he had some narrow escapes, for one enemy soldier drew his bow at him at such close quarters that Amano Yasukage, one of the five, kicked it out of his hand from the saddle, while Ieyasu himself sent an arrow into another who ran at him with his spear. And in the heat of the battle he had not been unmindful of the apprehensions of those at home, and chose a very characteristic way of cheering them up. One Takagi Kyusuke had taken the head of a cowled warrior and brought it to him for inspection. "Take that head back to Hamamatsu at once and proclaim it as the head of Shingen," he ordered, and so it was done. Riding up to the castle gate he shouted out loudly, "Head of Shingen, the enemy commander, taken by Takagi Kyusuke!" And all the people there were greatly relieved, for they had heard that the enemy was victorious and were beginning to get very anxious. And soon after this incident Ieyasu's squire came up and knocked loudly on the gate and called out: "Yakata Sama O Kaeri ari!" ("Our lord has deigned to return!") And at this those in the town were still more reassured.

To this squire, Kuroyanagi Takeshige, who had been close by him all through this trying day, Ieyasu now handed the fan he was carrying as an earnest of an increase in salary, and also presented his helmet and two bows to the three brothers Tsuzuki, who had thrown themselves against an overwhelming number of the enemy to facilitate his escape, and had rather miraculously survived. Torii Mototada was just giving orders for the gates to be shut and barred when Ieyasu interrupted him and told him to leave them wide open. "Leave them open and light great flares inside and out," he ordered; "that will make it easier for our men to find their way back. And as for the enemy, they are more likely to be puzzled and kept out. To shut the gates looks as if we were frightened of them."

These precautions taken, Ieyasu went into his mansion, "where a maid-in-waiting named Kuno served him with a meal of boiled rice in hot water, of which he took three bowls, after which he lay down and immediately his loud snores resounded through the apartment."

Sure enough when the two leaders of the vanguard of the Takeda forces, Yamagata Masakage and Baba Nobuharu, came up to the castle and saw the gates open and the illuminations they were puzzled. "Tokugawa Dono is renowned as the greatest general on the Tokaido coast," said the latter, "and you may be sure he is up to some cunning trick or other. So be wary." "And see what men these are," he went on. "Look at their dead bodies. They all lie facing the enemy. Not one of them has turned away. Those who fell in the advance lie on their faces, while those who were killed in the retreat lie on their backs looking up to the sky. They are foes to be reckoned with."

Neither were the defenders entirely passive, for that night Okubo Tadayo and Amano Yasukage got together a band of volunteers, sixteen matchlockmen, and about a hundred other foot-soldiers, and stole out to get round on the flank of Shingen's army where it lay bivouacked for the night on the upland of Sai-ga-dani, and as they knew every path and knoll they got in quite close and suddenly opened fire and attacked, so that a small panic started among Shingen's men, and some bolted and some fell over some crags and were killed. The main body of troops was, of course, not affected at all, but a certain amount of apprehension spread among them, and Shingen seemed in doubt as to the real strength of Ieyasu and the reason for his confidence after a severe beating. And so when he held a council with his leaders as to what their course should be, they eventually concluded that it was rather unwise to stay where they were, for it would evidently take some time to overcome the resistance of the Mikawa men, and meanwhile who knew whether Nobunaga was not marching to attack them in the rear? And if they waited longer Uesugi would be quite likely to march into their province, for they knew that he was in league with Ieyasu and Nobunaga. So they decided to go back home and return again with an even larger force next year. But for Shingen there was no next year, since he died not long after, most conveniently for Ieyasu, as several others like him were to do. But the immediate result of the fight was that Shingen sent the head of Hiraide Norihide to Nobunaga, whose troops he had led, with an angry letter denouncing him for assisting his enemies and openly breaking off their up till now apparently friendly relations. Neither was he pleased with the Shogun, and when the latter, possibly influenced by Nobunaga, urged him not to make this open breach, he wrote an abrupt refusal, citing as his justification a list he drew up of the "Five Sins of Nobunaga." These sins being, as is usually the case with things people denounce, acts that he had found inconvenient. Nobunaga, not wishing to be behind in vituperation, wrote out "The

Seven Sins of Shingen," and forwarded the document to the Shogun.

In January 1573 Shingen was again in the field against Ieyasu, and entered Mikawa and laid siege to the fortress of Noda. Suganuma Sadamasa, its commander, defended it well, and held out for a month till want of provisions forced him to surrender it. Meanwhile Shingen was taken ill, according to some reports, while according to another and more picturesque though not necessarily more trustworthy account he was wounded by a bullet fired by a sharpshooter from the castle. Shingen was fond of music as of the other arts, and hearing that someone was playing the flute very well at a symposium the defenders were holding to drink up their liquor before surrendering, this being all the provision they had left, he went out and got quite close to the ramparts to enjoy the melody, thinking perhaps that no very vigilant watch would be kept. But a couple of guards on duty saw him, took careful aim, and hit him in the head. At any rate, he died in April of this year, and a great load was lifted from the shoulders of Nobunaga and Ieyasu. But they still had to deal with his son Katsuyori who, if not as formidable as his father, was still leader of a powerful clan and in no way wanting in boldness.

CHAPTER 8

KURODA JŌSUI, OR SIMON KONDERA

KURODA MOTOTAKA, father of Jōsui, is described as a warrior family of the Uda Genji, though some say he was a drug dealer. Both may be correct statements. He left Fukuoka in Bizen to escape a tyrant of those parts, and went to Himeji in Harima, and took service with Kodera Masamoto, taking also his name. Hence his son was first styled Kodera Kambyoye, the source of the "Kondera" of the Catholic missionaries. In 1576 Kambyoye, aged thirty, thus gives his opinion of the prominent personages, and their chances of coming to the top, with a view to joining the most promising. "Hojo Ujimasa is too stupid; Tokugawa Ieyasu is too small, though promising; Uesugi Kenshin is too remote; Shimazu is only great in his own opinion. Mori and Oda are the most formidable, but Mori is only the son of his father, not too able himself, and content with holding what he has got. Oda is the man to follow. Mori is supported by 'the Two Rivers' (Kobayakawa and Kikkawa), it is true, but he is not the man of the hour." He therefore put himself in the way of getting an introduction to Nobunaga through Hideyoshi. To Nobunaga he said: "Harima is the strategic point here. And the two chief families in it are Bessho of Miki and ourselves. If we join you several smaller houses will follow us, and we can take Miki from Bessho, who holds it for Mori. Then the rest will be like splitting a bamboo, when one or two knots go the rest follow." Naturally Nobunaga was pleased to hear this, and told Kambyoye to consult Hideyoshi about arrangements, and Kambyoye's son Nagamasa, then aged ten, was sent to Azuchi as a hostage. In the course of the discussion with Hideyoshi both recognize the other's ability, and soon after Kambyoye fulfils his promise by making a sudden attack on Bessho and taking his castle.

But Araki Murashige, the Christian lord of Itami in the next province of Settsu, took the opposite side, because he resented being treated with suspicion by Nobunaga. Both Kambyoye and Hideyoshi, who was a friend of his, tried to win him over to the Oda party, but Kodera Masamoto, on the contrary, was for Mori, and intrigued with Araki to get Kambyoye assassinated, persuading the latter to go to Itami to try and influence its lord. Kambyoye escaped with his life apparently because he was a fellow Christian, but he was kept in close confinement there for nine months, and when at last he made his escape he fell from the walls, and this with the effects of his imprisonment rendered him lame for the rest of his days, though we read that he went for treatment for some time to the hot springs of Arima.

Hideyoshi often referred to him as "the little cripple," or later on when he showed himself even disconcertingly capable as "that damned little cripple." Araki Murashige resembled him in being an aesthete as well as a Christian, for he was one of the Seven Disciples of Rikyu, and both of them were converted to the faith by Takayama Ukon, another of the Seven. But Kodera or Kuroda knew how to keep both these hobbies in their proper place, and seems to have become less of a Christian and more of an aesthete as he grew older. So that he lived a long and distinguished life, and died, of syphilis it is said, honored by the two Japanese religions as well as the foreign one.

CHAPTER 9

IEYASU'S FAMILY TRAGEDY

IEYASU'S wife, the Lady Tsukiyama, was, like her son, a jealous and wilful personality, a virago who would have dominated a less decided character than her husband. As time went on she became if anything more embittered, bearing Ieyasu a grudge for the death of her father among other things, while he, on his part, was not specially attentive to her, and was no more monogamous than any other Japanese noble of the time, though that should not have worried her had she possessed a sense of proportion. But this, like all egoists, she lacked. And women played little part in the life of Ieyasu except as conveniences. She had lived apart from him for some years at her residence at Tsukiyama at Okazaki while he had been at home at his capital of Hamamatsu. Since her first name is not recorded, it is by that of this residence that she is usually called, or by her former surname of Sekiguchi.

Her son Nobuyasu had married the eldest daughter of Oda Nobunaga, and they got on well together, and had two daughters. This harmony of theirs angered the mother-in-law, and she immediately began to interfere. "A great Lord must have sons," she said. "What is the good of daughters? And it is not fitting for the Lord of a Province to have one consort either. He should have many children. It is his filial duty for the sake of the family and his fief." She had little sense of humor, for this advice apparently did not apply to that distinguished feudal lord her husband. It seems that her son thought it was his filial duty to fall in with her suggestions, and it may be he did not find it a very hard task. Anyhow his mother arranged for another consort for him in the person of a daughter of Masatoki, retainer of Takeda Katsuyori. She was his daughter by a concubine, and had been driven out of her family by the slander of another such stepmother, and was at a loose end, and thus Tsukiyama Dono was able to introduce her to Nobuyasu. The rather natural result of this was that Nobuyasu's wife became the bitter enemy of his mother, and determined to get even with her. This her stepmother's indiscretion enabled her to do.

Now the Lady Tsukiyama had occasion to consult a Chinese doctor named Genkei, with whom she became very friendly, and their relations soon became rather more than those of doctor and patient. And as if this were not enough, she began to use Genkei to plot with Takeda, requesting that he attack Ieyasu and Nobunaga and exterminate them, and then give her one of his most distinguished captains as a second husband. But unfortunately one of her ladies-in-waiting was a sister of a maid of honor of the wife of Nobuyasu, and she delivered to her the twelve incriminating letters in which the plot was elaborated. These were handed to Nobunaga forthwith by his daughter, and in them there was quite enough to prove the Lady of Tsukiyama was against him, but there was a little ambiguity as to whether her son Nobuyasu was quite willing to follow her. Just then Sakai Tadatsugu arrived with a present of a horse from Ieyasu, and Nobunaga immediately showed him ten of the twelve letters and asked him what he knew about the plot. Tadatsugu showed no surprise, and said he knew all about it, and that the letters were no doubt genuine. He did this because he himself had a grudge against Nobuyasu, who "threatened his father's old retainers like dirt" at times. And also it may be he had another reason. He had taken a fancy to one of the ladies-in-waiting to Nobuyasu, and through the good offices of his wife she had been able to enter his house—his wife being probably not sorry to see her go as she was very attractive. And this did not please Nobuyasu, and he expressed his displeasure with a freedom that angered Tadatsugu all the more. So when this chance came to him he put in a word against Nobuyasu; he did not tell a lie to save him, as would have befitted a loyal retainer. Nobunaga, therefore, was quite satisfied that there was a plot against him, and sent Tadatsugu back to Ieyasu with a demand that Nobuyasu be told to put an end to himself at once. Ieyasu was not exactly pleased at this, and reproached Tadatsugu with not having known how to lie to save his son. And Tadatsugu was married to Hirotada's younger sister, Ieyasu's aunt, and so great-uncle to Nobuyasu. But Ieyasu did not think it politic to break with Nobunaga, and so consented to follow his recommendation. Hearing this decision, Nobuyasu's tutor, Hiraiwa Chikayoshi, interposed with the request that he be allowed to die instead. But Ieyasu refused. Nobunaga would not be satisfied, he said, and that would mean the sacrifice of two valuable lives instead of one. So he had Nobuyasu removed from his castle of Okazaki and put under guard.

A retainer then went and put the Lady Tsukiyama to death in Tōtōmi, and she was buried in the temple of Sairaiji at Hamamatsu. But when the retainer, Nonaka Shigemasa, reported to Ieyasu he observed that she might perhaps have been given the option of becoming a nun, at which Nonaka was very apprehensive, but it is not recorded that any harm came to him in consequence.

Nobuyasu had been sent first to Ohama and then to Futamata, and thither in the ninth month of 1579 Ieyasu dispatched Hattori Hanzo and Amakata Michitsuna to see that he committed suicide. Before doing so he told them that there was no truth in the accusation that he had been concerned in the plot with Katsuyori, and that after his death it would prove to be merely a slanderous tale. He asked Hanzo, who was his retainer and friend, to be his second, but he was overcome with emotion and could not act, whereupon Amakata took his place and cut off the young man's head that the matter might be finished quickly. And he gave the blow with a sword by Muramasa, the famous swordsmith whose blades were considered unlucky by the Tokugawa house. When Ieyasu heard the details he observed: "Even such a devil as Hanzo does not care to cut off the head of his master." This seemed ominous to Amakata, who fled to Mount Koya, and afterwards took service under Hideyasu in Echizen. Nobuyasu was in his twenty-first year while Ieyasu was now thirty-seven. Whether Nobuyasu's death was much of a loss to his family is questionable. That he was a brave and capable soldier and a born fighter is clear. He was in the field with his father against Shingen at the age of sixteen, and in the retreat from the Oigawa was very indignant when Ieyasu at first refused him the responsible post of honor of commander of the rearguard. "It isn't the thing for a young and strong man to see his father's life endangered," he objected. So Ieyasu let him have his way, and he charged the enemy at the head of a hundred horsemen and drove them back headlong. And he served just as boldly and impetuously against Takeda Katsuyori. When he faced the enemy his face used to change color and his hair bristle up, so that his father nicknamed him "Marishiten," the name of a not very pleasant-looking Buddhist deity. But he was wayward and violent, and cruel by nature. When he found out that one of his wife's ladies had informed her of his liking for the other consort he forced his way straight into his wife's apartment and stabbed the offender to death before her eyes, splitting her mouth asunder at the same time with the remark, "You are the sort of animal that makes trouble between married people." Certainly a very salutary warning to the loose-tongued.

Then again, because he did not approve of something in the costume of a dancer who was entertaining him, he shot an arrow at her and killed her on the spot. He was said to be a very good judge of dancing. Again, when he was out hawking on one occasion he caught nothing but met a priest. Taking this for cause and effect he neatly lassoed the ecclesiastic and urged his horse to a gallop, and so dragged him to death. Even Sakakibara Yasumasa had a narrow escape when he reproved him for some misconduct, for Nobuyasu seized his bow and fitted an arrow to shoot him. Yasumasa, however, was not moved, but merely observed that he had done it for his good, and if he shot him his father would probably be highly displeased. Still, if his remonstrance was so ineffective perhaps he deserved to be shot. This speech calmed Nobuyasu, and he laid down his bow. But his want of control did not make him popular with the councilors, and was not a hopeful sign in the future leader of the clan. He objected, too, to the marriage of his sister through the mediation of Nobunaga to Okudaira Nobumasa, who was, in his opinion, beneath her in standing, since he was only the lord of a castle, though his defense of it was one of the three famous sieges of Japanese history.

Still Nobuyasu had his good points, for it was he who brought about the introduction of his younger half-brother Hideyasu to his father. He was the son of O Man, lady-in-waiting to Ieyasu's wife, who had her stripped and bound and so left in a field outside the castle when she learned that she was going to have a child by Ieyasu. Here she was found and rescued by Honda Shigetsugu, who was sympathetic and who took her to a distant village and looked after her when the child was born. As the face of the baby reminded people of that of the fish called Gigi *(Pseudobagrus auriantiacus* is the only name given for it, and it was not handsome) he was called O Gi Maru.

Nobuyasu was indignant that the child was not recognized, and made it his business to introduce him to his father in 1577, when O Gi Maru was three years old. He instructed the child how to disport himself, and then suddenly introduced him through one of the sliding doors and brought him to where Ieyasu was sitting, saying, "I wish to introduce my younger brother." Ieyasu was surprised, and for him rather disconcerted, but he recovered himself quickly and did not refuse to receive O Gi Maru, greatly to the satisfaction of Nobuyasu.

When the two inspectors returned and reported to Ieyasu, not without emotion, he said nothing. Tears stood in the eyes of all in attendance, but Honda Tadakatsu and Sakakibara Yasumasa could not restrain themselves, and wept aloud. "And of what make was the wakizashi with which the second struck off the head?" inquired Ieyasu. "Muramasa," was the reply. "How ominous!" he remarked. "It was with a Muramasa blade that Abe Yashichi struck down my grandfather Kiyoyasu. And when I was a child at Miyagasaki in Suruga I cut myself with a sword by accident, and that was a Muramasa blade, too. And now my son is killed with one. Muramasa blades bode ill to our house. If any of you possess one he had better get rid of it."

HONDA NAKATSUKASA-NO-TAIYU TADAKATSU

CHAPTER 10

NAGASHINO AND THE FALL OF THE HOUSE OF TAKEDA

It now remained to deal with Takeda Katsuyori. He was no less valiant a warrior than his father, but quite lacked his subtlety and resource. "A brave commander," observed Ieyasu, "but unadaptable and with only one strong point, and so he was undone." The capacity of his father was a drawback too, for the retainers had been trained by Shingen and had every confidence in him, but they found it difficult to feel the same about the son or to co-operate with him, since he was extremely self-willed and did not consult them. Therefore, renowned as were the Ko-shu warriors, confronted by a combination like that of Nobunaga and Ieyasu there could be but little hope for Katsuyori. The only question was whether he would meet his fate on the defensive or offensive. He chose the latter, as might be expected of him. And it says much for him that he held out for ten years against these redoubtable foes. "The destruction of his clan was not his fault," comments Yamaji Aizan, "for man's fate is 90 percent luck, and when the destiny of a province is to be conquered one man cannot save it. If the powder behind the bullet that struck Ieyasu when he was fighting the Monto sectaries had been a little stronger he would have gone down to posterity as a fool who lost his life like Togashi of Kaga in a faction fight with a pack of fanatics."

So in pursuit of his forward policy, in the seventh month of 1571 Ieyasu attacked the frontier fortress of Nagashino, and took it within a month, while Suganuma Sadayoshi, the commander, fled to the temple of Horaiji.

Just then Okudaira and his son Sadamasa went over to Ieyasu. They had originally been of his party, but were compelled by Shingen to join him, but now he was dead they were very glad to return to their old allegiance. They held the castle of Tsukude nearby, and as an intimation of their change of views they fired heavily on a contingent of Takeda's men who were garrisoning the main ward of it and then departed with their relatives and valuables. The Takeda men, naturally irritated, followed them up, whereupon father and son turned on them with their two hundred horsemen and smote the Takeda five hundred to some effect.

When Katsuyori heard of this he flared up and crucified Sadamasa's wife and younger brother, as well as a girl relative who happened to be hostages with him. He then made a raid into Tōtōmi but found Hamamatsu too well guarded to attack, so he swung round and went against Imamura in Mino in Nobunaga's territory, one of a string of forts that defended his frontier. Nobunaga, hearing of this, went out with his son Nobutada to take Katsuyori in the rear, but owing to the difficulty of the country and the state of the roads could not get there before the place was surrendered owing to the treachery of its commander. So he had to retire, and in the first round it was Takeda who scored. Katsuyori also managed to take the strong castle of Takatenjin, which was defended by Ogasawara Yohachiro, of Anegawa fame.

Ieyasu called on Nobunaga to send assistance so that they could go together to relieve it, but while he was waiting for him to arrive Katsuyori stormed it with such ferocity that Ogasawara, "having been assured of the safety of his own domains elsewhere, and having run out of ammunition," thought it best to surrender. Again luck was on the side of Takeda. Since Takatenjin was only thirty miles from Hamamatsu, Ogasawara was perhaps naturally indignant that no help was sent from that quarter. However, Ieyasu restored a fort not far away from it, and put Osuga Yasutaka there to keep an eye on it, and though Takeda made another raid up to the Tenryu river with seven thousand men he thought better of it and retired again. Then Ieyasu appointed Okudaira Sadamasa commandant of the castle of Nagashino. This castle, made famous for all time by the circumstances of its defense on this occasion, was at the junction of the rivers Takigawa and Onogawa, with the upper reach of the Toyokawa, and guarded the gate leading from Kai and Shinano through Mikawa and Tōtōmi to the capital. It had changed hands more than once, and been held by both Takeda and Tokugawa.

Now the reason that Takeda brought a large force against it on this occasion was the treachery of Oga Yashiro. Oga had begun his career as a Chugen or attendant of Ieyasu, but owing to his skill in administration and his genius for finance he had been promoted from one position of trust to another till he came to have charge of the exchequer of taxation and of local government as Daikan of Mikawa, and in this capacity he had charge of affairs both in Okazaki and Hamamatsu. So indispensable was he that it became a saying in these regions that the sun could not rise properly without Oga's assistance. As usual Ieyasu recognized his ability and put him where it would be useful. But unfortunately there was another side to him. He became extravagant and overweening, and ended in falling so low as to plot against his lord. He sent a message to Katsuyori suggesting that he lead an army against

Okazaki, when he would open the gates to him and he could enter and put Nobuyasu who commanded it to death. It is possible that dislike for Nobuyasu, which was rather rife among the retainers, may have had something to do with his treachery. Then if Katsuyori took hostages from Mikawa and Tōtōmi the men of these provinces would follow him. In that case Ieyasu would no longer be able to hold Hamamatsu, and would have to retire to Owari or Ise. This plan was very pleasing indeed to Katsuyori, who lost no time in setting out with an army of about thirteen thousand men to carry it out. Unfortunately for Oga someone gave him away to Nobuyasu, and he informed his father, who as a preliminary seized Oga's wife and four children and crucified them. As his wife had tried her best to dissuade him when he told her about the plot at which she was at first incredulous, this seems regrettable, but such was the way in these days. As for Oga himself, he was tied on a horse with his face to the tail with a banner attached inscribed with his offence, and so paraded through the streets of Okazaki attended by a band of drums, bells, and fifes to advertise the procession adequately. He was then taken to Hamamatsu, where the exposure was repeated, and after it he was buried up to the neck in the ground at the cross-roads at the entrance of the town, his fingers cut off and spread out on a board in front of him, and the muscles of his legs cut. His neck was stuck through a board and a bamboo saw laid beside it which passers-by might pull. The samurai retainers would not do this for they detested him and his ways too much, so the populace seem to have obliged, and on the seventh day he died. Not a pleasant story at all, but this kind of treachery struck at the roots of military society; he was not a soldier, and he must have known well enough what he risked. And he seems to have met his end with calmness and fortitude, for when his wife was crucified he only remarked, "You have gone on first. You are lucky. I must follow after you." Like all his race he had no sense of sin, only of failure. This Oga in his early days and Okubo Nagayasu later on were the only two of his trusted retainers who took Ieyasu in, and both were financial experts. It was difficult to find officers with this kind of ability who were honest.

Now Takeda Katsuyori did not hear of the discovery of this plot till he was well on his way, and when he did he thought it would not look well to turn back again, so he went on and laid siege to Nagashino. This was rather a formidable task, for it was a strong place with a main castle and three subsidiary wards, and the rivers in the angle of which it lay were from sixty to a hundred yards wide, with high, precipitous banks. It was held by a force of about five hundred. And Okudaira Sadamasa, who was only twenty-four, was full of energy and spirit, and

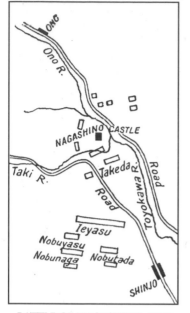

BATTLE OF NAGASHINO, 1575

a fine soldier, and was supported by Matsudaira Chikatoshi and Matsudaira Kagetada of his lord's house.

The siege began on the eighth day of the fifth month of 1575, and the Takeda men made several attacks, trying to mine the main castle and launching rafts full of men on the rivers, but the defenders countermined the one and overturned the second, so that Katsuyori lost some eight hundred men without any advantage at all. But all the same Sadamasa thought it wise to withdraw his men to the main castle. More assaults on this followed, the assailants bringing up towers to overtop the ramparts, but these the defenders demolished by gunfire and still held their own. On the fourteenth, again, the attackers made a general assault, but it failed with heavy loss, and they now sat down round the place to reduce it by starvation, setting up palisades on the land side and stretching cables across the rivers "so that not even an ant could get out." Since the defenders had only food for four or five days they had already called on Ieyasu for help, but so far no answer had come. He had sent to Nobunaga for assistance, but as yet had received no reply. Some of Nobunaga's councilors thought it a useless risk for the troops, but Sakuma Uemon advised sending a force. "It will be defeated all right," he observed, "but if we don't Tokugawa may ally with Takeda and then we shall be in a fix." According to the Mikawa Go-Fudoki this possibility was definitely suggested by a messenger sent by Ieyasu himself, who pointed out that though the Tokugawas had heretofore always been on the side of Nobunaga, present conditions might dictate an understanding with Takeda. Wherefore Nobunaga hesitated no longer. However, this is perhaps only conjecture, for it was certainly to Nobunaga's interest to support Ieyasu. So he started out from Gifu on the thirteenth and was at Okazaki the next day.

Meanwhile the condition of Nagashino was becoming more critical, and it was felt that something must be done at once, so Torii Suneemon, a retainer of Sadamasa, thirty-four years old, and famed for his bravery and enterprise, volunteered to take a message to Ieyasu.

Slipping out of the Yagyu gate at midnight on the fourteenth, he swam down the river, cutting the cables quietly with his dagger, and at sunrise on the fifteenth was able to light a beacon on Mount Kambo as arranged to let the garrison know he was safely through. Then he hastened to Okazaki and told Ieyasu that they had plenty of ammunition and their spirits were high, but there was only food for two or three days in the castle, and when that came to an end Sadamasa could only offer to commit seppuku to save his men. Ieyasu introduced Suneemon to Nobunaga, and they both commended his devotion, promising him to start the next day.

So Suneemon immediately took his leave, saying that he must let his commandant know as soon as possible that help was at hand, and on the sixteenth he again lighted three fires to apprise the besieged that a force was on its way to relieve them. But the besiegers had also perceived his first signal, and took measures accordingly. They spread sand on the river banks and watched it carefully for footprints while they stretched more cables across the rivers with bells attached to them, with the result that this time he was caught.

Brought before Katsuyori, he told his tale quite straightforwardly. Katsuyori praised his exploit, and suggested that he take service with him. That, said Suneemon, would suit him very well. "Then," pursued Katsuyori, "you will go and call to the castle garrison and tell them there is no hope of succor from Ieyasu and Nobunaga, so they had better surrender at once and their lives will be spared."

Suneemon promised to do this, and was taken close up to the castle, one account says unbound with an escort of soldiers and another hoisted up on a cross the better to attract attention, as well as to be reminded of the consequences of any deviation from his agreement. What he did was to shout out to them that both Ieyasu and Nobunaga were well on their way to deliver an attack on the investing army, and in three days they would be relieved. Those inside were much encouraged and determined to hold out, while as for Suneemon, he was naturally crucified, whether there and then or after being brought back and condemned by Katsuyori against the wish of several of his generals is a question. But his deed has never been forgotten, and among the records of the Japanese samurai his fame stands high. "Crucifixion," comments Tokutomi, "was common enough in those days." It was the alternative to seppuku or beheading. But of all the many who suffered it in this period, of all ages and both sexes, Torii Suneemon alone stands out in unique distinction. A certain retainer of Takeda is said to have been so struck by admiration for him that he had a picture of him painted on the cross and used it as a banner.

Now they realized that the enemy were advancing on them rapidly Takeda and his generals held a council of war, but they were not all of one mind. One party was for retiring, thinking it unwise to oppose their fifteen thousand men to the combined armies of thirty thousand of Nobunaga and eight thousand of Ieyasu. These were Shingen's veterans, Baba, Naito, Yamagata, Oyamada, and others. On the other hand, Atobe Oinosuke took up the usual fighting soldier's cry that has destroyed so many armies of advance and be damned to everything. "For twenty-seven generations from Shinra Saburo to Shingen the Takeda chiefs of the Genji of Kai have never turned their backs to any foe, and to do so now would be an everlasting shame." Naturally this advice commended itself to Katsuyori. Baba thought that if they must fight the best plan would be to carry the castle by assault regardless of cost. "They have not more than five hundred matchlockmen," he said, "and if you reckon on them all hitting at the first volley, and also at the second, for usually after that men shoot wildly, we shall not lose more than a thousand killed and wounded, and that is nothing much, and then we can swing the whole army round to deal with the new arrivals. And if you don't want to retire we can occupy the castle ourselves and hold out there, and Nobunaga will soon get tired of that and will want to get back to the capital." "When did you hear of Nobunaga retreating when he had once started out to fight? If he attacks what will you do? Fight to the death, of course. Well, then, if we have to fight it is better to start by attacking." And so Katsuyori decided. "Tomorrow we will stake everything on a battle," he declared, and Baba and Yamagata and the rest could do nothing but resolve to sell their lives as dearly as they could.

In opposing his fifteen thousand men to the thirty-eight thousand of the allies the odds may not have been so great if the fighting quality of the armies was considered, for the men of Kai were extremely formidable, and their prestige was great, and it was not likely that Nobunaga's levies from the district of the capital would have been able to withstand them in close fight. But Nobunaga had made his plans accordingly. Before starting out he had chosen three thousand specially selected marksmen from his whole force of ten thousand matchlockmen, and put them under the command of Sasa Narimasa, Maeda Toshiie, and three other experienced captains, and had also equipped all his men with stakes and rope for making stockades.

He gave strict orders that the sharpshooters were to hold their fire until the enemy were close up to the stockades, and that they were then to fire volleys of a thousand men alternately. This was a device that only one who possessed the resources of Nobunaga, and knew how to use them, would have been able to afford, for these weapons were expensive. And as he knew that the strong point of the Koshu troops was their charge of their well-trained cavalry he had arranged to deal with it in this manner.

Katsuyori drew up his men with right, left, and center, each consisting of three thousand, with another three thousand in reserve. The rest were manning the field-fortifications that had been thrown up round the castle.

The battle took place on the high ground of Shidara-ga-hara that stretches from the foothills of Mount Gambo to the Toyokawa River, and is rough and uneven and not at all easy for men or horses to negotiate. Nobunaga drew up his men behind a stockade facing a small and rather rapid stream that falls into the main river, with gaps at every forty or sixty yards for the convenience of counter attack. But on the left he placed Sakuma Nobumori with a force outside the stockade to entice the enemy to attack him, while on the right Okubo Tadayo, of the Tokugawa force, was posted also in front of it with three hundred matchlockmen to make a flank attack.

Meanwhile, Sakai Tadatsugu came to Nobunaga as he sat in council with his generals, and suggested that he be permitted to make an attack on the beleaguering part of the enemy force in the rear. But Nobunaga berated him for his presumption, and he retired crestfallen. However, he sent for him privately afterwards and told him he approved of the plan, but thought it best that it should be kept quiet. Even those in his council he did not entirely trust, it seems. He also gave him five hundred matchlockmen as a reinforcement, and he set out with about three thousand men in all. Under cover of a heavy rainstorm he worked round behind the enemy and divided his force into three detachments, one being sent against one position at Nakayama, which they at once bombarded so that those holding it were seized with a panic at the sudden attack and fled to the other entrenchment at Tobigasu, which was then attacked by the other two detachments which had been despatched thither, with considerable loss to the enemy and the death of the commander, Takeda Nobuzane.

Meanwhile at five o'clock on the morning of the twenty-first day Katsuyori's men began the attack on the allied armies. About two thousand men under Yamagata, Ogasawara, Atobe, and others threw themselves on the Tokugawa men under Okubo Tadayo who were outside the stockade by the bridge, but the steep banks of the river and the heavy fire of their opponents prevented them from advancing far, and the two flanks only became locked together in a hand-to-hand struggle that swayed backward and forward inconclusively. Then the Takeda center made an attack in its turn, but everywhere they were driven back by a hail of bullets from behind the stockade. And on the left wing Sakuma Nobumori was engaged with the enemy right under Baba, and soon he made a feigned retreat to draw the Takeda men on, which was successful enough, for they followed and seized a small eminence in triumph and then launched an attack against the adjoining stockade. Here, however, they were repulsed, and meanwhile another force under Shibata Katsuie and Hashiba Hideyoshi which had been detached for just this purpose made a move against their flank and rear, with the result that they lost heavily and many of their leaders were killed.

Katsuyori then threw in his reserves and ordered an attack all along the line, but as before it made no headway owing to the heavy fire of the Oda and Tokugawa troops, and was reeling when Sasa Narimasa gave the signal to Nobunaga that the crisis had come and he in turn ordered his army to turn to the attack. The Oda troops issued from the gaps in their stockade and the Tokugawa men round their flank and fell on the shaken enemy, who soon gave way at the shock and fled. And so by about three o'clock in the afternoon the fight was over, and of all the Takeda forces only about three thousand escaped, and their opponents took about ten thousand heads. For in the assaults on the stockade they had been shot down in heaps, and Baba and Yamagata and Naito and the Sanada brothers and many other of his veteran leaders were killed and the Ko-shu armies largely crippled in this battle. And the Oda and Tokugawa forces lost no less than six thousand.

It was a triumph for Nobunaga's modern methods and clever tactics compared with the conventional mass attacks of his opponents. The chief drawbacks in the matchlock were its short range and slow loading, so that there was a danger of the troops being rushed and broken by a vigorous charge before they had time to reload. But this defect Nobunaga overcame by the use of the stockade and by training the men to withhold their fire till the enemy was quite close and to pour in alternate volleys. It was the machine gun and wire entanglement of those days, and according to the views of Lieutenant-General Oshigami writing in 1913, not much improvement on Nobunaga's methods has since been made. And as there is always a good supply of generals of the Takeda type, perhaps there has been little need for it.

Ieyasu's comment on the battle was this: "Nobunaga and I were superior in numbers, and yet though we had a triple stockade in front of us he must needs come charging down on it. Naturally he got beaten. But if he had taken up a position behind the Takigawa River he could have held us up for ten days anyhow, and we should have had to retire. Then he could have launched an attack on us, and ten to one it would have been successful. It is a pity he was such a fool."

And one of the current lampoons expressed the popular opinion with the usual puns:

> Katsuyori to nanoru Takeda no Kai mo naku
> Ikusa ni makete Shina no warusa yo!

The Takeda called Katsuyori is quite worthless (he has lost Kai)
He has lost the battle for his quality is bad (Shinano is no good).

As soon as he saw how the battle was going, Okudaira Sadamasa and his men sallied out of the castle and attacked the besieging troops, who were soon beset on the other side as well by Sakai and his detachment, so that those who were not destroyed broke and fled with the others. And so the siege was raised.

After the battle Ieyasu complimented Okudaira Sadamasa on his distinguished exploits, and granted him considerable estates and the right of audience for his family after him. Beside this he presented him with the Yoshimitsu sword that he himself had received from Nobunaga after the Anegawa victory, and also at the request of Nobunaga he gave him his eldest daughter, O Kame, in marriage. Nobunaga also received him, and presented him with one syllable of his name, so that he was afterwards known as Nobumasa.

Nobunaga also requested Ieyasu to be good enough to put out of the way his uncle Mizuno Nobumoto, lord of Kariya, since this warrior had been inconsiderate enough to sell rice to Akiyama, lord of the Takeda castle of Iwamura in Shinano, which was being besieged by Nobunaga's orders. Or at least so Sakuma Nobumori alleged, quite possibly slanderously. Ieyasu did not particularly love this hot-tempered elder brother of his mother's in all probability, but anyhow he wished to oblige Nobunaga, so he sent Hiraide Chikayoshi, who killed him, just how is not stated.

For the next seven years, until the final campaign against him, Ieyasu was engaged in a desultory series of operations against Takeda Katsuyori, each making raids into the territory of the other, but usually retiring before there was an opportunity for any considerable collision. On one of these occasions it is recorded that in 1578, when he was attacking the castle of Tanaka, Ii Manchiyo, aged eighteen, first did distinguished service in battle. He was the orphan son of Ii Naochika, lord of Iidani, who had been put to death by Imagawa Yoshimoto, and was to become in after years the famous Ii Hyobu-shoyu Naomasa, one of the chief pillars of the Tokugawa house.

Now Uesugi Kenshin had fallen out with Nobunaga on account of the interference of the latter in the affairs of Echizen, which Kenshin considered his sphere of influence, and also through the machinations of the Shogun Yoshiaki, who was persuading him to adopt this attitude, and when in the early spring of 1578 he mobilized all his forces it appeared that he was going to try conclusions with him, though what he was apparently really about to do was to march in the other direction and attack Hojo, when at high noon on the ninth day of the third month of this year he was struck down in his lavatory with an attack of apoplexy, and without recovering consciousness he passed away on the thirteenth. It seems that liquor hastened his end, for this chaste and vegetarian Galahad of Japan liked wine as he disliked women, and so died in middle age without an heir.

So fortunate was his death for Nobunaga that as usual it was suggested that the time and place being the same the real cause of death was an assassin and not disease. But there is no proof of this.

The next thing Takeda Katsuyori did was to make an alliance with Kenshin's adopted son, Kagekatsu, who asked if he might marry Shingen's daughter, to which request Katsuyori gladly assented. This alliance offended Hojo, and he at once threw in his lot with Oda and Tokugawa. Why Katsuyori should have done such an unwise thing is not easy to fathom, for it laid him open to attack on both sides, but it was perhaps in keeping with his fearless unthinking nature.

In 1579 Katsuyori led out an army of sixteen thousand men to cut off Ieyasu, who had led a force into Suruga to co-operate with Hojo Ujimasa. But when he thought he had him Ieyasu suddenly crossed the river Oi back into Tōtōmi. "If I could have caught him in Suruga and destroyed him!" he exclaimed, shedding tears of baffled rage. "Nobunaga alone would not have been able to do me any damage. And if I had got Mikawa and Tōtōmi I would have been in Owari after Nobunaga next spring. Ah, what a pity!"

The next thing Ieyasu did was to prepare to take the fortress of Takatenjin, a stronghold of Takeda situated less than fifteen miles from Hamamatsu. Owing to its position Katsuyori was strongly dissuaded by his generals from trying to relieve it lest another experience like that of Nagashino should be the result. So he did nothing. Therefore in the autumn of 1580 Ieyasu had the place completely surrounded by a moat and rampart, and this again by a manifold stockade with a soldier posted at intervals of six feet. And to guard against any possibility of attack from a relieving force he built another rampart facing in the reverse direction.

And so things remained until the third month of the next year, when some of the besieged tried to force their way out and a general attack was ordered and it soon fell, thus returning to Ieyasu eight years after it had been surrendered by Ogasawara Yohachiro to Katsuyori.

A characteristic incident of this siege was that the garrison heard that Ieyasu had in attendance on him the famous Noh player, Saiwaka Yosaburo, and sent a message asking that they might have the pleasure of hearing him since any day might now be their last on earth, and they would greatly appreciate this final treat. Touched by this tasteful request, Ieyasu told Saiwaka to perform before them, and suggested that he choose pieces expressing pathos suitable to the occasion. So the great singer went up as close as he could to the fortress and the defenders crowded up into one of the towers, and all listened with deep emotion. When the performance was over a single warrior wearing a madder-colored haori came out of the castle and handed Saiwaka a present of specially fine paper and embroidered work. And the very next day the general attack took place, in which all the garrison fell after fighting with the greatest valor, and especially the warrior in the madder-colored haori. And in its dungeon was found one Okawachi Masamoto, who had been confined there ever since, because he refused to give up his allegiance like Ogasawara, and who had lost the use of his legs in consequence. He was brought before Ieyasu, who rewarded him for his loyalty with presents of gold and a pair of swords with his own hands. But he was not satisfied with his own conduct, it seems, for he shaved his head and became a recluse, taking the name of Kaiku (All Vanity). It was on this occasion, too, that Ieyasu was able to pay back an old score on Haramiishi Mondo, who was taken alive by one of Okubo Tadayo's men. He had not forgotten how this former retainer of Imagawa had insulted him when a boy by saying, "I am sick of the sight of that Mikawa youth," and now recalled it, saying, "And you are a person for whom I have no earthly use either." And so they put him to death.

Takeda Katsuyori now built a castle at a place northwest of Nirasaki, and in the twelfth month of the same year, 1581, he proclaimed it his new capital and moved into it. This was an entire departure from the ways of his father Shingen, of whom it was said that he never had a fortified capital. A residence with one moat was enough for him. The whole province of Kai was in fact his castle.

Moreover, Katsuyori had been becoming more and more unpopular in his province, and not only had the people less confidence in his ability to defend them, but as he was wayward and careless in his administration and judicial decisions, very different from the strict and impartial though stern and severe rule of his father, both the retainers and the populace generally became more and more discontented, and not only lost hope of holding out against the Oda and Tokugawa alliance but rather began to look forward to a change of masters and to prepare for it like the proverbial rats, for after all their own interest was apt to come first when the lord was distrusted.

The first definite step was taken by one Kiso Yoshimasa of Shinano, descendant in the twenty-second generation of the famous Kiso Yoshi-naka, who held the castle of Kiso-Fukushima and who had become a tributary of Shingen, one of whose daughters he had married. At the beginning of 1582 he revolted, and transferred his allegiance to Nobunaga. Upon this Katsuyori mobilized about fifteen thousand men and marched into Kiso, but was unable to make any impression in this rough mountain country and was repulsed. The next month Nobunaga sent word to his allies Tokugawa and Hojo to take the field with him against Takeda. He himself was still otherwise occupied, so his eldest son, Nobutada, led his divisions. As soon as these allied forces moved into the Takeda territory the commanders of the forts began to surrender to them. In a way that Tokutomi stigmatizes as common enough in Chinese history but very rare in Japanese his great vassals left him for the obviously winning side. Even his near relations deserted him for Anayama Baisetsu, who now threw in his lot with Ieyasu, was Shingen's nephew and Katsuyori's cousin and brother-in-law. It may be that he was incensed with Katsuyori for breaking off the engagement of his daughter with his own son, for some reason, though perhaps for eugenic reasons he should not have resented it.

Two uncles also at this crisis found they had urgent business else-where, and left their castles and made their way rather hurriedly into the neighboring provinces. In this way it was not long before out of his large army of nearly twenty thousand men Katsuyori was left with not many more than three thousand. It is true that one of his younger brothers, Nishina Nobumori, put up a very fine fight indeed at his castle of Takato in Shinano. So fiercely did his men assault the besiegers that Nobutada had to take a sword himself and put himself at the head of a strong party which eventually broke into the fortress with some difficulty. No quarter was given, and all the garrison fell fighting with their women and children, several of the women throw-ing themselves into the *mêlée* with the men like seasoned warriors. Four hundred heads were taken by the victors. Nishina himself, after standing up on one of the castle turrets and telling Nobutada just what sort of a man his father was, putting his relations to death, and burn-ing the Enryakuji and killing multitudes of both priests and laymen, prophesied his death very shortly, and then cut himself open in the form of a cross and died.

Katsuyori had been relying on this stronghold for a refuge, for now he had to retreat from his new capital, since its fortifications were not sufficiently advanced to be of any use, and there seemed no place left that could be defended.

Ieyasu now advanced with Anayama Baisetsu as a guide through Kakegawa, Makino, and Tanaka, which latter place surrendered to him, and then on to Sumpu. Hence he penetrated to Monjudo in Kai.

Nobunaga, too, started out in the third month to take part in the hunting down of Katsuyori. He left Gifu and proceeded to Inuyama and from there to Iwamura. His leisurely movements showed that he did not anticipate much trouble, and indeed it was rather strange that by this time Katsuyori was practically left alone, for none of his relatives and friends attempted to assist him against the hostile forces that were now closing in on him on all sides. The rest of his family fled to Komoro castle and shut themselves up there, leaving him to shift for himself.

So in the third month, after setting fire to the buildings of his new capital, Katsuyori tried to decide where to go, but his few remaining retainers could not make up their minds. He started out with some five hundred samurai, but these began to desert him before they had gone far, and eventually only about forty were left. Oyamada Nobushige offered him shelter in his castle of Iwadono, and Katsuyori decided to accept, but Oyamada slipped away in the night with his mother, who was a hostage with Katsuyori, made his way to his castle, and then shut the gates against his lord. Truly Katsuyori could not find anywhere to lay his head.

Meanwhile Nobutaka had entered the province of Kai and seized and put to death most of the Takeda family and their great vassals he could find, sparing only three of them. Katsuyori and his wife and his son Nobukatsu and a number of ladies-in-waiting with a few faithful samurai led by the three brothers Tsuchiya who followed him to the last, were making their way through the rough mountain country seeking some place in which to make a last stand. It was a painful and exhausting experience for the ladies, accustomed only to the elegance and comfort of feudal mansions, to have to trudge along footsore over the rugged paths in the hills. Unable to proceed any farther, they were surrounded and brought to bay at a place called Tago. The women were taken and put to death and Katsuyori and his son and the three brothers, after a last desperate fight in which they inflicted some loss on the enemy, ended their lives by seppuku. Katsuyori's young wife, nineteen years old, first stabbed herself and her husband acted as second and cut off her head, after which he killed himself and his son followed suit, the brothers Tsuchiya assisting them. This done, the three brothers made another assault on the enemy and drove them back, and then they, too, committed suicide.

So did an unwise autocrat bring about the ruin of one of the greatest feudal clans, for without the loyal co-operation of retainers and vassals in these days no feudal lord could keep his fief. Katsuyori lacked those qualities that were most conspicuous in Ieyasu, shrewdness and adaptability and self-control or patience. Shingen's share of them he did not inherit, but only his fearlessness, which unqualified did him no good. No doubt the lesson of his failure was not lost on Ieyasu while he gathered in the material fruits of it.

When Takeda Katsuyori committed suicide his head was brought to Nobunaga for inspection, and when he saw it he shouted angrily, "Your father was discourteous to me more than once, and now his rudeness has come home to roost on you. So much the worse for you, isn't it? Your father was anxious enough to come to the capital, but it is your head that will be taken there and stuck on the gibbet." Then he turned to his men and remarked, "Just look at this head. You can imagine how immensely it pleases me to see it like this!" On the other hand, when it was brought round to Ieyasu for his inspection he got up from his campstool and had it put on a ceremonial stand and set on the dais. Then with a respectful salute he addressed it, "Ah, I never expected to see you thus. It is because of your youthful impetuosity in not heeding the advice of your veteran councilors that this has happened to you." And he gave orders for it to be buried in the Kogan-in at Nakayama, since for fear of Nobunaga the Takeda family temple of Eirinji dared not receive his remains. And he further ordered a shrine to be built in its honor, which he called Tendosan Keitoku-in, and gave some rice-land as its endowment. Naturally the Oda retainers contrasted Ieyasu's delicacy with their master's boorishness, and but eighty days after this Nobunaga himself fell in the tragedy of the Honnōji.

CHAPTER 11

DEATH OF NOBUNAGA.
IEYASU'S FLIGHT THROUGH IGA

IEYASU now went up to visit Nobunaga at Azuchi, taking with him Anayama Baisetsu, formerly chief retainer of Takeda Shingen. Here he was splendidly treated and shown round the castle, and taken up to the top of the keep to enjoy the splendid view over the surrounding country, after which he inspected the landscape gardens, of which Nobunaga was very proud. He was also entertained at a Noh performance, and the usual valuable presents of horses, weapons, and gold were tendered by him. Nobunaga served him at dinner with his own hand, as was usual with highly honored guests. Akechi Mitsuhide was the supervisor of the entertainment.

They spent six days with Nobunaga, and then went on to see the sights of Kyoto and Sakai, accompanied by Hasegawa Togoro, one of Nobunaga's chief officers, as guide. At Kyoto they were directed to stay at the house of Chaya Shirojiro, a wealthy merchant venturer. His house had been called Nakashima originally, but the Shogun Yoshimasa always spoke of it as Chaya or Tea-house because he used to go there for tea-meetings, and so that came to be its name. He became a lifelong friend of Ieyasu and did him many services in the course of his life. He is also inseparably connected with his death, for it was after eating the delicacy he recommended that the old Shogun was attacked by his last illness.

It was on this occasion that the alleged insult to Akechi occurred that is said by some to have been the reason for his revenge on Nobunaga. He had prepared the best feast he could for Ieyasu's welcome, and had it all set out ready for serving when Nobunaga came in to inspect it, and immediately called out that the fish and fowl stank, and without more ado kicked the lot over all about the apartment, while he abused Akechi and finally relieved him of his office, and told several other retainers to act in his place. Seeing that it was the hottest season of the year and Nobunaga was a fanatic for cleanliness, this was not so surprising.

On the thirtieth of the fifth month of 1582 he was at Sakai, and received a message from Nobunaga inviting him to stay with him in the capital. So he sent Chaya Shirojiro on first, and then Honda Tadakatsu with a message to Nobunaga. His chief retainers, Sakai Tadatsugu, Ishikawa Kazumasa, Ii Naomasa Sakakibara Yasumasa, and Okubo Tadachika, were with him. Now Honda had but just set out when he met Chaya coming back on a packhorse. "This is what the world has come to!" he exclaimed as soon as he met Honda. "This morning Akechi revolted and burst into the Honnōji where His Highness was staying and set fire to it so that he committed seppuku. His heir was also surrounded in his lodgings, and after a fierce fight he, too, cut himself open. I have hurried back with the news." Honda at once brought him to Ieyasu, and he, excluding all but the chief retainers, listened carefully to the whole story. He then called Hasegawa, and told him that his sense of loyalty and his regard for Nobunaga made it his duty at once to march against Akechi and avenge his death, but unfortunately, with his small following, that was quite impossible, so nothing was left for him but to go back to Kyoto, make his way to the Chion-in, and there commit suicide to accompany him to the other world. "Much more reason is there," replied Hasegawa, "that I should kill myself first and be your forerunner." And he called to Honda, and they all set out, Honda and Chaya leading. But they had not gone far when Honda turned to Sakai and Ishikawa and suggested that they advise their lord that, though it was no doubt correct to do as they intended, it would be much more effective if they could make their way back to their fief and put themselves at the head of their troops there and lead them against Akechi. To lay his head before Nobunaga's spirit would be the most gratifying service to their late chief. Ieyasu agreed, but objected that they were in unknown territory abounding in bandits, so that they could hardly hope to get home safely. Here Hasegawa interposed that he could probably take them through, for he had been guide to Nobunaga when he was on campaign in these very parts.

So they decided to attempt it, and turned off in the direction of the coast, with the exception of Anayama Baisetsu, who took another road and, sure enough, was intercepted by a band of highwaymen and put to death with his following not far from Uji.

Hasegawa sent forward a messenger to Toichi Gemba Tomitsu of Izumi for assistance, and they went on by the country roads, Honda Tadakatsu brandishing his halberd "Dragon-fly Cutter" in the faces of the rustics with a view to eliciting reliable information about the route, and Chaya Shirojiro distributing money generously with the same purpose. Both were apparently effective in their fashion. Thus, when they came to the Kizugawa there was no proper ferry, so Honda used the business end of his halberd to haul out two brushwood boats, in which they got across, when he carefully pounded them into splinters with the butt to prevent any uninvited pursuit. So they went by the Sagara district of Yamashiro around the Tsuzuki district to Hachiman-yama, where they came on the not unexpected bandits, who confronted them to the number of several hundreds, but here again Honda did good service and succeeded in scattering them. That night Ieyasu put up with Hattori Sadanobu, priest of the Gofuku shrine. Next day they came to the Uji river, where again there was no ferry, but they discovered a ford and also a small boat for Ieyasu, and got over safely. An escort from the castle of Seta prevented any more attacks of the banditti, and so they went along by road across the pass into Iga. One of Ieyasu's men, Hattori Hanzo, was a native of Iga and knew the country, and was able to take them through. It was a fortunate thing for Ieyasu that the year before when Nobunaga had been on campaign there and had ordered a thorough extermination of the local samurai, a number of these had fled into the Tokugawa territory and had been kindly treated there. So that when they heard of the presence of Ieyasu among them, several hundred at once hastened to meet him and reinforce his small band. And so he had a comparatively easy journey to the small port of Shirako on the Iga coast. Here those who had escorted him were dismissed with suitable presents of valuable swords, while the heads of a few eminent brigands were presented for the inspection of Ieyasu as a return compliment, so that both sides parted in a happy frame of mind.

At Shirako there happened to be the merchant venturer Kadoya Shichirojiro with a big ship, who took them on board, and a fair wind bore them without delay to the port of Ohama in Mikawa, and so home. They beguiled the pleasant voyage with a merry discussion of the hardships and dangers they had surmounted, though this experience was considered the greatest hazard of Ieyasu's life. They were six days in all on the journey to Okazaki. The voyage was fortunate for Kadoya too, since Ieyasu afterwards gave him a monopoly of the carrying trade in those regions.

There is a Kodan story that relates how the ship was searched by agents of Akechi, who were on the watch to kill Ieyasu. He was hastily hidden under the cargo in the hold, but one of the searchers plunged his spear down into the interior several times to make sure, and one of the thrusts wounded Ieyasu in the thigh. Without a moment's hesitation he pulled out a towel and carefully wiped the blade of the spear as it was withdrawn, so that the soldier, seeing no tell-tale blood on it, went off convinced that his quarry was not there.

CHAPTER 12

IEYASU GETS KAI AND SHINANO

A WEEK after arriving at Okazaki he marched out again against Akechi, and got as far as Atsuta, when a messenger reached him from Hideyoshi with the news of the battle of Yamazaki and the defeat and death of the slayer of Nobunaga at the hands of his forces, so as there was no further need of his assistance he returned again to Okazaki.

Just then, fortunately for him, a rebellion broke out in Kai against Kawajiri Hidetake, who had held the province for Nobunaga after the defeat of Takeda Katsuyori and, relying on his support, had behaved arbitrarily, so that the men of Kai, whose temper was none of the mildest, would put up with him no longer. After Nobunaga's death, Ieyasu sent Honda Nobutoshi to him suggesting that if he wished to go to Kyoto he would give him a safe conduct through the Mikawa territory in the event of his own people besetting the raids of Kai to stop him. This rather broad hint did not please Kawajiri at all, for he no doubt guessed that his subjects considered putting themselves under Ieyasu rather than tolerate him any longer, so he made Honda drunk and had him killed, after which he attempted to march out of Kai with his retainers, whereupon the people precipitated themselves on him and his men and put them all to death.

Ieyasu did not hesitate, but stepped in and took possession without more ado. At this Hojo Ujimasa, considering this expansion a matter that could not be passed without protest, moved a large army through Shinano into Kai. He had about fifty thousand men to Ieyasu's seven thousand, but there was no comparison between the leaders, for Hojo was unprogressive and sluggish, so his greater force was able to make no impression, but was led a goose chase by Ieyasu's generals until he was tired of it, when his brother Ujinori, who had become a hostage with Ieyasu with Imagawa, began negotiations between the two houses, which resulted in Ieyasu taking the provinces of Kai and Shinano, while the Hojo got Kazusa, and Ujinori was married to the daughter of Ieyasu, which alliance was more useful to the latter than the former. Hideyoshi had meanwhile come to an open rupture with Shibata Katsuie over the question of the succession to Nobunaga, but in the campaign that followed, and that resulted in Katsuie's defeat and suicide,

Ieyasu took no part. He was busy with his newly acquired territory and had no wish to intervene, though Shibata sent him a message of congratulation on the increase of his domains, with a present of twenty tan of Chinese brocade, a hundred bales of cotton, and some fine shark skin, accompanied by the suggestion that he would do as well to join him. But Ieyasu did not think so.

On the other hand, he sent his congratulations to Hideyoshi on his victory, as was only courteous perhaps, and some say even started out with some troops, just as Shibata's career ended, and with it the career of Nobutaka, the third son of Nobunaga, who, with his elder brother Nobuo, had been appointed guardian of the small child Samboshi, later Hidenobu, who was the heir. As a present Ieyasu sent Hideyoshi the excellent tea-jar Hatsubana, while Hideyoshi responded with a fine sword by Kuniyuki.

This year (1583) Ieyasu was promoted to the Upper Fourth Court Rank and to the office of Sakon-e-gon-chujo, and in 1544 he was again advanced to be Sangi of the Lower Third Rank. Hideyoshi's rank was not so high, for he was only Sangi of the Lower Fourth Rank, but probably he wished to place Ieyasu under some obligation and so bind him to himself, for it must have been with his consent at least that he was promoted.

When he acquired the province of Kai, Ieyasu appointed Hiraide Chikayoshi Daikan over it, with Naruse Masakata and Kusakabe Sadayoshi as Bugyo. He made Iwama Okurazaemon Metsuke, but under these officers of his he appointed a number of others from Kai as advisers. This, he said, was the best way to keep the province peaceable and in order. "The Chinese characters that make up the word 'Sata' ('decision') are composed of the elements signifying 'pebbles,' 'sand,' and 'earth,' and to resolve these, he explained, you must sift them and wash them in water so that the earth is removed and the stones appear. And if they don't it is because they are not washed properly. And it does not matter if people take a little by the way if they do not inconvenience the lord." Then he examined and found out just how loyal the Kai retainers had been in Shingen's time, and those who had been faithful were employed again, some at their original stipends and others at slightly smaller ones. And as he restored the Takeda temple and built a shrine for Katsuyori as well, they realized his benevolent disposition and were entirely docile and submissive.

CHAPTER 13

LORD OF FIVE PROVINCES.
IEYASU OPPOSES HIDEYOSHI

So now, as the result of his alliance with Nobunaga and his victory over Takeda by which he obtained Tōtōmi and Suruga, and then by his astuteness and enterprise in the confusion that followed his death that gave him Kai and Shinano, Ieyasu was lord of five provinces in a fine strategic position for profiting by any other favorable circumstances that might arise, and second only in reputation to Hideyoshi. Of course, Hideyoshi's rise was the more striking, for whereas Ieyasu had been Nobunaga's ally he now found himself in a position of inferiority to Hideyoshi who had been merely a vassal who had risen from the ranks. It was one that he could hardly find pleasant, and it needed all his shrewdness and patience to hold his own dignity and domain with one of Hideyoshi's genius. The first steps he took were to ally himself with Oda Nobuo in Owari, his western neighbor, while in the same year (1583) he married his daughter to Hojo Ujinao on his eastern frontier; and since beside his trusty Mikawa samurai he now had Shingen's old retainers, who had apparently no objection to serving two masters, and who brought to him all the experience in military and administrative affairs that they had acquired from their former lord, he could face the future with some confidence.

Hideyoshi was similarly allied with Uesugi of Echigo on his northeastern and Ieyasu's northern frontier, and with Mori who held the rest of the mainland to the west of his territory.

Ieyasu and Nobuo were then the only powers he had to fear, and he tried to deal with them first by diplomatic methods, for he is said to have offered Ieyasu the two provinces of Mino and Owari if he would throw in his lot with, or actually under him, but he could not be tempted. On the other hand he made overtures to three of Nobuo's chief councilors to undermine their allegiance, and this it was that led to an open breach. Nobuo had them put to death and appealed to Ieyasu to help him against Hideyoshi. Ieyasu at once consented. No doubt he anticipated a collision sooner or later, for Hideyoshi's ambition was not compatible with any equal in the Empire, and calculated that no better occasion was likely to present itself than this.

It might appear that he would have done better to have thrown in his lot with Shibata, for their allied forces might easily have overthrown Hideyoshi, but in that case the question would hardly have been much nearer solution, for Shibata was also formidable, and then there were the irreconcilable claims of the two brothers, Nobutaka and Nobuo. Now the stage was clearer, for the former was out of the way and Nobuo was in reality quite commonplace and not very strong, so that while he appeared to be the leader he really was only a tool of Ieyasu.

It certainly looked better to fight for Nobuo's rights than for his own advantage, for, anyhow, he would get some credit for loyalty to the memory of Nobunaga, while at the same time he was likely to gain more in a contest with so powerful an antagonist as Hideyoshi even if he did not emerge the victor. And Hideyoshi was certainly at a disadvantage in fighting against the son of his late lord.

Ieyasu now made arrangements with the feudatories on Hideyoshi's rear to rise and embarrass him. Sasa Narimasa was to attack Kaga and Echizen and so paralyse his allies Niwa and Maeda in these provinces, while Chosokabe Motochika and Kasokabe in Shikoku were to cross over to attack Hideyoshi from the east, and he offered the Hongwanji monks and also the Shingon temples of Saiga and Negoro their former possessions in Kaga and elsewhere if they would join in. Hideyoshi was not slow in starting the same kind of negotiations. He sent word to Uesugi Kagekatsu to advance on Sasa, and at the same time to menace the Tokugawa rear, while Maeda and Niwa attacked Sasa on the other side. Nakamura Kazumasa, Hachisuka Iemasa, and Kuroda Yoshitaka were detailed against the monks, while in Awaki Sengoku was to intercept Chosokabe and his ally, and in Okayama Ukita Hideie would deal with Mori and block his advance. In the Kwanto, Satake was called on to join Uesugi and attack Homo and Ieyasu. The feudatories of Ise and Iga were on his side, and also his old colleague Hosokawa Tadaoki, Inaba Ittetsu, Gamo Ujisato, and Hori Hidemasa. The nearest to him were Ikeda Nobuteru (Shonyu) at Ogaki and Mori Nagayoshi at Kanayama in Mino. Altogether his allies outnumbered the Tokugawa party nearly three to one.

Ikeda at first hesitated when invited by Nobuo to join him, and consulted his retainers. One said that they ought not to forget their obligations to Nobunaga's house and ought to support his heir, for both he and Mori were hereditary vassals, having served Nobunaga's father Nobuhide; but another councilor objected that though this was so they must consider the future of their own house first, and Hideyoshi was the rising power. While Nobuteru hesitated which side to support, a messenger arrived from Hideyoshi offering the provinces of Owari and

Mino (before offered to Ieyasu), and this decided him. An unfortunate decision for him, for it cost him his life. "By this you can judge the rest," comments Tokutomi, "for they were all a lot of cat-watchers." Probably Ieyasu knew well enough that he had no chance of defeating Hideyoshi, but if he did not lose he would make a great name for himself, and if he did it would be in the best of causes. For his men were first-class fighters, and his side had more cohesion, a central position, and fewer self-seeking trimmers. Both leaders were in their prime, Hideyoshi forty-nine and Ieyasu forty-three. Nobuo was no soldier, though skilful enough at elegant and unpractical accomplishments.

Ieyasu made the first move by marching to Kiyosu and joining Nobuo, while Hideyoshi remained at Sakamoto in Omi, evidently because he was uncertain of the reliability of some of his allies, as a long letter to Niwa Nagahide in Echizen about his dispositions makes clear.

The fighting began in western Owari and Ise, where Nobuo took a few strong places held against him by the relatives of the councilors he had killed, and then awaited Hideyoshi's onset. He strengthened the castle of Mine in Ise with five thousand men, but Hideyoshi sent ten thousand against it under Gamo Ujisato, cut off part of its garrison who had sallied out to fight him, and invested it. Tsutsui Junkei also starved out the castle of Matsugashima, one of these fortresses in Ise, though it held out for nearly three weeks and its defenders sallied out and inflicted considerable loss on his men.

But the first important move was made by Ikeda Nobuteru in taking the castle of Inuyama, of which he had formerly been the lord and so was well acquainted with its defenses. It had a small garrison but was very well protected by the river and by marshy land. However, Ikeda arranged with some friends he had in the neighborhood to ferry a company of his men across the River Kiso and land at a place left unguarded by an accomplice inside. A Zen priest led the defenders and did valiantly, for the commander had been killed in a private feud shortly before, but he was at length slain and his men overpowered, so that Ikeda and his son Terumasa entered in triumph, much acclaimed by the citizens and farmers of the district, who seem to have had happy memories of his rule. Terumasa had been a hostage with Nobuo, but he had been foolishly sent back to his father to demonstrate Nobuo's good will, thereby making it easier for Nobuteru to join the other side. And so they all had a feast of fish and liquor before the gates and were very merry. The taking of this castle was regarded as a very smart piece of work well executed, since, for example, Ikeda did not himself lead the attackers for fear of a trap, even though he had taken hostages from his accomplice; and as soon as they had entered Inaba Ittetsu was detailed to go and hold the gates to prevent any possible attempt to retake it by an ambush from outside. They left little to chance.

Then Ikeda's son-in-law, Mori Nagayoshi, also wishing to distinguish himself, pushed out with some five thousand men to Haguro with the intention of making for Komaki. Sakai Tadatsugu, who was watching his movements, reported this to Ieyasu and asked him if he might strike a blow immediately at this isolated force and destroy it before it could be supported. Ieyasu consented and Sakai, Okudaira Nobumasa, Sakakibara, Osuga, Honda Yasushige, Matsudaira Ietada, and Matsudaira Ienobu and other leaders went off by night with another five thousand men, and by dawn the next day came up with Mori and at once launched an attack. The battle began with an archery and matchlock action across the river, and then Okudaira, seeing that the enemy were shaken by their fire, made a charge followed by the others, and succeeded in making them give ground considerably. Then Mori rallied his men in some old trenches in the village and another stiff fight took place, but once more he was driven back, and Sakai with a couple of thousand men made a circling movement at his rear, with the result that he made precipitately for his base in no good order, losing some three hundred men in the action and in the pursuit, which was continued for some distance. This was a distinct score for Ieyasu.

Sakakibara then pointed out to his lord the advantage of taking Komaki Hill, a rounded eminence less than half a mile away, about 280 feet high, and surrounded by marshy land, which commanded all the surrounding country and had formerly been used as a castle by Nobunaga before he made his headquarters at Kiyosu. This was done and Sakakibara's men spent a week digging trenches round it and also making two entrenched positions to the east of it as well as repairing two other old forts at Hira and Kobata, one to protect their communications with Kiyosu, and the other those with Mikawa.

After taking Komaki, Sakakibara Yasumasa made proclamation as follows:

Hashiba Hideyoshi, son of a peasant from a thatched cottage, who began life as a foot soldier, was favored exceedingly by Nobunaga, who raised him to be a commander and gave him a large fief, his grace being as extensive as Heaven and Earth. But after his death Hideyoshi straightway forgot all his obligations to his former lord and intrigued to take possession of the Empire. His son Nobutaka he has put to death, and now is leading an army against Nobuo. Such treachery is contrary to all decency and beyond description. My master Ieyasu, out of deep regard for his ancient friendship with Nobunaga, sympathizing with the unfortunate plight of Nobuo, has allied with him to smite these rebels, and let all who cannot endure such evil and will not thus shame their fair ancestral reputation join his righteous array.*

Meanwhile, the ecclesiastics of Negoro and Saiga, to the number of 30,000, had divided into three armies, one of which marched on Otsu in Izumi and was repulsed, another attacked Sakai, and the third Kishiwada and Kuroda. Hearing of this Hideyoshi started from Osaka on the twenty-first with 25,000 men with the intention of striking at Ieyasu and his main army. By the twenty-sixth he was at Gifu, marching from there to Unuma, where he crossed the Kiso on a bridge of boats and entered Inuyama on the twenty-seventh. Then he pushed out to Ninomiyama on the hills overlooking Haguro to examine the country and determine the positions of his divisions, which these under Hosokawa, Niwa, Gamo, Hori, Inaba Ittetsu, and his son, proceeded to take up and entrench. By this time his force amounted to some 80,000 men.

---

* *Annals of the Sakakibara House.*

CHAPTER 14

THE KOMAKI CAMPAIGN

IEYASU then took part of his army to Komaki, strengthening the communications between this place and Kiyosu, where the rest was stationed, and making a strong post at Taraku against the enemy position at Nijubori opposite, and laying down a military road between this place and the stronghold of Utatsu.

Hideyoshi on his part built a rampart 15 feet high and 3 feet thick between Nijubori and Iwasaki-yama, a distance of nearly a mile and a half, with several gates in it, so that he could hold the position safely against attack while he considered his next move. His own headquarters he made at an old fort called Gakuden, well behind these lines, and thus the two armies dug themselves well in and lay opposite each other, both fearing to repeat the mistake of Nagashino by making a frontal attack.

The first move was not planned by Hideyoshi, but made at the request of Ikeda Nobuteru, who suggested that as they had about half of the Mikawa men opposite them their province was laid open to a sudden attack, and if they moved into it behind Ieyasu and burned and ravaged it quickly and thoroughly the enemy would be drawn off and could then be attacked with every prospect of success. And quite probably he wished by this to retrieve the failure of his son-in-law at Haguro.

This type of encircling movement had been a device of Nobunaga, who had employed it successfully, but when his retainers tried it they always failed, so that it was not considered a safe maneuver, especially since Shibata had been defeated by it at Shizugatake. However, Hideyoshi gave his consent, though he warned Ikeda of the danger of penetrating too far and cautioned him against over-confidence. He then prepared to make a demonstration against Ieyasu's position as a feint to engage his attention to his front.

Ikeda had 20,000 men divided into four. The first part of 6,000 he himself led, the second of 3,000 was under Mori Nagayoshi, the third of 3,000 under Hori, and the fourth of 8,000 under Miyoshi Hidetsugu.

They started off at midnight of the sixth of the fourth month (May 15th), and by the next morning were camped at Kanijo village, where Ikeda proclaimed to his allies that Hideyoshi had promised him 50,000 koku as a reward. At ten o'clock they resumed their march in three columns, crossed the Yadagawa and then the Kanaregawa, and were in the neighborhood of Nagakude before dawn on the ninth. Here they encountered the fort of Iwasaki, held by Niwa Ujishige, brother of the commander Ujitsugu, who was with Ieyasu. When Ujishige saw this host, he at once concluded that its movement was not known to head-quarters, and determined to hold out with his 239 men until they all fell, trusting that the news of the fight would get through to the castle of Obata, and thence to the base at Komaki. So to that end he sallied

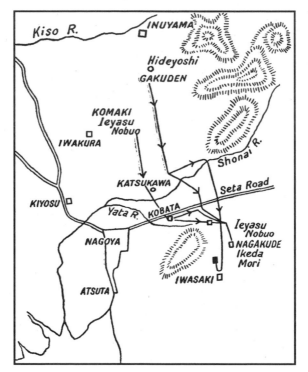

BATTLE OF KOMAKI, 1584

out and opened fire on them with as much noise as possible. Naturally his few defenders, with their little fort only about a hundred yards long, were soon overwhelmed by numbers, and after they had fought valiantly from 4 A.M. to 6 A.M. they were all killed.

Only the vanguard of about 2,000 had been engaged, the others resting and breakfasting while the fight went on, about a mile along the road, and without any idea that the enemy might be on their track.

But at 4 P.M. on the seventh a couple of farmers from Shinogi had come into the camp of Ieyasu at Komaki, and told him of a large army of Hideyoshi's men camping at Kashiwai. His first instinct naturally was to disbelieve them, thinking it was a ruse to draw away part of his army and so break through easily, but at dusk a spy he had sent out to Mori's camp to investigate returned and confirmed the report, so at once he threw out scouts to reconnoiter the country round Kashiwai, while he issued orders for his men to be ready to march immediately.

From what he heard from the scouts he concluded that the enemy was aiming a blow at his capital of Okazaki, and he determined to intercept them, so leaving Sakai Tadatsugu, Honda Tadakatsu, and Ishikawa Kazumasa with 5,000 men at Komaki, with 1,500 of Nobuo's army, he sent on the first division of his army of 4,500 men under Mizuno Tadashige, while he himself followed with 6,300 and Nobuo with 3,000.

"The enemy is near Kashiwai," said he to Mizuno. "You can get into Kobata tonight and join Honda Hirotaka, who commands there. If they attack, hold out and wait till we take them in the rear. If they hold on toward Mikawa, go in and attack them. I shall not be far behind you." So Mizuno went on past Toyama and Katsugawa, slipped round the enemy's left while he was resting at Kamijo, and was at Kobata at 10 P.M. Ieyasu followed on with Ii Naomasa and 3,000 men, starting at eight at night from Komaki, and, passing through the villages of Ichinokuda, Toyoba, Aoyama, and Nyoi, halted for a rest at the Ryuguji temple at Katsukawa, and inquired about the lay of the land from the villagers while he signalled with torches to the fort of Kobata. "Oh, this is Katsukawa village, is it? A good omen. We shall win tomorrow." "Katsukawa!" (River of Victory) he exclaimed in high spirits as he buckled on his armor. Then he started off again, and was at Kobata at twelve o'clock that night. Then Osuga and Mizuno with one division left Kobata at 2 A.M., and went down by Inoko, Ishihara to strike at the right flank of Miyoshi Hidetsugu's rearguard, who were quite unsuspectingly preparing to breakfast at dawn at Hakusan, while Sakakibara led another division along the Seto high road and round by Inaba to menace their rear from the left. The operation was quite successful, for the enemy, taken off their guard, were thrown into confusion immediately by the violent attack from both sides at once and badly cut up and routed, Miyoshi himself saving his life with difficulty. Then the enemy's third division under Hori Hidemasa, hearing the sounds of the conflict, sent out scouts, and learned that it was Ieyasu on their track and not the Monto monks as they had at first thought. So they hastily swung round and marched back to Nagakude, and there took up a position in two companies on a hill, with the river Kanegawa in front of them. It was now 7 A.M. Hori ordered his men to wait until the enemy were within twenty yards before firing, and promised a hundred koku to anyone who brought down a horseman. Straight on to his front came the victorious Tokugawa troops, unheeding the orders of their leaders to advance steadily, to be met by a storm of fire, followed by a vigorous charge, and then another onslaught by the now rallied rearguard, which was so effective that they reeled back and then broke into two masses, and, unable to hold their own, turned and went to the rear precipitately in their turn.

But just at this juncture Ieyasu came up behind, and when Mori's men saw his standard they retired, fearing to be outnumbered by the main army, pursued by some of the Tokugawa men. By now Ikeda and Mori also had brought back their troops to the aid of the rearguard at Nagakude, and sent out patrols to get the routed detachments together again, but half of them were destroyed and the rest had no more stomach for fighting and retreated in haste, and did not stop till they reached their bases at Nijubori and Gakuden. Ieyasu and Nobuo had brought up their forces from Kobata along the Seto highway and, making a wide circle across the Yada River and then the Kanaregawa, emerged across the rear of Ikeda and Mori, taking up a position at Hotokegane and Maeyama, sweeping away the remnants of the troops of Miyoshi and Hori that they met as they did so, and also absorbing the rallying men of their own discomfited rearguard under Okabe and Sakakibara. It was now nine o'clock. Ieyasu led the right wing with 3,300 men, and Ii Naomasa the left with 3,000, while Nobuo was in reserve with 3,000 more. Against them were Ikeda's two sons, Terumasa and Yukisuke, with 4,000 on the right wing, Mori Nagayoshi on the left with 3,000, while Ikeda Nobuteru himself held 2,000 more in reserve. The battle began by a heavy fire from the Tokugawa side, which laid low between two and three hundred of their opponents, whereupon Ikeda's two sons threw their men against Ii Naomasa on the left, but without much effect, for brisk matchlock fire defeated all their efforts. Neither did a reinforcement of picked troops sent from their father's reserve help them much. Meanwhile Ieyasu on the right did not move, but looked on and waited, as also did Mori opposite him, thinking that Ieyasu would send some of his troops to the assistance of his left and intending to strike at him when thus weakened. But suddenly deciding that the right moment had come, Ieyasu divided his army into two and precipitated it upon Mori, so that his men were driven back fighting hard. Mori himself stood out conspicuous in a white costume, waving his baton to rally his breaking ranks, which one of the matchlock men in Ii Naomasa's ranks observing, he took careful aim and sent a bullet through his head, so that he fell dead from his horse, aged twenty-seven. And it was not yet twelve noon. Then Nobuo's three thousand men swept round and through Mori's hesitating ranks and fell on Ikeda Nobuteru's reserve as he was attempting to support his sons on the right, and the combined forces of the father and sons crumbled at his onset. A certain Nagai Dempachiro rushed on Nobuteru as he sat on his campstool resigned to his fate, and speared him and took his head. This was the end of the battle, for the rest took to flight, and Nobuteru's son Yukisuke was killed in the confusion, though his brother Terumasa escaped to become a great lord in the future. All was over by one o'clock, the action having occupied three hours. The loss on the side of the vanquished was 2,500 killed, and that of the Tokugawa and Oda forces 590.

Ieyasu then viewed the heads and waited to see if Hideyoshi would come against him, but as he saw no signs he marched back to Kobata.

Hideyoshi, however, at once issued orders to march to Nagakude as soon as he heard of the defeat of the first detachment under Miyoshi. The movement in his camp did not escape the notice of those holding Komaki, and at a council of war Sakai Tadatsugu proposed to send out a company to strike a blow at the reduced force in front and flank simultaneously, but Ishikawa Kazumasa, who was already very partial to Hideyoshi, declared that it was madness to attack what must still be a very formidable army. But Honda Tadakatsu declared that he would not stand idle while his lord was in danger, and whatever anyone else might do, he was starting at once for Nagakude to fling himself on Hideyoshi's pursuing force despite the consequences. "For if my lord dies fighting, I must at all cost die by his side." Ishikawa Yasumichi supported him, and the two rode off with less than a thousand men, and did not draw rein till they came to Ryusenji, south of the river and not far from Kobata. There they began to menace the enemy by firing on his flanks, and prepared to throw themselves on his main force. "Now," said Honda to Ishikawa, "all we have to do is to sell our lives as dearly as possible, for every hour we can delay Hideyoshi is precious to our lord." They divided their little force into three and faced the enemy across the river. Hideyoshi at once saw how small a band they were, and divined their attention. "That's a fine fellow indeed!" he exclaimed. "He means to help his lord at any sacrifice. I wonder who he is." "That's Honda Heihachiro," said Inaba Ittetsu. "I remember his staghorn frontlet and white cloak in the forefront of the fight at the Anegawa." The tears stood in Hideyoshi's eyes. "He mustn't die," he said. "What's the use? I need men like him and his master as my supporters in the future." And he ordered his men to disregard their challenge and march on without crossing the river. And Honda sat watching the great host go by while his horse drank from the river. He then pushed on to Kobata, and found Ieyasu safe inside. All Hideyoshi did was to engage the rearguard of the Tokugawa army as it retreated into this place and inflict a loss of a couple of hundred on it.

Ieyasu did not stay long at Kobata. That night he slipped away back to his base at Komaki with Nobuo, leaving only three hundred men behind. And when Hideyoshi saw that he had eluded him, he too marched back to his base at Gakuden. Hideyoshi struck his hands together as he sat on his horse, partly in irritation and partly in admiration, so it is said. "Here's a leader you can't catch either with net or line!" he exclaimed. "He's smart and he's solid. You won't find another like him in the Empire, wide as it is. Well, I shall get him in Court dress at Kyoto sooner or later!"

CHAPTER 15

AFTER KOMAKI

THERE now ensued a stalemate, since neither side would attack first but waited for the other to begin, till at length, on the first of the fifth month, Hideyoshi withdrew his sixty thousand men to attack Nobuo's provinces, and moved on Kaganoi, the strongest place on the Kiso river, north-west of Kiyosu. On the sixth he had overcome the garrison by a heavy bombardment and was able to enter it.

He then attacked Takegahana, to the northwest of this, and as it was in a low situation surrounded by water, he applied his flooding method, and in exactly a month drowned out its garrison, so that it surrendered and was allowed to march away. He employed one hundred thousand workmen to throw up a dam so that the waters of the Kiso ran into it, and the inmates of the place were driven to make platforms in the trees and sit there to avoid drowning. After this he returned to Osaka. Ieyasu also returned to Kiyosu, for Hideyoshi had left enough men round Inuyama to prevent him moving to the help of these two fortresses, which he wisely refrained from doing. Meanwhile Hideyoshi's men had reduced most of the strong places in Nobuo's province of Ise, which he placed under his own generals, so that he now had possession of most of Mino, Iga, and Ise, a big material advantage, though he had sustained a great moral setback at the hands of Ieyasu which perhaps more than compensated for it, for that resourceful warrior was still as unsubdued as ever. And he now proceeded to score another point at Kanie castle, a place on the sea between Kiyosu and Nagashima, where Nobuo then was. This place was held for Nobuo by one Maeda Tanetoshi, who happened to be a cousin of Takigawa Kazumasa, whom Hideyoshi had pardoned after his share in the revolt of Shibata Katsuie and had taken into his service. Takigawa was now ensconced in the castle of Kamoe in Ise, and took advantage of his position to make advances to his cousin to come over to their side, and not unsuccessfully, so that he, with Kuki Yoshitaka, commanding the neighboring stronghold of Taba, suddenly marched in with three thousand men and took possession of Kanie, thus severing the connection between Nagashima and Kiyosu. He also sent boats up the river to attack the castle of Ono near by, but this attempt was frustrated by the commander, who had blazing torches flung into these boats and burnt them, as well as sent messengers to Nobuo and Ieyasu for help. Both of them at once responded, and despatched forces under Sakakibara and Oda Nagamasu to the aid of Kanie, which they soon beset on all sides and subjected to a fierce fire. They were not long in taking the outer works by storm, and from these they assaulted the main castle with matchlock fire and fire-arrows from towers they hastily erected there. The defenders ran short of food and ammunition, and then made overtures for surrender, to which the assailants agreed on condition that they were given the head of Maeda Tanetoshi. To this Takigawa agreed, and sent hostages to the Tokugawa army. Tanetoshi, perceiving his danger, tried to escape, but was taken and decapitated by his amiable cousin, who thus saved his own skin. It did him little good, however, for he found no cordial reception among his colleagues after thus surrendering his castle, and eventually made his way to Niwa in Echizen, where he died in obscurity. Ieyasu then garrisoned Kanie with his own men and destroyed its two subsidiary fortresses, put Ishikawa Kazumasa into Kuwana, and again retired to Kiyosu.

Hideyoshi now determined to employ diplomatic means to get Nobuo to conclude a separate peace, so that Ieyasu, thus deprived of his pretext for opposing him, might be landed in a dilemma, so on the seventh of the eleventh month he sent messengers to Nobuo to sound him. Nobuo in great delight eagerly grasped the opportunity, and at once consented to a reconciliation without consulting Ieyasu. The terms were that Hideyoshi was to return the four districts in north Ise that he had occupied and adopt Nobuo's daughter, while he was to send Oda Nobumasu, his uncle, Sakuma Masakatsu, Takigawa Katsutoshi, and others as hostages, as well as hand over the three districts in Iga to Hideyoshi, while both armies were to demolish the strongholds lately constructed in Ise and Owari.

Ieyasu was just about to start out again to Nobuo's assistance when Sakai, who had marched to Kiyosu with that intention, apprised him of the new development. He must have been surprised, but he did not show it. On the contrary, he merely observed that it was an excellent arrangement and no doubt everyone would rejoice to hear it, and he forthwith disspatched messages of congratulation to both Nobuo and Hideyoshi.

Thus encouraged, Hideyoshi at once asked Nobuo to make overtures for an amicable settlement with Ieyasu too. Since it was ostensibly on Nobuo's behalf that he had been fighting, he could hardly refuse. So he consented to allow his son, O Gi Maru, to become the adopted son of Hideyoshi. On the twelfth of the twelfth month this son of his, with the sons of Ishikawa Kazumasa and Honda Shigetsugu, left for Osaka in charge of Ishikawa, and arrived there on the twenty-sixth. O

Gi Maru was given the name of Hashiba Hideyasu and a fief of 10,000 koku in Kawachi. Nobuo then proceeded to thank Ieyasu for all his trouble in the war. And so this memorable campaign ended.

Hideyoshi at once turned his attention to the monks and the men of Shikoku when he was thus relieved of the menace of Ieyasu and Nobuo on the east, as well as of Sasa Narimasa on the north, for when that not very competent leader had attacked the castle of Suemori on the borders of Kaga and Noto, it had been valiantly held by Okamura Sukiemon, ably assisted by his wife, in the face of much greater numbers until Maeda Toshiie came up on his rear and defeated him.

Narimasa did, according to some accounts, brave the severe winter weather to cross the country to see Ieyasu and Nobuo, to suggest that they should resume hostilities; but all Ieyasu said was, "It is very kind of you to come all this way through the snow, but the fact is I have no personal enmity towards Hideyoshi. I only went to the assistance of Nobuo, and now he has made peace I can do no more." And as he found Nobuo no more responsive, there was nothing to do but to plunge once more into the snow on his way back to Etchu. The same refusal, too, awaited messengers from Chosokabe and the monks, and Hatakeyama, when Hideyoshi began his campaign in that direction. "Since peace has been made, I regret nothing can be done. Had it been earlier..." Ieyasu was quite determined to maintain the position he had taken up, at any rate till he saw a more promising opportunity than their co-operation was likely to provide.

Hideyoshi did not take long about subduing the monks, for within a month he had subdued Negoro and Saiga, the latter by his favorite flooding siege, though he did not proceed to extremities with them. He only administered a severe reprimand and burnt some of the Saiga temples. Towards the Shingon temples of Koya he was merciful, for he left them intact, partly owing to the skilful intercession of Kozan Shonin, better known as Mokushoku Shonin, who did him good services afterwards as an architect. Then came the turn of Shikoku. From three sides his invading armies of some 80,000, or it may be 12,000 of which Hidenaga was in chief command, assisted by Hidetsugu, Kuroda, Mori, Ukita, Kikkawa, and Kobayakawa, struck at the island of the four provinces. They were transported in 600 large vessels and 103 smaller ones. Shikoku had no force able to meet this great host, for it had been devastated by internal wars, and what men there were had inferior arms and insufficient commissariat.

In spite of all this, however, Chosokabe was for fighting, but his councilors could see no advantage in this course, so that it was not strange that when Hidenaga made secret overtures to them they set

themselves at once to break down their stubborn lord's opposition, and
in the end they prevailed. After a halfhearted attempt to relieve Ichinomiya fortress, which they were attacking, he sent in his submission
after a campaign of twenty-six days ending on the eleventh day of the
seventh month of 1585. Chosokabe was allowed to keep the province
of Tosa, but the rest was divided among the generals whom Hideyoshi
wished to reward, Awa going to Hachisuka, Sanuki to Sengoku, and
Iyo to Kobayakawa Takakage, with the exception of 23,000 koku which
was given to the ex-priest Ankokuji Eikei. Thus Chosokabe was very
effectively deprived of that chance of getting all of it under his control
for which he had defied Hideyoshi.

Scarcely was this campaign over when Hideyoshi was off to the
north to finish off Sasa Narimasa, whom Maeda had so far held in
check. Again his force was so great and his advance so rapid that there
was no question of serious resistance. Sasa was, as Tokutomi puts it,
"like a dried sardine gnashing his teeth" in his impotence. But Hideyoshi again showed magnanimity, and not only pardoned him when he
surrendered, but even restored one district to him and treated him in
the friendliest manner.

The origin of the dislike of the Lady Yae, wife of Hideyoshi, for
the Lady Yodo, his favorite consort, is said to have been the present of
a black lily by this Sasa Narimasa to the former lady as a compliment
when he was presented with the fief of Higo. This was an unlucky gift,
for it led to an insurrection there owing to which Sasa was ordered to
commit suicide. Hideyoshi's wife was so pleased with this rare flower,
which he had got from Kakusan in Kaga, that she gave a Cha-no-yu
party in its honor, to which she invited Yodo. But Yodo made careful
inquiry as to where it could be obtained and then sent for a large quantity, whereupon she gave a flower-show and invited the Kita-noman-
dokoro, and when she saw a lot of these black lilies mixed up casually
with other quite ordinary blossoms she felt very annoyed and nursed
a grudge against both the Lady Yodo and Sasa as well. The suggestion
has been made that Hideyoshi only gave him the province to placate
the old retainers of Nobunaga who were his companions, and that he
knew very well that a revolt would follow, which he then made a pretext to get rid of Sasa altogether. It is more likely, however, that he sent
him there because he credited him with the capacity to keep order in
the province, but owing to his conceited self-sufficiency he disobeyed
Hideyoshi's orders and treated his advice with contempt. So the revolt
flared up, and Hideyoshi, who had pardoned him twice already, now
lost patience and made an example of him, especially as the rebellion
might easily have spread and involved further disorder. He brought his

fate on himself, for he was behind the times, a defect not confined to him but a weakness always difficult for strong characters to avoid. His suicide is thus described: "Sasa Kuranosuke went out into his garden and sat down on a stone. Calling his equerry, he gave him thirty gold pieces and told him that he could have his wardrobe also, directing him to advertise the fact that this stone was the one on which Kuranosuke sat for the last scene of his life. Then he cut his belly in the form of a cross and tore out his guts, 'Now is the time!' he exclaimed when this was done to his satisfaction, and stretched out his neck, whereupon Todo Izumi, who acted as his second, struck off his head."

CHAPTER 16

ISOLATION OF IEYASU

I⟩ was by no means pleasant for Ieyasu to stand by and view these triumphs, for by them he was now completely isolated, as it was intended he should be, for he was the most formidable antagonist Hideyoshi possessed. And then, not content with subduing his allies, Hideyoshi also made attempts, and not without success, on the loyalty of his retainers. The defection of Sanada and of Ishikawa was a disquieting threat to Ieyasu.

Sanada had been, like his father, a retainer of Takeda Shingen, and at his death went over to Nobunaga, when he was assassinated to Uesugi, thence to Hojo, and then transferred himself to Ieyasu. He had ability, and was a cunning, restless fellow, anxious to find the best market for his talents. There was not much of the Bushi's objection to serving two masters about him, and Tokutomi styles him "the kind of freak natural in this period." He had held the fort of Numada for Ieyasu, by whom he had been ordered to hand it over to Hojo, in accordance with their agreement that the Sakuma district of Shinano should go to that Daimyo, but he refused. This angered Ieyasu, who had given him back his family possession of Ueda as a reward for his action in cutting off some of Hojo's men after he had left the service of that commander, and thought this ought to be enough. But Sanada insisted that he had a right to Numada too. However, Ieyasu insisted, since he wished to avoid a difference with Hojo while he was at variance with Hideyoshi. So Sanada made overtures to Hideyoshi through Uesugi. This was very welcome, and Uesugi was ordered to support him. So when Ieyasu, who would not stand disobedience from a vassal for a moment, sent out a force of some seven thousand men under Okubo Tadayo and Torii Mototada against Ueda to chastise him, they found another body of Uesugi's picked troops of approximately the same number awaiting them in addition to the garrison. Luring them on to the attack, Sanada gave the signal for the reinforcements to move on their rear, while a third detachment, made up of farmers and people of the place, made a demonstration to suggest that a third army was present. The result was that the Tokugawa army was thrown into confusion and had to retreat. They then surrounded the castle and prepared to besiege it when Ieyasu recalled them. This was because Sanada asked Uesugi himself to move to aid him, and Hideyoshi backed him up, whereupon Ieyasu, unwilling thus to be embroiled with Uesugi, thought it politic to withdraw.

But much more serious a defection was that of Ishikawa Kazumasa, who was not a turncoat fief-hunter like Sanada, but one of the chief councilors of the Tokugawa house. His family were hereditary vassals, and as a child he had been a companion of his master in exile, since then following him in his various campaigns, to the success of which he was a powerful contributor. He was renowned for his personal daring in the field, and on many occasions he had most gallantly risked his life in his lord's service, as, for instance, when he had rescued Nobuyasu from the clutches of Imagawa Ujizane, with whom he was a hostage, when Ieyasu had left his former ally for Nobunaga. And in the fight at Mikata-ga-Hara, too, he had played a great part. It was, therefore, the more inexplicable that at the end of the year 1585 he should suddenly desert his post of warden of the castle of Okazaki and go off with his family to Hideyoshi at Osaka. Fortunately, his example was not followed by Sakai Tadatsugu, his colleague, or any other of the chief councilors, and Matsudaira Chikamasa, whom he invited to follow him, at once informed Ieyasu at Hamamatsu, while Matsudaira Ietada marched into Okazaki and guarded it with his retainers till Ieyasu ordered Okubo Tadayo to proceed there to take over the command abandoned by Ishikawa.

The only influence of this disloyalty was the defection of Ogasawara Sadayoshi, another trimmer, who was one of those whom circumstances had always compelled to follow the stronger side, and so had drifted from Uesugi via Hojo to Ieyasu. And another former supporter, though not a vassal, who was fascinated by Hideyoshi was Ieyasu's uncle, Mizuno Tadashige, who had become lord of Kariya after the death of his brother Nobumoto. He was a capable soldier who had done good service to Ieyasu against the Ikko party and against the Hojo and in the Komaki war, and with Ishikawa held the office of Musha-bugyo or Army Commissioner.

The defection of these men merely showed the way things were going in the Empire, and was perhaps not exactly a surprise to Ieyasu; and Tokutomi thinks the only reason that there were no more such deserters was because of the parish-pump outlook of the Mikawa retainers, who knew and cared for nothing outside their immediate surroundings, so that the more cultivated existence that centered round Hideyoshi and the capital had no attractions for them. But Ishikawa had seen a good deal of Hideyoshi and gained a wider outlook, and so his ambition to share in this greater and more brilliant world triumphed over his hereditary loyalty. Ever since Ieyasu had sent him to escort the tea-caddy "Hat-subana," which he was sending as a complimentary gift to Hideyoshi on the occasion of his victory over Shibata, Kazumasa had been attracted by the magnetic charm of the latter, and in consequence had not been unsuspected by his colleagues. And this suspicion had doubtless intensi-fied his growing disgust at the bucolic clumsiness of his surroundings.

Of course, it may be argued on behalf of Kazumasa, as it may be for Judas, that he was doing his master a service as well as himself by betraying him, though what his master thought he did not entirely express. What he is reported to have observed is merely this: "Ishikawa is disloyal to leave me, but we must not despise his military ability."

From the end of 1584 to the end of 1586 the relations of Ieyasu and Hideyoshi underwent no change, though the power of the latter continued to increase and to render it necessary for Ieyasu to devise some counter measure if he was to retain any semblance of independent action. He could now rely on none of the feudatories of the west and north, so it was natural that he should consider a closer agreement with Hojo of Odawara, who was as yet unaffected by any of Hideyoshi's ma-neuvers, in order thus to elude the encircling movement he feared. For the present he refused to go to Kyoto himself or to send any of his re-tainers, though this latter course was suggested to him by Nobuo more than once, no doubt at Hideyoshi's instigation. In the first month of 1585, for instance, Oda Nagamasu, Takigawa Katsutoshi, and Hashiba Katsumasa went to Mikawa to sound him. Ieyasu was hawking in the country, and there they followed him. Hawk on wrist, he rejected their proposal unceremoniously. They retired to their lodgings, and the next day Hashiba tried again. "You're still here, are you?" said Ieyasu irritably when he saw him. "But I'm doing you a service," replied Katsumasa, "for if you don't submit Hideyoshi will bring a huge army against you. And you spend your time hawking! Your castle and fortresses are not in the best repair either." "Look here!" retorted Ieyasu, "I've had enough of this. He can't bring more than a hundred thousand men if he does come, and I have thirty or forty thousand. But he doesn't know the country about here and I do. So if he risks it he'll get the beating of his life. He seems to have forgotten Nagakude pretty quickly. And as for you, I advise you to make yourself scarce at once, or you will be in even greater danger." Hashiba did so without delay.

This happened a few months after Ieyasu had called a council of his retainers and they had unanimously advised him not to submit and as-sured him of their united support. And if the account of this interview is not strictly accurate, it probably represents his standpoint.

CHAPTER 17

IEYASU'S SECOND MARRIAGE AND ALLIANCE WITH HŌJŌ

HIDEYOSHI was apparently of the opinion that Ieyasu's position was a strong one, for he did not venture to attack, but tried to conciliate him by proposing a marriage with his half-sister Asahi-hime. She was the daughter of his stepfather Chikuami, and she was not consulted as to her views, though she happened to be married already. It is not quite clear who her husband was, it is true, for there are several versions of the affair, and they refer to different men. One says he was one Saji Hyuga-no-kami, and that he committed suicide owing to the slight put upon him by the unceremonious recall of his wife. Another calls him Soeda Jimbei, commander of the fortress of Tai in Tajima, and relates that she was taken away from him because he lost his castle and that he did not complain. And since many lost what was more irreplaceable than a wife under these circumstances, he would have no reason. Again, a more pleasing version has it that Soeda, who was now the lord of Karasu-mori in Owari, waived his claim to his wife and gave her up gracefully at Hideyoshi's request, because she was needed for greater things—the unification of the Empire, to wit. And that Hideyoshi generously offered him an income of 50,000 koku as a solace, but that he refused all reward, retired from active life, and became a recluse.

However this may be, the former envoy, Hashiba Katsumasa, again proceeded to Yoshida in Mikawa, and proposed the alliance to Sakai Tadatsugu, who reported it to his master. Ieyasu's reply was that he was not unwilling provided Hideyoshi agreed to three conditions. In the first place, that his heir, Naganaru, now seven years old, and later to be known as Hidetada, should succeed him even if another son were to be born of this union; in the second, that this heir should not go as a hostage to Hideyoshi; and, thirdly, that he should inherit all Ieyasu's four provinces intact. To heighten the effect, the Mikawa Fudoki says that Hideyoshi sent Asano Nagamasa as far as Kiyosu with an agreement conceding just these conditions, which he handed to Ieyasu as soon as he stated them, thus clearly demonstrating Hideyoshi's remarkable capacity for appreciating the Tokugawa chief's forethought. Naturally even he was unable entirely to conceal his surprise. Anyhow, these conditions prove that Ieyasu intended even at this early age to make Hidetada his heir, and this was quite natural, seeing that his eldest son, Nobuyasu, had died in the year Hidetada was born, and Hideyasu had already been adopted out of the family. The latter was the son of a secondary consort, it is true, but so was Hidetada, and so were all the rest, for Asahi-hime had no children. This was not remarkable seeing that she was a mature lady of forty-four, but one year younger than Ieyasu, and probably not robust, for she died four years later. Still, Ieyasu was in the habit of leaving nothing to chance.

Asahi-hime had a splendid wedding, as befitted a sister of the greatest lord in the Empire, and in the long procession that accompanied her, bearing the customary presents and articles of furniture, were more than a hundred and fifty ladies-in-waiting. Honda Tadakatsu went to take the betrothal presents to Hideyoshi, and was very cordially treated and handsomely rewarded.

However, Hideyoshi and Ieyasu did not meet at the ceremony and there was no visible change in their relations. Only Asahi-hime went willy-nilly as a gesture towards a better understanding, and no doubt Ieyasu treated her as such, and with all the most correct etiquette if nothing more. Still, he did not let this formal relationship lull him into any sense of security, and immediately applied himself to the business of knitting more close the ties that bound him to the family of his son-in-law Ujinao, so that if he did have to face Hideyoshi in battle he would not be unsupported. And this was the more necessary since Hōjō might easily suspect the possibility of what actually happened later, a combination of Ieyasu and Hideyoshi against himself, the only independent power left on the Takaido. Ieyasu had to be very wary indeed to avoid the fate of being forsaken by one ally and then attacked by the other.

Consequently he struck an attitude of extreme amiability, and sent to inform the Hōjō family that he would like to pay them a friendly visit. This meant crossing the frontier into their territory and therefore paying court as an inferior, as his councilors pointed out, but that was no matter. On the twelfth day of the third month of 1586 he arrived at the Kisegawa, which was the boundary between his domains and theirs, and was received by all his Hōjō relations in a specially erected mansion on the eastern bank. His son-in-law Ujinao especially greeted him most affectionately, and he was entertained lavishly with all the ceremony and courtly dignity on which the conservative Hōjōs so prided themselves.

Both sides made each other the usual valuable presents of rich material, and fine swords by famous masters—a katana by Moriie and a tachi of Ichimonji make—as well as a damascened gun of "western barbarian" iron from Ieyasu, and twelve hawks and ten horses and two ceremonial suits from Hōjō. Ieyasu left nothing undone to convince the Hōjōs, whose infatuated conservatism and easy-going arrogance made it an easy task, that he was their most devoted servant. He insisted on taking a seat lower than that of his son-in-law Ujinao, and proceeded further to abase himself by taking the part of the Chinese retainer in the Noh entitled *Jinen Koji,* well knowing, no doubt, that his rotund figure made him distinctly ridiculous in such a role. The burden of *Jinen Koji* is that a begging priest of this name undertakes to supplicate a slave dealer to return a girl he has bought. He prevails at length by performing an extravagant dance. The last words of this Noh are very significant: "And so from the ship that bears us to the Farther Shore of Enlightenment, tapping the drum whose sound symbolizes the waves of the Sea of Rebirth, together we will go the Capital." The trouble with Hōjō was that he would not by any means go up to the capital, with or without Ieyasu. His councilor, Sakai Tadatsugu, too, imitated his master, and danced an odd measure called "the prawn-fishing dance," so that they were all much amused, and the retired lord, Ujimasa, in an ecstasy of liquor and merriment, cackled in his cups when his chief retainer, Matsuda, murmured: "Ah, see how the lord Tokugawa regards us as his suzerains." And he shuffled up to Ieyasu and pulled out the sword from his belt, informing the company with a grin of alcoholic glee, "Great triumph of Hōjō Ujimasa! Without getting to his feet he disarms the first warrior of the Coastland!" Neither was that all, for when he started for home Ieyasu requested that one of Hōjō's senior councilors might go part of the way with him, and when they came to the frontier castle of Numasu he gave orders that it should be dismantled and all its defenses thrown down before the man's eyes, assuring him that there was no need of any fortress between them when Ujinao was his son-in-law. Hōjō's satisfaction at the success of this diplomatic visit was probably only equalled by that of Ieyasu.

Meanwhile Hideyoshi was preparing for his campaign against Shimazu of Satsuma, and was not disinclined to make further overtures to get Ieyasu to come up to the capital and submit and become his ally. He determined, therefore, on what was a distinctly novel step for one in his commanding position. He suggested that his mother, to whom he was most devotedly attached, should "pay a visit" to her daughter and her husband at Okazaki, thus, of course, becoming a hostage there, while Ieyasu visited him at Osaka. This plan was opposed by Hideyoshi's relations, and especially by Hidenaga, his step-brother, as undignified, but Hideyoshi considered it worth his while to make even this concession if he could so get his way without fighting, though at the same time, according to the Taikoki, he had an alternative plan if this diplomatic measure did not succeed of building fortresses in suitable places, transplanting his own men to the rear of Ieyasu's territory by the Tenryugawa, and there keeping them supplied by water, while at the same time he encouraged the farmers through the Monto sect of Buddhists, to which most of them belonged, to rebel and divert their crops from their lord to himself, so instituting a blockade both military and economic. And quite possibly some rumors of this plan may have been allowed to reach Ieyasu, for he too, in spite of a similar opposition on the part of his councilors, determined that the wiser course now was to acquiesce. Both reasoned on the same lines that war was expensive and uncertain and that the country needed peace.

In Ieyasu's speech in reply to the opinion of Sakai Tadatsugu that they need have no fear of the issue of a clash with Hideyoshi's armies and ought not to wish to avoid it, he drew quite an impressive picture of himself as a sacrificing servant of the people. "If war breaks out again between us, well, you can never be absolutely certain of the result, since the unexpected so often happens. And then we must consider that it will mean more suffering for the people the longer it goes on, and what would the loss of my one life matter compared with the avoidance of suffering and death to so many innocent ones? It would be a splendid thing indeed to sacrifice myself for the common good."

How could the simple Mikawa warriors maintain their intransigent attitude in the face of such magnanimous altruism? Ieyasu's judgment of the right time to make a concession certainly justified the saying that he "won the Empire by yielding" ("Ieyasu makete tenka wo toru").

CHAPTER 18

HIS SUBMISSION TO HIDEYOSHI.
HE VISITS THE CAPITAL

As a first move some members of the houses of Ii, Honda, and Sakakibara proceeded to Osaka to prepare the way before him, and incidentally to act as hostages. At Hideyoshi's suggestion the Court advanced Ieyasu to the rank of Gon-Chunagon on the fifteenth of the tenth month of 1586.

The O-mandokoro, the mother of Hideyoshi, left Osaka on the tenth and arrived at Okazaki on the eighteenth, where she was met and greeted by her dutiful son-in-law and his wife, who had proceeded thither from Hamamatsu. That neither Ieyasu nor any of his entourage knew the old lady very well seems apparent from the characteristic advice tendered by that very suspicious warrior Honda Sakuzaemon Shigetsugu: "You have to be careful, my lord, for there are a lot of elderly ladies-in-waiting about the Court, and Hideyoshi may quite likely have picked out one of them and sent her as a substitute for his mother." But they were all reassured when Asahi-hime could hardly wait for the doors of the palanquin to be opened before she fell on her mother's neck in tears, which were heartily reciprocated by the old lady, and spread by contagion to most of the spectators. They gave Asahi-hime credit for no histrionic powers.

This interview over, Ieyasu left Ii Naomasa, Honda Shigetsugu, and Okubo Tadayo in charge of the castle of Okazaki and his mother-in-law, and left for Osaka, accompanied by Honda Tadakatsu, Sakai Tadatsugu, and Sakakibara Yasumasa, arriving there on the sixteenth and proceeding to the mansion of Hidenaga. But it would not have been Ieyasu had he omitted to provide for eventualities, and at the first stop at Yoshida he gave Ii careful instructions as to what was to be done if Hideyoshi practiced any doubledealing. If he suspected any attempt to seize him, he would slip away to Higashiyama, where it would be difficult to find him, and in three days could apprise them at Hamamatsu of his danger, and they were to send one army of ten thousand men by Hino and Seta to Higashiyama, and another of the same size to cut in by Nyoigatake, so that Hideyoshi would be forced to make for Osaka for safety, when, if they pushed on, they ought to be able to cut him off before he reached the Katsuragawa.

Unconventional as ever, Hideyoshi paid Ieyasu a visit incognito the very night he arrived, and told him quite simply and frankly how matters stood. "I have risen to all this greatness from the most menial position, as you well know, and my officers don't really respect me, for they were all my colleagues not long ago. So I want you to greet me before them all in the most deferential manner, for that will impress them as nothing else would. And I on my part will treat you with the greatest consideration." And he patted Ieyasu cordially on the back. "I have married your sister, and now I have come to visit you. These are the acts of one who wishes you well," replied Ieyasu guardedly; "and for your kind expressions I am very much obliged. You can rely on me to support you whole-heartedly." And they sat down together and helped each other to drink in the most intimate manner.

Ieyasu had quite made up his mind to oppose Hideyoshi no more. The strenuous resistance he had made had been very profitable so far, and no less would a submissive attitude be now. So far he had taken all he could from Hideyoshi, and now he would give him all the assistance in his power, but with the reservation of getting his own back again some day if the occasion offered. That night when the servants in the mansion of Hidenaga shut the amado with the usual pattering of feet and rumbling and banging of the shutters, the country samurai of his guard sprang up in alarm. "Sate koso daiji da!" ("Hullo, something's up!") they exclaimed, and they did not relax again till this unaccustomed routine was explained to them. Such refinements as outside shutters were evidently unknown outside the capital even then.

"On the twenty-seventh day the Great Lord entered the Castle of Osaka. Hideyoshi came to meet him in the courtyard. Nobuo the Naidaijin of Owari came to the castle at the same time. The Great Lord greeted Nobuo and would not advance. Nobuo hung back and would not proceed. Hideyoshi took the hand of the Great Lord and led him before Nobuo. At the wish of Hideyoshi the retainers of the Great Lord all entered the Reception Hall. The retainers of Hideyoshi were unable to enter." This made it clear that nobody in the Empire was to take precedence of Ieyasu. "The Kambaku sat on the Dais. Shinjo Tsuruga-no-kami came forth and presented on behalf of the Great Lord a gold lacquered tachi, ten horses, and a hundred pieces of gold." And Ieyasu bowed low in deep reverence as arranged. "And when the Daimyos saw that even the Lord Tokugawa, to whom the mother of the Kambaku herself had gone as a hostage, thus did obeisance, they realized that Hideyoshi was indeed the Lord of the Empire, and their regard for his authority was increased a hundredfold."

Hideyoshi presented Ieyasu in return with the Tea-jar "Shiraku-

mo" (White Clouds), a short sword by Masamune, and a long one by
Miyoshi Go, beside many fine hawks and a brocaded haori. As to this
last present, it is said that Hidenaga and Asano suggested to Ieyasu
that he should ask for it. "The Kambaku was wearing a red war surcoat
(Jimbaori) ornamented with the Paullownia crest in brocade. Before
all the assembly Ieyasu asked for it to be presented to him. 'This is the
surcoat I wear when I go out to war,' replied Hideyoshi. 'But now I
am by your side, you need never go forth in armor any more,' replied
Ieyasu. Hideyoshi was delighted. 'I am indeed fortunate to have such a
brother-in-law,' he exclaimed, 'and so have no more occasion for fighting.' And he took off the haori and handed it to Ieyasu."

From Osaka Ieyasu proceeded to Kyoto on the first of the eleventh
month, and on the fifth was promoted to the Upper Third Court
Rank, while Honda Tadakatsu and Sakakibara Yasumasa were awarded
the lower grade of the Lower Fifth Rank and created Nakatsukasa-taiyu
and Shikibu-taiyu respectively. He returned again safely to Okazaki
on the eleventh day, and the day after Hideyoshi's mother terminated
her "visit" and started back for the capital escorted by Ii Naomasa.
Orders were also given for a mansion to be prepared for Ieyasu's use
near Hideyoshi's Juraku mansion, and Todo Takatora, chief retainer of
Hidenaga, was appointed Commissioner for this work with an income
of 30,000 koku. Todo was afterwards to become one of Ieyasu's most
trusted advisers, and it was he who suggested later on that the Daimyos
should be ordered to build their mansions round Edo castle.

As to Hideyoshi's mother, she can hardly have been very sorry to
leave Okazaki, if the story of the behavior of one of her guardians is
true, and there seems little reason to doubt it. Her ladies were much
surprised to find their lodgings surrounded by a huge heap of brushwood, and naturally inquired its significance. Ii Naomasa, who was
always most courteous to them, said that he really did not know. He
was only twenty-six then, and often inquired kindly after their wants
and made them presents of fruit and fish. But they inquired elsewhere,
and learned that this brushwood had been put there by order of the
other officer of their guard, Honda Shigetsugu, that die-hard country
samurai who never spoke a word to them but whose loud voice was
often heard shouting orders to the soldiers to keep a sharp watch over
them. His intention was to set fire to it and burn the whole company
alive should anything happen to his master in the capital. Naturally
their dislike of him was redoubled, and they must have thought his
nickname of "Oni Sakuza" or "Devil Sakuza" well deserved. When they
got back they related all this to Hideyoshi, and his only comment was
that it was just like the fanatic loyalty of the Mikawa samurai. But he

complimented Ii very highly, and it may not be entirely unconnected with this incident that when Ieyasu went to Edo, Hideyoshi especially asked him to give no fief to Honda, since he never showed him any courtesy.

He was not the only one so nicknamed, for there was a country "pestle-and-mortar" song that celebrated some of these Tokugawa retainers that ran:

Tokugawa Dono wa yoi hito-mochi yo!
Hattori Hanzo was Oni Hanzo!
Watanabe Hanzo wa Yari Hanzo!
Atsumi Gengo wa Kubi-tori Gengo!

The Lord Tokugawa has a fine lot of men!
Hattori Hanzo called Devil Hanzo!
Watanabe Hanzo called Spearing Hanzo!
And Atsumi Gengo, Head-taking Gengo!

And it was this same Oni Sakuza who rebuked Ieyasu with his usual outspoken vehemence when he told him to send three of the big iron pots which Takeda Shingen had used to boil great criminals alive to be distributed to the three provinces of Suruga, Kai, and Mikawa. "I think you must be possessed by the devil,' he burst out, "to waste money on the transport of such worthless things. We want no more of the savage ways of that old lay-priest. I am going to break all those pots up and throw the pieces into river."

When Ieyasu came home again after his entertainment in the capital the weather was cold, and he asked for a haori. Kondo Nuidonosuke's son brought him one that had been presented to him by Hideyoshi, embroidered with a design of plum-blossoms and storks, but he made a very wry face. "That can be worn in the capital if one wants to be fashionable," he remarked, "but to put on such a gaudy thing here is against my family traditions and won't do at all." His objection was certainly very fitting, for somehow one can hardly picture him attired in this kind of costume.

During the next year or so Ieyasu was able to live quietly on his domains, visiting the capital on such ceremonial occasions as that of Hideyoshi's entertainment of the Emperor at the Juraku mansion or his famous tea-meeting at Kitano. He took no part in the campaign against Shimazu of Satsuma, which was now occupying the attention of the Kwambaku, for the house of Mori was selected for the "embarrassing favor" of assisting in this operation with men and munitions owing to its suitable geographical position. Ieyasu's loyalty and submission made it possible, of course, for otherwise no such great body of men could have been moved to this remote part of the country. And it was this very remoteness, as well as his pride in his ancient lineage, for Shimazu is among the very oldest of the great feudal families, that prompted the lord of Satsuma to refuse homage to Hideyoshi, though quite apart from this he was a most formidable adversary, for his fierce and well-trained clansmen, led by the three spirited brothers, had defeated the best of the other feudal levies of Kyushu under Otomo and Ryuzōji, so that they had become entirely dominant in the island. This was quite contrary to Hideyoshi's principle of making the central government under himself supreme in every part of the Empire, and so he did what no one else in the history of Japan has ever been able to do, threw a great land and sea force into Kyushu and drove the Shimazu brothers to capitulation. It is possible that the Satsuma samurai were as good fighting men as the Mikawa clansmen, but their leaders lacked the insight and diplomatic skill of Ieyasu or perhaps they would not have been thus humiliated.

In the third month of the year 1586 Ieyasu got a carbuncle on his back. He told his pages to squeeze it between two clamshells to get rid of the matter, but there was no improvement, for it only grew bigger. It was extremely painful and resisted all his efforts to heal it, so that his councilors began to grow anxious and it was rumored abroad that his condition was serious. Then Honda Shigetsugu suggested that he see one Kasuya Chokan, who had treated him successfully for this complaint, but Ieyasu would not take his advice. This exasperated Honda, who burst out in his usual forcible manner: "If you don't take proper care of this illness you'll die a dog's death, so there! Here are all the doctors saying that the chances are ten to one against your recovery, and you don't seem to realize how precious your life is. Well, I shan't stay here to see to your obsequies, for I am going on to prepare the way for you, so this is the last you will see of me in this life." And he was going off abruptly when Ieyasu in some surprise told the attendants to stop him. "What are you so excited about?" he asked. "I may be ill, but I'm not dead yet. And if I do die, what is the good of your committing suicide? Veteran councilors are too valuable for that. You have to look after things after I am gone, and guide the steps of my heir. Pray reconsider your decision." "That depends on circumstances," replied Honda, in whose face emotion now fought with anger. "If I were a young man of twenty or thirty there might be no need to accompany a heedless master like you, but I am nearly sixty now and from my youth I have been at your side in all your battles. I have lost an eye and some fingers and am lame in one leg from wounds. I have got about all the damages one well can in one body, and it is only owing to my lord's favor that life is at all tolerable. So if you go to another world I have no support left. Your relatives the Hōjō and all your other neighbors have got their eyes on your provinces, and how can we face powerful foes like these when we are without your strength and inspiration? It means that your house will be ruined, and then what would become of me, the too old servant of a fallen family? I should be a little better than a beggar. Look at Asari, the once honored retainer of Takeda. He has had to come over to us, and beg to be taken on as a humble follower of Honda Heihachiro. Do you think I want a miserable fate like that?" This argument impressed Ieyasu, and he consented to see Chokan. He came, and put some medicament on the carbuncle, and afterwards prepared a huge moxa as big as a dice-box, which Honda himself applied, as well as some internal remedy, with the result that the abscess burst in the night and discharged a large quantity of matter as required. After this Ieyasu felt much better and recovered rapidly. Honda was so delighted that he literally wept for joy, a fairly rare phenomenon in people of his temperament. And Uesugi Kagekatsu's men agreed that it was well that Ieyasu was spared to the Empire, for now that Shingen and Kenshin were both dead his was the most commanding personality they knew.

CHAPTER 19

THE KWANTO CAMPAIGN

HIDEYOSHI had now to deal with the last unsubdued powers in the land, the Kwanto under Hōjō, and beyond that Date Masamune in Mutsu, two chiefs who somewhat corresponded to Mori Terumoto and Shimazu on the west. Hōjō was an imposing figure, but too easygoing, and inclined to stand on the defensive, an attitude that had so far served well against Takeda and Uesugi, who could not devote enough time and sufficient troops to make the siege effective, but was not at all a safe policy against Hideyoshi, who had ample means and time at his disposal and no enemies behind him. But this difference does not seem to have penetrated Hōjō's mentality, and he did not realize the might of Hideyoshi and the fact that in eight years he had subdued all the great houses in the Empire, so, when in his turn he was called on to go as a vassal to the capital, he only made excuses and did not go. Ieyasu seems to have advised him to do so, but he took no heed, and the only member of his family who visited Hideyoshi was Ujinori, uncle of the young lord Ujinao, and captain of the castle of Nirayama, the chief outpost of Odawara to the east. This was quite likely the result of the representations of Ieyasu, who was not at all anxious that the Hōjōs should be overthrown. They were his neighbors, and as the adage says: "If the lips are destroyed the teeth are cold." Ujinori was a fine soldier, and an old friend of Ieyasu, for they had been fellow-hostages with Imagawa. Ieyasu was himself at the capital when Ujinori came up to apologize to Hideyoshi for the dilatoriness of his brother Ujimasa and his other relations. Ujimasa had some reason for being disinclined to make the journey, for he had retired and declared that his health was not good. Besides his apologies he wished to obtain a decision in the matter of Sanada, that is to say, that Sanada should hand over the castle of Numata to the Hōjōs as Ieyasu had bidden him to do in accordance with the agreement they had made. Ujinori got a shock when he was received in audience by Hideyoshi, for he and his family had not altered their style or their costume for decades; they were quite satisfied with themselves as they were. So he was ushered in to find the Kambaku seated on the dais surrounded by all the great lords in Kariginu with great crests, in all the dignity of Court Rank and costume.

But since he had no special relations with the Court and no rank he could only be treated and addressed as a simple military noble, and announced as Hōjō Sukegoro Ujinori, having to take a very low place indeed, much behind the retainers of Hideyoshi and others with their Court titles, Hyobutaiyu, Uneme-no-sho, and so on. And his obeisance was acknowledged only by a silent bow from the Kambaku, whom the Hōjōs were still thinking of as Nobunaga's horse-boy risen to be an able general. And now Ujinori felt like a country squire in the presence of elegant courtiers. Not that he appeared at all in an unfavorable light, for he was of fine presence and easy manners, as well as eloquent of speech. As was his custom, Hideyoshi came to see him privately that evening, and pointed out how desirable it was that his family should in their own interest come up and make their submission, since, as he could see, they were otherwise unable to take their proper place among their equals, but would have to come after everyone with Court rank and office. "This," said Hideyoshi, "is because you have not paid proper respect to the Court, but remained isolated in your fief."

Ujinori replied quite courteously that he would carry the Kambaku's recommendation to his family. "He hoped they would be able to fall in with it, but if they did not he certainly would not desert them, but would vigorously oppose Hideyoshi's armies, with the utmost of his capacity." And so they parted, Hideyoshi full of admiration for his fine character and bearing.

Hōjō Ujimasa, the elder brother, still remained obdurate, however, and would not listen, trusting to the strength of his position. So Hideyoshi sent him a letter formally accusing him of rebellion, and declaring his intention of crushing him as he had done Akechi, Shibata, and the rest. "I will certainly punish you at once," it concluded; "next year I will march against your fief with my armed forces, and will cut off the head of Ujinao, and that without delay."

This letter also contained his judgment in the matter of Sanada, and it was rather favorable to Hōjō, for Sanada was only to keep one-third of the territory with the castle of Numada, while Hojō was to be given the other two-thirds. The two-thirds required to make up Sanada's fief were to be supplied out of the territory of Ieyasu. This seemed unfair to Ieyasu and generous to Hōjō, but since Hideyoshi had made up his mind to confiscate all Hōjō's domains and place Ieyasu there it was not quite what it seemed.

This letter was sent to Ieyasu to deliver to Hōjō, and he forwarded it to Odawara with a reproach for disregarding his advice, and a recommendation to apologize even at this late hour. Hōjō, however, again ignored it, thinking with some reason that if Hideyoshi had treated

Ieyasu, whom he regarded as a tributary, with such condescension, this threat was no more than bluff. With a strange obtuseness he failed to realize how the situation had changed in the last six years.

Even before despatching the ultimatum Hideyoshi had begun preparations for the campaign by ordering all the wives and families of his vassals to assemble in Kyoto as hostages. He also issued orders to the lords of the Kinai, or district of the capital, and province of the east and north of it, to mobilize their troops. In Icyasu's fiefs the proportion of men required was the highest of all, seven men per hundred koku. For the northern provinces it was six, and for the Chugoku four.

The plan was for Ieyasu, Nobuo, and Gamo Ujisato to advance along the Tokaido road, while Uesugi and Maeda went by the Tosando. Probably Ieyasu was not surprised to find the heaviest burden on his shoulders, since he was the nearest to Hōjō and in the most convenient position to attack him. Moreover, he was the father-in-law of Ujinao, and for this reason likely to be suspected of having leanings in his favor if he did not prove the contrary by energetic action against him. So, thoroughly consistent in his submission as he had been in his opposition, he threw himself whole-heartedly into the campaign, and willingly consented to lead the van.

To begin with, at the end of this year (1589) he sent his heir Nagamaru, now aged twelve, under the escort of Ii, Sakai, and others to the Juraku mansion as his hostage. Nagamaru was a handsome youth, and Hideyoshi received him with every consideration. His wife, the Lady Yae, herself redressed his hair and presented him with a fashionable suit of clothes and a gold-hilted tachi, and when arrayed in them she stood back and looked him over approvingly, and said to Ii: "The Dainagon is indeed fortunate in having such a large family, and Nagamaru has beautiful manners, so he must have been well brought up. But his hair and clothes, you know, are a bit countrified, so I have taken the liberty of fitting him out in proper Miyako style. Still I am sure the Dainagon will be anxious if his son is so far away from him, so please take him back at once." In this way Nagamaru was given his Coming-of-age ceremony, and received as a compliment the first character of Hideyoshi's name, being henceforth known as Hidetada.

But Ieyasu insisted on sending a hostage all the same in the person of Honda Yasutoshi, his cousin.

And just about the time that Nagamaru reached Kyoto, Asahi-hime, the wife of Ieyasu and sister of Hideyoshi, departed this life at the age of forty-eight. She was buried in the Tōfukuji, and given the posthumous title of Nammei-in. There was no public mourning for her owing to the military preparations. She died quietly as she had lived, for nothing is said about her. It is unlikely that Ieyasu was prostrated with grief. Still, he never married again; there was no particular need. It might have been embarrassing for Ieyasu had she lived. She died at the right time, and he was fortunate as usual. And he had plenty to occupy his thoughts, for he had literally to prepare the way for Hideyoshi. The Tokaido highway had to be cleaned up and new resthouses built along it, and all the castles in the way renovated so that they could be handed over for the time to the Kambaku in a suitable condition. This work was Ieyasu's real return for the restoration of Hidetada to him. The transport arrangements were superintended by Ina Tadatsugu, an experienced engineer, who threw a floating bridge across the Fujikawa at the same time.

Hideyoshi intended to make another of his impressive exhibitions by this campaign of the same kind as his reception of the Emperor at the Juraku, his building of the Great Buddha, and so on. The Sanjo Ohashi Bridge at Kyoto was rebuilt for his departure as the inscription that remains on its "Giboshi," or bronze pillar bosses, yet testifies.

In the second month of 1590 Ieyasu started out and reached Yoshi-wara in Suruga on the fifteenth, where he camped to await Hidey-oshi, for whom a residence had been built there as a temporary base. Thence he threw out his forces to get into touch with the fortresses that formed the outer defense of Odawara, the Hōjō capital. By this time the fleet under the command of Chosokabe Motochika, Wakizaka Yashiharu, Kato Yoshiaki, and Kuki Yoshitaka had arrived at the coast of Odawara to institute a blockade on that side. The last three of these commanders were later in charge of the naval operations in the Korean campaign. Meanwhile Hideyoshi himself had made a characteristically showy departure from the capital. Clad in scarlet-laced armor, with a helmet shaped like a Chinese head-dress, with a huge gold quiver on his back, his teeth blackened, and a wig on his head, he bestrode a horse gaily decked in golden tasselled mail with ornaments of green and red. With his scarlet lacquered bow in his hand and a sword ornamented with "Noshi" by his side, he rode over the Sanjo bridge, followed by all his high officers equally splendidly attired, and also by the Great Court nobles; while all the people of Kyoto and from the country round thronged to see the sight, and stands were erected along the highway as far as Yamashima and Fushimi. In this connection Tokutomi offers an interesting comment: "We present-day Japanese, with our lack of skill in propaganda, may think this all very odd. But we must remem-ber that our reticence and dislike of display are things that we owe to the restraint of the Tokugawa government, and that they were wholly unknown in the days of Hideyoshi and Nobunaga." This is, of course, very true, but it seems in this matter Ieyasu and his successors were only returning to the severity of the Hōjōs and Ashikagas. Momoyama flamboyance, like Victorian vulgarity, was perhaps no more than an episode.

So Hideyoshi moved in stately fashion along the Tokaido road until he reached the domains of Nobuo and Ieyasu, being splendidly entertained by their representatives at the chief towns, while in Sumpu he was met by Ieyasu himself, who returned from the front specially to receive him in his capital, and having done so immediately hurried back to his men. It was an opportunity for Hideyoshi to inspect and admire the famous sights of the Tokaido, and to exercise his poetic gift on them, but at the same time he never relaxed his strict precautions against any possible surprise. The Mikawa Fudoki says that Ishida warned him against entering the castle of Sumpu because Ieyasu meditated treachery, but Asano and Otani reassured him. There is also a story repeated in more than one record that when Ieyasu and Nobuo met him there he jumped down from his horse and laid his hand on his sword with the exclamation: "I hear that you two are traitors. Come on, then! I am ready!" Whereupon Nobuo flushed and was silent, but Ieyasu, quite unruffled, replied in ringing tones: "And a very fine and suitable gesture for Your Highness when beginning a campaign! Long life to you!" So that Hideyoshi rode on quite assured. The ground for this suspicion may well be that related in the *Myoryokyohan* that Nobuo suggested to Ieyasu that if they made an arrangement with Hōjō and attacked Hideyoshi in front and rear simultaneously they would have an excellent chance of getting rid of him. But Ieyasu replied that he could not betray anyone's confidence in this way, and the same reply he also made to a like suggestion from Ii Naomasa, who observed that Hideyoshi rode with only fifteen attendants, and it would be easy to assassinate him. "The Empire has its destiny," said Ieyasu, "and it is not to be tampered with by man's agency!" And Ii was abashed at his want of insight. His master could see how little there was of the Empire maker about Nobuo or Hōjō. Hideyoshi was quick to quash any rumors of discord by visiting the camps of Ieyasu and Nobuo in gay civil costume, with only a short sword in his belt, making merry with them both in the frank and hearty way that came so natural to him.

Meanwhile the great host of 150,000 men were encircling the fortified town of Odawara and Oda Nobuo, Oda Nobukane, Hosokawa Tadaoki, Gamo Ujisato, Fukushima Masanori, Hachisuka, and others, with about 40,000, were attacking Nirayama, its strongest defense on the Tokaido road. They never succeeded in taking it, though they constructed a wooden tower to overtop it, and take it with fire, but the 3,640 men of the garrison not only held out stoutly, but sallied forth and inflicted severe loss on Fukushima's detachment. So after a while Hideyoshi withdrew Nobuo, Hosokawa, and Gamo with half the force to help invest the main castle. In the other regions he was gradually taking all the subsidiary fortresses, with the exception of Oshi, and before very long Odawara was almost completely isolated. Oshi only capitulated after the main fortress fell, though Ishida applied Hideyoshi's favorite flooding tactics to it. But to reduce Odawara was not easy, for it was well situated and admirably fortified and organized for defense. So Hideyoshi settled down for a long siege, and to prevent his men becoming bored by it he had resort to aesthetic methods, and inaugurated a picnic campaign. Hōjō had relied on the failure of supplies for such a large army, but several thousand ships were employed for the commissariat, and there was abundance of everything. The various commanders built themselves quite handsome residences with Shoin reception-rooms and tearooms surrounded by landscape gardens, while the men laid out vegetable patches, where they grew melons and eggplants and varieties of beans, while tradespeople from the western province towns came and set up shops, not only for everyday commodities, but for curios and European imported articles as well. And these were followed by the keepers of inns and restaurants, while, of course, strumpets were in proportion to the rest of these non-producers. Hideyoshi also told his attendant lords that they could send for their wives, he himself setting the example by writing a letter to his consort Yae asking her to send his favorite, the Lady Yodo, to keep him company. His own headquarters on Ishigaki was a most imposing and permanent-looking structure. It appeared hardly inferior to the Juraku mansion or Osaka castle with its white plastered walls on stone foundations and its lofty keep and embattled gates, while on its roads horsemen could ride ten or fifteen abreast. The defenders in Odawara made the most of their impregnable position, and laid themselves out also to be as merry as possible, for they, too, had plenty of supplies, and were in high spirits; "though at times there might be silence in the city, soon it would be broken by the strains of a flute or the twang of strings or the click of the Go, or chessman, or the sudden shouting of drink-smitten dancers." And there was no profiteering in food in Hideyoshi's camp, for though Ieyasu with his usual foresight had ordered rice to be stored the year before and forwarded to Numazu for the use of his men, Ina, in his headquarters, reported to him: "Rice is as cheap in these hills as it is in Numazu, there is no need to go to the expense of transporting our own." "H'm," replied Ieyasu, "that's Nagatsuka Masaie. He's no soldier, but he knows how to manage that sort of thing."

Ieyasu appears at one at least of the Cha-no-yu parties that Hideyoshi gave so often during this campaign, with Hosokawa Fujitaka, father of Tadaoki, and Yuki Hōkyo, the diarist, to whose descriptions we owe so much, and Sen Rikyu the chief Tea-master, on which occasion the Tea-jar Hashidate and the Tea-caddy Gyokudō, very eminent vessels both of them, were used. There was of course some fighting to be done. Ieyasu had marched by the Tokaido through Hakone and taken the forts that barred his progress, and then worked round to the eastern side of Odawara to conduct the siege of that section. He brought some miners from Kai and undermined one part of the works, so that a sudden storm brought them down, whereupon Ii Naomasa and Matsudaira Yasushige forded the River Ashiko and burst in and set fire to the buildings. The Hōjō men sallied out to meet them, and a fierce fight took place, the Tokugawa side losing three hundred men, and the defenders four hundred.

That they took some pains over this attack seems evident from the story of Ieyasu's curious inquiry about the bridge over the moat in this region, which Ii thought might be useful for the advance. Ieyasu called him and said: "The bridge! The bridge!" and no more. Ii thought he meant that the depth of water under the bridge ought to be examined, so he drove in a stake to make sure. But when he reported it, Ieyasu only repeated his former interrogation. It took forty days, the narrator informs us, for Ii to conclude that his anxiety was about the bridge itself, and when he did so he slipped out on to it under cover of darkness and felt that it was unsafe. When he informed his lord of this a smile illumined his not always expressive features. This method suggests a Zen "Koan," and the Mikawa men seem to have been not a little naïve. But the siege only resulted in the throwing down of one or two towers and pieces of the wall by mining, and the defenders were quite able to repulse the attacks with some loss. So by the sixth month not much had been done, but Hideyoshi relied more on his ability to sap the confidence of the defenders than their works.

The two armies always stood on terms of courtesy and consideration for each other. Both Ukita and Kurodoa made representations to Hōjō about capitulation, and on each occasion they sent him many kegs of fine liquor to cheer him, and he responded with the delicate compliment of a present of powder and bullets, naturally more needed by them, since from their high vantage ground they kept up an incessant bombardment, though apparently without much effect. Kuroda Jōsui paid a visit to the Hōjōs in civil costume, quite unarmed. Ujimasa presented him with two of the treasures of their house, a sword and a conch, "one of the war conches of the Empire" it was called, as well as a part of the historical work *Azuma Kagami,* while Ujinao gave him a lute. This on account of his effort to arrange a peace. Already Hōjō's chief councilor, Matsuda Norihide, had been reported by his own son to be plotting to let the assailants in, and though the son only informed on condition that his father's life should be spared, this condition was not respected. But Hōjō's confidence was badly shaken, and he could see that more treachery was likely as his chances became less, so he made up his mind to come to terms. That is to say, Ujinao and his brother Ujifusa did, and they went out to Ieyasu to negotiate a surrender. Ujinao proposed that he should commit suicide, and that his father and the garrison should be unharmed. This proposal being communicated by Kuroda to Hideyoshi, he, in consultation with Ieyasu, emended it as follows: Ujinao to be pardoned, and Ujimasa and Ujiteru and the two senior councilors, Matsuda Norihide and Daidōji Masashige, to commit seppuku. It appears that Ujimasa was obstinately opposed to surrender, but that his sons came out to negotiate without his knowledge. No doubt it was as son-in-law to Ieyasu that Ujinao was spared, though Ieyasu did not care to seem importunate on his behalf lest he too should be suspect. The first and least unpleasant part of the decision to be carried out was the order to put Matsuda to death, on the sixth day. "On the tenth the Great Lord (Ieyasu) took up his quarters in the castle and inspected it."

On the eleventh Ujimasa and his younger brother Ujiteru, who had been sent on the ninth to the house of the physician Tamura Ansei, were recommended to commit seppuku. The arrangements were in charge of Ieyasu, Ii, and Sakakibara. Fifteen hundred men were ordered to mount guard over the two. This was a broad hint. "It is evidently considered," observed Ujiteru, "that it is time for us to depart." So both took a bath, dressed themselves correctly for the ceremony, and made their parting verses. Ujimasa's ran thus:

> Autumn wind of eve,
> Blow away the clouds that mass
> O'er the moon's pure light
> And the mists that cloud our mind,
> Do thou sweep away as well.
> Now we disappear,
> Well, what must we think of it?
> From the sky we came.
> Now we may go back again.
> That's at least one point of view.
>
> UJIMASA, aet. 53
> Posthumous title:
> *Jiun-in den.*

As both stabbed themselves and drew out the dagger, Ujinori as second cut off their heads at a blow, and then went to turn his sword against himself when Ii Naomasa seized his hand and prevented it. Ujinao was sent to Mount Koya at first, but was afterwards given 10,000 koku in Kawachi, but he died of smallpox, aged twenty-nine. Of course it was said that he was poisoned, but this does not seem likely. Ujinori also was given a fief of 3,000 koku in Kawachi, and afterwards another of 10,000 at Sayama. But all the great fiefs in the Kwanto were confiscated to be conferred on Ieyasu.

For this Odawara campaign the following Field Orders were issued by Ieyasu:

1. If anyone advances and reconnoiters without orders he shall be punished.
2. Anyone who presses on too far forward, even though to make a name for himself, is a transgressor against military law and will be punished with all his family.
3. Anyone who is found trespassing in another company without proper reason shall be deprived of his horse and arms. And if his master objects he shall be held extremely culpable. And when anyone has to pass through on some duty way shall be made for him and he shall go straight through without loitering.
4. When troops are on the march none shall go by byways. This fashion must be strictly impressed on them. If any move in a disorderly fashion their leader will be held culpable.
5. Anyone who disobeys the orders of the Bugyo will be punished.
6. When troops are on the march, all flags, guns, bows, and spears are to be carried according to fixed order, and they are to march at the command of the Bugyo. Any disorder will be punished.
7. Except when in the ranks it is forbidden to go about carrying long spears. One spear not of this type may be carried before the commander when on horseback.
8. Anyone letting a horse stray loose in the camp will be punished.
9. As to the baggage train, strict orders are to be given that they are to be allotted a proper place so that they do not get mixed with the troops. Any who do will be put to death on the spot.
10. Without orders no one may seize any man or woman and take them. Should anyone take and conceal any such person his master shall correct the matter, and if any case shall come to light of his neglecting to do so that leader's fief shall be confiscated. And the vanguard shall not, without orders, set fire to any house in enemy territory.
11. Violence and intimidation of tradespeople is strictly forbidden. Offenders will be put to death on the spot.
12. Anyone who strikes camp without orders will be punished.
    May all the Gods of Japan both great and small pay attention!

May they blast without pity any who transgress the above orders!

So be it.

Tensho 18.2. (1591)

IEYASU.

That the enforcement of such orders was not left to heaven alone an incident in the division of Gamo Ujisato makes quite clear. Ujisato noticed that the troops did not march in good order as they might, so he himself rode right round the division from front to rear to inspect them. He noticed that a fellow with a helmet crested with several tiers of catfish tails was not keeping his place, and ordered him sharply to do so. On his return he saw him out of it again. Without a word he drew his sword and struck off his head. The helmet he gave to another man. There was no more disorder.

CHAPTER 20

IEYASU ENTERS EDO

DURING the campaign of Odawara, Hideyoshi offered Ieyasu the lordship of the Eight Provinces of the Kwanto, and he accepted it. This meant that he would move to the eastward beyond the barrier of Hakone, and would relinquish his ancestral fief of Mikawa with the provinces of Tōtōmi, Suruga, Shinano, and Kai, that he had conquered himself, and these would naturally then come under the control of Hideyoshi. The offer is related in the Kwan-hasshu-kosen-roku as follows: "One day Hideyoshi went out with Ieyasu, who was in charge of the main army there, to inspect the castle of Odawara. Taking Ieyasu's hand he said: 'See, we shall soon overthrow the Hōjō now, so I promise you as your fief the Eight Provinces of the Kwanto.' 'Good. Let's piss on the bargain, then,' replied Ieyasu, and the pair of them went over toward the castle and pissed together. So to this day the children speak of them as the 'Pair of pissers on the Kwanto' (Kwanto no tsure-shōben)."

Hideyoshi's gift may have seemed spontaneous magnanimity, and that is the impression he liked to make, and usually did make, but actually this transaction was dictated by far-seeing policy as usual. Of the eight provinces only four were really free, for Satomi was in Awa, Sano in Kozuke, Utsunomiya and Nasu in Shimotsuke, and Satake in Hitachi, so that, though the territory was unquestionably more than his former holding, it was not then so big as it seemed.

Moreover, since the Kwanto had been under the beneficent rule of the Hōjōs for some time and owed fealty to that house, Hideyoshi might well hope that when a new lord was put there a certain amount of opposition to him would arise, as in the case of Sasa Narimasa, and as he was not very familiar with the country it would at the least keep him busy at home, and might even weaken him so seriously that the Taiko would have an excuse for rearranging things to his advantage. Thus he would use the condition of the Kwanto to safeguard himself further. So says the Tokugawa Jikki, and there may be some truth in it, for Hideyoshi seldom acted with a single aim, but at the same time he may have meant no more than to make Ieyasu warden of the Kwanto to uphold his power there as had been done by the Ashikaga Shoguns when they appointed a Kamakura Kubo. Anyhow it was an embarrassing favor, or a polite infliction, to be asked to leave his five home provinces, one of which was his ancestral fief and the others his sword and diplomacy had won, and which he did not owe to the favor of anybody. However, in accordance with his principle in life of yielding for a while to superior strength, and of being wary enough to know superiority when he saw it, he made no objections. Hence presumably arose the proverb: "Ieyasu won the Empire by retreating."

It was natural that Hideyoshi should reward Ieyasu for his exertions in the Odawara campaign as he had done in the case of Kobayakawa Takakage, for instance, when in return for his services in Kyushu he bestowed Chikuzen and Hizen on him. Anyhow, by so doing Hideyoshi fulfilled three different purposes. First, he rewarded Ieyasu and so conciliated him. Then he removed him from his strategic position on the Tokaido and shut him in behind the Hakone pass, thus preventing him from becoming a menace to the capital should he have the intention at any time.

It was noticeable that when Ieyasu was giving fiefs to his chief retainers after the rearrangement, and he gave Odawara to Okubo Tadayo, Hideyoshi immediately asked that Hakone be given to him also with the intention of putting Ieyasu's most trusty retainers under an obligation to himself, so that they would be on his side if any difference arose. At the same time he prevailed on Ieyasu to send Honda Shigetsugu (Devil Sakuza), against whom he had a grudge, into retirement instead of giving him a fief, and Ieyasu did not think it politic to refuse.

However, as soon as Ieyasu had vacated his former provinces Hideyoshi put first Kato Mitsuyasu and then Asano Nagamasa into Kai, the most central position, and Hidetsugu into Kiyosu that commanded the Tokaido nearest the capital, while further east, on the same highway, he put Horio into Hamamatsu, Tanaka into Okazaki, Ieyasu's old castle, Yamanouchi into Kakegawa, and Nakamura into Shizuoka, thus completely closing the throat of the Kwanto by posts in the hands of his most reliable retainers. There is little doubt that it was for all this that Hideyoshi embarked on the Odawara campaign, and when it was done he had finished his task.

After Odawara he started on a tour of inspection of the north, and on the way looked round Masashi and Edo. It was then that he told Ieyasu what a high opinion he had of the strategic position of Edo, and how he thought he ought to make it his headquarters, when, with Odawara in the hands of a trusted subordinate, he would be powerful and secure indeed. This advice Ieyasu took also. He no doubt saw the possibilities of this now small city, and in making a virtue of necessity at the same time was well satisfied to be in a situation so favorable for future development. He had, it is true, Oda Nobuo in front of him and Date behind him, but these might be dealt with later on. It is highly improbable that he was in the least unaware of any of Hideyoshi's schemes.

His own retainers seem to have been surprised by his choice of Edo. Had their advice been taken Odawara would have been made the capital, or, failing that, Kamakura. The former was a strong and populous city, and seemed to the casual eye best suited. The town was a ri long, and well furnished with every kind of shop and trade able to supply the luxuries as well as the necessities of life. The picture of Edo is a great contrast. Beside the castle built by Ota Dokwan a hundred and thirty years before, and taken by Hōjō sixty-two years ago, which was extensive but dilapidated, there was but a straggling town that was hardly more than a village. To the north of the castle was Kanda Hill, while on the east was a reedy swamp completely covered by water at high tide. This came up to what is now Hibiya. Beyond was the wide flat plain of Musashi, "where the moon rose and set in the grass, with never a peak to hide beyond," as the popular verse had it. The town was no more than the village of Hirakawa, from the present Ote machi and Eiraku-cho to Yuraku-cho, and consisted of some hundred houses or so. The shrine of Kanda Myojin was where the Treasury now is in Nagata-cho, and near it was the Nichirinji, and there were some fifteen or sixteen temples and two or three shrines scattered about between this district right up to the present site of the Fukiage park. There were more temples and shrines than enough for such a handful of people, and their festivals were hardly crowded, but the Festival of Kanda Myojin, on the fifteenth day of the eighth month, was, then as now, the most important event in the year.

So when on the first day of the eighth month of 1590 Tokugawa Ieyasu made his official entry into his new capital, it was an auspicious event for this little place. He had not lost much time about it, since it was only on the fourteenth day of the seventh month that the Eight Provinces were formally handed over to him. His rapidity of decision and movement astonished Hideyoshi. "The Lord Tokugawa's way of doing things is really extraordinary," he exclaimed when he heard it.

Now as Ieyasu entered his new capital by the western highway, preceded and followed by a long train of followers and retainers of all ranks, he noticed a priest standing in front of his temple gate at Kaizuka, not far from where the Hanzo Gate is now. For some reason he stopped and inquired who he was. Some narratives improve on the story by insisting that his horse stopped of itself like Mohammed's camel, and would not go on owing to some divine inspiration. The priest explained that he was one Son-ō, abbot of the Shingon Temple of Kōmyōji. "Then," replied Ieyasu, "perhaps you are the disciple of Kan-ō, the abbot of Daijuji, in my province of Mikawa?" The priest answered that this was so, whereupon Ieyasu dismounted and remarked that he would rest there a while, so Son-ō, highly delighted, made him a cup of tea, which he drank, and after a while resumed his progress, declaring his intention of coming back the next day.

He made his headquarters in the Nichiren Temple of Hō-ōnji, a more comfortable place than the disused castle. This temple of Daijuji, of which he spoke, was the one founded by Chikatada, his ancestor of the sixth generation in the village of Kamota, in the Nukada district of Mikawa, which had ever since been the chantry temple of the Tokugawas. Ieyusa had fled there for refuge after the battle of Oke-hazama, when Nobunaga's men were pursuing him, and Kan-ō had asked him what he would do if victorious over his enemies. The reply was that he intended to seize their castles and enlarge his territories. To this Kan-ō objected that it was an unworthy motive, and that the aim of a feudal lord should be the security and prosperity of his people. Thus Ieyasu obtained enlightenment, and determined to act in accordance with this good advice. Kan-ō then presented him with a banner, on which he wrote the Jodo text: "Separate from unholiness and cleave to the Pure Land," and under this Ieyasu triumphed. As a result he made Kan-ō one of his councilors, and it was not remarkable that he should show preference for his disciple.

Next morning he came again as he had promised, and Son-ō offered him a light repast of rice-gruel and soybean soup, the best the temple could provide. But Ieyasu was well satisfied, and after he had finished his meal told the priest that he wished to make this his chantry temple in Edo, and if Son-ō would not object to changing his sect from Shingon to Jodo, to which the Tokugawas belonged, the matter could be settled at once. And so it was arranged, for the happy monk did not consider such a detail of any importance.

His spiritual future thus settled, Ieyasu proceeded to inspect his temporal residence, the castle of Edo, accompanied by Honda Masanobu. It consisted of the Hon-maru or main castle with the Ni-no-maru and San-no-maru, surrounded by wide empty moats. The buildings were roofed with boards, and the kitchens and outbuildings thatched, the former much smoke begrimed. They had never been repaired since they were damaged in the siege by Hōjō, and the rain had leaked through the roofs and stained the mats inside. The entrance was of an even more unpretentious nature, a simple earth floor with three steps made of the same number of wide boards taken from an old ship. Its rustic simplicity might have rejoiced a tea master, or appealed to the severe tastes of the model Chinese Emperor Yao, but it seemed to Honda, little as he cared for luxury, hardly dignified enough for a great lord. "We may perhaps leave the interior for the present," he observed, "but the entrance really ought to be rebuilt. It is not seemly for the reception of the Daimyos when they come to pay their respects." But Ieyasu thought otherwise. With a hearty laugh he replied: "Now, Sado, it isn't like you to recommend such extravagance. Besides, the stipends of our retainers must be seen to before anything else." So all that was done was to fill in the moat between the Ni-no-maru and the main castle, and renew some of the floor mats. He then proceeded to apportion fiefs to his retainers according to their merits. Here Hideyoshi had shown a desire to be generous at his expense in some other cases beside that of Okubo Tadayo, so that the chief feudatories of Ieyasu should owe him some gratitude too. So he asked the latter how much he intended to give Ii, Honda, and Sakakibara. Now Ieyasu intended to give them about a hundred thousand koku each, but at once divining what Hideyoshi was after, he replied that he thought sixty thousand would be a good reward for them. "Oh," exclaimed Hideyoshi, "surely that's much too little. You must give them a hundred at least." So Ieyasu kindly consented to fall in with the suggestion, and so convinced Hideyoshi of his ever docile and altruistic desire to serve the house of Toyotomi, reflecting at the same time that he had saved a hundred and fifty thousand koku, for if he had said a hundred thousand Hideyoshi would certainly have capped it with a hundred and fifty.

He was considerate in ordering that retainers with small salary should be given properties near Edo, and in no case should their manors be farther away than a day's journey. Had this been so their salary would have been diminished owing to the expense of traveling. The majority received one village, and where two or more were given they were adjacent to each other, also that the holder might be saved inconvenience. As there was no room for families in Edo at present, Ieyasu recommended that these retainers should build a simple house for them on their fiefs and come to Edo for duty by themselves. So they came in with only horses and body-servants, and lodged where they could, some in the farmers' houses, and some in huts that they had run up hastily as temporary barracks. And so great was the crowd and so few were the houses in the district that the whole countryside was overwhelmed by them, and at first many could find no shelter nearer than from eight to twelve miles from the city. And since the roads were very bad or non-existent, these had a fair amount of hardship to put up with. Only Ieyasu and the very great vassals were able to afford the comfort of a temple.

All the arrangements of the fiefs and land Ieyasu entrusted to his commissioner Ina Kumazo Tadatsugu, making him Daikwan or District Commissioner of all the Eight Provinces. Honda Masonobu ventured to question the wisdom of this, seeing that he had had a Commissioner in each of his five provinces before. But Ieyasu would not listen to any objections, and only asked Honda to draw up a form of oath that he wished Ina to swear. So he wrote down the first article: "That he should administer the provinces as carefully as though they were his own property;" the second: "that he would be entirely impartial in his dealings with those under him;" and when Honda waited for the third his lord informed him that that was all. Ina Tadatsugu certainly justified the confidence reposed in him, and carried on the local government all his days until he died in 1615. He was always known as Kori-Bugyo, or Local Commissioner, the office he first held under Ieyasu. He first attracted the special attention of Hideyoshi by his skilful and prompt disposal of the hundred thousand koku of rice left by the Hōjōs at the surrender of Odawara, and handed over by Hideyoshi to Ieyasu. He was employed by Ieyasu in this campaign as Commissioner of Transport, and proved extremely successful, and afterwards also he made a name as an engineer like the Suminokuras, constructing dams and excavating river beds and watercourses and reclaiming land, improving the communications of the country, and increasing the revenue of the Kwanto. Besides these activities, he was equally efficient in putting down brigandage and administering justice. His son maintained the tradition, and handed it on to his descendants who filled the office of Gundai for many generations, and thus the family established a system of local government known as the Ina school, which, with another, the Hikosaka school, came to be called the Two Schools of Local Government of the Tokugawa Era.

Meanwhile Ieyasu, having settled the place of his enlightenment after death, immediately busied himself with searching for a Shinto shrine that might ensure the prosperity of his family in this world. With Sakakibara Yasumasa he started on a tour of the old castle to see what deities were honored in its precincts. Yasumasa remarked that he understood that there were a couple of little shrines in the northern quarter, so thither they made their way. They found them in a grove of plum trees, and glancing at the first they saw it bore a tablet with the name of Tenjin. "Ah yes," said Ieyasu as he passed on to look at the second, "Dōkwan was a poet, so he would have a shrine of the God of Literature." Dōkwan was not always a poet according to the well-known story of the raincoat, but Ieyasu never became one. But when he saw what was inscribed on the second, an expression of delighted surprise came over his face, and he bowed before it most reverentially; "Look here, Shikibu," he exclaimed to Yasumasa when that retainer had come to his side, "how wonderful this is. If I had not found a tutelary shrine here to my liking, I had intended to set up one to Sannō of Sakamoto on Heizan, and here I find one already established." Yasumasa agreed that it was most remarkable, and did not also fail to declare that it was without doubt a happy omen that betokened a splendid and prosperous future for the house of Tokugawa. Ieyasu nodded his head repeatedly in high good humor, and immediately ordered this shrine to be gazetted as the official guardian shrine of his house. Now the reason for his preference for this god was the belief that special importance attached to the seventh zodiacal sign from that under which anyone was born. The year of his birth was the year of the Tiger, and seven from this brings us to that of the Monkey. And as the monkey was known to be the messenger of the Sannō Gongen, it was natural that he should reverence his shrine above others. And so the Sannō shrine gained an importance in Edo, which it has never lost till the present day. Some may wonder why such a man as Ieyasu was thus superstitious, but Shinto has always been a most practical type of superstition, or religion, or observance, or whatever it is called, and certainly contributed to the good order of the land. The Sannō festival and processions were famous as opportunities of joviality and merriment for the Edo populace. For the Sannō Gongen is no other than the jovial Daikoku. Still one thing remained in the religious sphere, and that was an official Oratory where the Tokugawas could present their petitions to the Buddhas. The ancient temple of Sansōji at Asakusa, with its miraculously granted image of Kwannon, was obviously the place, and so Kinryuzan, as it is usually called, was chosen. Ieyasu issued an order that both this fane and also Kōmyōji should be maintained with all proper decorum, and that all irregularities should be discontinued. Evidently this was rather necessary in the case of Kinryuzan, for it is stated that among its thirty-six priests all but a few were decidedly not immaculate in their ways. In fact no more than ten could be said to be anything but hedge-priests. It was even suggested that it was not correct to make such a place the official oratory, but Ieyasu was not inclined to be severe with such peccadilloes, and all he did was to see that only the ten celibate and proper priests were invited to the castle for the reading of the Sutras on the appointed days. The others took the hint and retired in favor of their sons or disciples after a while, so that the temple then resumed the ascetic atmosphere deemed desirable for its new responsibilities. The temples were not, however, in most cases allowed to remain where they were, for the ground was needed for more weighty purposes than religion. Especially was the district called Tsubonezawa, about where the Imperial Park is now, a regular quarter of them, for there were five Nichiren, two Shingon, one Tendai, five Zen, and three other branch-temples, and from here across the town to Hirakawa there were also four Shinto shrines. So Ieyasu had not been in Edo more than a month when suddenly he issued an order for all these fanes to move outside the center of the new city, and though he provided them with fresh sites gratis, and also grants for moving, the rapidity of his decision seems to have made these leisure-loving ecclesiastics execute the quick change of their lives. It was not the only move they had to make either, for as the city grew in most cases they had to shift again, as in the case, for instance, of the famous Kanda Myojin, which went first to a place just outside Kanda-bashi, then in 1604 was removed to Kanda Hill, and eventually found rest at last in its present site on the height above Yushima. So, too, Hirakawa Tenjin was moved to outside the Hanzo Gate, and afterwards to its present position, thus giving the name Hirakawa-cho to this district. Sannō Gongen was left where he was for the time, but later on moved to Momijiyama, and when this was enclosed in the castle he was brought out beyond the Hanzo Gate also for the convenience of pilgrims, and only moved to Hoshigaoka, where his shrine now stands, after the Great Fire of 1650.

The ground thus cleared, the next thing was to find a place for the smaller retainers near enough to the castle for them to serve there as guards without inconvenience. Naito Kinzaemon and Amano Seibei were appointed Commissioners for this duty, and they proceeded to fix on the quarter to the northwest of the castle, now known as Bancho. This name was given to it because it was the quarter of the Guards, O-ban-shu. It was then decidedly hilly ground, and the Commissioners had it levelled so that the occupants would not be put to expense in building their residences. The numbers of the streets do not run consecutively because they were not arranged in order, but according to the place of residence of the different Companies of Guards. For instance, the First Company was located on the north of the Fifth, and on the west of the Fifth was the Second Company. On the north of the Second was the Sixth, on the north of this was the Third, while on the north of this again was the Fourth. It was this that made the Bancho quarter proverbial for its intricacy as noted in the well-known saying: "Bancho ni ite bancho shirazu" ("Living in Bancho and not knowing the way about it"). And these sites were arranged according to the express order of Ieyasu that the odd numbers one, three, and five should be in one line, since they were Yo or positive, while the even numbers, being negative, should be marshalled on the front and rear of them. At this time only the O-ban-shu guard existed. It was the bodyguard of the Shogun. Afterwards two other divisions were created, the Kosho-ban or Hanabatake-ban, which was on guard within the castle, and the Shoim-ban, for duty in the palace itself.

After his men were settled, Ieyasu instituted an inquiry into all the temples and shrines and their rights, for he signified his intention of granting sites to all those that had any connection with any of his ancestors. Very naturally this was a sign for a general rush on the part of all the religious foundations in the Kwanto, and the esurient ecclesiastics flocked to Edo "like clouds and mist." A very considerable number remained after those whose claims were but imaginary had been weeded out, and these took up their residence in the city and built their temples and shrines where in future very fervent prayers would go up for the preservation of the Tokugawa house. Nor was this all, for in many other ways the priests were expected to make themselves useful to the Shogunal administration.

Ieyasu next appointed the officials to superintend the weights and measures and the measures of capacity. The former office was given to one Shuzui Hyozaburo, a man of Kōshu, who was very prompt in presenting himself and requesting that this business should be entrusted to him. He was introduced by one of Ieyasu's retainers, Tamon Dempachiro, who was a native of Kōshu, and got the position apparently because Ieyasu admired his enterprise. Ieyasu's own cousin, one Mizuno Yasutada, who had a fine reputation as a soldier, was entrusted with the superintendence of the measures of capacity, as well as with the office of Controller of one division of the city and Daikwan of the villages of Sekiguchi, Kobinata, and Kanasugi in the suburbs. He was usually called Taruya, this nickname being given to him by Nobunaga because he had presented a tub (taru) of sake to Ieyasu in the Nagashino Campaign, which the latter had passed on to Nobunaga. A certain Naraya Ichiemon was appointed with him as Controller of the city, and in 1593 a third, Kitamura Hikoemon, was added.

The Tokugawa Jikki ascribes the regular use of convenient coins to Ieyasu, though it seems that Hideyoshi had already introduced much the same types. It says: "There had not been any coinage so far, but a large piece called Oban and gold dust. In Hideyoshi's days they collected various kinds of metal from all the provinces and brought it to Kyoto so that there it could be exchanged for silver, but this was very troublesome owing to the time required to examine it. In the Kwanto there were officials appointed to inspect the coinage, and there was also in use a coin called Kokuban, like the Ryo of later days. When Ieyasu became lord of the eight provinces of the Kwanto he brought to Edo one of the well-known Goto family of metalworkers from Kyoto named Shosaburo Mitsutsugu. Mitsutsugu was a smart and clever fellow, and soon became a great favorite, and was often consulted by his lord. One day Ieyasu told him that when he became lord of the Empire he might ask whatever he would, and it should be given him. Goto replied that there was nothing he particularly wanted for himself, but that everyone felt that the large size of the current gold coins was a great inconvenience, and if he could be permitted to cut them each into four pieces and mint a new variety it would be very much to the advantage of the country. Ieyasu agreed, and so these quarter pieces were made and called Koban. And afterwards, in 1606, also at Goto's suggestion, another coin called Ichibu, a quarter of these, was also made, and so well did they please everybody that they continued to circulate for more than two centuries." And somehow Goto seems to have become a millionaire.

"And from ancient days it had been the custom to use silver for currency in lumps just smelted as it came from the mine, and as there was no fixed price for it a good deal of inconvenience was caused to everyone in exchanging it. So in the sixth month of the year 1602 Sueyoshi Toshikata, the Daikan of Otsu, requested that the price of silver might be fixed by the Government so that the prices of commodities could be stabilized. This also Ieyasu approved, and ordered a Ginza or silver mint to be set up and made Toshikata its chief, so that he administered it just as Goto did that for gold, and issued coins called Chogin and Ko-tsubugin. And as everyone now brought the silver that they obtained by smelting and mining to exchange for the new silver, there was no lack of it for coining, and thus prices were able to be fixed, and all the people of the Empire felt the most fervent gratitude for the benevolence of the Government in granting them such a fine currency."

Ieyasu was never slow in taking the opportunity to put any of the powerful magnates under an obligation if one offered, and Date Masamune was an instance of this. Hideyoshi was incensed with Date about a rising in which he was concerned and summoned him to the capital, at the same time ordering him to remove from his fief in Mutsu to Iyo in Shikoku. This put Date in a pretty flutter, and his men too, and they could not think what to do about it, so Masamune dispatched his retainer Date Kozuke with only one attendant to consult Ieyasu. He felt that the fate of his house perhaps depended on how the matter was handled, and he asked Ieyasu to do anything he could for him. It was the eleventh month and very cold, and they came early in the morning and found Ieyasu sitting in the quilt-warmer, where he received them. "I suppose you haven't had breakfast yet," said he, "but I can give you some here if you don't mind it a bit simple," and his men were just going to show them into the next room to serve it there when he went on: "No, they can have it here with me," so they proceeded to lay places beside him and serve him. Ieyasu's rice had been put on the top of the quilt-warmer to prevent it cooling, and they took it and filled his bowl, and he told them to give Date and his companion some of it too, for it would be warmer than theirs. The only relish there was with the rice was some fish pickled in sake-lees, so the meal was certainly simple. When tea was handed at the end of it the two envoys rose as if to take their leave, and as they did so Ieyasu called out loudly: "To look at him anyone would think your master was a tough customer who knew his own mind, but the truth is that he is nothing but an ass without backbone or foresight. That's why he is in this dilemma. Well! He can go back to Shikoku and be food for fishes, or he can stay here and cut himself open. He had better think it over and make his choice." And then he went on to tell them in detail just what sort of answer ought to be given to Hideyoshi. With expressions of gratitude they went back and repeated it all to Masamune, and he made his preparations accordingly, and waited for the arrival of Hideyoshi's messengers.

When they did come they found Masamune's residence beset by a lot of retainers who were bustling about armed to the teeth with swords, bows, and spears of various sorts and sizes. He himself without any weapon by his side at all received them and led them up to the dais, and then explained to them with tears coursing down his cheeks: "My head is very much at the disposal of the Kampaku, should he wish to have it struck off, and I am very sensible of his great kindness in giving me another fief like this instead. I am very ready to receive it myself as you can well imagine, but the trouble is that these retainers of mine, a turbulent lot of headstrong country-bred samurai as you see, knowing nothing at all about the law of the Empire, object strongly to leaving their homeland where they have lived for many generations and going to an unknown part of the country. In fact they keep on declaring that it is a samurai's duty to commit suicide rather than meet such a fate, and won't be satisfied until I set the example. I have argued the matter with them in all sorts of ways, but like a lot of self-willed rustics they won't listen to me. I am afraid it is very discourteous to treat messengers of His Highness in this way, but you see, when I am censured my retainers won't obey me, so what am I to do?"

The envoys looked suitably impressed and hurried back to report to Hideyoshi. It happened somehow that Ieyasu was in attendance on him just then. "If it were only Masamune," he observed, "I would go and settle him myself all right, but there are about a thousand of his men there, a rough unyielding lot, set on resistance at all costs, and then he has got any number of them in his province as well, and they are just as determined not to leave it and hand it over to someone else. Of course, if you are certain of putting them down you can have your way, or, on the other hand, you might be generous out of respect for their very natural feelings. Perhaps that would be as well." After a little thought Hideyoshi agreed to take Ieyasu's advice. Masamune's gratitude knew no bounds, and in future he was very much on the side of the Tokugawa lord.

Okazaki Castle was the birthplace in 1542 of Matsudaira Takechiyo, who would later take the name Tokugawa Ieyasu. The castle was built by Matsudaira Kiyoyasu, Ieyasu's grandfather. Pictured here is the main keep of the castle. (Wikimedia Commons)

Matsudaira Kiyoyasu (1511-35) was Ieyasu's grandfather and the lord of the Matsudaira clan during the Sengoku period. He died at 25 years of age leaving his young son, Matsudaira Hirotada, as head of the clan. Horotada would also die young, at 22 years old, paving the way for Ieyasu's rise to power. (Wikimedia Commons)

Odai no Kata (1528-1602) was Ieyasu's mother. Her father, Mizuno Tadamasa, was lord of the Mizuno clan. She and Ieyasu's father, Matsudaira Hirotada, divorced as a result of political machinations that made the Mizuno and Matsudaira clans enemies. (Wikimedia Commons)

In this woodblock print by Utagawa Yoshitora from the series *Heroes of Mikawa Province* (1873), **Ieyasu** is shown in full regalia. It was in 1567 when he was daimyo of Mikawa Province, 36 years before he became Shogun, that Ieyasu took the surname "Tokugawa," thus becoming Tokugawa Ieyasu. (Wikimedia Commons)

Tsukiyama-dono (1542-79), also known as Lady Tsukiyama, was Ieyasu's chief consort. She was the mother of Matsudaira Nobuyasu, Ieyasu's eldest son. Lady Tsukiyama and Nobuyasu's wife, Lady Tokuhime, had a quarrelsome relationship which led Tokuhime to accuse her mother-in-law of conspiring with the rival Oda clan. In order to save face, Ieyasu had Lady Tsukiyama executed in 1579. (Wikimedia Commons)

Toyotomi Hideyoshi (1537-98) was one of the three great unifiers of Japan along with Oda Nobunaga and Tokugawa Ieyasu.
Hideyoshi, who had been a leading general under Nobunaga,
initiated a campaign to unify Japan which led to his effective rule
of the country until his death in 1598. Hideyoshi's son, Toyotomi
Hideyori, was defeated by Ieyasu at the Battle of Sekigahara in
1600. (Wikimedia Commons)

In 1564, Ieyasu (then known as Matsudaira Motoyasu) was forced to deal with growing conflict in Mikawa Province as tension erupted into fighting with a group of peasants, monks and warriors opposed to daimyo rule. In this print by Tsukioka Yoshitoshi, Ieyasu is shown on horseback leading an attack at the **Battle of Azukizaka** where the rebels were defeated. (Wikimedia Commons)

Asahi no kata (1543–90), also known as Asahi-hime, was Ieyasu's wife and the half-sister of Toyotomi Hideyoshi. Her marriage to Ieyasu in 1586 was arranged to ease tensions between the two powerful men, both vying for power after the death of Oda Nobunaga in 1582. The marriage would be a short one as Asahi no kata would fall ill and die in 1590. (Wikimedia Commons)

Oda Nobunaga (1551–82) was one of the three great unifiers of Japan along with Toyotomi Hideyoshi and Tokugawa Ieyasu. As the powerful leader of the Oda clan Nobunaga initiated a strategy to unify Japan in the 1560s. By 1580 he controlled most of the island of Honshu but his plans were cut short in 1582 when his general Akechi Mitsuhide betrayed him, forcing Nobunaga to commit *seppuku*. (Wikimedia Commons)

The Battle of Tenmokuzan (1582) was fought by the Takeda clan, led by Takeda Katsuyori, against the combined forces of Oda Nobunaga and Tokugawa Ieyasu. Katsuyori was decisively defeated in the battle, marking the end of a longstanding rivalry between the two sides. Katsuyori, his son and his wife committed *seppuku* as a result of the defeat. (Wikimedia Commons)

Emperor Go-Yōzei (1571-1617) reigned from 1586 to 1611 and was the 107th emperor of Japan. He was emperor during the rivalry of Tokugawa Ieyasu and Toyotomi Hideyoshi, two of the three great unifiers of Japan. In 1603, Ieyasu was named Shogun by Go-Yōzei ushering in the era of Tokugawa rule. (Wikimedia Commons)

Lady Saigo (1552-89) was Ieyasu's first consort and trusted companion. She held considerable influence conferring with Ieyasu on numerous issues. She was the mother of Tokugawa Hidetada, the second Tokugawa Shogun who succeeded his father in 1605. (Wikimedia Commons)

Intended as the administrative center of the Tokugawa Shogunate in Kyoto, construction on **Nijo Castle** began in 1603 and was finally completed by Ieyasu's grandson, Tokugawa Iemitsu, 23 years later. Pictured here is Ninomaru Palace, one of two palaces on the castle grounds. (Wikimedia Commons)

The Battle of Nagakute (1584). Ieyasu (seated, right) is shown here conferring at the Battle of Nagakute near the city of Nagoya. Fought between Hashiba Hideyoshi (later Toyotomi Hideyoshi) and the forces of Tokugawa Ieyasu and Oda Nobukatsu, this battle (along with the Battle of Komaki that same year)

marked the first conflict between Hideyoshi and Ieyasu. Even though Hideyoshi suffered significant losses, the conflict is seen as something of a stalemate and the two powerful men made peace soon afterwards. (Wikimedia Commons)

Tokugawa Hidetada (1581–1632) was Ieyasu's third son. His mother was Ieyasu's influential consort Saigo-no-Tsubone. Hidetawa succeeded his father in 1605 becoming the second Shogun of the Tokugawa dynasty. He would rule until 1623 when he abdicated in favor of his son Tokugawa Iemitsu. (Wikimedia Commons)

CHAPTER 21

THE KOREAN CAMPAIGN AND DEATH OF HIDEYOSHI

In the twelfth month of 1592 Hideyoshi declared his intention of sending an expedition to Korea, and appointed Konishi Yukinaga and Kato Kiyomasa to lead the vanguard. They were ordered to start in the third month of the following year, and the rest of the army of 270,570 men was to proceed under the various commanders from the base at Nagoya in Hizen according to plan. Hideyoshi left Kyoto on the twenty-sixth of the third month for this base, and arrived there in the third week of the month after. Here preparations had been hurried on for his reception since the year before, and everything about his quarters was imposing and splendid. Ieyasu was appointed to the supreme command of all the Daimyos of the Eastern Provinces, so he left his son Hidetada in Edo to act as Warden in his absence, with Sakakibara Yasumasa, Sakai Shigetada, Honda Yasushige, Matsudaira Yasuchika, and Miyake Yasusada as councilors, and appointed his other son Hideyasu commander over Uesugi, Date, Satake, Nambu, and the others whose contingents marched with the Tokugawa force, the whole amounting to about fifteen thousand men. For the first time Ieyasu appointed five O-bangashira to command the five divisions into which his army was arranged. He had a number of war-vessels built from timber that was brought from the forests of Izu, and for these Koriki Kiyonaga was made Commissioner. When Ieyasu arrived at the base at Nagoya he was at once summoned by Hideyoshi to take part in the council of war with Maeda, Gamo, Asano, and others.

Now it happened that quite close to his camp there was a spring of exceedingly fine water, and as the soldiers of the whole army got into the habit of going there to get it they soon started quarrelling, so sentinels were set to guard it by the Tokugawa officers to prevent disorder. Some men from Maeda Toshiie's camp came to draw water and were refused access by these guards, whereat they grew angry, and as Maeda's camp was not far off it was not long before a number of their friends came to their support. The Tokugawa men reinforced their guards in consequence, and soon there were several thousand men facing each other all armed and threatening to start a serious conflict at any moment. Honda Tadakatsu and other leaders of the Tokugawa force tried their best to get their own men in hand, and they were ably seconded in their efforts by Sakakibara, who had just arrived on a visit from Edo, but on Maeda's side there did not seem to be anyone with sufficient authority to restrain the brawling rank and file, and things went from bad to worse. In fact, Watanabe Hanzo with several other veteran officers of the Edo troops was just leading a body of three hundred musketeers with their weapons at the ready up to a hill behind Maeda's camp to open fire on it without delay, when Date Masamune, whose camp lay next, and who was on good terms with both lords, and especially owed a debt of gratitude to Ieyasu, sent several officers to both sides to try and get them to listen to reason. The result was that Maeda sent an officer to Ieyasu direct to say that the disturbance had arisen entirely from the brawl of common soldiers, and he was most anxious to suppress it, while he relied on Ieyasu to do likewise with his own clansmen. Ieyasu had gone up on to the roof of his quarters and been an interested spectator of the whole affair from the first, and there he received the envoy and gave him the required assurance. He then received Sakakibara Yasumasa and observed to him with a smile by way of greeting: "You see, we have been able to stage a nice quarrel as a diversion for you after the fatigue of your long journey from Edo."

After this incident Hideyoshi moved the camps of Maeda and Tokugawa next his own.

During the Korean Campaign which Hideyoshi carried on fruitlessly for six years from 1592 until his death in 1598, and which caused considerable loss and hardship to a number of the feudal lords, as it was possibly intended to do, besides sowing seeds of dissension among them, Ieyasu stayed in Japan, losing neither men nor resources, but on the contrary rather gaining prestige and advantage through the troubles of the others.

In 1591 Hideyoshi had retired from the office of Kambaku and become Taiko or Retired Kambaku, the former title being transferred to his nephew Hidetsugu, his adopted heir. Ieyasu, Maeda Toshiie, Ukita Hideie, Mori Terumoto, and Kobayakawa Takakage were appointed as a Council to advise him.

Ieyasu proceeded to Nagoya in Hizen, which Hideyoshi made the base for his operations against Korea and China, his intention being to force his way through the former country, conquer China, and seat the Japanese Emperor on the throne of "the great Ming."

Hidetada was left in Edo with Sakakibara and Ii Naomasa as councilors. On the way to Nagoya Ieyasu called at Kyoto and paid his respects to the Imperial Court. When he arrived Hideyoshi informed his generals in council that he would cross over to Korea and lead his armies himself, declaring that he would feel quite secure in leaving Ieyasu in charge at home. However, as the Emperor himself sent a letter requesting him not to leave the country, and his mother, to whose wishes he always paid great attention, did not like the idea of his being so far away, while the affairs of the Lady Yodo and her young children also occupied him, it ended in his never leaving Japan at all.

In the autumn of 1592 his mother died after an illness that was very profitable for all the great shrines and temples in the country, to which large gifts were made for prayers for her recovery. He then started negotiations with the Chinese envoys after his army had been forced to retire on the capital of Korea and his warships and transports had been destroyed by the efficient navy of that country under the command of the great Admiral Yi Sun Sin.

During this period of the negotiation with China Hideyoshi was very busy with aesthetic activities, buildings and entertainments, Noh performances, excursions, and Cha-no-yu. He gave the fêtes in the melon garden, the excursions to Mount Koya to visit the memorial temple to his mother called the Seiganji, to Yoshino to view the cherry blossoms, and various other visits to the great lords, these latter expensive honors that depleted their purses, but which they had to take with a good grace. And it all ended with the great fête at the Daigo Sambo-in, when for the last time he disported himself with his friends in the beautiful gardens that he had planned.

Hideyoshi was especially enthusiastic about Noh, and at times had a performance every three or four days. He had new pieces composed on the themes of the Yoshino cherry blossom party, the visit to Koya, as well as on the overthrow of Akechi Mitsuhide, Shibata Katsuie, and Hōjō. He had them written by Komparu Hachiro, and he himself with Maeda Toshiie, Ieyasu, Oda Nobuo, and other lords took part in them.

One of his ceremonial visits to Ieyasu is thus described: "His Highness proceeded in an ox car from his mansion of Juraku to that of the Divine Lord in Court dress, which was also worn by all his suite. As a present from the Divine Lord he received a war sword by Nagamitsu, an ordinary sword by Mitsutada, and a short sword by Yukimitsu, a fine war-horse with trappings, 30,000 ryo of silver, a hundred handsome costumes, five hundred bolts of silk, and three hundred of hemp. By Hidetada he was presented with one war sword, a horse, five hundred pieces of silver, fifty suits of clothes, and a hundred bolts of linen, by the Lady Denzu-in (Ieyasu's mother) with ten pieces of gold and ten suits, and by Hideyasu with thirty suits. The retainers of the Divine Lord also contributed from twenty to two suits each according to their salaries. The splendour of the entertainment pen and paper cannot describe." They would find it difficult, too, to describe the feelings of Ieyasu at all this lavish expenditure, but patience was his strong point, and he looked forward to the day when he could bleed others. And he could afford it better than most.

It was about this time that Hideyoshi gave the famous fancy dress garden party in the melon garden at Nagoya, when he himself was dressed as a melon-seller in a black hood, russet-colored robe, and wide sedge hat, and walked round among his guests crying his wares. All the other great nobles were likewise oddly attired, Ieyasu masquerading as a seller of reeds, while Maeda Toshiie was a begging monk, Hideyasu a pickled melon merchant, Maeda Gen-i a nun, and so forth. Ieyasu was as ready as any of them to fall in with the Taiko's whims, trying though they sometimes must have been.

He also assisted at the elaborate entertainments given to the Chinese envoys at Nagoya, while on the other hand he ordered his retainers at home to prepare a lot of iron plates for the warships that the Taiko was building. Then a little later on, when Hideyoshi went back to Osaka, Ieyasu and Maeda Toshiie went with him, and did not again return to Kyushu. The last few months of the year were spent in entertainments, usually parties for Cha-no-yu, of which Hideyoshi was extremely fond, and which Ieyasu attended, and even gave, but for which he was not as enthusiastic as some, though he knew the use of it for political purposes as well as anybody. And he knew the value of fine tea-caddies and tea-bowls, and possessed and acquired some very famous specimens at little cost during his life. He was also with the Taiko when the latter went to visit the Imperial Court in state with his great officers, taking a number of valuable presents, and being entertained at the palace with performances of Noh. Ieyasu then went back to Edo for the beginning of 1594, whither he then summoned the eminent Chinese scholar, Fujiwara Seikwa, son of the Court Noble Reizei Tamenori, and attended his lectures on Sung Confucianism.

Hideyoshi now saw fit to hand over Osaka castle to his infant child Hideyori, whom the Lady Yodo had lately borne. The only other child had died at the age of two, and all his hopes were now centerd on Hideyori, who was to be his successor. Therefore he determined to rebuild Fushimi, and the Daimyos as usual were called upon to provide materials and labor. Ieyasu was one of those thus honored. He transported timber from his domains round Fuji and stones from Izu at great cost, and not wishing to overwork the levies from his own territory he hired laborers from the Omi neighborhood, and though his contributions were not so profuse as some of the others owing to the distance of which he no doubt made the most, apologizing to the Taiko for his remissness, yet the latter seemed well pleased with the result. And that Ieyasu was taking notes of it all for future reference when he should be able to do likewise there can be little question. And so in less than a year the great fortress of Fushimi was finished at a cost of about two hundred and fifty thousand koku, perhaps about a quarter of a million sterling.

Ieyasu then proceeded to attend another series of entertainments given by Hideyoshi and Hidetsugu the Kambaku, who was a very keen aesthete among other things, at Kyoto, Fushimi, and Nara, all very charming places for the autumn scenery. At the end of the year he married one of his daughters, through the mediation of the Taiko, to Ikeda Terumasa. In the new year of 1595 he again returned to Edo.

At the end of this year came the tragic end of Hidetsugu, against whom his uncle the Taiko brought charges of treasonable conduct in attempting to form a coalition of Daimyos against him as well as others of homicidal habits and want of filial respect, banished him to Mount Koya, and then sent orders to him to commit suicide. And all this very largely because he stood in the way of the succession of Hideyori, whom the Taiko now wanted to make his heir. For Hideyoshi had adopted Hidetsugu only after the death of Tsurumatsu, his first-born son, born in 1589, when Hideyoshi was fifty-three years old, apparently thinking it unlikely that he would have another. And indeed there were those who were less confident than he was, for they denied him the paternity of either, and ascribed it to Ono Harunaga, or some other. But when Hideyori was born in 1593 he began to regret this arrangement, and possibly, as some suggest, incited further by Ishida Mitsunari, who wished to find favor with the Lady Yodo, proceeded thus to put him out of the way.

Ieyasu seems to have foreseen that there would be trouble between the uncle and nephew, and went back to Edo, leaving Hidetada and Okubo Tadachika in Kyoto, but advising them to be sure and take the side of the Taiko should any question arise, as he was certain it would before very long. So when Hidetsugu sent for Hidetada to go to him at the Juraku mansion he was told he was not in the house, and meanwhile he managed to slip away to Fushimi, and at once went to Hideyoshi. Ieyasu also lent money to Hosokawa Tadaoki so that he might be able to pay back his debts to Hidetsugu who had lent various sums to some Daimyos to win their favor, for it appears that many of them were chronically hard up for ready money. Probably he guessed what his uncle meditated against him and tried to take the only defensive measures he could, and may have intended to hold Hidetada as a hostage. Anyhow, Ieyasu safeguarded himself from any suspicion of being implicated in it. Hideyoshi had Hidetsugu's wife and consorts and children, some thirty persons in all, put to death on the common execution ground, an action that aroused some indignation among the people. It also drew a rebuke from Ieyasu, for, when on his arrival at Kyoto after the executions, Hideyoshi told him he would have liked to wait till he could have consulted him about it, but it was an affair that unfortunately could not be postponed, he replied: "I don't think you did well at all in this. If the Kambaku was at fault, could you not have banished him somewhere or other? It is a pity you acted with such harshness. You are getting on in years now, while Hideyori is only a baby. If anything untoward should happen the Empire would have been safe if the Kambaku had been alive." Hideyoshi said nothing. Hidenaga too was dead, and the future of his family indeed depended on the life of this one infant, whom Ieyasu himself in the fullness of time was to treat in much the same manner.

In the fifth month of 1596 Ieyasu was promoted from Gon-Dain-agon of the Lower second rank to Naidaijin of the Upper second. Hideyoshi entertained him to a banquet on the occasion of his becoming Naidaijin, and so anxious was he to make a good impression and show his friendliness that he had special vessels made with the Aoi and Kiri crests on them in gold lacquer. "What do you think," asked Ieyasu of Honda on the quiet, "is it better to look as though we were taken in, or shall we be distant with him?" "Have you then forgotten how you increased the fief of Ogasawara Yohachiro when he came over to our side?" was Honda's answer. Ieyasu nodded, and seemed quite satisfied. The case of Ogasawara Yohachiro was a very good example of their methods. Ogasawara was the chief among the country samurai in his district, and a daring warrior. He was also ambitious, and thought that if Nobunaga and Ieyasu were on good terms still, and the former had a big battle to fight in the neighborhood of the capital, that Ieyasu would send him large reinforcements. This would be an opportunity for him to take advantage of his weakness, and perhaps get hold of the province of Tōtōmi. But Ieyasu saw through his plan, and won him over as an ally by giving him a large fief. Almost immediately after followed the Anegawa campaign, and Ieyasu went to Nobunaga's assistance promptly enough, but he took Ogasawara with him, and since he had such a reputation as a soldier gave him the honor of leading the vanguard against Asakura, which he certainly did most valiantly, crossing the river before all the others, so that Ieyasu's men followed and gained a great victory. So did Ieyasu contrive to keep him under his eye, render him innocuous, and at the same time make use of him, while Ogasawara remained all the time convinced—or had to pretend he did—that he was being treated with great respect and confidence. It must have been difficult to play this game with Hideyoshi, however, for it was a favorite one of his own.

Then began the second Korean Campaign, because when the Chinese envoys came to Fushimi in the ninth month of this year, and only appointed Hideyoshi sovereign of Japan instead of China as he expected, he broke off the negotiations abruptly, declaring that he had been grievously insulted, and again declared war on Korea because this unfortunate buffer State was the cause of his quarrel with China, as he put it. Therefore in the beginning of 1597 he again dispatched his armies on to the mainland under the command of Kobayakawa Hideaki, another of his adopted sons. Ieyasu again took no part in the campaign, but only in the various entertainments that the Taiko and others gave in connection with it. In this way the year passed, and in the latter part of it Hideyoshi was mostly engaged in laying out the garden and buildings at the Sambo-in at Daigo, where he gave his famous spring fête, proceeding there in state accompanied by his wife, six consorts, and the child Hideyori, and all his great vassals, and viewing the cherry blossoms. But later in the year he became ill, and on the eighteenth day of the eighth month of 1598, before he could go again to Daigo for the autumn tints with the Emperor, as he had arranged, he became a guest in the White Jade Pavilion.

Hideyoshi's death is thus rather picturesquely described in the *Mikawa Go-Fudoki:*

On the fifth day of the fifth month of the third year of Keicho (1598), after all the Court and military nobles had paid a visit of ceremony to him at his Palace of Fushimi, Hideyoshi was suddenly attacked by illness. The Court physicians, Takeda Hoin, Tsusen-in, Seyaku-in, Yoan-in, and the rest all racked their brains to determine the best remedies, and then administered them to him, while all temples and shrines offered up prayers and supplications to the limit of their capacity, but unfortunately in both cases without effect. Meanwhile such a great crowd of notables of both Court and military circles came to inquire after his condition that the neighborhood of Fushimi was packed with them and their retainers, and there was not left room so much as to stick a gimlet....

And so the state of the Prince Toyotomi Hideyoshi, Chancellor of the Empire, and former Kambaku of the Lower First Court rank, went on growing more grave until the eighth month, when it became apparent that he could not last much longer. And on the eighteenth day of that month he called to his side the Bugyo Ishida Nagatsuka, Masuda, Otani, and Asano, and said to them: "I think it unlikely I shall last out today. When I am gone hold services for me as a Deity for five days, but for certain reasons I think it would be well to conceal my death as long as possible. And don't forget all I have told

you about Hideyori's succession." And then regrettably unable to wait for
the moon to rise he passed away. He was one who excelled both ancient and
modern in planning and execution, and made his martial might manifest even
to the far confines of Chosen and the Great Ming, and yet when the number
of years allotted him by fate was complete there was not one to attend him on
the journey by the dark road to the Yellow Springs. Alone we come and alone
we go is the way of this life, alas. His chief wife, it is unnecessary to state, as
well as the Ladies Yodo, Sanjo, Matsu-maru, and the rest had long ago agreed
to share the same lotus with him in the world to come, yet remembering the
universal law that to live is to die and to meet is to part, although they may
have declared they would accompany him, yet actually all they did was to join
with the other ladies-in-waiting in lifting up their voices without restraint, and
making as loud lamentations as they possibly could, while the men, as might
be expected of them, were doing their utmost to carry out his last wishes as
conscientiously as possible. So that night they prepared his remains and took
them out and buried them as secretly as they could on the eastern hills. The
only followers were Maeda, Tokuzenin, and Kozan Shonin of Mount Koya,
who were most attached to him. He was only sixty-three years old, which cannot be considered great longevity.

CHAPTER 22

THE SEKIGAHARA CAMPAIGN

WHEN Hideyoshi knew he had not long to live his chief anxiety was to safeguard the future of his child Hideyori. He had been appointed Kambaku at the age of three, and now the Taiko appointed a board of Five Regents (Tairo) to administer till he should be of age. They were Tokugawa Ieyasu, Ukita Hideie (his own foster-son), Maeda Toshiie, Mori Terumoto, and Uesugi Kagekatsu. Some maintain that Hideyoshi asked Ieyasu to become sole regent and to decide whether Hideyori was fit to succeed him, and that he refused to take the responsibility. But if Hideyoshi did ask him, it was probably one of his leading questions. The five Bugyo, Masuda Nagamori, Ishida Mitsunari, Maeda Gen-i, Asano Nagamasa, and Nagatsuka Masaie, remained as they were, but between them were appointed three Churo or Interveners, Ikoma of Takamatsu in Shikoku, Nakamura of Suruga, and Horio of Tottori, to see that all went smoothly between the two groups if friction occurred.

It is interesting to note that the Portuguese thought the best council would have been one composed of Ishida, Maeda Gen-i, Konishi, and Kuroda. But after Hideyoshi's death the animosities among these leaders that had so far been restrained began to show themselves.

It was not long before Ieyasu gave the other Regents cause for complaint in making several political marriages for his sons and daughters. This had been strictly forbidden by Hideyoshi as tending to form cliques. He now proceeded to marry his sixth son Tadateru to the daughter of Date Masamune, his adopted daughter, the daughter of Matsudaira Yasumoto, to Fukushima Masanori, and his granddaughter, who had been adopted by Ogasawara Hidemasa, to Hachisuka Muneshige, while another granddaughter was betrothed to the twelve-year-old son of Konishi.

This was a convenient way for him to provide a cause for division among the Daimyos and thus see how he stood. Ishida Mitsunari immediately complained of this infringement of the rules to Maeda Toshiie, and it came up for consideration by the Regents. Ieyasu admitted that it was not very correct procedure, but submitted that it was no more than a minor affair, and really showed no lack of loyalty to Hideyori. Moreover, the Bugyo themselves had been guilty of some negligence in failing to act when they ought on a previous occasion. As Horio, one of the Churo, was a friend of Ieyasu, the matter was smoothed over, though for a while things looked critical, and troops were massed in Kyoto and Fushimi. Ieyasu's supporters among the Daimyos were too powerful, so nothing was done. Had there been unanimous opposition to him things might have turned out differently, but he calculated correctly that this was not likely. Then Hosokawa Tadaoki, a friend of Maeda, and under an obligation to Ieyasu, was able to prevent a breach between these two protagonists, for Maeda was far more able and influential than any of the others in the opinion of Ieyasu. Kuroda and Hosokawa said to Maeda Toshinaga: "Toshiie and Ieyasu are the two great men. Ishida wishes to destroy Ieyasu. If this happens, your father will be left alone, but he is old and delicate, and will not live long, and you are young and would find it difficult to survive. Ieyasu is the finest leader of the day, and is supported by all the wisest and strongest in the land, so that to try and overcome him is like the worm resisting the wheel. To try and deceive Toshiie is a stupid intrigue." Toshinaga saw the force of this, and persuaded his father. It was Kuroda who first suggested this argument to Hosokawa, who was a special friend of Maeda. Kuroda owed Ishida a grudge for the "Go"* incident in Korea, while Hosokawa was under an obligation to Ieyasu for his assistance in the matter of Hidetsugu.

The other Regents now asked for the resignation of Ieyasu on account of these marriages, but he took no notice, so their relations became somewhat strained. He was residing in Fushimi, and Maeda, who was the guardian of Hideyori, was living with him in Osaka castle. About this time Ishida made some attempt on the life of Ieyasu, or rather schemed that someone else should do so, but his plan was defeated by the sharpness of old Jōsui, who suggested that Ieyasu should move into the castle enclosure instead of living outside among the others as he had been doing. He also supplied a guard to prevent any more such attempts. Ishida was also making arrangements with Uesugi Kagekatsu to attack Ieyasu from that quarter if necessary. Then, when Ishida went to Osaka castle in 1599 to see Maeda Toshiie, who was then on his deathbed, seven generals who disliked and despised him thought it would be a good opportunity to fall on him and put him out of the way once for all. They were Kato Kiyomasa, Ikeda Terumasa, Kuroda Nagamasa, Fukushima Masanori, Asano Yukinaga, Kato Yoshiaki, and

---

* Ishida was appointed Inspector-General of the forces in Korea, and in the course of his duties called on Kuroda, who kept him waiting some time while he finished a game of Go. This angered Ishida, who reported to Hideyoshi that Kuroda was more interested in Go than in the campaign. Hideyoshi reprimanded him, and Kuroda did not forget it.

Hosokawa Tadaoki. Ishida heard of their intentions and fled in a lady's palanquin and dress after Maeda died and took refuge with Ieyasu in Fushimi. Rather a strange thing to do. But there was nowhere else he could go, and Ieyasu was not given to showing his knowledge and feelings, so he thought there was a chance of safety in an appeal to his generosity. Sure enough Ieyasu responded, and not only protected him from his angry friends, but sent him home to his castle of Sawayama under the escort of his son Hideyasu. Some historians are so surprised at this that they think Ieyasu really was taken in, and was unaware of Ishida's plots against him, but this is hardly credible, for if so he would have been rather more slow-witted than the average, whereas he was more suspicious and calculating than most. There is evidence that his confidential councilor Honda Masanobu had advised him to give Ishida as much rope as possible, and probably old Kuroda was of the same opinion. There can be little doubt that Honda and Ieyasu considered Ishida the best person to bring the opposition to a head, for with him the same principles of loyalty were not involved as would be the case if the house of Toyotomi were directly invoked, at any rate just then, for Hideyori was only a child of seven. It was easy to represent Ishida as simply working for his own hand, as certainly he was, though he was not the only one. Ieyasu's next move was significant. He suggested that those who had borne the burden of the Korean war might like to retire to their fiefs to rest, whereupon Maeda Toshinaga and Mori, and old Kuroda and Ukita, and also Uesugi at once left for their respective provinces, there not so much to rest as to make their arrangements according to the side they supported. Ishida had, even while in Ieyasu's castle, called on Uesugi to mobilize and attack the Tokugawa position from the north, and this he proceeded to do.

When Maeda was dying his wife Hoshun-in brought a lot of Buddhist texts and said she would put them in his coffin because he had led a life of violence and had killed many people, and made very much evil Karma. He smiled at this and replied: "I was born in an age of strife, and I have fought all over the country it is true, but I have only killed those who would kill me, and I have not harmed anyone without cause. Therefore I have done nothing worthy of hell, and if the ox-head and horse-head jailers come and accuse me there are a lot of brave retainers of my house who have gone on before, and they will rally round me and show the devils a thing or two, and prove their valor on the dark road. I don't care about the next world, what I am worried about is what I leave behind in this. Hideyori is young, and his father is dead, and Ieyasu and I are his chief support, 'Grandpa Edo and Grandpa Kaga' as he calls us, and when I die I fear for his interests. If only I could live five or seven years longer he would be old enough to assume the rule of the Empire, but none has power over death. Ah, I wonder if there will be anyone to stand by him." And as his illness became more acute he suddenly seized a short sword by Kunimitsu that stood by his side and plunged it into his breast and expired.

After his death his retainers were brought over to the side of Ieyasu through the influence of Hosokawa. Still, as it was put about that Toshinaga meant to attack Ieyasu, the latter signified his intention of anticipating him. This rumor owed its origin to Ishida in all probability, but the affair was settled by the mother of Maeda and the son of Hosokawa going to Edo as hostages, which caused another protest from the other Regents as being forbidden by the rules of Hideyoshi. However, Ieyasu paid no heed to them, and went and stayed in the castle of Osaka with Hideyori for the first few months of 1600.

It was during this stay that Will Adams, the pilot of the Dutch ship *Liefde,* was first brought before him. Adams had been the Pilot-Major in a fleet of five vessels sent out to trade with Japan by a company of Rotterdam in 1598. The Dutch had started this kind of venture because Philip II of Spain and Portugal had forbidden them to trade with Lisbon on account of their successful war and expulsion of the Spanish invaders of their own country, which led to their becoming the greatest sea power of the time. Up to that time they had been the European distributors of the goods that the Portuguese and Spanish brought from the East, but now they began to participate in that process themselves.

They had started to develop as a sea power ever since the herring had favored them by transferring its spawning-ground from the Baltic to the North Sea in 1415. The fortunes of the Hanseatic League were built up on a foundation of herrings, as their crest of a dried stockfish and half an eagle surmounted by a crown fitly testifies. And as these herrings were well salted they caused a great demand for beer, and the fact that these two articles were the staple diet of sailors goes far to explain the high rate of mortality on the voyages of these days. It was in the very year that these Dutch ships were setting out for the East that the Hanseats had been turned out of the steelyard in London by order of Elizabeth, while in Russia Ivan the Terrible had dealt with them also after his manner, at the same time welcoming the English, who had opened up the port of Archangel, so that together the Hollanders and the English were breaking into these monopolies of Portugal and Spain and Germany on both sides of the globe.

The five ships that sailed from Rotterdam on June 27, 1598, were the *Hoop* (Hope) Flagship, Admiral Jacques Mahu, William Adams, Pilot-Major; *Liefde* (Charity), Captain Vice-Admiral Simon de Cordes;

Geloof (Faith), Captain Gerrit van Beuningen; *Trouw* (Fidelity), Captain Balthasar de Cordes; *Blijde Boodschap* (Good Tidings), Captain Sebald de Weert. There were other Englishmen in the fleet beside Adams, but none survived. In the fleet, too, was the first Dutchman to reach Japan, Dirk Geritszoon Pomp, who came on the Portuguese vessel *Santa Cruz* from Macao in 1585. But he was on the *Blijde Boodschap,* which was taken by the Spaniards in Valparaiso, as was the *Trouw* by the Portuguese in Tidor, while the *Hoop* went down, and the *Geloof* turned back again round the Straits of Magellan, through which they had all passed, and eventually got back safely to Holland. Only the *Liefde* managed to reach Japan, the first ship of any nation to do so by this Pacific route, and put into a port of Bungo province on April 9, 1600. Among the twenty-four survivors were the Captain, Jacob Jansz Quaeckernaeck, or Quack, Jan Joosten Lodensteyn, Melchier van Santvoort, the "Mr. Sandford" of Cocks, Jan Abelson van Oudewater, and others, whose experiences in this part of the Pacific were to be various. The *Liefde* is described as a vessel of 300 tons, with a crew of 100 men, and 18 guns, though Dirk Gerritz says she was of 400 tons and 26 guns. On arrival in Japan she had on board 500 matchlocks, 5,000 cannon-balls of cast iron, 300 chain-shot, 50 quintals (100 lb. to the quintal) of powder, and 350 fire arrows. On her stern was a picture of a saint with a book in his hand, presumedly Erasmus, and by his name she seems to have originally been called. As to Adams, much has been written of him, and he is well described as a typical Elizabethan seaman, though most, if not all, narratives of his career in Japan do not mention that he was actually in command of one of the English ships that operated against the Spanish Armada, the *Richard Duffield,* "a ship of 120 tons, with a crew of 70, taking supplies to the west to Drake's fleet." This experience cannot but have influenced his sentiments towards the Spanish and Portuguese, their trade, and their religion.

Anyhow, the chief result of the long and painful voyage of this fleet was to present Ieyasu with a very welcome supply of English guns and ammunition, as well as with a shrewd and well-informed and reliable adviser in European affairs, for he confiscated the ship "according to the laws of the country," and detained the crew. If the Portuguese thought he would take their view of what they insisted on was a party of piratical heretics, they were badly mistaken, for he had quite an open mind on the subject of foreigners, as of other people, considering only their possible use.

In his interview with "the great king of the land," as Adams styles him with happy foresight, he describes Ieyasu as very surprised and interested to hear of their voyage by way of the Straits of Magellan, after which he asked the significant question: "Had his country any war just then?" and receiving the answer that it was at peace except with the Spanish and Portuguese, he went on to inquire about the religious beliefs of Adams, and was told that he believed in "the Creator of Heaven and Earth," a safe and diplomatic reply. He gave orders that they should be kept securely but comfortable, and sent the *Liefde* round to Uraga, himself starting for the same region in June, but reaching it before them, though he by no means hurried on the way. And the reason for his move eastward was this.

When it was reported to Ieyasu that Uesugi Kagekatsu was very busy building a new castle at Kazashigahara owing to the position at Wakamatsu being less easy to defend, and for this purpose employing eighty thousand men working day and night on this place and seven strategic points round it, including a number of military roads, he sent him a request to come up to the capital and explain himself. But Uesugi showed no inclination to oblige him, and contented himself with making many excuses for staying where he was, while his Chief Councilor Naoe Kanetsugu wrote various letters to the effect that these preparations were only normal repairs that he found necessary on taking over the fief of Aizu from Gamo only a year or two ago. They certainly were not preparations directed at any particular person. It must be remembered, he said, that it is the way of country samurai to collect weapons, just as it is that of those of the capital to collect tea-things.

Ieyasu then sent an envoy, Fujita Nobuyoshi, to persuade Uesugi to visit him, but Naoe regarded him as a spy, and recommended Uesugi to have him put to death. But Nobuyoshi got wind of this, managed to make his escape, and went and reported first to Ieyasu, and then to Hidetada, and it is not likely he put Uesugi's intentions in a very favorable light. Uesugi's neighbor Hori Hideharu, lord of Echigo, who was engaged with him in a squabble about taxation rights in some territory he had ceded to Uesugi, also complained to Ieyasu that he could not guarantee the *status quo* in this region unless Uesugi were curbed. So that, considering all these things, when Naoe again sent rather a provocative letter of refusal to the repeated demand to come up and explain himself, Ieyasu decided that he must march east and take defensive-offensive measures against this recalcitrant, though there is little doubt he would have preferred to arrange it without fighting, provided, of course, that the settlement was favorable to his interests. Naoe and Uesugi must have thought they were quite safe in their firm stand since they were apprised by Ishida, who inspired them, of the arrangements he had made with his friends of the anti-Ieyasu party to rise in support, and when he started to march east they must have thought the game was won, but they did not realize his stealthy maneuvers through Kuroda, Hosokawa, and Date to neutralize much of this support. So he might well proceed rather leisurely toward Edo, flying his hawks as usual, and admiring the views.

He left Osaka, in fact, on June 18th, having received a famous sword and tea vessels, 20,000 koku of rice, and 20,000 pieces of gold as a farewell present from Hideyori. He did not hurry himself by any means, for he did not reach Edo till July 2nd, and he spent some days on the way enjoying the scenery at places like Kanazawa and Kamakura. The fact seems to be that he was more interested in the situation in the west than that in the east, and had his attention concentrated largely on that region. After a short stay in Edo he moved on to Koyama in Hitachi, where was the base of operations against Uesugi under the command of Hidetada. Here he held a council, at which Fukushima, Kuroda Nagamasa, Hosokawa, Ikeda, Kato Yoshiaki, and Asano assisted. Just then news arrived that Ishida had definitely declared war or rebellion in the west, and Ieyasu offered those whose families were in Osaka, and consequently in the power of Ishida, who held them as hostages, the alternative of throwing in their lot with the western party if they wished. Perhaps not unnaturally none of them did wish, but promised him their unswerving support.

At this council it was decided that the west was the most important field of action. The Tokugawa allies, Date, Mogami, Satake, and Maeda, had been called on to attack Uesugi from four sides, and though Satake went over to Ishida, and Maeda could not move owing to the attacks of hostile neighbors, the forces of Date and Mogami kept Uesugi so busy that he was never able to give Ishida any assistance. Meanwhile, to make certain, Hideyasu was left at Utsunomiya with a force of twenty thousand, while Ieyasu prepared to march west again with his main striking force.

Now as it was necessary for Ieyasu to have command of the two roads leading to the capital, the Nakasendo and the Tokaido, so that he could move his armies freely along both, the first thing he did was to send a mobile force to seize the strategic positions. This was composed of two divisions, one of about sixteen thousand men, commanded by Fukushima Masanori, with whom went Hosokawa Tadaoki, Kato Yoshiaki, Kuroda Nagamasa, Todo, Honda Tadakatsu, and Ii Naomasa, and a second of about eighteen thousand under Ikeda Terumasa, with Asano Yoshinaga, Yamanouchi Kazutoyo, Horio, Arima, and others. Their first objective was the castle of Kiyosu in Owari, which belonged to Fukushima, and was being held for him by a certain Osaki Gemba, popularly known as "Devil Gemba." Now this was perhaps the most

MODEL OF "DE LIEFDE" IN WHICH WILLIAM ADAMS REACHED JAPAN,
CONSTRUCTED FROM CONTEMPORARY PRINTS AND DESCRIPTIONS
BY THE AUTHOR

important place in the campaign, for whichever side held it commanded the communications between the two roads, which were not much
more than twenty miles apart here, and were joined by a cross-road that
ran not far away from Gifu to Miya or Nagoya. Ishida was by this time
at Ogaki, not far away, and had been attempting to persuade or fright-
en Oni Gemba into handing over the place to him, but this doughty
warrior refused most firmly, and sent messages to the east for help, with
the result that Fukushima and his men hurried up and entered before it
could be attacked. Ieyasu observed that his success in this campaign was
largely due to this loyalty of Oni Gemba. The fortresses of Inuyama,
Gifu, and Takegahana were held by the Westerners, whose headquarters
was in Ogaki. These places were only fifteen, eighteen, and ten miles
away, but the River Kiso ran between the two forces.

The castle of Gifu was held by Oda Hidenobu, grandson of Nobunaga, who had been persuaded by Ishida to come over to his side. Ieyasu
did not hurry himself to the front, not necessarily wholly because he
distrusted Fukushima and Kuroda, though it was not very easy to trust
anyone entirely, but because he wished these allies to do as much of the
work as might be so that he could keep his own army fresh. So after a
council at Kiyosu an attack was at once made on Gifu and Takegahana.
The force under Ikeda crossed the river in face of the enemy, while the
other lower down, under Fukushima, did the same. Then Fukushima
having taken Takegahana, the two of them concentrated on Gifu, almost coming to blows on the way because Ikeda got a little in advance,
whereas it had been agreed that they should advance together. Fukushima challenged Ikeda to a duel on the evening before the final attack on
Gifu, but the affair was adjusted by his being allowed to attack the front
gate, while Ikeda advanced against the back. After a stiff fight Gifu was
taken, and Oda Hidenobu captured and sent to Mount Koya, where
he died long after. They then pushed on along the Kisokaido, and by
September 30th were in possession of Akasaka, which they selected as
the best place for their headquarters, and sat down there to await Ieyasu.
This position flanked Ishida in Gifu, and menaced that of Ogaki. The
fortress of Inuyama also surrendered to them on the fall of Gifu.

Meanwhile in the west some of the Tokugawa followers had been
making a stout resistance that added to the difficulties of Ishida. Before
he left Osaka, Ieyasu had called on his old friend Torii Mototada, then
aged sixty-two, who was lord of the castle of Fushimi, and arranged
with him to hold this important strategic position to the end. No
doubt both of them knew what the end would be, and Ieyasu showed
more emotion at parting for the last time with this companion of his
early days than ever he showed before or since.

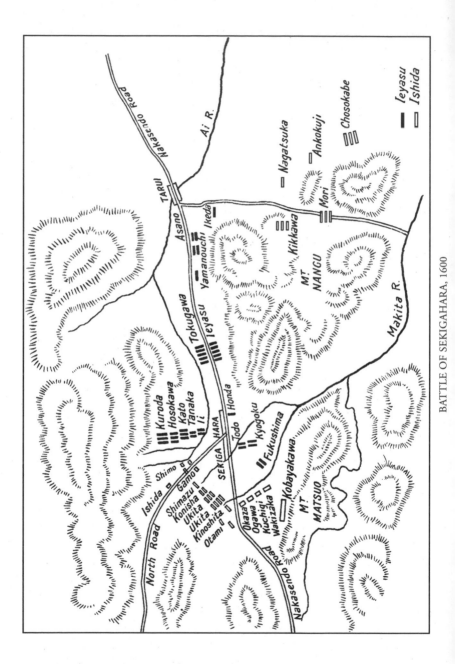

BATTLE OF SEKIGAHARA, 1600

Fushimi was the last castle that Hideyoshi had built, and so was a particularly strong place. Beside the main keep there were five other fortresses, called the Nishi Maru, San-no Maru, Matsu Maru, Nagoya Maru, and Jibushoyu Maru, forming a garrison of eighteen hundred men. Under Torii Mototada, the Commander, there were Naito Ienaga and his son Motonaga, Matsudaira Ietada, and Matsudaira Chikamasa. Beside these Kinoshita Katsutoshi, lord of the castle of Kohama in Wakasa, had been specially placed in command of the Matsu Maru by Ieyasu. There was also the martial tea merchant, Kambayashi Chikuan, who had asked to be allowed to take part in the defense, and who seems to have been stationed in the Drum Tower. Kinoshita, however, had a disagreement with Mototada and left the castle to guard Kodai-in, the wife of Hideyoshi. Shimazu Yoshihiro wished to be allowed to take part in the defense, but Torii did not trust him and refused, and when he sent Niiro, one of his captains, to the castle the garrison opened fire on him. Kobayakawa Hideaki was likewise anxious to assist the garrison, but Mototada was taking no chances, and repulsed his overtures also. So that these two leaders had to join Ukita and Nabeshima in assaulting the castle.

From the eighteenth to the twenty-eighth of the seventh month no impression was made on the defense. Then Ishida himself came from Sawayama to encourage the besiegers. At last one of Kobayakawa's men managed to set fire to one of the towers with a fire arrow, but Kato Kurozaemon, a retainer of Torii, climbed up a ladder and put it out, though he was burnt to death in doing so. On the first of the eighth month fire was seen to burst from the Matsu Maru and to spread to the Nagoya Maru. And this was not the Work of the besiegers, but of Koga no Goshi, Daikwan of the Tokugawa estates in Omi and a spy of Ieyasu, who was in charge of the Matsu Maru. And the reason was that Nagatsuka Masaie had seized his wife and children in Koga and sent a message to him into the castle on an arrow to the effect that he would crucify them if he did not betray his master, but that if he did so he would be rewarded. So to save them he consented to set fire to the tower he was holding, and also to break down the wall for a space of a hundred yards with the assistance of forty men whom he had persuaded to join him. Then under cover of the flames the main gate was assaulted and broken in, though the defenders resisted manfully with spear and halberd. Thus the Matsu Maru and Nagoya Maru were taken, and then Kobayakawa sent a messenger to propose a truce, but his overtures were rejected, and the attack again proceeded. In this Matsudaira Chikamasa and the valiant tea-merchant Kambayashi Chikuan fell fighting. Then the Jibushoyu Maru was taken by Shimazu's troops, and Matsudaira

Ietada, after fighting with one of Shimazu's captains and wounding him and then repulsing an attack made by overwhelming numbers, killed himself. By this time the main keep had been set on fire by fire arrows, and Mototada was asked by his staff if he did not think it was now time to commit suicide. He thought not, and putting himself at the head of some two hundred men he three times repulsed the attackers, receiving many wounds, and losing half his force. Then the besiegers ambushed parties of men on both sides of the gate, and when the defenders sallied out and drove the assaulting force headlong back again, these emerged and fell on them from both sides, so that most of them fell fighting where they were. By this time, after five counterattacks, the castle was filled with the enemy, and Mototada's men were reduced to ten. Now Mototada had sat down on a step to rest a moment when one Saiga Shigetomo ran at him with a spear, whereupon the old man called out his name, and Saiga waited respectfully while he put an end to himself, and then received his head. Three hundred and fifty men fell with him. Naito Ienaga in the Nishi Maru fought with his son Motonaga, and for a while repulsed the enemy, then mounting on the belfry and piling wood around it, he ordered Harada, one of his retainers, to make his escape and tell his eldest son Masanaga, who was with Ieyasu, of the fate of the fortress. He then committed seppuku, and Harada fired the pile, so that he was cremated in it. His son Motonaga, sixteen years old, unable to escape the fire, also cut himself open, and leaping on to his father's pyre was consumed with him.

Most of the garrison of eighteen hundred men were killed, and of the attackers three thousand, so that the castle had held out for almost a fortnight and inflicted such loss on the Western army that it was a victory of doubtful value.

The heads of Torii Mototada and Matsudaira Ietada and Matsudaira Chikamasa were exposed on the Kyobashi bridgehead at Osaka, placed on a "Kugyodai" or ceremonial stand of white wood as a mark of respect for their loyal conduct. But Sano Shiroemon, a cloth merchant of Kyoto, who had received favors from Mototada, came and bribed the guards, and stole his head, and brought it to his younger brother, who was a priest, and he buried it at his temple. Sano afterwards confessed to Ishida what he had done, but Ishida pardoned him. Mototada's son Tadamasa afterwards made this temple the family chantry of their house, and made the priest its abbot.

CHAPTER 23

HOSOKAWA TADAOKI, HIS WIFE, AND HIS FATHER

HOSOKAWA TADAOKI was not the only one of his family who did good service for Ieyasu at this crisis. His father Fujitaka Yusai was very useful, as was his wife Gracia.

Tadaoki was eminent as soldier, diplomat, and aesthete. At the battle of Makinohama he fought by his father's side when he was but eleven years old, and at the assault on the castle of Kataoka at the age of fifteen he again bore himself valiantly and won the praise of Nobunaga. He studied Japanese verse under his father, and was a disciple of Sen Rikyu for tea. By nature overbearing and violent, his domestic life was hardly ideal. He quarrelled with his father and brother, drove away his elder son, and killed his second, so that it was scarcely to be expected that his connubial relations should have been unruffled. His wife was the daughter of Akechi Mitsuhide, and it seems that when her father rebelled against Nobunaga, he wished Tadaoki to join him, but he refused, and sent his wife away, and both he and his father shaved their heads and prayed for Nobunaga's enlightenment after his assassination. Their marriage had been arranged by Nobunaga, their over-lord, so that the families of his two great retainers might be thus knit together. It was owing to the mediation of Hideyoshi that Tadaoki took his wife back again, but it is probable that she was not very well disposed to him and his house, since it was by taking advantage of her father's rebellion and defeating him and putting him to death that Hideyoshi was able to seize the supreme power in the Empire. Tadaoki's wife was introduced to Christianity unwittingly by her husband, who was a friend and Cha-no-yu companion of Takayama Ukon. Takayama explained the faith to Tadaoki and wished him to embrace it, but he saw nothing in it. But he repeated the discourse to his wife, who was very much impressed by it, and determined to become a Christian if she could. The opportunity occurred when Tadaoki was away on the campaign in Kyushu with Hideyoshi, when she herself took the initiative. According to the missionaries, Tadaoki was a very jealous husband, who did not allow his wife to go out and mix with other people. Possibly he was not so unwise in this in view of Hideyoshi's penchant for attractive ladies, for his wife was one of the famous beauties of the day, and her mental qualities were in no way inferior to her character or good looks. When he left for Korea he gave his wife this poem:

Nabiku na yo	Though the wind may blow
Waga sode-gaki no	From Otokoyama's heights
Ominaeshi.	Do not thou incline
Otokoyama yori	O my fair patrinia flower
Kaze ga fuku tomo.	Blooming by the garden fence.

However, the lady managed to slip out incognito with several of her ladies from the back gate of the mansion in Osaka and go to the missionaries' church. She listened to the teaching of the Japanese catechist Vincent, who was working under the Portuguese Cespedes, and asked him to baptize her, as she probably would not be able to come again. Meanwhile, the retainers had discovered her absence, and after searching all the Buddhist temples at last found her in the church, and brought her back under cover of darkness. The fathers thought she was a concubine of Hideyoshi, and feared to baptize her in consequence. However, as she could not go herself, she sent her ladies to church, and eventually seventeen of them were baptized. Consumed by a desire to receive baptism too, she got into a coffin and tried to get out that way, but the fathers dissuaded her and told her to wait. Then she heard that Hideyoshi in Kyushu had issued his ban against the missionaries, and determined at all events to be baptized before they went away. So she sent her lady-in-waiting Mary (daughter of Koyohara Daigeki, a connection of Hosokawa) and informed the father of her intention. He instructed the lady how to baptize her, and so she received the ceremony by proxy, and was named Gracia. She also baptized her second son. So she began to live like a nun, spending her days praying and reading the *Imitation of Christ,* and other religious books. She is said to have learnt both Portuguese and Latin, and was probably the most advanced lady of her time. But when Tadaoki came back from Kyushu and heard of all this he was very wrath, and ordered her to give up her faith or he would kill her, and even went as far as laying his dagger on her throat. But she remained quite calm, and said he might kill her but she would never renounce her faith. She seems to have thought of running away, but Father Organtino Gnecchi persuaded her to stay and submit to her husband as far as possible. She says in her letters to him that Tadaoki had cut off the hair of her ladies and turned them out of the house, and that he had cut off the nose and ears of her foster-mother because she opposed him in some trifling matter. So he must have been a trying companion.

It is not perhaps very surprising that when Ishida's men went to the mansion of Hosokawa in Osaka to put his wife and her household under arrest as hostages the retainer in charge of it, Ogasawara Shosai, should have first put Donna Gracia to death, set fire to the building, and then killed himself with the rest. This, doubtless done according to Tadaoki's instructions, is a more probable version of the tragedy than that which describes her as committing suicide, which as an enthusiastic Christian she was not at all likely to do. Since it was not correct etiquette to enter the room of his mistress, Ogasawara requested her to come near to the door, when, standing outside the threshold, he drove a halberd through her heart. And this uncompromising defiance made Ishida hesitate in his demands on the other families of the Tokugawa generals, and he did no more than post guards round their mansions so that the wives of Kato, Kuroda, and Ikeda escaped in disguise.

Hosokawa Yusai was now an old man of sixty-seven, a veteran soldier, and the most famous scholar and poet among the military nobility. It was his literary quality that proved most effective on this occasion. When he heard of the death of his son's wife and of the menace of Ishida's armies he at once entered his chief castle of Tanabe, or Maizuru as it is now called, in the province of Tango and put it in order for defense, though he had only a garrison of five hundred men. Before long he was invested by an army of fifteen thousand, who took up positions outside the castle and began to bombard it. But several of the enemy captains had been the old poet's pupils in verse-making, and their attacks were very half-hearted in consequence, many of them absentmindedly omitting to put the projectiles into the guns before firing. Quite a number, too, were more in sympathy with the Easterners than with Ishida, and did as little as they possible could. All this, added to Yusai's skill and experience in the tactics of defense, caused the weeks to go by without any impression being made on the fortress. Now Yusai had some very precious volumes of Japanese poetry in his possession, including a particularly rare and ancient edition of the Kokinshu, and he was afraid they might be damaged in the siege, so he sent a letter to Prince Tomohito, younger brother of the Emperor, asking him to send Maeda Gen-i to receive them and present them to the Emperor, the Prince, and the Court Noble Karasu-maru Mitsuhiro. This was done, and then the Court recommended Yusai to surrender. However, his duty as a soldier would not permit him to do anything but die at his post, so he maintained, and after a little more time was wasted an Imperial Edict was issued ordering the place to be surrendered and the defenders to march out unharmed, so anxious was the Court lest anything should happen to so eminent a scholar and poet. And so after two months' siege the Western troops marched away, but too late to take part in the decisive engagement at Sekigahara.

And there was another force that was not in time for the battle, that on the Tokugawa side led by Hidetada, who had set out along the Na-kasendo with about thirty-eight thousand men, and on the way stopped to take the castle of Ueda instead of masking it, and hastening on to join his father. This castle, defended by Sanada Masayuki, who was one who knew his business, held out long enough to delay Hidetada, and when he did decide to hurry on he was unable to arrive until after the victory was won. Ieyasu was naturally furious and refused to receive him, and had not Honda the younger interceded for him he might not have got off with only this implied reprimand. Masazumi insisted that it was his father Masanobu who was to blame, and asked Ieyasu to put him to death for it, and he Masazumi would commit suicide, so anxious was he to prevent any breach between father and son. This was effec-tive in calming Ieyasu's wrath, for the day afterwards he allowed him to come and apologize for his error of judgment. When he did so, Ieyasu replied quite calmly: "Well, the messenger sent to you may have made a mistake about the day fixed for the battle. So you need not take it to heart. These battles are like games of Go. If you get the essential piece it does not much matter what opening your opponent may have, or what pieces he holds, for it won't be any use. As long as we win this battle it doesn't matter what castles small people like Sanada may hold, for they will have to surrender them when they hear of it. Didn't any of your staff put the matter to you in this way?" Hidetada confessed that one Toda Issai had done so. Ieyasu at once had Toda summoned and presented to him, much to his surprise. So little did he expect such an honor that Hidetada had to shout at him at the top of his voice before he would come forward. Ieyasu took some cakes in both hands and gave them to him with the remark, "It was because your position was not high that your advice was not followed. I will make it so that it will be in future." Shortly afterwards he was made commander of the new castle of Zese at Honda's suggestion with 30,000 koku, whereas he had formerly only had only 3,000.

Again, in addition to the fifteen thousand before Tanabe, another fifteen thousand men were kept out of the main theatre of war by the resistance of Kyogoku Takatsugi in Otsu, just by Kyoto. This was a force under Tachibana Muneshige of Kyushu, who was ordered to take Otsu on his way to join Ishida in Owari. He did so in two days it is true, but this just made him too late for the battle which took place on the fifteenth day of the ninth month.* However, the assault provided an interesting spectacle for the people of the capital, who flocked out to the temple of Miidera on the hill opposite with their teapots and luncheon boxes and settled themselves there to watch the show to the end, both by day and night. They thought it at least as entertaining as a conflagration, and much more protracted, no doubt.

The Western armies did not do very much in Ise either, where there were also several partisans of the Tokugawa, and after taking one castle with difficulty the thirty thousand men under Mori Hidemoto and Chosokabe hurried on to join the main army, though they, too, proved of little use to it.

No doubt some of the procrastination of the Western army is to be put down to the suspicion some of the leaders had of the good faith of their companions, and their intelligence system suffered in consequence, so that they were quite surprised when they heard that Ieyasu had arrived at Akasaka on October 20th. In reality they had been hoping that he would be held up by Uesugi and Satake in the east, and so would not be able to march west at all, and their strategy had been influenced by their hopes, so that they had lost some measure of aggressive spirit.

Now the plan of Ieyasu was to mask Ogaki and march right on and break through so as to strike at their strongest point, Ishida's castle of Sawayama, or directly at Osaka if they should abandon this stronghold and retreat.

Ishida had sent an urgent messenger to Mori to come up, but he fell into the hands of the enemy. Then, fearing for the safety of his castle, he returned to it secretly to arrange for its defense, sending to Otani, who was in Echizen, to join forces with Kyogoku and Wakizaka. Meanwhile Masuda in Osaka recalled the forces in Ise and Kikkawa and sent them into Mino. Otani arrived in Mino on the third of the ninth month with his son and Wakizaka Yasuharu and his son Yasumoto, Ogawa Suketada, Ogawa Samano-suke, Kuchigi Mototsuna, Akaza Naoyasu, Hiratsuka Tameie, and Toda Shigemasa. On the seventh day Mori Hidenobu, Kikkawa Hiroie, Ankokuji Eikei, Chosokabe Morichika, and Nagatsuka Masaie, with thirty thousand men, came in from Ise and took up their position on Nangu Hill. By this time another messenger had been sent to Mori Terumoto urging him to hurry, and he came in to Osaka with his thirty thousand men on the thirteenth, but again delayed there as there was a rumor that Masuda was betraying his side to the Easterners. Shimazu Yoshihisa arrived on

---

* October 21st according to the Western calendar.

the thirteenth, but with only seventy followers. Shimazu was one of the most eager fighters, but was ill supported, whereas Mori Terumoto with his large contingent* had little enthusiasm. He had been brought into the fight by Ankokuji Eikei, who had been diplomatic liaison officer between the Oda and Mori. He seems to have pulled Terumoto one way, while Kikkawa Hiroie pulled him another, and unfortunately Ankokuji prevailed, with very bad results for Mori's estates and his own head. Ankokuji himself was pusillanimous, as was Nagatsuka, while Kikkawa Hiroie and Mori Hidemoto were only concerned with coming out on the winning side.

Since the Western army had not expected Ieyasu, they were uncertain whether to hold Ogaki or not, but Ishida did not wish to endanger his base at Sawayama for it, which would be "like holding on to an arm to lose the head." Tokugawa Ieyasu did not care which they did, for he let them know that he intended to push on anyhow, and if they evacuated Ogaki so much the better, but if not he would mask it and march past it, without further delay. It was at this juncture that Shimazu Yoshihiro proposed a night attack on the Eastern army. He had reconnoitered their camp, he said, and found them tired, and in some cases asleep on their armor, and considered that a sudden attack at night would be very effective, offering to make it himself with his nephew Yoshihisa. But Ishida would not entertain the idea since he had made up his mind by now to retreat to Sekigahara. His great strategist Shima Sakon observed: "Night attacks are for a small army against a greater, but the larger numbers are on our side, and we shall therefore win in a pitched battle." Probably little would have been gained, for Ieyasu took good care to guard against just such an attack by throwing out outposts and lighting flares, and the night proved rainy and foggy.

On the twentieth there took place a sharp skirmish by the River Kuisegawa. Shima Sakon and Gamo Bitchu led out a force, and having concealed ambushes in the villages of Kido and Isshiki, they crossed the river and defied the enemy. This was answered by some of Nakamura Kazuuji's men, who were drawn out and attacked them, whereupon the Westerners retired and drew their opponents over the river in pursuit. There the other two hidden companies sallied out behind them and caught them front and rear. Thus taken at a disadvantage they fought well, but lost heavily. Then Arima's men came to their assistance, and the Westerners also lost good men. Nightfall put an end to the fight, and the Easterners were withdrawn. Ieyasu was just about to dine when

---

* For the comparative might of Mori and Ieyasu compare the saying: "Ieyasu could make a road of rice from the Kwanto to the capital, and Mori could build a bridge of gold and silver to it from the Sanin and Sanyo."

this fight began, and having some doors brought up on to the roof of the barrack he watched it with some of his officers as he dined, becoming so intent at one stage that he even dropped some rice grains on to his knee. He commended the skill of Nakamura in handling his troops, but when they crossed the river in pursuit he at once observed that it was a false move.

So that night, October 20th, leaving seven thousand five hundred men under Fukuhara Nagataka to hold Ogaki, the divisions of Ishida, Shimazu, Konishi, and Ukita set out in this order for Sekigahara, taking every precaution to prevent their move being known to Ieyasu. They had a ten-mile march in the cold and wet along a narrow and steep road, with only the lights of Chosokabe's camp to guide them. All else was pitch-dark. Ishida himself rode first to Nagatsuka and Chosokabe, and then to the division of Kobayakawa on Matsuo Hill, where he saw Kobayakawa's councilor, Hiraoka Yorikatsu, and told him to charge down on the Eastern army when he should light a signal fire. Then he rejoined the rest and discussed the battle with Otani Yoshitsugu.

Ieyasu's commissariat arrangements at Sekigahara were, as usual, not elaborate. About sixty yards from his main headquarters was a structure of small bamboos covered with paper varnished with persimmon-juice, and containing utensils suitable for serving about three people. There were two pots, three waterbuckets, and a cauldron. Two cooks and three scullion boys were in attendance. It was the sort of equipage that a retainer of about 3,000 koku might have had. After the victory he moved to a village south of Sawayama, where Otani's quarters had been. Here he had a hut thatched with straw and with walls of plaited straw, without any door, but only a bamboo lattice on one side. They brought some mats from Sawayama to put on the floor, and where these did not cover it they put down some straw matting. Thirty mats were laid down on the grass outside to seat those who were received in audience. And these had to put their sandals on the ground behind them, for there were no attendants to look after the footgear. Neither were there any guns or other weapons in racks as was common. The Hatamoto bivouacked in the same simple way all around, while the rest found quarters in the houses of the people of the Sawayama fief a couple of miles or so away. But none of them made any regular camp.

On the fourteenth Ieyasu asked Keya Mondo, retainer of Kuroda Nagamasa, who had been sent to him, about the numbers of the enemy. Keya replied that all he could see was about twenty or thirty thousand men. "How is it that you make them out to be so few," said Ieyasu, "when the others say there are somewhere about a hundred thousand?" "Ah yes, the whole force may be a hundred thousand or thereabouts," replied Keya, "but the real enemy amounts to no more than I have stated, because all the forces of Mori and Kobayakawa are on our side. That's our secret." Ieyasu looked very pleased at this confirmation of the facts, and took a box of "Manju," or bean-jam buns, and handed them to Keya, who immediately sat down on the verandah and ate them all up. When he had gone, Ieyasu asked his attendants what was his proper name. They told him it was Keya, but he said that was not his real surname, but a nickname that he had got from a place in Echizen, where he had distinguished himself in a fight. The retainers were surprised at his extraordinary memory for such a detail about someone who was only a rear-vassal.

About midnight of the same day Fukushima Masanori sent his grandfather to Ieyasu to inform him that the enemy were moving out of Ogaki along the Makita highway to Sekigahara, and the battle would begin early next day, in which they would destroy them completely, so it were well that he should get to horse at once. So he proceeded to take some nourishment in the form of boiled rice and hot water, and prepared to mount. When they brought his helmet he would not put it on, but wore only a hood of brown crepe silk. "This big force would be scattered just like that he had formerly defeated at Nagakute," he foretold, and then, calling his chief retainers, he directed their attention to the great number of watch fires that showed how large it was. "But," he went on, "I shall smash them all and rout them in the morning, and do you see to it that the faces of your forefathers are not smeared with dung on your account!" "For us," they declared with fierce determination, "there are only two alternatives, either to come back with a bloody head in our hands, or to leave our own for the enemy."

Early in the morning the Western army was in position on the two roads that met at the village of Sekigahara. In the center lay the large divisions of Ukita Hideie and Konishi Yukinaga, while to their left were Shimazu Toyohisa in front and Yoshihiro behind him. To the left of them on the wing was Ishida with his professor of strategy, Shima Sakon, and Gamo Bitchu in front of him, and Oda Nobutaka and a body of troops of the Osaka garrison in support. All these lay at the foot of the hills and surrounding the north high road. On the right wing, and surrounding the Nakasendo, there came next to Ukita, Kinoshita, Otani Yoshikatsu, Hiratsuka, and Toda, with their contingents on one side of the road, and Akaza, Ogawa, Kuchigi, and Wakizaka on the other. Behind these on Matsuo Hill lay Kobayakawa Hideaki with his eight thousand men, and again behind Akaza and Toda, and facing the road and also incidentally Kobayakawa's flank lay Otani Yoshitsugu. The object of this disposition was to block the road, and at the same time hold the center of the attackers, and then descend on their flank and rear if possible. By daybreak the Eastern army had arrived along the Nakasendo and made contact in the mist.

The battle began about eight o'clock with an attack by Ii on Ukita, closely followed by Fukushima. Then Kyōgoku, Tōdō, and Terazawa flung themselves upon Otani, while Oda Yuraku and his son Nagataka, Furuta Shigekatsu, Inoko Kazutoki, and the brothers Sakuma and Funakoshi Kagenao engaged Konishi and Tanaka, Hosokawa Tadaoki, Kato, Kanamori, Kuroda, and Takenaka made at Ishida. At first Ukita drove back Ii and Fukushima, but they rallied their men and regained their ground, but again the Westerners came on, and the battle swayed backward and forward without much advantage to either side. Meanwhile Shima, who had led forward some of his men, had been subjected to a hot fire from the matchlocks of Kato and Togawa, and had to retire wounded. Then Terazawa drove in the van of Konishi on to the main force so that it lost formation, and following up this success rapidly threw the main body too into disorder. Then they swung round and made an attack on the flank of Ukita. All this time Shimazu had not moved, and Ishida sent to him for assistance, but he paid no heed. Ishida then rode over himself, but Shimazu replied that it was best that each leader should fight his own battle and rely on himself, for there was no time to watch the affairs of others, with which answer Ishida had to be content. But Otani's men, seeing that Ukita was hotly engaged, now crossed the stream and threw themselves on the advancing masses under Tōdō, Kyōgoku, and Oda, so that they bore them back, for they were a specially picked body of shock troops. And now Ishida thought the moment opportune to light the signal for Kobayakawa to throw his men into action to gain a decision, but with no result, for Kobayakawa did not move a man. Otani and Konishi both sent messengers urging him to advance, but again nothing happened. Ieyasu, too, was becoming anxious, and when he heard that there was doubt about Kobayakawa's intentions he bit his fingers hard as he sat on horseback, a habit he had when things looked critical for his side, and ordered some of his matchlock men to open fire on him and see what he would do. He also sent a messenger to Kuroda Nagamasa to learn his views, and this retainer, Yamagami Goemon, rode up and shouted unceremoniously: "Kōshu, Kōshu, is Chikuzen Chunagon coming over to us or not?" "I know as little as you do," replied Kuroda, "but if he does deceive us and throw his men against us, what of it? To cut through Ishida's men and then strike down Ukita and Kobayakawa won't take us very long. But I have my men to look after just now." And Yamagami retired and told Ieyasu what Kuroda had said, and it pleased him very much. "Yes," he remarked, "Kai is always like that." "That fellow," exclaimed Kuroda after Yamagami had departed, "evidently does not know what politeness is. We are in the middle of a fight it is true, but that is no reason for neglecting to observe the proper etiquette. What does he mean by calling out 'Kōshu, Kōshu' in that rude fashion, as though it were his own question and not the inquiry of the Naidaijin Ieyasu, to which a reply should be given only after dismounting?"

Kobayakawa was evidently convinced that the matter was urgent when Ieyasu opened fire on him, for he was not long in giving orders to his men to attack Otani's force below him. But Otani was quite prepared for this, and repulsed the attack with some loss. But when Ieyasu saw the Chikuzen troops turn against the Western army he ordered a general attack all along the line, and his men threw themselves into the battle with redoubled vigor. At the same time Kobayakawa attacked again, but Otani, assisted by Hiratsuka and Toda, who attacked on the flank, again managed to repulse him, but with considerable loss on both sides.

Now because he suspected Kobayakawa Otani had put Wakizaka, Ogawa, and the rest on his own right flank in case he should be threatened in that quarter, but now Tōdō, Kyōgoku, and Oda Yuraku attacked Hiratsuka and Toda in the flank, and at the same time made a signal to Wakizaka to join them, which he did at once, while Kobayakawa's men made yet another attack. Smitten on three sides, it was not long before these leaders were killed and their men scattered, leaving the way open for an attack on Otani, who had never dreamed of this last development.

When his men, too, were no longer able to hold their ground, Otani Yoshitsugu, who was a leper and disabled and half-blind through the disease, leaned half-out of the palanquin in which he rode and bade his retainer Yuasa Gosuke put an end to him, and be sure to hide his head. Gosuke did so, took off his head, hid it, and then killed himself. Otani's two sons had the same intention, but they were persuaded to escape instead, and managed to get away to Echizen. By this time the knowledge that they were betrayed had spread to the other armies and affected their fighting spirit, and confusion began to show itself. Finding themselves attacked in the rear, the divisions of Konishi and then of Ukita began to break up with cries of "Treachery!" Ukita Hideie himself, full of wrath at the defection of Kobayakawa, vowed he would not leave the field till he had fought him hand to hand, but at length he allowed himself to be overruled by the advice of his chief captains, and also hurried away to the rear. Shimazu alone was left, and when most of his men were killed and his brother Toyohisa had fallen Yoshihiro put himself at the head of the eighty or so that remained and cut his way through, in spite of an attack made on him by Ii Naomasa, who greatly wished to take his head, but was prevented by one of Shimazu's men discharging a matchlock at him at a distance of some fifteen yards and wounding him in the left arm. The Satsuma men took the road to the southwest of Mount Nangu, and crossed the pass to Osaka, where they commandeered ships to take them home to Kagoshima.

Ishida and Konishi, too, both fled to the mountains. As for the armies on Nangu Hill, it appears that Nagatsuka and Ankokuji had some inclination to move their men to take part in the battle which they could distinctly hear raging not very far off, but Kikkawa Hiroie, who was in command of the van of Mori's force, had already arranged with Ieyasu that he would assist him, and so did nothing, so that the rest were still waiting for him to advance when their outposts came into contact with the fleeing remnant of Shimazu's force, from whom they learnt that the battle was already lost. So Nagatsuka and Chosokabe retreated to Ise, while Mori led his men back to Osaka, and Ankokuji Eikei fled. It seems strange that he, who had been the agent who brought Mori into the fight, should have done nothing at all at the critical moment, but, like Nagatsuka Masaie, he was no soldier, but only a diplomat and schemer. Very likely he as well as Nagatsuka and Chosokabe found his courage fail him, and thought it better after all not to oppose Ieyasu. But the inactivity and doubtful sluggishness of Mori's comparatively large army of some seventeen thousand men makes a great contrast with the splendid though rather irregular and undisciplined dash of Shimazu.

As to whether the Westerners had any chance of winning, even if Kobayakawa had not fought for the East, Tokutomi considers it unlikely, for he points out that there were several reasons for their defeat. They had no real Commander in Chief, such as Ieyasu certainly was, and consequently there was no proper cohesion in the army, and their fighting spirit was badly affected, and even where it was not, as in the case of Shimazu, the lack of co-operation nullified the effect of their valor. And not only was there little coordinated movement between the different parts of the army, but the very name of Ieyasu seems to have struck one section of it with consternation, while that of Ishida, on the other hand, was so detested by the Easterners that it excited them to fury. So that the fact that Ishida was the chief figure in the Western army was a double drawback, for not only was he incapable of acting as a military commander, but he supplied a better focus for the hatred and contempt of his opponents than any other figure could have done. Hatred of his ways and desire to get even with him were stronger feelings than loyalty to Hideyori, and the more effective since few of the Westerners can have had a very strong antipathy to Ieyasu. Still in spite of all these deficiencies the Western army put up a good fight for four hours and made some of the best of the Easterners give way.

And when at about two o'clock (the hour of the ram) Ieyasu saw that the victory was won and his long-wished-for supremacy gained, he took off the hood he had so far been wearing and put on a light helmet, "Ura-shiro to iu ichi-mai-bari no on kabuto," a helmet of single thickness called "White Lining," which he fastened tightly, and taking a leading staff of Mino paper with a handle of green bamboo, he settled himself for the business, or rather ceremony "kubi no jikken shiki," of viewing the heads. It is from this action that has arisen the Japanese proverb, "After victory tighten your helmet."

First of all he called to Kuroda Nagamasa to come to him, and commended him before all the generals. "Today's victory," he said, "is entirely due to your loyalty and care, and as a reward for your great merit, as long as my house shall last the interests of the house of Kuroda shall never be allowed to suffer." And he handed him a short sword by Yoshimitsu, which he put into his belt with his own hand.

After Kuroda came Honda Tadakatsu and Fukushima Masanori, who were especially praised for their handling of the troops, and then Ieyasu's fourth son, Matsudaira Tadayoshi, and his father-in-law, Ii Naomasa, who had been wounded. "Hawks of a fine stock always turn out well," said Ii, as he spoke of the merit of his companion. "If they have a good trainer," replied Ieyasu, gracefully returning the compliment. He then produced a bandage from his portable writing-case, and with his own hand applied it to the arm of Ii. But he would not consent to his men singing the customary song of victory until they had entered Osaka and set free the families who were held as hostages. Which consideration was greatly appreciated by all ranks of the army. Soon Kobayakawa Hideaki approached and knelt before Ieyasu and expressed regret that he had been unable to fight on the right side at the siege of Fushimi, begging that he might be allowed to lead the van in the attack on Sawayama. Ieyasu rose from his campstool and greeted him warmly, assuring him that he had done splendid service that day, and readily granting him permission to lead the assault on Sawayama.

This took place two days later, when Kobayakawa, Kuchigi, Waki-zaka, and Ogawa with some Mino troops attacked this place from the landward side, while Tanaka Yoshimasa and Miyabe Nagahiro led their men against the water gate. In all there were some fifteen thousand men under the direction of Ii Naomasa, who was Ikusa Metsuke or Overseer of Operations. On the next day (the eighteenth of the ninth month) it was agreed that the lives of the garrison should be spared on condition that Mitsunari's elder brother Ishida Masazumi, who was in charge, committed suicide. However, as some recalcitrants set fire to the keep of the castle, Masazumi and the other relations of Ishida put an end first to their wives and children, and then to themselves. Mitsunari's wife was killed by one of his own retainers, who afterwards followed her. This they did in the blazing keep of the castle so that their bodies were consumed with it. The conquerors remarked that in Ishida's castle they found no money. He had indeed lived up to his favorite maxim: "A retainer should spend all he gets from his lord. If he does not he is a thief. If he spends too much and makes debts he is a fool."

As to Ishida himself, he fled into the country round Mount Ibuki to the northwest of Sekigahara, with the intention of getting away to Osaka, and from thence to Satsuma, where there would be a chance of raising another army with the assistance of Shimazu, but a three days' diet of husks and exposure to the weather gave him dysentery, and he was soon handed over in rags to the officers of Ieyasu. Konishi was apprehended even more rapidly, and when it was suggested that he might like to commit suicide he refused on the grounds that he was a Christian. Ankokuji Eikei, too, had his hiding-place revealed by a Ronin, who bore him a grudge for turning his former master out of his fief. He tried to escape in a palanquin to the temple of Toji, but was beset, and his two attendants stabbed him and then fought till they were killed. Good as were their intentions, he seems not to have entirely acquiesced, for he was not very badly injured and was brought in alive to the Tokugawa headquarters. How gratified Ieyasu was may be gathered from his presenting ten pieces of gold to the Ronin, who at first emphatically refused to take it, declaring that his motive was only the very proper one of revenge, and that he did not wish to profit otherwise. But Ieyasu would not take a refusal, and so he received this quite large sum, but distributed it among the people of his village in true recluse style.

Nagatsuka Masaie, who had taken no more part in the fighting than had Ankokuji, and whose specialty seems to have been commissariat, retired to his castle of Mizoguchi after the defeat of his side, where Ieyasu sent an officer to him submitting that he put an end to himself without delay, which he did, seeing that any other course was hardly feasible, leaving behind him quite a large treasure in gold, silver, and other valuables, showing him to have been a soldier of a saving disposition.

When Ishida had been brought to Ieyasu's camp and given medicine and suitable clothes and made comfortable, Honda Masazumi went to see him. After the usual compliments he began: "Since Hideyori is so young, it would have been better if you had done what you could to bring about agreement between the Tairo and Bugyo, and so prevent disorder in the Empire, but instead of that you go and stir up a profitless rebellion like this and stake everything on one battle and lose it. That doesn't look particularly wise. I wonder what advice or reasons led you to take such a course?"

"A secondary vassal like you," retorted Ishida, "isn't likely to have any ideas about the stability of the Empire. You are like a well frog that can't see the ocean, so planning an affair like this and carrying it out would be quite beyond you. Anyhow, it was because Ukita and Uesugi and Mori, and then Maeda Gen-i and Masuda and Nakatsuka could not agree that it all came about. And I can tell you at once that I and nobody else was responsible for it all. So you can tell Ieyasu to take my head off, and pardon the others, for they were not the authors of the plot. They did their best, but when it came to the fighting some betrayed us, and others were not there in time, and so we failed. But had that not been so, and had they acted in harmony and good faith, it is your side that would have been the losers. But as we have been beaten and are prisoners in your hands, you can criticize us and deride us for being beaten, but even so, in spite of those traitors, Ukita and Otani and Shimazu and I held our ground and fought on without confusion to the very last, and never let our defeat become a rout. So whatever abuse is leveled at us we have nothing to be ashamed of."

"You have certainly put your case adroitly," replied Honda, "but a wise commander must know his men and be a judge of human nature. If he starts on a campaign without any insight into the minds of his generals he can easily be upset by traitors. It is proverbial that victory depends on the loyalty of retainers, and though Ukita and Nakatsuka and yourself may have set out from Owari to do or die as you say, in the end the others retired and left Otani to be killed, and here are you taken prisoner. Was that all according to plan?"

Ishida laughed. "It's quite true that there's no excuse for anyone who is taken in by treacherous subordinates," he admitted, "but you are a bit narrow-minded in blaming Ukita and myself for retiring and leaving Otani to be killed. As you know, he has been an invalid for years, and there was little reason why he should not die a bit sooner than later. We ran away to fight again another day, that's all. When Tanaka's retainer came to my hiding-place it would have been easy enough to have stabbed him and then committed suicide. But I thought it a better plan to give the enemy the trouble of putting an end to me if it must be, and meanwhile I should be able to hear about the gallant deeds, or otherwise, of the others, so that I shall have something entertaining to tell the Taiko when I meet him in the

underworld. And that's all you'll get out of me this side of Hades!"
And he shut his mouth resolutely and said no more.

In due course he and Honishi and Ankokuji were beheaded in the
riverbed at Kyoto, after being exhibited in Osaka and Sakai placarded as
disturbers of the peace of the Empire. They were the only ones thus treated, for Ukita was exiled, and it is to be noted that they were all upstarts.

Ishida's pertinacity persisted to the end, if the record of his last
discourse is to be believed. Offered a persimmon on his way to the
execution-ground, when he had stopped and asked for a cup of tea, he
refused it on the ground that it would injure his digestion.

"It hardly seems necessary to consider one's digestion just before
decapitation," observed Konishi dryly. "That shows how little you understand," was the retort. "You can never tell how things will turn out
the next minute, and so while you have breath in your body you have
got to take care of yourself."

That Ieyasu considered it politic not to be too drastic in his penalties appears from his reply to Honda Masanobu's suggestion that Naoe
Kanetsugu deserved to be punished, since he had been one of the
chief instigators of the rebellion. "No doubt," replied Ieyasu, "and not
only he, but the chief councilors of Mori and Shimazu and the others,
because they all egged on their lords at Ishida's instigation. And if I
punish Naoe the others will get upset and run away to their provinces,
and we may have all the trouble over again."

CHAPTER 24

KURODA JŌSUI AND KYUSHU

MEANWHILE Kuroda Jōsui in Kyushu was by no means idle. He called for volunteers for the campaign against the Ishida party in that island, and all classes of society were encouraged to join, Ronin, old men, Inkyo, traders, farmers, and artisans, since all the able-bodied samurai were with his son Nagamasa in Ieyasu's camp, and they responded willingly. Those who had no proper armor came in paper haori, on the back of which they had painted their crests, and picked up any old discarded equipment they could find, while some who had no helmets wore split bamboo hats with birch twigs stuck round the brim. The horses they rode were in many cases thin and sorry-looking but they made as brave a show as they could, riding up gaily brandishing their spears. In all, three thousand six hundred men were thus collected. Jōsui greeted them all personally with compliments suitable to the occasion, if they were old telling them that their experience would be most useful and congratulating them on their enterprise, and if they were young observing that their vigor was remarkable and their spirit beyond all praise. Each horseman received 300 me in silver, and each foot soldier a kwambun of Eiraku coins. Jōsui himself presented them with the money, and spoke a few words to each, never repeating himself, and when some of his officers informed him that some had come forward more than once so that they could receive more money and that it would be well to mark them in some way, he replied that he was well aware of it, but considered that on such an occasion it was not advisable to make any invidious investigations.

When he announced that he would set out on the ninth day Mori Taihei and Inoue Kuroemon, two of his oldest councilors, said that the day was unlucky, and also that it would be well to Wait till Ieyasu had set out for the west. But Jōsui answered that if he did that he would look like a trimmer, and as for unlucky days he had set out on the ninth before and been victorious, as they might remember. If they did not like it they could wait for what they considered a lucky day and follow on after him. So they agreed to start with him, saying that they were always ready to die for him at any time, but it was his safety they were considering. Jōsui laughed and called for drink, and they toasted the success of the campaign.

First of all he proceeded by sea to Kitsuke, the castle of his neighbor, Hosokawa Yusai. This castle being given to Hosokawa was a case where Ieyasu had outwitted Ishida, for it was Ishida who had suggested that the fief in Bungo be allotted to Yusai, pretending that it was the dying wish of the late Taiko. His real reason for pressing this was that he wished to divide and weaken the forces of Yusai, whose position in Tango enabled him to menace Osaka and Sawayama, and whose staunch friendship for Ieyasu was well known. Ieyasu saw through this scheme it appears, but made no objection because he also saw that it could be made to cut both ways, for he afterwards said to Yusai: "Ishida has divided your fief in this way, thinking to weaken your forces by taking some away to the west, but there in Kyushu I have only one supporter, and that is Kuroda Jōsui. Now your new fief is next his, so be sure you send a few good men down there so that you can combine to some effect when the need arises." Yusai sent his captains Matsui and Ariyoshi to take charge of Kitsuke, and when the war broke out they wished to go back to his assistance, leaving the castle in the charge of Jōsui; therefore they went to him at Najima for ships to take them round by Shimonoseki and the Sanin coast, since all the mainland was in the hands of the enemy. Jōsui, however, told them he could not spare any, though he would give them money to hire some if they could find them. But there were none to be had, and so they had to return to Kitsuke. Jōsui went off thither and told them to hold out, but not to make any attacks outside, giving them three pieces of cannon or large matchlocks. He assured them that if they were besieged he would send them assistance in three days. He then assisted Kiyomasa's wife, who had escaped from Osaka, giving her clothes of which she was in need, and sending her safely home. He also sent news of the fall of Gifu, which he had heard from his son Nagamasa who was with this part of the Eastern army, to Kato Kiyomasa, with the result that he gave up fortifying his castle and determined to take the offensive too.

Beside his activity on land, Jōsui had some ships at sea too, and it chanced that as Shimazu was retiring after Sekigahara three of his transports, containing mostly women and children, were intercepted by them, the main body getting away. They made a sign to surrender, but perhaps it was not understood for the Kuroda fleet of some twenty ships, a few of his own, and others he had persuaded the pirates of those parts to lend him, attacked them forthwith. So the Satsuma men fought back hard as was their way, and it was not till late afternoon that the action that had begun at daybreak ended in their ships being set on fire and sunk with the loss of all on board. Jōsui's men lost about a hundred in this desperate fight, and when they reported the victory to him he exclaimed in indignation, "What's the use of this sort of thing? Quite an unnecessary piece of work. And killing women and children is inhumane, too!" But it was not long before his face cleared, and he observed that it was difficult to blame men who had fought so toughly. Meanwhile he took the strong places of Takaku, Usuki, Saeki, and Kokura and entered the next province of Chikuzen, while Kato Kiyomasa moved against Udo, the castle of Konishi Yukinaga. Kato had already been advised by Ieyasu that he had better stay in Kyushu and conquer the neighboring provinces of Higo and Chikugo, which he would then give him as his fief. Udo eventually surrendered after receiving the news of the victory of Sekigahara. Jōsui also stirred up Ito Juhei in Hyuga to rise up in that province also, so that he took the important town of Miyasaki. This done, he and Kiyomasa went and beleaguered the castle of Yanagawa in Chikugo, the capital of Tachibana Muneshige.

Here they were joined after a while by his neighbor, Nabeshima Katsushige, son of Nabeshima Naoshige, lord of Saga. Nabeshima had fought on the wrong side, for though he had offered to join Ieyasu he was recommended to stay at home in Kyushu. However, he sent his son Katsushige to do what he could for the Eastern army. But on his way through the Kansai his small force was halted and surrounded by the troops of Ishida, who were by this time on the move, so he thought it more discreet to join them for a while, and was sent to assist in besieging Fushimi and Anotsu. So busied he was not in the Sekigahara fight, and when he heard of the victory he hastened to Osaka to Ieyasu and begged pardon for his ineluctable lapse. Ieyasu granted it on condition that he go and attack his neighbor Tachibana.

However, Jōsui and Kiyomasa were old friends and companions-in-arms of Muneshige in the Korean campaign, and were by no means anxious to damage him if it could be avoided, so they suggested that he surrender and join them in a campaign against Shimazu. After some discussion they convinced him that they would secure his pardon from Ieyasu, and so it was arranged. Muneshige was another who had taken no part in the fighting at Sekigahara, for he was delayed in besieging Otsu.

But when they were just preparing with Nabeshima to advance on Satsuma they got a letter from Ieyasu and two more from Ii Naomasa and Honda Tadakatsu all expressing anxiety for their health if they ventured on a campaign in the winter weather that was now near, for it was already November, and advising them to stay where they were. Seeing that Satsuma is the warmest part of Japan and has a Riviera-like climate, this was amusing, and merely Ieyasu's way of hinting that he saw through Jōsui's energetic fishing in troubled waters. He may quite likely have had a plan to conquer Kyushu and then cross over and oper-

ate in the Kansai district if anything should happen to Ieyasu, and seeing his connections there he would have been in a very strong position.
He is said to have asked Ii Naomasa to suggest that his son be given
Ukita's fief in Bizen or some other territory in the Kansai, while he and
Kato kept the land they had taken in Kyushu, but however that may be
he quickly realized that it would not be wise to let too much obvious
self-seeking show through the loyalty of his support, and so from now
on he became the very complete altruist philosopher. "Aha, he knows!"
he is reported to have exclaimed when told that Ieyasu's enthusiasm for
his continued activity in the field was not very apparent. Date Masamune, who was about his equal for cunning at the other end of the Empire, quite frankly admitted to Ieyasu when taxed with it that he was
out to snatch something for himself in the conflagration if he could,
though he was not very successful. No doubt Jōsui's failing health, for
which contemporary opinion blames the spirochaete, had much to do
with his graceful retirement, but in all this modest self-effacement he
showed considerable wisdom, for he must have calculated that though
he was as capable in many ways as Ieyasu and now perhaps the only
one who might have contested the Empire with him, yet he really stood
no chance of success as affairs had turned out, and any other conduct
would only have put the future of his house in jeopardy.

So when he went to Osaka later on at the invitation of Ieyasu, and
was received with great cordiality, and Ieyasu said: "It is entirely owing
to the military prowess of yourself and your son that the Empire is thus
unified and restored to peace, I have arranged, therefore, to give you
a large reward in territory, and shall petition the Court to grant you
high rank also," Jōsui respectfully declined. "I am old," he explained,
"and my health is poor, so I have little strength left for further activity.
My son will support me from the bounty with which you have been
pleased to endow him, and I have no further ambition for wealth or
possessions. All I wish for is permission to spend my remaining days
in peace." This Ieyasu was delighted to give him, and we are told that
Hidetada greatly admired this detachment, comparing him to the Chinese sage Chorio.

Evidently he was quite satisfied with his son's discretion, for he once
said to him: "I served Nobunaga and Hideyoshi, and three times I had
differences of opinion with them and went into retirement. But you
have managed to agree with Ieyasu and his son without any disputes.
I have been a great gambler. To get the Empire I would have staked
anything, even your life. But you need not run risks of this kind. I used
not to think very deeply before acting, for I rushed in with a sandal on
one foot and a clog on the other, so to speak. And you have plenty of

ability and your full share of prudence and foresight, so you think out things well and calculate your chances deliberately."

For some little time Jōsui lived in a villa in the Ichijo district of Kyoto, and indulged his taste for aesthetics and philosophy in the place best fitted for it. And he mixed this with works of benevolence, too, for he interceded with Ieyasu for the life of Otomo Yoshimune, the not at all worthy offspring of Otomo Sorin whom the latter would have certainly put to death otherwise, so that he was only banished, and afterwards his descendants were appointed Koke or Masters of Ceremonies to the Tokugawas with the erstwhile great houses of Imagawa, Kira, and Rokkaku. Shimazu was another on whose behalf he interested himself. It happened that Jōsui and Shimazu had a mutual friend in Konoe Ozan, the famous poet and calligraphist, who had spent three years in exile in Satsuma, and he, too, exerted himself on behalf of Shimazu's revenues. But probably these were safeguarded anyhow by geography and the balance of power in Kyushu, for Ieyasu had no desire to see some other lords there too strong and Shimazu was notoriously difficult to attack.

But Ieyasu could not resist a joke at Jōsui's expense, for he invited him to a banquet at Fushimi with some other nobles, and in the room he set out four or five tea-jars of great rarity and value. After dinner he looked at Jōsui and remarked that he would give him any one of them he fancied if he would carry it home himself unaided. So the little cripple picked up the biggest one and carried it home, much to Ieyasu's amusement. This is the jar called Nanjo, which is still one of the great treasures of the house of Kuroda.

After going for a while to the Daitokuji and sitting in meditation there under the great Zen master, Haruya Osho, "considering the origins of life and death and thereby gaining extreme peace of mind," Jōsui again returned to Kyushu, not to his son's castle of Najima in Chikuzen, but to the historic Dazaifu, where he built himself a small tearoom in front of the shrine of Tenjin, the deified poet Michizane, and there made tea and poems and diverted himself with the simple pleasures of the scenery.

In 1603 his son Nagamasa determined to build a new castle, since he thought Najima, though a strong place, was too small. The place he chose was a site not very far away, then called Fukusaki. At first Jōsui was inclined to oppose the project as laying too heavy a burden on the people, but later on gave way. No doubt Ieyasu favored it as providing work for the other lords of Kyushu who had to build it. This is the now famous town of Fukuoka, it being given this name by Jōsui because his ancestor had gone to Fukuoka in Haku-gun in the province of Bizen, and he maintained that to commemorate one's origin was one of the duties of filial piety. It was one of the strongest places in the country, and its main keep and six supporting castles took seven years to finish. Jōsui assisted considerably in superintending the communicating roads that were needed in connection with it, and some time later he departed this life, having claims on both the Buddhist and Christian heavens, as well as on Shinto deification, though he is perhaps best known in his mortuary chapel in the Daitokuji, the Ryūko-in.

After Sekigahara, Ieyasu proceeded to rearrange the country in accordance with his plans for its future. This meant confiscating the fiefs of his opponents and increasing those of his supporters, not by any means always consistently with their merits or the reverse, but more with regard to the exigencies of the time. So many of these grants of territory were only provisional, made with an eye to revision or resumption in the future as occasion might dictate. As usual Ieyasu went warily, "tapping even a stone bridge," for there was still a good deal of pro-Hideyoshi sentiment that it was advisable to respect.

Shimazu was the most fortunate of the Westerners, for he was persuaded to surrender after retiring to his fief and resisting his neighbors for a while, and was allowed to keep his revenues untouched or even a little incremented, for he was left with 605,000 koku. Next to him came Kobayakawa, who was given 574,000 in Bizen, which, however, he did not long enjoy. Maeda was also increased to 1,195,000 koku, making him the wealthiest of all the feudal lords, and Mogami from 240 to 570,000, though it is difficult to regard the services of these, especially of the last two, as of anything but a negative kind. Date Masamune was not badly off with 605,000 either, though this was only 25,000 more than he had before. The greatest loser was Mori, for though at first Ieyasu informed him through Kikkawa that nothing would happen to his emoluments if he went home quietly, when he had done so he changed his mind, observing that he could not overlook his rebellious conduct, and deprived him of all his fiefs except the two provinces of Suwo and Nagato. This meant that he lost 836,000, being reduced from 1,205,000 to 369,000, while Uesugi lost even more, for he was transferred from Aizu of 1,200,000 to Yonezawa at 300,000, so losing 900,000. Satake, too, was moved from Hitachi to Akita, 205,000, losing 339,000 on the way. But ninety smaller lords lost everything, and at their expense Ieyasu benefited to the extent of 4,464,000 koku, not all of which he could keep, however, for he had to reward his friends.

Kuroda was given Chikuzen vice Kobayakawa with an income of 523,000 koku, and Hosokawa Buzen in the place of Kuroda with some additions that brought him up to 369,000. Nabeshima remained in

Saga with 357,000, which was lucky seeing that he had fought against the Tokugawa forces for a while at Fushimi, though apparently under compulsion. Fukushima got Hiroshima with 498,000 koku in place of Mori, and Asano 395,000 at Wakayama in Kishu. Todo Takatora went to Imaharu with 203,000 and Yamanouchi to Tosa with 202,000 vice Chosokabe, who retired to Kyoto into private life. Yamanouchi had done nothing much in the campaign but give advice to other lords that they should surrender their castles to Ieyasu, and for this he was indeed well rewarded. Kato Kiyomasa was increased to 520,000 at Kumamoto, and the two Churo Horio and Nakamura were removed from Hamamatsu and Shizuoka, now resumed by Ieyasu, to Matsue and Yonago in the Sanindo with 170,000 and 145,000 respectively. Gamo got Aizu with 600,000 for no particular reason.

It may seem rather strange that Ieyasu did not give very large fiefs to his loyal family retainers Ii, Honda, Sakai, Sakakibara, Okudaira, and Takeda. But this was part of his policy. They were, however, given important strategic positions on the high roads or round the capital Edo. Ii was at Hikone (180,000), Sakai at Takasaki in Kōzuke (50,000), Honda at Kuwana on the Tokaido (100,000), Sakakibara at Tatebayashi in Kosuke (195,000), the Okudairas at Utsunomiya (100,000), and Kano in Mino (also 100,000), while Torii was at Iwakidaira in Mutsu, on the road to the north. Two other Hondas were also at Okazaki and at Otaki in Kazusa, each with 50,000. To these fudai damyo or close retainers of the house of Tokugawa the control of the administration was to be entrusted, a great honor and responsibility, but no great wealth.

To his own family Ieyasu was somewhat more liberal, for Matsudaira Hideyasu got Echizen with 751,000 koku and Tadayoshi Owari with 520,000. In 1602 Ieyasu married his son Hidetada's daughter to Hideyori, and this naturally enabled him to keep a close eye on the young man by means of her retinue, though he professed great friendship for Hideyoshi's heir. This he thought advisable, since any attempt against him would alienate the late vassals of the Taiko such as Kato Kiyomasa, Kuroda, Fukushima Ikeda, and without the support of these he might be in a difficult position. He also inaugurated the shrine of Hideyoshi as Shin-Hachiman. But later on when he dared he was to deprive this new war-god of his position.

In 1603 Ieyasu was formally proclaimed Shogun by the Emperor, and he requested that his title of Naidaijin should now be transferred to Hideyori. The last Shogun, Ashikaga Yoshiaki, had only died in 1597, though he had been deposed in 1575 by Nobunaga. But Nobunaga had never been more than Vice-Shogun, for he was not of the Minamoto house. It seems that Todo Takatora constituted himself the fugleman in this as in other such cases, for when Ieyasu did not show any signs of assuming the office of Shogun some of the daimyos were credited with suggesting that he should do so, and Takatora and Suden laid the matter before him. "We hear on all sides," said they, "that the lords are impatiently waiting for the good news that Your Highness has been appointed Shogun." Very characteristic was the reply: "There is no hurry about that. The country has to be set in order, and the welfare of the people seen to. That is the most urgent need. Then the various lords have to be settled in their new fiefs. When all that has been done it will be time to look to my own personal status."

A little before this, in 1600, the Emperor Go-Yozei had consulted Ieyasu about the succession. His Majesty personally wished his successor to be his second son Masahito, whose mother was the daughter of the former Kwampaku Konoe, but there was an elder son whose mother was the daughter of the Dainagon Nakayama Nobutsuna, and this Dainagon had enlisted the sympathy of Maeda Gen-i and got him to persuade Hideyoshi to arrange for the Udaijin Kikutei Harusue, who was a great friend and benefactor of the Taiko, and had got him promoted to Kwampaku, to issue an order proclaiming the elder prince heir to the Throne. This meant that the second son would have to enter a monastery. Now Ieyasu did not specially care to see the elder son, Yoshihito, succeed on account of his sponsors, so he gave his opinion thus: "It has always been understood both in ancient and modern times that the best judge of a son is the father. I myself have many sons, and in selecting my heir I never consulted anyone else, but decided the matter by myself alone. And similarly there can be no question but that the Heirship to the Throne should only be decided by your August Opinion." Naturally the Emperor agreed, and Prince Masahito was proclaimed Imperial Heir, afterwards succeeding as the Emperor Go Mizu-no-O to the satisfaction of both Emperor and Shogun, at least for a while.

CHAPTER 25

THE BUILDING OF EDO

No great change took place in Edo for some years, for it was merely the capital of the Kwanto and Ieyasu was well occupied with other matters, but after the death of Hideyoshi and the battle of Sekigahara its lord became the greatest power in the Empire, and in 1603 was appointed Shogun. Thus Edo became the chief city of Japan and the center of administration, and Ieyasu at once set about making it worthy of the position. It had in 1602 suffered its first fire, and in consequence orders had been given that its houses were in future to be roofed with boards and not with thatch as heretofore. It was at this time that one Takiyama Yajibei wishing to distinguish himself, roofed the side of his house facing the main street with tiles, leaving the other side boarded, whereat the Edo folk nicknamed him "Half-Tiled Yajibei." This seems to be the first use of tiles in the city.

So in July 1604 Ieyasu issued orders to all the daimyos to hold themselves in readiness to supply labor and materials to build the castle and reconstruct the city, and at once they began to collect timber and men and construct ships for transport. To face the moats and ramparts a large amount of stone had to be brought from Izu, and for this these much-burdened noblemen had to provide three thousand ships. Shimazu of Satsuma alone provided three hundred beside a large gift of money. Each of these ships carried two stones that needed a hundred men to handle one of them, and made two journeys to Izu and back each month. For every 100,000 koku of their income the daimyos were required to send 1,120 of these hundred-man stones, the equivalent in money being 192 gold pieces; 385 ships would be needed to handle them.

Meanwhile, to prepare the site for the large population that now flocked to it, Ieyasu determined to reclaim the area about two miles square that lay between Fukagawa and Hibiya, that was nothing but a sea-washed swamp. To do this Kanda Hill, round the present Surugadai, was leveled flat and the whole of the earth composing it carried away and planted in this low-lying ground. So was formed what is now the larger part of the business quarter of the city. For this immense work the daimyos were divided into ten companies each under

SAKAKIBARA KOHEIDA YASUMASA

a leader. For each 1,000 koku of their income they had to provide one man, so that as their combined resources can hardly have been less than 10,000,000 koku there will have been some 10,000 men engaged in the work. When finished the city was a more or less level plain from Kudan Hill to Shinagawa on one side and Asakusa on the other. It is true the filled-in area was hardly choice residential land, but it was good enough for the townspeople, and the worst of it was kindly donated for the amusement quarter of the city, as elsewhere recorded.

It was at this time that Nihon-bashi, the well-known center of the city, was built. As the channel was somewhat wide, it was banked out with stone on each side and the bridge thrown across the narrowed space. Even then it was 226 feet 5 inches long and 26 feet 5 inches wide. One explanation of the name is that it was given because all Japan had a hand in making it, which seems as good as any other suggestion. The fact that this name would also refer to the sunrise and would be suitable to it as the point from which distances were reckoned would be a recommendation no doubt to a people who love words of many meanings. It is likely that the names Owari-cho, Kaga-cho, and Izumo-cho given to the blocks nearby refer to the lords who had the embarrassing privilege of working on these places. That the building of the castle was a crushing burden on these lords may be well seen from the letters that have survived in which they refer to details of the corvee and their anxiety lest the result of their efforts should not come up to the requirements of the superintending officials, kept up to a standard by the ever-critical eye of the old Shogun himself, and after he retired to Shizuoka, of his son Hidetada. Morning and evening did this latter go round the works and inspect everything, tearooms being provided for him to rest in here and there by the way. Most of these letters end with such expressions as, "Indeed it is a most anxious time," or "The greatest care must be taken," or "We must not relax our vigilance for a moment." "Of late," writes Masuda Motoyoshi, chief councilor of Mori Terumoto, who had gone down to Izu to superintend the loading of the stone ships, "Ogosho Sama (Ieyasu) has been short-tempered, and I am very apprehensive. I fear I am clumsy and incapable in all these affairs, and that is why I feel so uneasy. We must, indeed, be very careful. And again, Mori and Kikkawa were not in time with their supplies. It is nothing to laugh at. The arrangements have got out of order, and I am very anxious about it." And if these great lords found difficulty in raising money and ships and delivering their supplies in time it is not probable that the smaller feudatories found it any easier. Fourteen hundred yards of stone ramparts between 70 and 80 feet high were required for the castle at this stage, and the price of stone in Edo rose with the demand, for Asano complains that it is "dearer this year than last, for a hundred-man stone costs twelve pieces of silver now, and a six-foot cubic measure of cobble stones cost three ryo of gold." And sometimes the ships were wrecked in a sudden squall, and that was a further loss and vexation. On one occasion several hundred stone ships were sunk on their way to Edo: "a hundred of Nabeshima's, forty-six of Kato Yoshiaki's, thirty of Kuroda's, and any number of flotillas of four or five belonging to lesser people." Kato Kiyomasa, too, lost seven ships off Edo in a hurricane, but in this case since they sank only ten miles off Shinagawa the fishermen salvaged the ships after the stone had sunk to the bottom and apparently were very pleased at the windfall.

In 1606 there was another order to start work again after a rest of a few months, and Todo Takatora, lord of Imaharu, as usual volunteered to superintend operations. Now the great keep was started, and a large part of it was done by Kuroda Nagamasa, while half a dozen others constructed the main castle (Hommaru).

In the sixth month of 1606 most of the first part of the building was finished, and the Shogun complimented those who had taken part in it and made them presents, but the only one who got anything very substantial was Todo Takatora, who received a fief of 20,000 koku in Bichu in the ninth month for his energetic supervision of the others. By this time the main castle and its palace and ramparts, the Ni-no-Maru or second castle, the third castle or San-no-Maru, and the stone ramparts from the Pheasant Gate on the northeast to the Tameike reservoir on the southwest were constructed.

Then in 1607, after a rest of a year or so, orders were issued to start work again as before under the superintendence of Todo Takatora. This time the brunt of it was borne by the lords of the east and north, and not by those of the west as heretofore. Those of the Kwanto who totalled a million koku were divided so that 800,000 koku was allotted to providing stone and 200,000 to finishing the great keep. Date, Uesugi, Gamo, Yogani, Sataki, Mori, Mizoguchi, and Murakami of the north are the daimyos who are now requisitioned. The stone was brought from Kanase in Kosuke, 20 tsubo for each 1,000 koku. Beside the keep, the ramparts that had been built already about 48 feet high were raised to 60 feet, their width being 120 feet. Then was built the great front gate (Ote-Mon) and the Chushaku Gate. Also the outer earth wall that surrounded the whole was raised 12 feet to 40 feet in height, and the outer moat from the Pheasant Gate on the northern side to the Tameike reservoir on the southeast was dug out and widened. Work was also done on the northern side. As the castle of Sumpu (Shizuoka), to which Ieyasu retired to live this year, was being reconstructed too, the strain on the daimyos was heavier even than before. For between 1602 and 1614 not only was the castle and city of Edo completely reconstructed but the following castles were built also: Zese was built and Otsu demolished in 1601; Fushimi in 1602, and again in 1604; Hikone in 1604; Nagahama in 1606; Sumpu in 1607; in 1611 Takada in Echide. All these castles were erected by the tozama or outside lords, whose revenues suffered accordingly, though it seems that the ordinary people were pleased by the demand for their labor.

In 1611 another call was made on the northern daimyos, and Date Masamune himself superintended the construction of more ramparts and moats round the Nishi Maru. Honda Masanobu was in charge of everything, and Hidetada as usual personally inspected all that was done every day. This time the work was pushed on with great energy, for the Shogun was in a hurry and a very large number of workmen were employed, who, we are informed, were eminently satisfied with their wages; that is, of course, the farmers and townsfolk in the Edo district. Probably the same classes in the provinces who had to pay for the work to some extent at least, were not so satisfied, though the Shogun certainly obtained a lot of money from his mining properties which would go some way to mitigate the burden in his own domains.

The next year, 1612, several lords in Shinano and the neighborhood were requested to supply a quantity of timber from that part for the further activities of 1614. So at the end of 1613 Sakai Tadayo, Doi Toshikatsu, and Asano Shigenobu issued orders to the daimyos of all provinces in the west, including Kyushu, Shikoku, Sanyodo, and Sanindo, to supply materials and labor for a last great effort to complete the fortifications. What had been done so far embraced a fairly large area, the Nishi Maru, Kita Maru, the defenses in front of the Ote Mon or Main Gate, and the moated enclosure, called Daimyo-Koji, where were the residences of the great lords with the outworks in front of the Nishi Maru, in all about five miles in circumference and fifty acres in area. But there still remained a certain amount to be done to bring this to the condition required by Ieyasu and Hidetada, that is practically as it is today, for it needed no strengthening afterwards, and what was added in the time of Iemitsu and Ietsuna was only the moat that enclosed the outermost part of the fortified area on the northern side. So these western lords took in hand the Main Castle, the stone rampart on the upper part of which was built by Hosokawa Tadaoki, while Shimazu constructed the high stone wall round it. Hachisuka Muneshige, Kuroda Nagamasa, Matsuura Takanobu, Arima Toyouji, Ikeda Tadatsugu, Todo Takatora, and Tsuchiya Toshinao were all set to the Main Castle as was Nabeshima Katsushige, who had to look to the Tora Gate as well, his business being to build stone ramparts in these places as well as some others, in which he had Ito Sukeyoshi to assist him. Mori Hidenori worked on the Ni-no-Maru and the Inner Sakurada Mitsuke. Others were detailed to finish the ramparts on front of the Nishi Maru and the Ni-no-Maru. Unfortunately for them it was the rainy season, and in consequence of the heavy falls some of the ramparts gave way, in one case crushing a hundred and fifty of Asano's men under the ruins. Several other daimyos had a similar experience, and their trouble and expense were considerably augmented. At last in the ninth month of this year they were dismissed to their provinces with presents of money, clothing, and horses as well as compliments, for soon they were to have another demand made on them to supply troops for the Osaka campaign.

The following notice was posted where the work was going on:

During the rebuilding all must dismount here. But women and children are not included.

Long swords are not to be worn. This does not apply to the Commissioner of Works (Fushin Bugyo).

It must be understood that the prohibition of smoking and covering the face (Hokarage) that was enforced before must be observed.

Anyone transgressing these regulations will be severely punished.

By order of the Commissioner.

But that Hidetada might not be unduly fatigued by his exertions in inspecting the works every day, tearooms were erected here and there and trees planted round them to make a Rōji. Here, surrounded by gold screens, he could rest and drink tea ceremonially. Ieyasu disliked smoking, and like his contemporaries James I and Akbar he issued an edict forbidding the use of tobacco, introduced apparently during the decade before Sekigahara by the Europeans, regarding it as an economically unsound indulgence, a waste of time and of money. Under this anyone selling it was to have house and property confiscated, and those who detected any in transit were to be given the horse and vehicle that carried it. But though the Tokugawa Shoguns could eradicate gambling and Christianity, they were powerless to prohibit the habit of smoking, which soon became firmly established, and eventually they gave up the attempt. Liquor they were content to regulate.

The beginning of the residence of the daimyos in Edo, which added so much to the prosperity of the city, was not exactly owing to any compulsion on the part of the Shogunate, though certainly the requests of these lords for grants of ground there were made from a desire to curry favor with the Bakufu. And the origin of the fashion was that in 1600 Maeda Toshinaga sent his mother the Lady Hoshun-in with the wives and children of his councilors to reside in Edo as a sign of his good will to Ieyasu. And Hidetada was so pleased at this that he gave him a fine site opposite the main gate of the castle. And Toshinaga soon built a mansion there. This was before Sekigahara, and his example was immediately followed by Todo Takatora, Hori Hidemasa, Asano Nagamasa, and Hosokawa Tadaoki. After that epoch-making engagement practically all the rest, headed by such great lords as Mori and Nabeshima, and of course Date Masamune, asked to be permitted a residence in the new capital. Before this they used to lodge in temples when they went up there, it seems, for Mori Hidenari is described as moving to his new mansion at Sakurada from the Tentokuji temple in Kojimachi where he formerly used to stop. Very much to the satisfaction of the Abbot of the Tentokuji apparently, since he had often, quite respectfully no doubt, but earnestly, requested Mori to vacate it. A daimyo and his retainers in these days might not be the most comfortable companions for Buddhist priests.

According to one account, Ieyasu did not at first favor this flocking to Edo on the part of these lords, and told them that if they had a residence at Osaka they did not need one at Edo, but they were insistent, and so he assigned the Outer Sakurada quarter of the city, afterwards called Daimyo-koji, for their mansions. This land was covered with brambles and very rough and full of hollows, so that for a while it was difficult to use, but when they widened and deepened the castle moats in front of it the soil that was dug and dredged out was used to level it, and so good sites for the mansions and their grounds were obtained. Here were situated the Yashiki of Kato Kiyomasa, Kuroda, Nabeshima, Mori, Shimazu, Date, Uesugi, Asano, Nambu, Ito, Kamei, Kanemori, Sengoku, Mizutani, Akita, Hijikata, and in fact everyone of any importance, because of its convenience for going on duty in the castle, a service which the lords had to take it in turn to perform. Since it became a collection of lords from all over the Empire some wit dubbed it Saito Musashi Bo or Musashi quarters of the East and West, whence by association it became known as Benkei-bori and is so still.*

At first these lords used to call at Osaka and pay their respects to Hideyori and then proceed to Edo to do the same by the Shogun. Since this was the end of their journey they would stop there some time before starting out again to return to their province or castle. So they began to bring their ladies and establish them at Edo, and it was not

---

* Saito Musashi Bo Benkei means Benkei of the Musashi Cell of the Western Pagoda, but "to" also stands for "higashi" = East, hence the pun. Compare the name Ikkoku bashi or One koku bridge, which owed its name to the fact that two lords both named Goto had their houses beside it. "Go-to" means five "to," and ten "to" make one koku. Kioi-cho also harbored the mansions of Kii, Owari, and the lord Ii.

long before all the Fudai lords had their families there.

And these early residences were very imposing. The house of Ii obtained two that had belonged to Kato Kiyomasa, using one as their Upper Mansion, this being by Benkei-bori, and the other as their Middle Mansion, farther away by the Yotsuya Gate. The Middle Mansion survived untouched by fire for two hundred years or so, and was therefore seen and described by the author of the *Ochibo-shu*. The Upper Mansion has a great gate, 60 feet long, of two stories, and ornamented with five carved and gilded rhinoceros as big as small horses, while the tiles of the barracks surrounding it had gilt bell-flower crests that shone brightly even in the dark. They must have been like the 3-foot golden tiger on the front of the gate of his Middle Mansion, which was so luminous that it frightened away the fish in Shinagawa Bay and made the fishermen complain that it prevented them earning a living. In front of the entrance porch of this latter mansion in Yotsuya there was a stone pavement right up to the front door instead of the usual wooden "Shikidai." This was so that Kiyomasa and his friends could jump right on to their horses at a moment's notice. Above the gate, too, was an apartment called the Chamber of the Envoy. It had Shoji of the old-fashioned style solid halfway up (Koshi-shoji), the frames of which were strengthened with rods of iron on the outside and furnished with fastenings of the same metal. Those who came with messages or samurai of other clans who were not very well known were shown into this room and so the retainers could hear what they had to say, and if they thought it advisable could draw these shoji and drop the bolts so that the intruder could not get out. This was like Kato Kiyomasa. These great mansions with their lofty gables and carved and gilt gates were quite in the Momoyama style as represented by the surviving gates of Hideyoshi's mansions at Fushimi and Juraku, but were almost all destroyed in the various fires and rebuilt much more plainly.

As to the districts of Edo, that called Mikawa-cho was where in these early days the lesser retainers of Mikawa used to come and stay in turns when on duty. Hirakawa was a village outside the Hirakawa Gate that was so called from the stream of the same name, and with Kojimachi seems to be one of the oldest place names. Sarugaku-cho was called after Kanzei Taiyu, the master of Sarugaku or No, whose residence was there. The well-known Hanzo Gate is called after Ieyasu's retainer Hattori Hanzo, but it does not seem that Yuraku-cho has any connection with Oda Yuraku, as often stated, for it was under water in his days.

The city itself seems to have grown from the soil excavated from the moats, for as these were made from Nihon-bashi towards Dosabori this soil was left piled up and prospective tradesmen were given a site and allowed to take away as much as they wanted and built it up for their shop and residence. At first there were not so many volunteers for this rather laborious pioneering, but before long the men of Ise came forward in large numbers, attracted as they always were by the possibility of gain, so that it was said that half the establishments in one block might have the name Igeya on their shop-curtains.

Naturally these early settlers had their reward, as the city filled up, and it is recorded that in twelve years a site bought for one or two ryo was sold for from one to five hundred. And when ground grew so valuable the question of boundaries became acute, for the lines had been carelessly marked out in the early days and forgotten, so that a lot of litigation resulted, and neighbors squabbled and became estranged.

The city of Edo was not originally well off for pure water, and especially on the filled-in ground the wells were brackish from the infiltration of sea-water but even before he entered the city Ieyasu had given orders to Okubo Mondo Tadayuki, a water expert, to construct aqueducts. This he did by making a dam under the hill of Mejiro and bringing the water of the Takada river into the north-west districts of the city through Kobinata, Koishikawa, Yushima, and along under Kanda Hill. More water was brought also from the Tameike or Reservoir of Akasaka to supply the southeastern quarters. These were sufficient for the city for another half-century or so, when the Tamagawa aqueduct was completed.

CHAPTER 26

THE COMING OF THE DUTCH

Of the Dutchmen who came in the *Liefde* with Adams several were taken into the service of Matsuura Shigenobu, lord of Hirado, to make guns and ammunition for him, but after a while the Captain Jan Quaeckernaeck and the Supercargo Melchior van Santvoort obtained permission to go home again in 1605. Adams wished to go also to arrange for English ships to come to Japan, but Ieyasu found him so useful for shipbuilding and information on other matters that he would not let him. He thought that this communication with Europe could be negotiated by those who were not so indispensable. Quaeckernaeck was killed in a fight with the Spaniards, but Santvoort went to Patani and sent a letter with an invitation from Ieyasu to Dutch merchants to come to Japan, and in 1609 the *Brack*, with Captain Spex, came to Hirado because Matsuura had kindly provided the junk on which the Dutch had been able to leave Japan. In the seventh month of this year Spex was received by Ieyasu at Sumpu, and presented a letter from the Stadthalter of the Netherlands with presents of goblets, silk, lead, and ivory. To it he returned this reply:

From the Lord of Japan, Minamoto Ieyasu, to His Highness the Lord of Holland.

Though your letter has been written so far away, when I open and read it it is as though your High Presence is before me. And especially am I extremely delighted with the four presents you have sent me. Now the warship that you have dispatched from your honored country, with its commander and officers and numerous crew, has arrived at the port of Matsuura in this Empire to inaugurate friendly relations with this little country in accordance with my desire. If both our countries have the inclination, though separated by a thousand myriad miles of ocean, they may by yearly communications become not dissimilar. And in our country we correct the worthless and bring them back to the right way. Therefore those who come across the seas to trade with us may certainly live unmolested. So if you will select people and send them to this land we will on our part supply suitable ground to erect a factory and a harbor where the ships may find shelter wherever your countrymen may wish. And I trust that our relations may become ever more friendly. For the rest I shall rely on the discourse of the Captain. It is now autumn, but the heat is still severe. Spare yourself as the weather changes.

Fourteenth year of Keicho (1609).
Seventh month. Twenty-fifth day.

At the same time four copies of a license (Go-shuin) were handed to the four Dutch officers couched in these words:

When Dutch ships come to Japan they are hereby authorized to enter any harbor they like, and according to this ordinance they may go wherever they like without let or hindrance. Let none disregard this. So be it.

And so the commercial relations with Holland that were to last for three hundred years while the country was closed to all other nations began. Naturally this welcome to the Dutch was not at all to the taste of the Portuguese and Spanish, who at once took pains to point out that they were an undesirable race of pirates who sought to interfere with the peaceable trade they had carried on with Japan for so long, trying to intercept their ships from Macao and so on. But Ieyasu took no notice. He was able to get information about the real condition of affairs between the nations of Europe from Adams, who seems to have been rather impartial in his comments, for he was quite friendly with all these nationals.

Later on in 1612 Spex came again with Hendrik Brouwer, who was to be chief of the Dutch factory, bringing another letter from "Mauritius de Nassau Lord of Holland to Minamoto Ieyasu Lord of Japan."

You who are a great noble without equal in this age, and famed especially for martial prowess, lord of a prosperous country whose history stretches back a thousand years. My pen cannot express the feelings of gratitude with which I have received your honored epistle sent from a realm so far distant. And I am beyond measure thankful for the gracious permission that you have given to the Dutch merchants who have arrived in Japan to trade freely in your domains. Were our country nearer Japanese might be pleased to visit it also, and in that case we would give them a most hearty welcome. When as yet you did not know about our country Captain Jacob Quackernaeck was driven starving on to your shores, and though the Portuguese said that the Dutch were robbers and pirates besides other evil things, you did not listen to them but assisted our men, and for that also we owe you a debt of gratitude.

Some of our people went to China to trade, and once our envoy was received, but the Portuguese made presents to the officials and intrigued in various ways so that though they made three attempts in all they had to sail away without accomplishing anything. And when the Portuguese and Spaniards go anywhere and the Dutch have followed them, the former say that they have been merchants for a long time and are experienced, but the Dutch are only beginners, and so business with them will only result in loss. But that is a lie. The fact is that they have done as they liked in the world so far, and then the Dutch came and they thought by saying these things that they would get everything in their own hands again. But in this matter, as you have been kind enough to say, we are honest. But whatever the Portuguese may say they are not likely to do anything. We at any rate will carry out whatever you may wish. When the Dutch went to Bantam and Patani, where the Portuguese had already been, they were courteous to them, but the Portuguese hindered them in various ways. They told lies and so go there no longer, but the Dutch are still doing business on good terms with everyone.

And the intentions of the Spanish and Portuguese are difficult to understand because they are hidden deep in the minds of the Padres who reveal nothing, and this is a matter that you should consider very carefully. And the intention of the Padres is to convert all Japan to their faith by degrees, and as they hate other religions there is sure to be a struggle between the sects and a great disturbance in the country. And then the Padres hope to turn matters to their own advantage.

Now the Dutch who come to your country will do whatever you may please to require of them, and consider it a pleasure to do so. And so they will continue to do in the future.

We are people who wish to do business with far-off lands, and we should much like to go to Korea, so for this purpose we trust that you will do us the further favor of granting us your license to trade there also.

We have to apologize for many of the things in this letter, but we have written everything in detail without any reserve.

Please let us know what we can do for you whatever it may be.

Feb. 18th, 1610.

Here did the Dutch not only rebut the accusations of the Spaniards and Portuguese, but proceed from defense to attack, and there is little doubt that these statements helped to confirm the Shogunate in its views that the activities of the missionaries were a menace.

So the Hollanders set up their factory in Hirado and did not move to Uraga as Ieyasu urged them. Brouwer admitted that it was a convenient place, but they had already sunk a good deal of money in buildings and presents in Hirado, and the people there were very amiable to them, as they might well be. In a letter to Pott, the Governor of the Dutch East Indies, he encloses a map of Japan given him by Adams, who had it from Honda Masazumi, who had been directed by Ieyasu to see to it that the advantages of Uraga and its relation to Edo were thus properly advertised. Incidentally Brouwer remarked that Ieyasu's frequent invitations to them to go up to the capital were to see what kind of presents they would bring him, for he was an avaricious old man and liked to have valuable things given him, though he could not easily bring himself to give a high price for them. However that may be, it is clear that he was not a favorable subject for what may even then have been considered "the fault of the Dutch." For instance, he was asked if he would buy six brass and six iron cannon, but he thought them dear and could not make up his mind because these metals were rather cheap in Japan. But Brouwer was just then recruiting cheap Japanese labor for the Indies, for he says in a letter to the same official in 1613:

I am sending you as you ordered by this ship a small Japanese boat, and sixty-eight men. Japanese are clever and their wages are low. They only need rice and salt fish to live on. Of these men nine are carpenters, three are smiths, three are plasterers, and the rest sailors and soldiers. And if you find them useful I can send as many as you want for the Emperor has given his written permit for any who wish to go abroad.

CHAPTER 27

IEYASU AND NEW SPAIN

WHILE Ieyasu was hoping to increase the trade with the Spanish colonies it happened very providentially for him that in 1609 Don Roderigo Vivero y Velasco, who had been serving for a while as Governor of Manila, was wrecked in Japan owing to the *San Francisco,* the ship in which he was returning to Novispania, being blown out of its course and cast on the shore of Iwawada in the province of Kazusa, quite near to Edo. Of the other two vessels that were accompanying her, one, the *San Antonio,* held on her course, while the other, the *Santa Anna,* was beached in the province of Bungo. Don Roderigo was hospitably received by Honda Tadatomo, lord of the castle of Otaki, and by him sent to Edo, where he was presented to the Shogun Hidetada. He was then brought to Sumpu to undergo a similar honor before Ieyasu. All the arrangements for these ceremonies were made by Adams, who coached the Don in the procedure of the Shogunal Courts. In his report of his experiences we get a glimpse of Ieyasu and his surroundings as they appeared to this cultivated Spanish nobleman. The population of Edo, he says, is one hundred and fifty thousand, and that of Sumpu one hundred thousand, and the buildings of Edo are the finer. "The day after I arrived at Sumpu the Emperor sent a minister to me at the house of the officer with whom I was lodged, bringing a present of a dozen beautiful costumes and four swords and the assurance of his best consideration. At half-past two," he continues, "arrived a palanquin and an escort of two hundred matchlock men. At the order of the captain this was set down and I got in. A squad of thirty men under another officer marched with it through the town till we came to a formidable ironbound gate. At the officer's order it was opened and we saw another company of two hundred matchlock men drawn up in line. The captain led me between their ranks, and about five hundred paces farther on we came to a second moat with a drawbridge. Here I was handed over to another officer. Again the gate was opened to us and we entered to find a company of two hundred spearmen drawn up and supported by a number of matchlock men. From thence onward we were received by most respectful salutes as we passed on to the portal of the Palace. Within the first corridor or entrance hall there must have been a thousand men-at-arms and soldiers of various kinds. We passed through some eight or nine chambers, in all of which there were officers and chamberlains-in-waiting. The style and decoration of these apartments was a thing worth seeing. The ceilings were bright with gold, and on the walls were paintings like those on the screens that have been sent to Spain from Japan, but much better executed. Two ministers now came to meet us and asked me to rest for a while. They then returned to consult with the Emperor, and appeared again after about a quarter of an hour. His Highness, they informed me, would accord me the honor of a reception so far unprecedented in the Empire. And then I was ushered into his presence. In the center of a spacious apartment was a dais of three tiers. Round it was a double railing. In Spain such things are only gilt, but in Japan I understand they are of pure gold. On the dais the Emperor sat on a round seat of green; on his right hand about six paces distant was another seat of the same kind of velvet. He wore loose robes of green satin ornamented with gold brocade. In his belt were two swords, and he had no hat on his head, but his hair was done up in a knot with a colored band. The pattern embroidered on his robe seemed to be of stars and a half moon. He was a stout, heavily built old man between sixty and seventy years old, with a most dignified bearing. His face was like that of the Shogun, and he had a pleasing expression. In accordance with what I had been told I did not approach and kiss his hand, but stood some six or seven paces in front of him. He signed to me to put on my hat and be seated. Then after scrutinizing me for a while he clapped his hands twice, and one of the dozen or so chamberlains who were prostrated within the railing advanced and called to the minister who was seated beside me. The Emperor then turned to his minister and told him he was pleased to see me, and trusted that I was not perturbed, for it was not the wont of soldiers to be affected by mishaps at sea; that if there was anything I wanted he hoped I would inform him as freely as though he were the King of Spain. To this I replied that though I had been to some extent troubled by my loss and misfortune yet the pleasure I felt at being thus received by such a great monarch had quite banished all this from my mind, while I looked forward to a happy continuance of his favors." Pressed further by Ieyasu and also by the minister to express his wishes without reserve, Don Roderigo then put forward three requests:

That the Christian fathers and brothers in Japan should not be persecuted, but should be granted as much security to preach as the Japanese Buddhist monks enjoyed.

That since the Dutch pirates who frequented Japanese ports were enemies of the Spanish king, it was not right that they should be granted the protection of the Emperor any longer, and he trusted they would be expelled without delay.

That in pursuance of the policy of friendship between Japan and Spain, a welcome should be extended to ships from Manila.

The Emperor listened to all this, and said he would give a reply later. "He was about to give me permission to retire," says Don Roderigo, "when he bade me wait awhile, and a daimyo from some province accompanied by a retainer carrying a tray piled with gold pieces prostrated himself at the door of the apartment, apparently kissing the ground in his humility. I understand the value of the gold to be some 100,000 ducats. The Emperor then gave orders that I was to be shown over the Palace.

"Two days after Kozuke Dono brought me the Emperor's reply to the effect that no harm should be done to Christian missionaries; that he was not aware that the Dutch were pirates; that they had already received his permission to enter Japanese ports for a period of two years, but when that had elapsed he would consider the matter; that since he greatly desired the friendship of so powerful a monarch as the Spanish king he would be glad to make an agreement to trade and to do all he could in other ways to facilitate the coming of merchant vessels; that if there was any article I wanted I was to let him know at once. He also again suggested that we should arrange to send some mining engineers."

The Spaniard then made counter proposals. He would request the King of Spain and the Governor of Novispania to send fifty miners. But if they came they should receive half the profits of the mines while the other half should be divided between the King and the Japanese Emperor. And in order that the King of Spain might control this income he should be able to send officers to Japan; that they should be permitted to bring with them priests of any order and have services performed publicly. That the Hollanders should be expelled from the Empire since they were the enemies of the King of Spain. That the Spanish ships should have the right to have the same freedom to go wherever they pleased as those of the Japanese Government; that for building ships to send to the Moluccas and Manila both the necessary materials and men should be provided for the King of Spain; that the Captain and the Envoy that Spain would send should receive treatment in Japan proper to their rank, and that they should have the right to bring missionaries and hold service openly in their chapels. That the Spanish residents in Japan should have their own courts of justice, and should be able to punish any offenders themselves.

Ieyasu refused at once to expel the Hollanders, but told Don Roderigo he would consider the other requests. Eventually, though the

Spaniard considered that the King of Spain's share of the silver would certainly amount to a million and more, Ieyasu would not consent to this division of the profits. Ieyasu had intended to send Father Alonzo Munós as an envoy to Novispania with Father Sotelo, but as the latter was ill he arranged that Don Roderigo should go home in the 120-ton ship that Adams had built and take Munós with him. After a stay of several months in Sumpu Ieyasu sealed the agreement to all his requests except the two objectionable ones. The Spaniard was to sell the ship when he reached home if he got an opportunity to do so profitably, and with the money to buy goods and send them to Japan. He suggested that the ships should come from Manila and winter in Japan, and then proceed to Novispania. He promised to pay due respects to any envoy sent either by the King of Spain or the Governor of Novispania, and to provide anything they might need in the way of labor and materials for shipbuilding, and also residences at current prices, and to allow no extortion. In return he requested special treatment for any Japanese who went to Novispania. A present of three suits of armor and a sword was sent to the Spanish king. The document was signed by Honda Kosuke-no-suke Masazumi. Another epistle was also sent by the Shogun addressed to the Lord of Spain. This ship left Edo Bay in August 1610, and in it were twenty-three tradesmen, including one Ryusei, a vermilion dealer, and Tanaka Katsusuke, of Kyoto. The crew numbered eighty, and the vessel was named *Santa Buenaventura*. They had, it seems, a warm welcome in Novispania, and came back again with Sotomayor the Envoy, who arrived there a year after. According to Tokutomi, Don Roderigo also returned with him, and reported that he had sold the ship as requested, bringing a lot of goods in a new vessel, as well as handsome presents for Ieyasu, the Kuno clock, wine, scarlet cloth, cloaks, portraits of the King of Spain and his heir.

The first advances that Ieyasu made in the direction of Novispania were through the Jesuit Hieronimo de Jesus, who was deported by Hideyoshi but came back again when he heard that the Tokugawa house now ruled, owing to the reputation Ieyasu seems to have had for broad-mindedness, though his was the sort of broad-mindedness easily misunderstood. Anyhow, Ieyasu was not displeased to see him, and after inquiring about things in Manila suggested that he go back there and exert himself a bit to promote trade, at the same time engaging any shipbuilders, pilots, captains, or mining engineers who might be available for service in Japan.

Ieyasu was not altogether satisfied, for nothing much was said about trade or mining. "We don't want them to preach Buddhism (Christianity)," he said to Suden; "what we want is ships for trade. Write them a letter to that effect." Suden did so, and thus he wrote:

To His Excellency the Ruler of Novispania.

Your fragrant epistle is before me, and I have perused it without delay. The presents also I have received safely according to the invoice. During the past year the merchants of your honored country have been shipwrecked here from time to time owing to the severe gales on our shores. I have sent them back to you again, and rejoice to hear that they arrived safely. Your honored country and mine are thus strengthening the bonds of friendship, and if ships come every year and exchange the valuable commodities of our two territories even the best government cannot equal the benefit that will ensue to the land and its people. But this land is a Divine country. Since the beginning it has reverenced the Gods and respected the Buddhas. For these Gods and Buddhas are in reality one and the same, being but original form and extraneous manifestation. In the way of loyalty between lord and retainer, and in making firm and trustworthy agreements between the rulers of provinces the Deities are adjured to be witnesses of their faith. And those who do right they reward and those who do evil they punish. Their wondrous efficacy is as plain as an outstretched palm. Is not this the way of Benevolence, Duty, Etiquette, Knowledge, and Sincerity. But the religion that your honored country uses has tendencies of quite a different kind. There seems to be no affinity with anything in this land. In our texts it is written: "People of no affinity are difficult to estimate," so that as regards propaganda on reflection it seems better to cease from it and employ it no more. But the mutually profitable trade that will follow the arrival of merchant vessels is in the highest degree desirable. Therefore we have no objection to your ships calling at any port in any of our provinces. I have given strict orders to this effect to my officers, so set your mind at rest and banish all suspicion and doubt. I send you some products of this country in the accompanying package, which I trust you will accept. Pray take care of yourself in the increasing heat.

July, 1612.

There is no mistaking the meaning of this letter, though it is conveyed courteously enough. And it represents a convinced opinion that has not changed from that day to this. Tokutomi says of Ieyasu that his views on trade would have won the approval of Cobden and Bright and the Manchester School, and that he could see no ill results but only profit from association with foreign countries. But against Christianity he set his face as firmly as Hideyoshi had done, and for the same reason. Its beliefs and aims were quite incompatible with the past history and culture and the mentality of his people. It is not likely that Ieyasu would have objected to the Sermon on the Mount and similar things had he known of them. He would certainly have said they were summed up in the one word "Benevolence." But institutional Christianity was another matter. For that the Japanese never had any use at all.

Sotomayor, the envoy from New Spain, who arrived in 1611, preferred the following demands:

1. That the Spaniards be allowed to build what ships they liked in Japan.
2. That they be allowed to survey the Japanese coasts.
3. That the Spanish ships be allowed to sell their goods where they please and should not be searched.
4. That the Dutch be forbidden to trade in Japan, and that the Spaniards be allowed to send their warships to burn the Dutch vessels.

Ieyasu granted 1 and 2 and said nothing about 3, and told them that he could not interfere in the quarrels of foreign nations or expel any of them from Japan.

But the next year Ieyasu changed his policy with regard to foreign priests for several reasons. There was, in the first place, the affair of Okamoto Daihachi, secretary of Honda Kozuke-nosuke, who was a Christian, and who was bribed by Arima to get him back the territory he had lost. Okamoto forged a document handing over the lands to Arima and afterwards said it had been revoked owing to the slanders of Hasegawa Sahyoye, Governor of Nagasaki, and a disliker of Christians. This angered Arima, and he appealed directly to Ieyasu, who ordered investigations to be made so that the whole thing came out. The result was that Okamoto was burnt and Arima turned out of his fief, which was given to his son, who thereupon apostatized. Old Arima was afterwards exiled to Kai and eventually executed. In consequence of this Ieyasu turned out all his officers who were Christians. Another thing was his discovery of a conspiracy to use foreigners to overthrow the Shogunate. This was made on the death of a certain Okubo Nagayasu, who died in 1613. He had originally been a player of Sarugaku Noh in the family of Takeda but had been promoted to the rank of samurai and then to that of daimyo of Hachioji near Edo, with 30,000 koku, on account of his skill in working the mines for Ieyasu, and providing him with money for his campaigns at Sekigahara and Osaka without the necessity of taxing the people. He was appointed daikan of Izu in 1606. Ieyasu was rather fond of money, and it was a sure way to his favor to provide him with it. Now Okubo was a Christian, and it is by no means unlikely that there was a connection between his religion and his knowledge of mining, and as he was trusted by Ieyasu, who does not seem to have bothered about looking into the accounts very deeply, he took advantage of this to appropriate a good deal of money instead of paying it over. Becoming wealthy and luxurious, he went in for a number of concubines, to whom he was said (by them) to have promised large sums of money when he died. But when this sad event happened they did not get it, for the heir insisted that government accounts must be settled first. The concubines appealed to the Shogun, and Okubo's books were examined and his defalcations discovered, and also letters showing that he had proposed to call in foreign soldiers to overthrow Ieyasu. So, not unnaturally, his fief was confiscated and his sons put to death. Now Okubo's son had married the daughter of the chief retainer of Matsudaira Tadateru, daimyo of Echigo, sixth son of Ieyasu, and himself became one of his chief retainers, and this Tadateru had married a daughter of Date Masamune, who sent the embassy to Spain. Hence Tadateru also fell under suspicion with several others in connection with this affair, and was removed from his fief of 620,000 koku to a small one of 30,000, and kept under strict supervision all his days, which were many, for he lived to over ninety, and must have been thus the longest lived of all the Tokugawas, and he was rather fond of drink, too, it is said. But he was suspected of trying to plot against his brother Hidetada, and also in the Osaka campaign he did not behave at all well. At this siege Hideyori had on his side a number of Christian warriors with standards bearing Spanish insignia.

When Ieyasu asked Will Adams why the Spaniards wished to survey his coasts he was told this would be considered an act of hostility in Europe, and also that these priests had been expelled from England, Holland, and Scandinavia and part of Germany. Adams gave him an account of their doings in South America and the Indies, and this confirmed the boasts of Captain Landecho,* of the *San Felipe.* And since the Spaniards and Portuguese were on bad terms with each other, they gave each other away in their desire to do each other damage, and so corroborated what Adams had said. Moreover, there were several Japanese priests and Jesuits who repudiated their faith when they returned from Europe. And Ieyasu was a Jodo Buddhist, and favored several distinguished priests, especially Tenkai, afterward Lord Abbot of Ueno, and Takuan, and the first thing he did when entering Edo was to establish his family temple there, and it was his policy to use the Buddhist priesthood to assist him in the government. Like the Soviet Commissars he apparently regarded Buddhism as opium for the people, but unlike them he approved of it. Ieyasu had also sent a certain tea master, Nishi Soshin, to the West to investigate Christianity in the Keicho era (1596–1614), and he stayed there three years and became

---

* Enraged at the appropriation of his cargo by the Japanese, Landecho tried to impress on Hideyoshi's envoy an appreciation of the might of the King of Spain, and pointed out the extent of his dominions. Then in answer to the question how he had obtained them, he stated that priests were first sent to convert the people and afterwards soldiers who operated with these converts, and thus conquered the country.

a Christian, and then returned and gave Ieyasu a full account of all his experiences and views.

In 1614 Ieyasu issued an order that all Jesuits should leave Japan, but not foreign merchants, and though he forbade samurai and nobles to profess Christianity, he did not prohibit it in the case of farmers and tradesmen. In the September of this year sixty-three Jesuits and some Japanese Jesuits went to Manila accompanied by several distinguished Japanese, who were sent away to dic abroad. Among these were John Naito Hida-no-kami, aged seventy, his sister Julia, and his son Thomas, and Don Justo Takayama Ukon, who died soon afterwards in 1615.

CHAPTER 28

LUCHU AND FORMOSA

IN pursuance of its policy of creating opportunities for commerce both near and far the Bakufu encouraged operations against Luchu and Formosa as well as communications with Europe. In 1608 Shimazu Iehisa, who had recently been favored by Ieyasu with the gift of the first syllable of his name, and was perhaps anxious to show that he deserved it, sent a communication to the king of Luchu, calling his attention to the fact that he had not sent any envoy with tribute for a long time, though for ten generations he had stood in the position of vassal to the house of Shimazu, and should, as such, send an embassy every year to the Shogun in the usual way. This was, in fact, inspired by the Bakufu itself, which also suggested that if the Luchuan king did not agree to the proposal an expedition should be sent to compel him by force. The messengers sent by Shimazu were two Buddhist priests and a layman, and these went and confronted the king, Sho Nei, and his three generals, and explained their position, and demanded tribute. This, however, was refused, so the priestly envoys, having made a map of the islands and stolen a statue of Benten on the Waves carved by Nisshu Shonin of Ozumi in which the king put great faith, hurried back again to Shimazu.

Shimazu at once decided to send a force, and in the second month of the next year dispatched one of 1,500 men, 734 of them being matchlock men with 37,200 rounds of ammunition, under the command of Kabayama Hisataka, one of his chief retainers. Their firearms and their fighting capacity soon made short work of the Luchu men, though since the Satsuma side lost 300 men they evidently did what they could. The king was captured with his capital, and by the fifth month the campaign was over and the king being escorted to Japan, while Ieyasu was apprised by letter of the happy result. He sent a reply of truly martial brevity, conferring the conquered territory on Shimazu in two lines. It ran thus: "Concerning the matter of Luchu. That you have reported the subjugation in such a short time I consider a meritorious feat, and the country is hereby presented to you as will be more fully set forth later. Seventh month, seventh day, 1609. Ieyasu." This was an addition of land yielding between 80,000 and 90,000 koku to Shimazu's territory.

So the next year Shimazu Iehisa came up to Sumpu to return thanks to Ieyasu for this favor, bringing the Luchuan king with him. The king brought an offering of 10,000 ryo of silver, beside a very large quantity of various fabrics and a sword. Iehisa, too, presented other valuables, and they were elaborately entertained by Ieyasu for two days, his two younger sons, Yorinobu and Yorifusa, dancing before them. Iehisa was given a pair of swords by Sadamune. Clearly the old man was pleased.

Then the performance was repeated at Edo, where they were received in audience by the Shogun. To him also were given ten thousand pieces of silver and rich brocades and fabrics and swords for himself and his son Iemitsu. He, too, entertained them to banquets and to a Cha-no-yu party, at which he gave them tea with his own hand. Iehisa then sent a special letter to the Luchu officials, impressing on them how much the Shogunate wished for trade with China, and pointing out that they were well qualified to act as intermediaries in encouraging ships of both countries to call at their ports and finding out what commodities were most suitable for exchange.

Another project of Ieyasu was to use Formosa as a trading center for Japanese, Chinese, and Portuguese ships, for which its position made it very suitable since it was about halfway between Macao and Japan and just opposite to the important harbours of Fuchow and Amoy on the coast of China, to which country it paid tribute. And for this also he found Arima Harunobu a willing catspaw, and as the result of the suggestions of Honda Masazumi he prepared to send an expedition to the island to obtain information and if feasible establish a base there. In the articles of the instructions he issued to his officers, still extant in the annals of his house, his object is very clear. They begin by giving the usual pretext that Formosa had omitted to send envoys to the Japanese rulers bearing their compliments and presents, as it was the duty of all decent foreigners to do, and the omission of which was a definite sign of rascality. Therefore this was to be first demanded of them. As to the presents they might be what they pleased. Then a suitable site for a port was to be decided on, and arrangements made for Chinese ships to trade there. The island was also to be carefully surveyed from one end to the other, and a map of it drawn up. The people were to be treated kindly and given anything they might like to have to put them in a good humor, but if they should be unreasonable and refuse to do what they were asked hostages were to be taken forcibly and brought back to Japan. It ends with the order that anyone in the expedition who is refractory or disobedient shall be told to commit seppuku at once, and is dated in the second month of 1609, the same month as the Luchuan expedition of Shimazu. But though the purpose of the two expeditions was much the same the results were very different, for the savage inhabitants of Formosa added violence to impoliteness, and attacked and very roughly handled Arima's men, of whom many were killed and wounded, though they did with some difficulty manage to take several aboriginals prisoner. These they took back to Japan and presented to Ieyasu, who freed them, gave them presents, and sent them back home. Japanese ships seem to have called at Formosa frequently after this, but no attempt was made to conquer the island till 1616, when with the permission of the Bakufu Murayama Tōan the daikwan of Nagasaki sent another expedition consisting of thirteen vessels, but they were dispersed by a violent storm and some were wrecked on the China coast and only a few reached Formosa, where again their crews were attacked and most of them killed by these sturdy aboriginals, who have been a thorn in the side of Japan ever since, for they are animals who defend themselves very decidedly when attacked.

CHAPTER 29

THE "MADRE DE DIOS" AFFAIR

THOUGH Ieyasu's relations with foreign countries were almost uniformly those of courtesy he did not refrain from punishing what he considered an insult when he thought it advisable. There was, for instance, the affair of the *Madre de Dios,* the Portuguese galleon that he caused to be destroyed at Nagasaki. Ieyasu wanted some of the incense wood called Kyara, and requested Hasegawa Fujihiro, the Bugyo of Nagasaki, to get it from Champa. But as none had arrived from there lately this was not possible, but Arima Harunobu happening to hear of it sent some that he had which Ieyasu was pleased to accept, and as a token of his appreciation sent him a present and a sum of money with which to procure more.

So at the beginning of 1609 Arima fitted out a ship under the command of a naturalized Chinese named Kyubei and with six of his retainers on board it set out for Champa. But on the way they put in to the port of Macao, and while waiting there for a favorable wind a quarrel broke out between the Japanese and some servants of the Portuguese factory and some of the latter were killed. Then a lot of Portuguese sailors retaliated by attacking the Japanese, killing five of them and taking their property. At this Kyubei fled to China, and thence went back to Nagasaki, which he reached in the ninth month.

In great wrath Arima took him up to Sumpu and laid the matter before Ieyasu, who told him to report the arrival of the next Portuguese ship at Nagasaki. This was the *Madre de Dios,* under command of that very Pessoa who had been governor of Macao when the trouble occurred. Arima at once sent word to Sumpu and Ieyasu ordered Arima and some other neighboring feudatories to attack and sink it. But Arima regarded it as a special enemy of his own, and requested that he should be allowed to avenge the insult single-handed, to which Ieyasu agreed. His first intention was to lure the captain on shore and take him prisoner, and at his request Hasegawa invited Pessoa to discuss business matters, but the missionaries warned him and he would not come. Moreover, he at once made preparations to set sail again. He had a cargo valued at a million crowns on board, as well as a dozen Jesuits, and no doubt felt his responsibilities both toward God and Mammon.

Then Arima, declaring that he would have to commit seppuku if Pessoa escaped, ordered two of his men to go on board apparently unarmed, but with daggers concealed in their clothes and so assassinate him. But this also failed, for the Portuguese opened fire on the boat and set sail. They had to anchor before they had got out of the bay, however, owing to a contrary wind and sea, and then Arima sent out a flotilla of six war vessels to attack them. His younger brother Sumitada took command of them as his deputy. First of all they tried to burn the *Madre de Dios* by sending a number of fire ships down the wind against it. They were fishing boats loaded with hay and the thatch and debris of some peasants' houses that were pulled down for the purpose, but they were not effective. Then Arima procured two big sailing vessels and built a tower on them to the same height as the foreign vessel, and at eight o'clock in the evening of the ninth of the twelfth month with these and his six other ships he launched a general attack on it. The Portuguese went to throw fire-pots at the towers to destroy them when one burst on the ship and set fire to the sails and rigging. The Japanese ships sheered off to escape the flames and the explosion they expected to result. So Pessoa, surrounded by his enemies and unable to do anymore, fired the magazine, and the galleon blew up and sank two hours after the battle commenced. The losses on the side of the Japanese were sixteen men, and two hundred went down with the ship.

Arima immediately set out for Sumpu and reported to Ieyasu, who congratulated him heartily, and presented him with a sword by Nagamitsu and the goods recovered from the galleon. It was then made known to Hidetada and he, too, through Honda Masonobu sent his thanks. Altogether the lord Arima must have been well recompensed for his trouble as well as revenged, for the goods recovered included 200,000 ryo of silver, the same number of pounds of silk thread, gold chains and rings, damask and brocade, weapons and musical instruments, and so forth. And the loss was at the expense of the missionaries, who lost the supplies that they were expecting by the annual ship and had to curtail their expenses, shut up their schools, and in some cases live on charity. And incidentally the price of silk thread in Kyoto rose to exactly double on account of the shortage.

Naturally the Portuguese authorities could not let this incident pass without a protest, and in 1611 an envoy came from Goa to Ieyasu bringing letters from the Governor-General there and also from the Governor of Manila asking the reason for the destruction of the *Madre de Dios,* requesting the resumption of trade relations and assuring him of their respect and goodwill.

They were well received by both Ieyasu and the Shogun, though according to the Dutch account Ieyasu received their presents but said not a word in return. Anyhow, according to all accounts the demands for an indemnity and the dismissal of the Nagasaki Bugyo who had given incorrect information, as the envoy maintained, were resented by Ieyasu, who said that he had no objection to the resumption of relations but he could not allow any interference by outsiders with the government of the country. A written reply was also sent drawn up by Hayashi Doshun as from "Nihon-koku Shitsuji Kozuke-no-suke Fuji-wara Masazumi, i.e. Honda Masazumi the Administrator of the Empire of Japan," in which he pointed out that the captain was the only person against whom they had any grudge, and that it was only because he had refused to answer the summons of the Government to discuss the matter, though invited more than once, and not only so but had fired on them, that they proceeded to attack his vessel to arrest him according to the law of the country, and that they had had no intention of attacking or damaging anyone else, so that it was only Pessoa who was responsible for what had happened. Appended to this was the Shogun's licence to trade in the following laconic form:

Messengers have come from Goa with the request that the black ships be allowed to come to this country, to which there is no objection. According to the rules of commerce they may trade as in former days. If anyone opposes this he shall be punished as a criminal. Let this be well known.

Sixteenth year of Keicho (1611)
Season of Spring.
August Red Seal.

In the second month of 1610 the four families were permitted to give a subscription Noh performance in the grounds of Momijiyama, and Ieyasu himself was to be present. All the great daimyos and house retainers were given boxes to see it. When the plan of the boxes was submitted to the Shogun beforehand he at once remarked: "Why are the houses of Mizutani and Minagawa omitted? I don't see their names. They are retainers that have followed my house ever since the old Mikawa days, and are equal to any veteran vassals." Honda Masanobu and Okubo Tadachika, who were in waiting, replied that both of them were absent on guard duty at Kasama castle. "But warriors are very jealous of prestige," replied Ieyasu, "and if they are not invited to the performance they will be hurt. If they themselves cannot attend, then invite their chief councilors and give them a box. It will prove that they have not been overlooked." And they did so, and the two families were deeply gratified at this consideration.

In the third month of 1612 Ieyasu was by Imperial Edict appointed Chancellor of the Empire (Sōkoku), and permitted the use of the Chrysanthemum and Paulownia crests. He declined the title of Chancellor, however, but requested that of Chinjufu Shogun for his house ancestor, Nitta Oinosuke Yoshishige, and that of Dainagon for his late father, Okazaki Jirosaburo Hirotada. His filial feeling was much admired by the Emperor, who at once consented. With regard to the grant of the use of the Imperial crests, too, he expressed his sincere gratitude, but urged that since the dividing of the Nitta and Ashikaga branches of the Minamoto clan the Ashikaga had seized the military power and acted despotically, and Takauji had received the grant of these crests from Go-Daigo Tenno and the family had continued to use them ever since, but that he, representing the loyal house of Nitta, did not consider it proper to follow the example of such predecessors.

After proceeding to the capital to return thanks for these honors in the eleventh month of the same year, he sent Doi Toshikatsu and Naruse Hayato to Nitta in Kazusa to search out the tomb of Yoshishige, and built a temple there which he called Gijusan Taiko-in (Giju = Yoshishige), which he endowed, and there he had the Edict of Imperial Appointment deposited. He also built in Okazaki the Shōōji temple, and in the first month of the year following (1613) he proceeded from Suruga to Mikawa, and went to the Daijuji and inspected his ancestral monuments, scraping off the moss that had encrusted some of the most ancient ones with his own fingernail and examining them closely. He then visited the Shōōji to inaugurate the new mausoleum of his father, presenting silver and other things to the abbot. And all this was of the greatest value in impressing on all the Empire the great importance of filial duty, so that all were stimulated to be mindful not to neglect their ancestors and the observance of respect for them became universal. No doubt, especially during the period of civil war, ancestors had been treated with as little respect as living parents sometimes were.

CHAPTER 30

THE FALL OF OKUBO TADACHIKA

IF Ieyasu did not hesitate to deal drastically with members of his own family when they failed to live up to their responsibilities or did anything that might jeopardize the Tokugawa interests, it was not likely that he would be less severe with his old retainers. Though he was an autocrat who decided everything of any importance himself, and could not be said to have any ministers, he depended on these veteran councilors for advice and information, and they were very much in his confidence. Moreover, it was to their families that he looked to support his house after his death, so the elimination of any doubtful one would be very necessary. These fudai retainers did not get very large fiefs, and this seems to have caused some discontent among them at first if some of the current stories are to be believed. One is to the effect that Ii, Sakakibara, and Honda Tadakatsu had their estates surveyed after they received them, and were informed by the surveyors that they were actually worth in each case about 80,000 koku less than their face value. As they were all about 200,000 koku, this was a considerable loss, and they were not pleased. The contrast between the large revenues of the Tozama daimyos like Shimazu and Maeda and others and their own modest stipends was rather glaring, but Ieyasu could hardly interfere with these just then, though as time went on means were found to harass them financially. It is significant that when Ii, Honda, and Sakakibara, and Sakai were first given daimyos' fiefs Hideyoshi had asked Ieyasu how much he was going to give them, and he, remembering Hideyoshi's trick of trying to put other people under obligations to him, told him just half the amount he had decided on. As he expected Hideyoshi at once recommended that they be given double and Ieyasu agreed, thus gaining an increased reputation for docility with Hideyoshi without paying anything for it, for had he said what he originally intended to give Hideyoshi would certainly have doubled that. Nothing further happened in the case of these fudai lords, however, but though Okubo Tadachika was an equally trusted councilor and his house had been retainers of the Tokugawa family from the earliest days, this did not save him when their suspicions were really aroused.

Tadachika was the son of Okubo Tadayo, who had been always at the side of Ieyasu as a warrior and as a councilor, and the son followed in his steps. He fought with Ieyasu at the Anegawa and at Mikata-ga-hara, and at Nagakute was with him as captain of his bodyguard, and on all these occasions acquitted himself with distinction. He was made guardian to Hidetada, and it was his presence of mind that saved him from being enticed by Hidetsugu to his mansion and made a hostage. His son Tadatsune was married to Ieyasu's granddaughter, the child of Okudaira Nobumasa and O Kame. But he did not get on with Honda Masanobu. This was said to have started from a quarrel they had when both were on the staff of the division that Hidetada led at the Sekiga-hara campaign, and which was held up by Sanada so that it could not take part in the battle. But anyhow they were rivals, and that alone may have explained it. And so Okubo's downfall is sometimes attributed to the slanders of Honda. Probably, however, Ieyasu would not be so easily influenced by any individual, and had much more weighty reasons for the action he took. It was from Tadachika that Okubo Nagayasu,* the superintendent of the gold and silver mines who had worked such large frauds, had his surname, for in his early days he had been without one, and his patron seems to have been suspected of having been privy to or at least very careless about these defalcations.

He cannot very well have been ignorant of the very notorious lux-ury and arrogance of Nagayasu, and though he was supposed to be a confidential adviser of Ieyasu he neither rebuked his namesake nor said anything about his conduct. Then, again, when his son Tadatsune became ill he remained at Odawara, the fief that he had inherited from his father, who had been given it at Hideyoshi's suggestion. It was a small one, only 45,000 koku, but an important place strategically, and the former capital of the Kwanto. For three years he did not come

---

* Okubo Nagayasu appears to have been one of a company of Noh actors who were brought from Kyoto to give a performance in the castle of Edo when Ieyasu was entertaining a large company both of his retainers and also of the townspeople to whom he gave some refreshments as well, and over them would appear to have chatted amiably. In the course of these remarks he observed that he had been fortunate enough to get on so well that beginning with only a half of the province of Mikawa he had come to be lord of the eight provinces of the Kwanto. In fact only Mori Terumoto now had as broad territories as he had, but all the same great as his landed possessions were he could not get as much gold and silver as he wanted. And without this he was apt to be cramped in his enterprises. To be able to save money one needed full storehouses, but that alone would not enable one to keep a lot of retainers. And without a large following one could not make either defensive or offensive war successfully. How to get this money, then, was what he would best like to know. These remarks were overheard by Okura Taiyu of the Komparu part of Noh actors, and through one of the Bugyo he sought an interview with Ieyasu suggesting that he knew of a way to make money. When admitted to audience he pointed out that to get capital from mining was the best way, since exacting it from the people by taxation would only make him unpopular, while if he conducted a survey of various likely spots and found precious metals there this would, on the other hand, make those places prosperous and his government more appreciated. Ieyasu naturally agreed, and inquired where he could find experts in this business, and was told that there were many in the neighborhood of Kyoto. He then asked Okura Taiyu whether he would not give up his present occupation and become Commissioner of Mines. To this he consented, and handing over his artistic heritage to his pupils started to organize the search for gold in Izu.

TOKUGAWA HIDETADA, IN COURT DRESS

to Edo at all, and he also dug another moat round part of the castle. And a short time before this a certain Yamaguchi Shigemasa had had his fief confiscated for marrying his son to the adopted daughter of Tadachika without the permission of the Bakufu, and this apparently angered Okubo so that he adopted a sulky attitude toward them. And when his son died a very large number of the Edo officials who had been his friends went down to Odawara to pay their respects without asking permission of their superiors, which annoyed Hidetada so much that he "gated" a number of them. Okubo had been for some time very profuse in his hospitality to the various daimyos of the region round the capital and gave expensive entertainments and kept open house to all and sundry. This also was not to the liking of either Edo or Sumpu.

So when at the end of the year 1613 as Ieyasu was on his way from the one to the other an old man named Baba Hachiemon, who had been a retainer of Anayama Baisetsu of Kai, stopped him and handed him some accusation against Okubo which he took so seriously that he went back to Edo and held a secret consultation with Hidetada and also with Honda Masanobu: soon after this an order was issued to Tadachika bidding him go to Kyoto and see that the inquisition against Christianity was being properly carried out. He therefore left Odawara and went to Kyoto accordingly.

The Bakufu then issued a statement to the effect that owing to his having arranged a marriage without the consent of the Shogun his son was to be evicted from the fief, and without any delay both Ieyasu and Hidetada, attended by the other councilors, the Hondas, Doi Yoshikatsu, Ando Naotsugu, and Ando Shigenobu, went to Odawara, and after another consultation there ordered the castle to be dismantled at once, and the walls and gates and other defenses were soon thrown down and destroyed by workmen impressed in the locality, assisted by a very large number brought down specially from Edo. Okubo himself was then ordered to proceed to Edo, and his samurai were all disbanded. Then in the second month of 1614 a pledge for the daimyos was issued by the Edo Bugyo in this form:

We have not the slightest suspicious intention toward the Shogun or the Retired Shogun. If we should come to know of anyone who has any such evil intentions or who transgresses the laws they have laid down even if they are our parents or children or brothers we will at once report it without concealment. Since Okubo Sagami-nokami has incurred the displeasure of the Shogun we will hold no communication with him or his son.

Sakai Uta-no-kami.
Sakai Bingo-no-kami.

Mizuno Kemmotsu.
Inoue Kazue-no-kami.

Doi Oi-no-kami.   Yonezu Kambei.
Ando Tsushima-no-kami.   Shimada Hyojiro.

Such was the fate of any daimyo who ran counter to the wishes or policy of the Shogunate, and such it continued to be for the next two hundred and fifty years. Exactly what was the real accusation against Okubo is not clear, but evidently for various reasons his removal was considered advisable. Ieyasu must have thought some danger threatened, for when he and Hidetada travelled back to Edo from Odawara they had the Tokaido highway closed from Mishima to Oiso and Hiratsuka, while along the Hakone pass guards armed with bow and matchlock were posted every 30 feet, a precaution hitherto unknown. In the annals of the house of Okubo it is written that Katagiri Katsurnoto informed Ieyasu through Baba Hachiemon that Tadachika was making treasonable communications to Hideyori, and though this does not seem very probable, it is more than likely that one of the counts against him was that he sympathized with the house of Toyotomi and dared to oppose Ieyasu's plan for overthrowing it. At any rate, this sudden and severe punishment of one of the oldest members of the inner circle of the Shogunate council was meant to be a very salutary example to any others who might be inclined to behave in an independent, ostentatious, or disrespectful manner, and so imperil the solidarity of the governing body.

CHAPTER 31

THE ENGLISH COMPANY

WHEN the English merchants of London heard that the Dutch authorities had received a letter from Ieyasu inviting them to trade in Japan, they thought that they too might share in the venture, and ordered John Saris to proceed there to try his luck. He was to rely on the assistance of Adams, who had sent letters home describing the situation.

The English East India Company, founded in 1600, was nothing like as wealthy as the Dutch, the capital of the latter being about £600,000, while the English had only £70,000. It is interesting to note that as far back as 1583 Queen Elizabeth had sent John Mildenhall with a letter to the Court of Akbar, the Mogul Emperor of India, born in the same year as Ieyasu, rather like him to look at, and perhaps the greatest monarch of his age. On his way Mildenhall had called also on the Sultan Ahmed at Constantinople, another great monarch, for Turkey, owing to the might of a succession of extremely able Sultans, among whom the previous ruler, Suleyman the Magnificent, was most distinguished, was supreme from Mecca and Baghdad to Budapest, Cairo, and Algiers. In fact the world was then a very Mongol-dominated one. And in India, too, the Jesuits had bribed the ministers of Akbar to hinder the English envoy just as they had tried to do in the Far East, but without success, for he managed to circumvent them, and eventually an edict was issued granting him the privileges he wanted.

Later on, in 1611, three English ships under John Saris and John Best had beaten four galleons and twenty-six galleys of the Portuguese off Surat, thus clearing the way to the Far East, and lowering the prestige of the Portuguese in the eyes of the Great Mogul.

In 1613 the *Clove* with Saris on board arrived at Hirado, where the Dutch had been persuaded to establish their factory through the persistent maneuvers of its lord Matsuura Shigenobu, who gave them also a warm welcome. Ieyasu, when informed of their arrival by Adams, expressed his satisfaction, telling them that he rejoiced that strange nations had such a good opinion of his country as to come so far to see it.

Adams went down to greet Saris, who was rather offended by his refusal to stay in his house, for he preferred to put up with the Bugyo Zenzaburo—the Zanzibar of Saris—and generally gave the impression

of being very pro-Japanese in all his ways. Saris was then escorted by
him to Sumpu and presented to Ieyasu, after which he was taken to
Edo and received in audience by Hidetada. Adams then took him to
his own estate at Uraga.

The description of the reception of the mission runs thus: "On
the fourth day of the eighth month of the eighteenth year of Keicho
(1613) the envoy of the King of Ingarateira came to Sumpu to pay his
respects. It was the first time anyone had come from this country. He
brought a letter written on heavy waxed paper 2 feet wide by 1(½) feet
long, with pictures on the margin on three sides, folded in three, and
then again folded in two, with seals attached by paper. The writing was
in the 'Namban' letters, and could not be understood, so we got 'Anji'
(Adams) to write it down in Kana. It ran as follows:

"King Zemeshi (James) writes to say that by the grace of Heaven he has
been King of Great Britain, France, and Ireland for eleven years. And since
the might of the Shogun of Japan has become widely known throughout the
world, it has of a certainty been heard of in our country. Therefore we have
sent Captain General Juan Saris as our representative across the seas to bear our
greetings to the Shogun of Japan, and if so it may be that the affairs of both
our countries can thus be widely made known our satisfaction will indeed be
great. If, therefore, it can be arranged that several merchant ships can be sent
every year from henceforth the merchants on both sides will be more friendly
and will be enabled to buy and sell the commodities they mutually desire.
And moreover if it be the wish of the Shogun Sama of Japan by his goodwill
merchants may be allowed to remain in his country and so increase the harmonious intercourse between the two peoples. And then we will freely invite
Japanese merchants to come to our country that they may buy and sell, and
that we may always be able to communicate with Japan frankly and without
any reserve. This is what I would have you understand.

"The King of Great Britain
At his Castle of Westminster
James Rex.

To the Shogun Sama of Japan."

Anxious as Ieyasu was to profit by foreign trade, and willing to be
liberal to the countrymen of Adams, he proceeded to make out for the
English a very generous patent for trade with the following letter to
the King:

Minamoto Ieyasu replies to His Highness the Lord of Igarateira.

I have for the first time received tidings of Your Highness by the envoy
who has made this long and wearying journey. The Dominion that proceeds
from Your Honored Palace as set forth on paper is obviously one that is on the
right lines, and especially so in its activity in the matter of shipping whereby
great prosperity has been achieved.

And I am most pleased to accede to your wishes concerning the encouraging of communication between our countries and the provision of facilities for maritime trade. Though separated by myriads of miles of sea and sky we may in this way well be said to become like near neighbors.

Some small complimentary gifts I send in a separate package. This is just a small token of goodwill. Spare yourself as the climate changes.

Oct. 8, 1613.
August Seal.

Accompaniment. Five sets of Gold Screens.

The licence to trade contained seven articles:

1. As to these ships that are the first to come to Japan, they are permitted to trade in all commodities. They have all official permission for navigation.
2. As to the freight that they carry this shall be landed as they will.
3. There is no objection to their landing at any port in Nippon, and they may put in to any haven or shore if they should chance to meet with storms or be disabled in sails or gear.
4. They shall be granted land and premises in Edo if they wish, and shall be permitted to build houses and reside there and engage in trade. Moreover, the Englishmen shall return home whenever it may seem good to them, and the houses they have built shall be disposed of as they will.
5. Should any of the Englishmen die in Japan, his property shall be handed over without question.
6. In the matter of their goods there shall be no forced selling or lawless conduct.
7. Should there be any disorderly fellow among the Englishmen, the degree of his guilt and punishment shall be judged by the English General.

Keicho, 18.8.28.   August Red Seal.*

However, in spite of this invitation to make his headquarters in the Edo district Saris determined to stay at Hirado, evidently thinking that he would be more independent of Adams there, for he suspected that the Pilot would try to work matters to his own advantage and to that of his friends the Dutch and Japanese, and try to use the Company for his own purposes. Saris was a headstrong and self-opinionated person, who did not realize that considerable special knowledge was necessary to trade successfully in Japan. He did not perceive, for instance, that it would be a much more expensive business to give presents to the daimyo and his councilors than to the Shogun, who was not in want

---

* Ieyasu also inquired whether the English were intending to try to find the North or Northwest Passage, and promised to give them in that event an introduction to his officials in Ezo.

of money. "A present for the Emperor, one for the King, and two or three others for the secretaries" was all that was needed there, and these latter, the Hondas, were famous for their indifference to such offerings, as well they might be under the keen eye of such a master. But it was the business of the government to keep the daimyos short of funds, and Saris soon found that beside the many complimentary presents he had to make, Matsuura was always trying to borrow money, or raise it at his expense to meet his various commitments, "being at his shifts," in the words of the diary, to go to Edo and for other reasons. For "Old King Foyne," as the English styled him, was only a small lord, and was chronically hard up. Moreover, at Edo there was no Dutch competition, and it is possible that the Company would have been better treated later had it been in the capital.

However, Saris thought it better to employ Adams, "we being wholly destitute of language," and after some haggling he was given a salary of a hundred a year, though Saris would not allow him to handle any money. Adams* was now quite reasonably well off, though he never accumulated much wealth in Japan. Still he was a hatamoto, or direct retainer, of the Shogun, with a village and eighty or ninety farmers to work for him at Hemmi, near Uraga. He had a house in Edo too, the site of which has been commemorated by the name Anjin-cho, given to a street in Uogashi in Nihon-bashi ward, just as the well-known street Yaesu-cho recalls his Dutch contemporary Jan Joosten Lodensteyn, who also won the favor of Ieyasu. He had the privilege of audience with Ieyasu at all times, "even when kings and princes are kept out." Ieyasu seems to have used him as a kind of Metsuke, for Cocks in his diary writes: "November 1615. Captain Coppindall advised me how well the Emperour (Ieyasu) did receive the present he carid him, and gave him another of 5 kerremons, 10 pike heads, 100 arrow heads, and 3 waccadashes, and hath given his letter to the King of Shashman (Satsuma) for trad into all his dominions." He also writes: "He, the Emperour, sent Capt. Adames to Edo to the padres to know wherefore they are com in to his dominions, he having formerly banished all of their coate out of his dominions. He also hath made proclamation under pain of death that no Japon shall goe into New Spaine from henceforward. These padres are com now out of New Spaine."

Still there is no evidence that Adams ever used his position at Court

---

* Adams had married a Japanese girl who is said to have been a Catholic, the daughter of one Magome Kageyu, who was superintendent of the packhorse exchange at Demma-cho, and apparently a man of some means though what his rank was is not clear. Probably the family of one who devised communications on land was considered suitable for alliance with one who did the same for those on the sea. Magome is probably the "Migmoy," nicknamed "Machiavelli," of Cocks's diary. He seems to have been an agent for the Company at Edo, but evidently not a particularly trusted one judging from what is there said of him.

to make money as Saris suspected. Murdoch evidently thinks of Saris in terms of the less desirable foreign merchant of later days, summing him up as "at bottom not much better than a mere dollar-grinding Philistine with a taste for pornographic pictures." But his position was a difficult one, for the Dutch competition, backed by much greater capital, was too much for him and his successor Cocks. As the Dutch had a monopoly of trade with the Moluccas, they used to capture English ships that tried to trade there and bring them in to Hirado as prizes, which hardly added to the respect in which the Japanese held the English. And after the death of Ieyasu the attitude of the Government to foreigners altered. Hidetada considered that the Europeans, their religion, and their trade were likely to be a menace to the nation and to the house of Tokugawa, and commenced to hamper them and refuse facilities of doing business. As the letters well put it, "things were not as they were in the old man's days." Trade was restricted to Hirado, and could not be carried on elsewhere. However, in 1619 the Dutch and English made an agreement called the Treaty of Defense, which was actually a treaty of attack upon the Portuguese and Spanish ships and Chinese junks trading with the Philippines. They made more by this than by honest trading, for they took some £100,000 worth of plunder from their two expeditions against Manila and elsewhere. But the English could not afford to put their share of money and ships into this profitable enterprise, and so in 1622 they fell out. In 1623 took place the massacre of Amboyna, in which the English captain with nine others and nine Japanese and one Portuguese were tortured and then executed on a charge of having plotted to surprise the garrison. Amboyna had been the principal base of the Dutch until they founded Batavia in Java in 1619. This massacre forced the English to retire and concentrate on India. And so they left their buildings and their bad debts, and Hirado several thousand pounds out of pocket by the adventure, but perhaps not sorry, for being restricted to Hirado and Nagasaki was irritating. Anyhow they introduced the potato into Japan, this still being known as Jagatara-imo, or Jacatra potato, to distinguish it from the Satsuma or sweet variety. And they left voluntarily, and were not subjected to any of the humiliating conditions which attended the conserving of their trading privileges by the Dutch in Deshima. That was something.

CHAPTER 32

DATE MASAMUNE'S MISSION TO EUROPE

MEANWHILE the Western daimyos were not the only ones who saw the advantages of encouraging trade with Europe, for in 1613 Date Masamune, the "One-eyed Dragon" of Sendai, contrived to send one of his councilors, Hasekura Rokuemon, on an embassy to the Pope, accompanied by Father Sotelo, a Franciscan monk, who had been condemned to death for coming back to Edo and preaching there after this was prohibited by the Shogun, but whose pardon Date had obtained for purposes of his own. Sotelo had a knowledge of medicine, then as now used as a bait for religion in the East, and had cured one of Date's ladies of some disease, which pleased him greatly, so that he offered the father a large reward in gold and silver and silk, which the priest refused, declaring that these things were done for the sake of his "Way." Whereupon Date received him and some other missionaries in audience as a great honor, and they presented him with many pounds of bread and cloves and candles and pepper, and became very friendly with him, and he gave them a temple in Sendai, and even deigned to go and hear Sotelo preach. The friar seems to have spoken Japanese very well. Then Date suggested that he should conduct a mission to Rome on his behalf, and consulted Ieyasu about the matter, and he agreed. In this way Date saw a chance of opening up trade relations with New Spain, which lay directly opposite his fief, and it is also not impossible that he thought he might thereby get assistance to overthrow Ieyasu, or anyhow he was suspected of some such design, and was certainly cunning enough for anything. But Ieyasu, as usual, thought he too saw an opportunity of using Date to encourage this commerce for his own benefit. Father Sotelo thought he would use the pair of them to get the means of proceeding to Europe as Ambassador to the Pope, and so get himself appointed Archbishop of Japan. And there was yet another person who wanted to use this mission to get a free passage home, and that was Sebastian Viszcaino. He was a Spaniard who had been sent out to bear a message of thanks to Ieyasu for his kindness to Don Roderigo, and at the same time to search for the Isles of Gold and Silver, which were supposed to exist in or near Japan. He brought various presents to Ieyasu of portraits of the King and Queen of Spain, clothes, wine, and the famous clock which is still preserved at Kunozan but he did not bring what Ieyasu had so specially asked for, experts in mining. However, when he asked for permission to survey the Japanese coasts to find this El Dorado he obtained it, and Ieyasu had a letter given to him requesting the coastal daimyos to give him every facility. When they heard of this the English and Dutch said it was only an act of espionage on the part of Spain, and a preparation for sending an army to conquer Japan. Ieyasu replied that he did not fear foreign countries, for he had quite enough troops to deal with any of them if they did come. He would have been very pleased if Viszcaino had at his own expense found islands of these precious metals, for if they had been in Japanese territory he would have claimed them. And if not, he still saw possibilities of trade with New Spain. So Viszcaino surveyed the coast from Akita to Nagasaki, and in so doing he met Date, always on the alert, and was persuaded to act as the commander of the ship as he had such experience in navigation. It goes without saying that he found no treasure islands, all he met was people like Ieyasu and Masamune, of little use to anyone like him. And so he was distinctly disgruntled, and his feelings towards the Japanese were anything but friendly. So he was not sorry to be engaged as captain of the ship by Date perhaps only for want of a better, and he did his best to quarrel with everyone on board. With some reason does Tokutomi describe this ship's company as directed by a combination of those who wished to use trade for the Kingdom of Heaven and of those who wished to use the Kingdom of Heaven for trade.

Ieyasu's own admiral, Mukai Shogen, went to Sendai to superintend the building of the ship, which was of cryptomeria wood, 36 feet wide and 108 feet long, with a mast 99 feet high. So Hasekura Rokuemon and five other officers of the Sendai clan, with five more of lower rank, for their surnames are not given, as well as ten retainers of Mukai Shogen and forty "Southern Barbarians" embarked in it, one hundred and eighty in all, beside some merchants.

The voyage was not exactly a harmonious one, for so little could the commander Viszcaino agree with the Japanese that they quarrelled openly and threatened his life, so that he had to retire from his post as captain and become an ordinary passenger. And he took the first opportunity he could of getting off at the first port they reached, which was that of Zakatula, and went home to his father in Spain. His diary exists in an unpublished collection of documents relating to the discovery, conquest, and organization of the Spanish dominions in America and Oceania.

They went on from Zakatula to Acapulco, which they reached in January 1613. Thence to Mexico, where seventy-eight of Hasekura's

IEYASU'S CLOCK, PRESENTED BY THE SPANISH
ENVOY. INSCRIBED "MADE IN MADRID, 1581"

suite were baptized in the cathedral of S. Francisco. Hasekura was anxious to join in, but was advised to have it done in Madrid, where it would be more ceremonial and produce a more striking effect. They then crossed the isthmus to Vera Cruz and set sail once more from S. Juan de Ulloa. Then to Havana, Seville, Cordova, Toledo, and Madrid. All through Spain their expenses were paid by the Spanish king, and Sotelo and Hasekura were received in audience by him, Sotelo presenting an old dispatch from Ieyasu that he had been given in 1610, when he had intended to go, but was prevented by illness. Hasekura was baptized in great style by the Royal Chaplain, acting as deputy for the Archbishop of Toledo, his godfather being the Duke of Lerma and his godmother the Countess of Barachia. They stayed in Spain eight months, visiting Alcala, Guadalajara, Zaragosa, Lerida, and Barcelona, and then to Italy to Savoia and Genoa, where they were welcomed and fêted much as the former embassy of the Kyushu daimyos had been. Then they proceeded to Rome, and were received by the Pope, and Hasekura also received the honor of Roman citizenship, the Latin document conferring this being still in existence in Japan in the annals of the house of Date, just as the originals of Masamune's letters are still preserved in Spain.

In these he observes that he has great respect for Christianity, though he is hindered in becoming a convert by an obstacle. In another place he says: "There is a great obstacle to my becoming one, but I wish to make all my vassals Christians, and in order to do so I wish you to send me some 'baterens' of the order of S. Francis. I will treat them kindly." The obstacle was, of course, Ieyasu. He goes on to say that he will send ships to New Spain every year, and hopes they will be assisted by the king. It is by this route that he supposes the Franciscans may come.

However, the bona fides of the embassy were distinctly suspect, for the Jesuits wrote home objecting to it, saying that it was not from the ruler of Japan, but from a subject. Moreover, Sebastian Viszcaino also lifted up his voice in accusation, declaring that its real object was nothing but trade, and that the Japanese had little love for Christianity, and worst of all that Ieyasu and Hidetada were Protestants. That Date had sent these people without the knowledge of Ieyasu or the other missionaries, which was not true. He said that Sotelo was quite misrepresenting the case when he said that the Japanese wished fathers to come, for they did not, and recognized that Christianity was quite incompatible with the lives they led, and had no liking for it. He referred also to the slanderous statements of the Dutch to Ieyasu and Hidetada that the Spanish king meant to use converts as a means of trying to annex Japan. This appears, too, from the letters of the Venetian Ambassador in Rome, Simon Contarini, who says that the mission is not satisfied because of the three requests it made only one was granted in a modified form, and that was that His Holiness should receive under his protection Date Masamune "as a Sovereign Prince, who was on his way to ascend the throne of the Mikado!" The Pope excused himself in the matter of the other two things by saying he must consult the King of Spain before appointing a bishop or sending monks. The Venetian thinks he fears that the king will try to make these places Spanish territory rather than papal. He also says that Sotelo said that "his king, being next in power and dignity to the Emperor (Shogun), would try to supplant him, and then he would not only declare himself a Christian and the obedient servant of the Church of Rome, but would afterwards compel all other princes of the country to do the same." This is very reminiscent of Hideyoshi's intentions towards the Chinese if the Portuguese would sell him a couple of galleons to assist in conquering them.

Bishop Cercyra, too, in his letter to the Jesuit general, deplores this mission, and says he has done all he could to prevent it, for its real object is not any propaganda at all, but only "the expectation of great material benefits on the part of Masamune by the arrival of Spanish ships in his ports, and there is danger if it is successful, seeing that the Lord of the Empire and the Prince his son do not want any Franciscans in the Kwanto, and if they come it may exasperate the king against Masamune and cause him to suspect that there exists some ominous alliance between him and the Spaniards so that he may give vent to his indignation in causing the total ruin of the latter, for his estates are entirely dependent on the king's good-will, who may deprive him of them as well as of his life whenever he may think it convenient to do so." When the embassy arrived again in Japan Christianity was less in favor than ever, and the report of Hasekura was that in Europe it was "nothing but a vain show." So none of the promoters of the mission gained much, except it was the Bakufu that profited by the information it brought back. Which was just what Ieyasu had intended.

CHAPTER 33

IEYASU AND HIDEYORI

HIDEYORI was residing in Osaka castle with an income of 637,400 koku, and after the death of Maeda Toshiie in 1599 Katagiri Katsumoto became his guardian. Katagiri was given a fief of 28,000 koku at Tatsuta in Yamato by Ieyasu, and it may be he that managed to keep Hideyori clear of the schemes of Ishida. In 1601 Ieyasu had built the castle of Nijo to dominate Kyoto, already flanked by those of Fushimi and Zeze. In 1603 Hideyori was married to Sen-hime, daughter of Hidetada. Then in 1605 Ieyasu retired from the office of Shogun in favor of Hidetada, and the new Shogun came up to Kyoto to receive his commission from the Emperor with an army of seventy thousand men. On this occasion Ieyasu tried to get Hideyori to go to Edo and visit his father-in-law, and certainly he would have no fear on the way with such a large escort, but his mother Yodo saw through the plan and objected strongly, declaring that she would cut her son open herself rather than that he should leave Osaka.

At the end of Hideyoshi's life there were in the Empire two hundred and fourteen lords of more than 10,000 koku, and of these eighty-seven fought for the Western army at Sekigahara. Eighty-one of them lost either their life or their fief or their freedom as the result, and only seven were left to be a possible thorn in the side of the Tokugawas. But only Shimazu and Nabeshima still kept their original incomes, while Mori and Uesugi and the others were much reduced, and all regarded themselves as lucky and had no wish to tempt providence again, so that the new Shogunate had nothing at all to fear from their activity. On the other hand there were now a hundred and ninety new daimyos of more than 10,000 koku, and of these half consisted of members of the Tokugawa house and its hereditary retainers, while of the other Tozama daimyos more than two-thirds were in practically the same dependent position as the fudai, and had no interest in identifying themselves with the fortunes of the Toyotomi family.

Moreover, they were kept hard at it emptying their pockets over the building of Edo and the other castles, for which work they hastened to offer their willing services lest they lose favor in the sight of Ieyasu and worse befall them. They were, too, all domiciled in Edo with their families, making the best of their position as hostages in the city they had been at so much pains to build.

It was characteristic, perhaps, that in 1609, second month, Date Masamune made proclamation that he had changed his name to Matsudaira Mutsu-no-kami from his former style of Hashiba Echizen-no-kami, assumed during, and in honor of, Hideyoshi. There was no better weathercock in Japan than Date, and Ieyasu must have grinned when he heard of it. Date paid well for the honor too, for he presented a hundred pieces of gold, two horses, ten embroidered nightdresses, and two short swords, as well as five pieces of gold each to five of the ladies-in-waiting, since so much of the business was done through their good offices nowadays.

And that was not all. Unfortunately for Hideyori almost all of the old friends of his father proceeded to die one after the other. In 1611 Asano Nagamasa (aet. 65), Kato Kiyomasa (53), and Horio Yoshiharu (69) went off to their white jade pavilions, and in 1613 Ikeda Terumasa (50) and Asano Yukinaga (38) followed them, while the year after Maeda Toshinaga (53) departed also.

How far the most influential of these, Kato Kiyomasa and Asano Yukinaga, would have gone to prevent the tragedy of Osaka is of course not easy to decide, but their opposition or mediation might have caused Ieyasu to hesitate, and with their departure the way lay unobstructed by any but Fukushima Masanori, whom it was not difficult to detain as a precaution in Edo. In fact, so convenient was their death for the Tokugawa party that Ieyasu has been accused of having brought it about by poison, administered to them at entertainments that he gave for that purpose, at the suggestion of Hiraiwa Chikayoshi, who is credited with having acted as host and shared the poisoned dishes with them and died accordingly. But as a considerable time is, even so, said to have elapsed before they died, it seems that no more credence is to be placed in this story than in other similar ones of the period. The actual truth seems to be that they died of a different kind of poison, for Kato and Asano, as well as Ikeda and Okubo Nagayasu, are elsewhere declared to have died of the "Chinese pox,"* as also are Tokugawa Hideyasu, Kuroda Jōsui and Honda Masanobu. Since this disease, which the Japanese were as much inclined to disown as anyone else, was probably only introduced comparatively lately, it was likely to

---

* This international though nationally repudiated disease, was attributed by the Japanese to the Chinese, as it was by the French to the Italians, to the Italians by the French, to the Poles by the Russians, and to Europe by the Turks, while Europe refers its origin to America. Its appearance in Europe about 1495, the period of the beginning of the voyages of the great explorers, gave it particular opportunities to spread about the world.

be severe, and seems to have accompanied other important diversions into the mansions of the great. And Ieyasu was lucky as usual. Even the spirochaete was on his side.

Ieyasu had already begun to take measures to isolate Hideyori and diminish his importance for some time before he had issued orders to the lords of the west and central provinces in the first place not to stop at Osaka and pay their respects to Hideyori before visiting Sumpu or Edo, in the second not to bring a conspicuous number of retainers with them, and third not to wear so much beard on their faces. Kiyomasa, however, objected that to omit his visit to Osaka would be unchivalrous, that the size of his escort must depend on circumstances, and that the helmetcords were more comfortable when wearing a beard.

In 1611, Hideyori was invited to the Nijo castle, where Ieyasu was staying, and Yoshinao and Yorinobu, Ieyasu's seventh and eighth sons, were given as hostages into the hands of Hideyori's generals, so he ventured to visit the old man, who was considerably impressed, and probably not very delighted with his cleverness. Katagiri had so far given out that he was quite incapable and dull. Ieyasu had already tried to make Hideyori spend as much money as possible by persuading him and his mother that it was the proper thing to rebuild the Great Buddha at Kyoto, though he did not apparently wish to be identified personally with the project, and that for a very practical reason, for it is recorded that when Hideyoshi's Buddha was burnt in 1602 the Lady Yodo sent a message to her sister Sogen-in, the wife of Hidetada, suggesting that they might help her to rebuild it, and through Honda Masanobu the request was passed on to Ieyasu, who was very indignant with Honda for mentioning such a thing. "This Buddha," he burst out, "was a piece of eccentricity of Hideyoshi's, and there was no need to rebuild it at all. If they thought there was they could do it themselves, for if every shrine in the country were to come asking the Shogun to assist it he would soon be bankrupt, and why make any distinction between these fanes? To keep the Empire in peace and quietness was a much better way of using money than building Buddhas." Actually he liked to make other people bankrupt by making it difficult for them to avoid building these things, and so again ensure the peace of the Empire.

So by the spring of 1614 the new Great Buddha and its temple were finished, and the last part of the task, the casting of the great bell suitable for such an institution, was taken in hand. This was successfully carried out too, and a rival to the other great bells at Nara and elsewhere, fourteen feet high and seventy-two tons in weight, was cast. As usual, it had an inscription written in elaborate Chinese text, the work of Seikan, a priest of the Nanzenji, famous for his learning, who had been a great friend of Kato Kiyomasa, and been patronized and dispatched to Korea by Hideyoshi as an envoy, and in consequence was much envied and disliked by many of the other prominent ecclesiastics. One of these, quite possibly Tenkai, must have conceived the idea of bringing misfortune on Seikan, and at the same time providing a pretext for a break with Osaka, and so gaining the gratitude of Ieyasu. For it does not seem likely that he would have thought of it unless so prompted.

In keeping with the importance of the affair a great ceremony of inaugurating both the Buddha and the Temple was to be held, and all arrangements had been made for it, and incidentally Tenkai is found trying to get some of them altered so that he shall not have to yield precedence to the functionaries of the Shingon sect, who had been favored by the house of Toyotomi. Great, therefore, was the surprise and agitation of everyone when Itakura, the Governor of Kyoto, interposed with a demand for the postponing of all the celebrations on the ground that the inscription on the bell was an insult to the dignity of the Shogun and his family.

The objections formally made to the inscription on the bell were that:

The name of Ieyasu was split by the character *an* in the phrase *Kokka anko*.

The name of Ieyasu ought to have been written immediately after the name of the era.

From time immemorial such inscriptions have been written by an eminent priest of one of the five temples. That this should be written by a rustic shaveling was an unheard-of thing.

It is unpardonable that the inscription should have been composed without informing the authorities of the five temples and obtaining their sanction.

In both China and Japan it has always been the custom to avoid using the characters of the Emperor's name, and in this realm taking the name of the Emperor or Regent or Shogun in vain cannot be overlooked.

Objection was also taken to the expression Ho-shin-kun-Shison-I-sho-raku ("Rulers and subjects prosperous and glad and all their progeny happy and glorious"), which they maintained was intended to suggest the reading "Rejoicing in the resplendent glory of the progeny of the house of Toyotomi as our rulers."

Also, "In the East it greets the pale moon, and in the West bids farewell to the setting sun" was interpreted as alluding to the lord of the east as the lesser luminary.

On September 16, 1614, Katagiri was then summoned to Shizuoka by Honda Masazumi, and told to bring about a settlement between the two parties, and also to see that the offensive inscription was effaced. At the same time Yodo sent Lady Okura, mother of Ono Harunaga, and two of her ladies to tender her apologies. These deputations also

Ieyasu handled so as to further his own ends, for to the ladies he said nothing about the bell, but was most cordial, merely asking them that Hideyori refrain from his military preparations and from attracting unattached samurai to his service. It seems that his uncle, Oda Yuraku, had been sounding the daimyos about supporting Hideyori, and this had been reported to Ieyasu. But Katagiri he did not receive at all; only Honda saw him, and intimated to him that he must find some way of placating his master, besides the effacing of the inscription and an apology, but would not say anything definite. Only he observed that he thought himself that it would not be a bad thing if Katagiri suggested the removal of Hideyori from Osaka to some other province. Naturally Katagiri could not decide anything without consulting the others, and so both parties left for home. On the way back they met at Tsuchiyama, a town in Omi, and Katagiri told them what was evidently required, but remarked that he did not favor it at all, for he thought it would be better for Hideyori or Yodogimi to go to Edo as hostages. Since his experience of the Edo authorities was so very different from their own, they perhaps not unnaturally thought that he had put forward this plan himself so that he might profit at the expense of the house of Toyotomi.

The ladies got home before Katagiri, though whether this was because Ieyasu purposely delayed him by getting him to visit Itakura on the way is a question, but anyhow they had time to tell Yodo about his suggestions that Hideyori should take another fief, or she should go to Edo and presumedly to add something unfavorable as well. They seem to have suggested that Katagiri was trying to arrange for her to become the wife of Ieyasu, which made her so angry that she said she would have his head. Since Katagiri was connected by marriage with Ieyasu, and had had his income increased by him, the tale seemed more plausible. Ono Harunaga, Yodogimi's secondary husband, shared her indignation, for he was jealous of Katagiri, and ordered the generals to assassinate him, but they refused, and then Katagiri explained himself. He said his plan was to gain time until Ieyasu should die, for if it was arranged that Yodo was to go to Edo, it would take a long time to prepare a residence for her there. And moreover, when it was prepared, she would probably be taken ill and be unable to travel, and the preparations for the journey would take a long time too, so long that Ieyasu would hardly live to see her arrive in his capital.

Hidetada they regarded as a man of principles on which he himself acted, whereas none could say how Ieyasu would act except that it would be in a way that suited his advantage. His principles were sound and respectable enough, it is true, but they were for other people to follow in very many cases, but Hidetada they thought had only inherited the rather conventionally righteous mentality that Ieyasu sometimes saw fit to assume, without any of the adroitness with which he was always liable to temper it. And if Ieyasu died, Hideyori would have excellent prospects with his own intelligence and the prestige of his father. They seem to have underrated Hidetada's capacity, judging by his actions after his father's death, but anyhow these possibilities were just as well known to Ieyasu, and therefore it was that he had come to the conclusion that he could not afford to wait any longer, but must force matters to a decision.

And as usual his treatment of the situation was effective, for the result was that, after having been invited by his friends to make an attack on Ono and his party, and having refused to split the camp thus, for he was really loyal to Hideyori, there was nothing left for Katagiri to do but retire to his fief. He was not able to do any more for the family of Hideyoshi, and in the two campaigns before Osaka his men fought on the side of Ieyasu. He tried, however, to save Hideyori and Yodogimi, and when he found this impossible he committed suicide because he had failed to bring about an agreement between the two houses.

So Ieyasu kept on circulating rumors of Hideyori's intention to rebel against the Shogunate till at last the Osaka leaders, seeing that a clash was inevitable, no longer hid their defensive preparations, which Ieyasu then declared to be a *casus belli* and attacked. It was he who forced on the rupture of relations, and was active in preparations for the conflict, as becomes evident from the accounts of the English Company, which describes a strong demand for their guns and ammunition from Ieyasu long before Osaka showed any signs of wanting any.

CHAPTER 34

OSAKA. THE WINTER CAMPAIGN

HIDEYORI issued an appeal for assistance to all the daimyos, but not one of them responded. He had to rely on his ninety thousand freelances to defend the castle, whereas from all over the country, east and west and north and central Japan, the lords of provinces and castles sent their contingents to join the Tokugawa forces, which are usually computed at ninety-four thousand men. Ieyasu led one army from Sumpu and Hidetada the other from Edo, and before long Osaka was completely surrounded on all sides. However, no very great efforts were made to take the fortress by storm, and the amount of fighting in this campaign was not great. In view of the strength of the castle this was not surprising.

The outer defenses were about eight and three-quarter miles round, and everywhere it bristled with guns of all sizes, from the two great cannon called Taro and Jiro, that were mounted in the tower before the Sakura Gate in the Ni-no-maru, and are described as the biggest in the Empire, to the "great and small ordnance" that fired through the embrasures cut everywhere in the many walls and towers, while every hundred yards or so there was a fire-projecting mangonel. Sanada also built out a barbican in front of the Hachome Gate with a wall and an empty moat, and threefold palisades, one on each side of the moat and one in the middle, with towers and embrasures to command this part of the wall. It was called the Sanada Barbican (Sanada no Dejiro) after him.

Thinking to stimulate the spirits of the defenders, the Lady Yodo dressed herself in armor and got three or four of her ladies-in-waiting to do so likewise, and went round with them inspecting the posts. But the soldiers seem to have regarded this demonstration with mixed feelings, and rather as a suggestion that they were hard up for leaders. Rather more curious is the statement that Oda Yorinaga, son of Yuraku, went the rounds of the guards at night with a mounted escort attired like himself in armor of gilt, with lacing of autumn-tinted thread, and accompanied by a woman warrior clad all in scarlet armor with swords in scabbards of the same color, and a red "horo" or arrow-catcher on her back, whose business it was to spank any samurai caught asleep. Neither did Hideyori himself rouse much enthusiasm, since for long he did not meet his staff or officers at all, and when it was suggested to him that it would encourage them considerably if he did, he consented to do so, but when they were all mustered to receive him and sat expectant in the hall of audience, though they felt their spirits rise when the great golden gourd standard of the late Taiko was borne in, when Hideyori himself followed and merely uttered the two words "Mina Kuro" ("Thanks for your trouble") and then retired again, they could scarcely feel very exhilarated. Though this incident may be apocryphal, it probably represents the sentiments of those in the castle pretty accurately.

Now the opinion of Ono Harunaga was that the best plan would be to take the offensive and seize Kyoto and the country round it, for, judging by the movements of Ieyasu at Sekigahara, he would not arrive in time to prevent it. This Sanada doubted, for now that he had all the resources of the Empire at his back he was not likely to hesitate, therefore he considered that they ought to hurry and throw out their forces so as to take the strategic points of Uji and Seta, capturing Fushimi and burning Kyoto, for this definite action might impress some possibly wavering daimyos and bring them in on their side. Goto also agreed, but apparently this bold policy did not appeal to the majority, for nothing was done.

On the way to the Osaka Campaign, as Ieyasu was going to cross the Kuragari Pass in Yamato, someone remarked that it was commonly said that no one had ever won a victory after going over that pass, so immediately he avoided that road and took another path through the rice-fields, thinking it as well to humor the popular superstition and avoid anything of evil omen.

In a discussion that took place on the possibilities of the situation Hosokawa Tadaoki seems to have summed it up pretty shrewdly. When it was suggested that Ieyasu would have a difficult task seeing that under the Ikko monks it withstood Nobunaga for seven years, he said: "Yes, but the times are now rather different. The fact is that Hideyori is only a child, and it is his mother who is in command. Everyone of any importance is bound to Edo, because their relations are hostages there. And of the loyalty of those freelances in the castle I am not very much convinced. Nobunaga had enemies all over the country, and was in constant danger of attacks in his rear, so he could not concentrate his forces in one place. But now the whole Empire is united under Ieyasu, so that without doubt even this strong place will not hold out long."

Before setting out for the West, Hidetada issued a number of regulations for his army. These insisted on obedience to officers, and prohibited grumbling and disorder and trespassing of one contingent on the path of another, as well as the premature advance of any individuals to get credit at the expense of the rest, ill-treating and plundering civilians, and omitting to pay for requisitions, and so on. These articles were submitted to Ieyasu by Honda Masazumi for his criticism, and he remarked: "Yes, that is what you would expect of the Shogun, I suppose. When I was young I never issued any detailed orders like this. If they act according to orders and things go badly, you can't scold your men, and if they act contrary to them and are successful, if you praise them it brings the orders into contempt. It may be best to leave the details to be settled according to circumstances."

We learn, too, from a further series of orders issued about billeting that 3 mon were to be paid by each man for a night's lodging if he burnt the host's wood, but nothing if he provided his own. Soldiers brought their own supplies, and to facilitate this orders were given that rice, beans, bran, straw, and other articles of the kind were to be on sale by the roadside, so that there should be no difficulty about food for both men and horses. For the latter, 6 mon were to be paid to the host. Ieyasu himself left the Nijo castle on the fifteenth of the eleventh month and proceeded to Osaka by way of Nara, where he stayed a night at the Horyuji temple, and so to Tennoji, where he had a conference with his generals, and determined to make his headquarters at Chausuyama, a small eminence facing the front of the castle. Here he arrived on the eighteenth and met Hidetada. "The inner part of the castle is very strong," he said, "and will be difficult to take, even if we carry the outer. We must adopt a waiting policy, and hem them in by fortified works, and so cut off all their communications. Let the Shogun see to this, and I will go hawking meanwhile in the Kinai district." And he went off back to Sumiyoshi.

The next few days nothing much was done except to receive the Emperor's message of consolation for all the trouble they were taking, and to discourage a messenger from within the castle by cutting off his fingers and branding Hideyori's name on his forehead, and in this plight sending him back.

Ieyasu then ordered his chief architect, Nakai Masatsugu, to have the houses at Semba pulled down to build quarters for his men, and also to see to the construction of his own temporary residence on Chausuyama, or Tea-mill Hill. This eminence was, as its name suggests, a somewhat steep-sided hillock with a top only just spacious enough for Ieyasu's own quarters, and with no spare room for those of his personal staff, who had therefore to live at its foot.

The building he ordered to be set up was a living and sleeping room of twelve mats, facing north and south, with a lean-to 6 feet by 18, and a verandah 5 feet wide. At the foot of the hill was a palisade with an entrance gate, and inside this an outer guardhouse of twelve mats facing east, with a porch 18 feet by 30, having a tokonoma in it. To the west there was a tearoom of four and a half mats, and on the south side a storeroom 12 feet square, while on the east was the bathroom, also 12 feet square. On this side also was a twenty-mat apartment for the councilors. The kitchen on the north side completed the buildings.

On the fifth day Ieyasu issued orders that a rampart should be made in front of the moats and stockades set up to protect it, and that none should risk being killed or wounded by the enemy's fire. Also, that Kuki Moritaka should station a guard-ship at the mouth of the river so that none of the enemy could get out that way. That night he told Masamune that he had decided to make a general attack before long, and that plenty of scaling ladders should be ready.

Hidetada was very anxious to make this attack, and to carry the castle by storm, so he told Doi Toshikatsu to request Ieyasu to order it and to fix a day, since he thought Hideyori was inclined to sue for peace. But all Ieyasu replied was that it must be impressed on the Shogun that he should not underrate a foe because his numbers were not great. At which Hidetada was by no means pleased.

After a consultation with his staff Ieyasu ordered a bombardment to be carried out for three consecutive days at ten o'clock at night and at dawn, while miners were set to work to undermine the towers. To undermine the confidence of the defenders as well arrows were shot into the castle carrying messages urging them to surrender as the wisest policy. Both Ieyasu and Hidetada on many occasions carried out a reconnaissance of the castle from the front lines, and exposed themselves to considerable danger in doing so. They went up one of the siege towers on Arima's front one day, and when some of the defenders saw the Tokugawa insignia flying there, for they apparently advertised these visits, doubtless to encourage their men, they not unnaturally directed a hot fire from ordnance of all calibres on the tower, some of the shot being up to a thirty-two pounder, though with no result.

What fighting there was took place mostly at Shigeno and Imafuku on the north side of the castle, where Satake and Uesugi proceeded to storm and take some stockaded defenses and drive out the defenders and consolidate the position. But the next day these, under Kimura Nagato and Goto Matabei, brought up reinforcements, and working up under cover of their sandbags, suddenly made a charge and drove them out again. There followed some more actions of the same kind, and again the defenders were the more successful, and Satake's men were once more forced to retire. However, they in turn were reinforced by Sakakibara and Horio with a few hundred men and gained some small successes. After a volley from five hundred matchlockmen, for instance, his spearmen charged and broke through, and pushed back the enemy with some loss. By this time Ieyasu concluded that Uesugi would do well to fall back into reserve and rest his men, so he sent orders to Horio to take up the attack in his place. But this idea Uesugi much resented, replying indignantly: "It may be the order of Ogosho Sama, but I was born in a warrior house, and it is our tradition never to retire when a fight has once started." But all the same, when at the conclusion of these operations an officer who had been with Uesugi returned to headquarters and before everyone accused him of delay and neglecting opportunities to make a successful assault, Ieyasu rebuked him pretty sharply and told him he would hear nothing against Uesugi's martial qualities, "especially from a damned fool like you who gives his opinion unasked."

Meanwhile Ieyasu had begun to negotiate with the enemy while he bombarded and otherwise menaced them: the policy that is described as "gripping the throat and stroking the back." He tried to bribe several of the opposing leaders, Sanada among them, but unsuccessfully. Then he turned to Oda Yuraku, who was a friend of his, and who later on openly joined his side. He also sent word to Edo that Acha-no-tsubone should be sent up, since she was a great friend of Yodo's sister Maria Kyogoku, whose son was one of Ieyasu's commanders. And he thought one woman would be mentally suitable to cope with another. Yodo was imperious and ambitious, and made a fair show as Lady Regent, but she was in fact, like most of the high-born ladies of her day, inclined to be narrow-minded from want of experience of the outside world as well as superstitious and emotional. Ieyasu, whose knowledge of women was pretty comprehensive by this time, regarded her as the weak point on which to concentrate. On the fourteenth day of January Acha-no-tsubone arrived at Osaka, and on the sixteenth a hundred great guns started to bombard the castle systematically, so that the noise they made prevented those within, and especially the ladies, from getting much rest. In addition to this, they would fire sudden volleys and raise a great war-cry at various times during the night to give the enemy the idea that they were just going to launch an attack. They were getting pretty tired of all this when a great shot fell into Yodo's apartment and caused another commotion. She was taking morning tea with several of her ladies at the time, and the cannonball struck and smashed to pieces the tea-cabinet they were using. This filled the ladies with panic, and Yodo became very much inclined to pacific suggestions.

Meanwhile, through Goto Shosaburo, Ieyasu had put forward the suggestion that one way of terminating the deadlock would be that either Yodo go as hostage to Edo, or else the moats and walls of the castle be entirely levelled so that it would no longer be a menace to him. Ono Harunaga and Oda Yuraku thought that there was something in the first suggestion, hoping no doubt to gain time, and said that in that case they would like a grant of more territory since they had to pay so many loyal supporters. But this idea did not appeal to Ieyasu at all, neither did the desire of the Osaka leaders that Hideyori should have two provinces of Shikoku if he left Osaka, so he countered by the offer of Awa and Kazusa in the east, a rather obvious maneuver which was very definitely declined.

Again on the eighteenth, it being the anniversary of Hideyoshi's death, it was almost certain, thought the officers of Katagiri Katsumoto, whose contingent was by the Kyobashi Gate, that Hideyori would go to the shrine in the castle, and at this accordingly they aimed when they considered the time was favorable. The great shot did not strike Hideyori, but hit and splintered a pillar in Yodo's apartment in the keep so that it fell and crushed to death two of her ladies. So both sides were inclined to negotiate, but Ieyasu did not wish that anyone should consider him at all precipitate. On the contrary, when on the seventeenth of the month the Emperor Go Mizu-no-O sent two courtiers, the Denso Hirohashi Kanekatsu and the Imperial Envoy Sanjonishi Saneeda, to the headquarters at Chausuyama, to request Ieyasu to come to Kyoto and make peace, he refused promptly, though, we are told, respectfully. He afterwards added as an explanation that should the negotiations not be successful it would seem disrespectful to the Throne, so it was better not to start any. But, according to a letter of Suden, he did not receive the envoy, and remarked that he did not want any intervention of the Court.

Meanwhile, by the eighteenth of the month, Acha-no-tsubone and Honda Masazumi were busy at the camp of Kyogoku Tadataka putting their case before his mother, Yodo's sister, whose names are significant, for she was known to the Jesuit missionaries by her Christian name of Maria, but to the Japanese chroniclers by her Buddhist posthumous one of Jōkōin. And the terms they proposed were to the effect that the Ni-no-maru and San-no-maru enclosures of the castle should be levelled, leaving only the Honmaru or inner bailey, that Ono Harunaga and Oda Yuraku should send hostages for their good behavior, but that none of the other leaders or retainers, whether veterans or recent adherents, should be in any way affected. And to this, after some discussion, the defenders agreed. So the letters of Suden and the Japanese chronicles of the siege.

The Jesuit missionaries' account of the matter seems to exaggerate the military successes of the defenders, for it puts the attackers' loss at thirty thousand, and asserts that many of them ran away, and that the cold was more than they could endure, so that Ieyasu feared lest the generals fighting for him should decide to forsake his camp for that of the young and vigorous Hideyori. So they say he was forced to come to terms, which Hideyori's commanders accepted because they, too, had not the resources for a long siege, and doubted the loyalty of many of their adherents. And the terms were, they allege, that the second and third moat systems were to be filled up, and Hideyori was to swear not to start any more rebellions, but to keep the peace for all time. And they also add that it was indeed a rare thing in Japan for two armies to come to terms unless one was completely beaten, and in this case the Shogun had no intention of keeping to the agreement, but only of depriving the castle of its defenses so that he might attack it more successfully later on. It was indeed "not a treaty to ensue peace, but a covenant to prepare for further war."

Even now it is not clear why the defenders permitted these moats to be filled in. Either they were persuaded that there would be perpetual peace or else they thought Ieyasu's suggestion only applied to the outer moats. So many men did Ieyasu concentrate on the work, however, making them labor at it night and day, that all the defenses except the inner ones were levelled. One account says the defenders tried to complain to Honda Masanobu but he was too ill to see them and thus procrastinated till all was finished, and so they were tricked and Ieyasu's real purpose in this campaign was accomplished. Anyhow, the "Winter Campaign of Osaka" has become a byword ever since for the folly of pacifists.

So on the eighteenth and nineteenth days Honda Masazumi met and discussed the terms with the Lady Jōkōin and Acha-notsubone, and on the twentieth Jōkōin with the two ladies Niino-tsubone and Acha no tsubone proceeded to Ieyasu's headquarters at Chausuyama and received the agreement from him. They presented him with three costumes and thirty bolts of damask, and Honda Masazumi served them with liquor, and Ieyasu gave them an agreement signed with blood taken from his little finger. This document stated that Hideyori's status should not be affected in any way, and that the incomes of his men should not be touched, while there should be no more want of confidence or double dealing between the two parties. The two sons of Oda Yuraku and Ono Harunaga were also sent as hostages, and the three ladies agreed that Hideyori should provide men to pull down the ramparts and towers of the Ni-no-maru, and that Kyogoku Tadataka should be the Commissioner to see that this was carried out.

The next day Kimura Nagato, Oda Yuraku, and Kori Shume came

to Okayama and received a similar agreement from the Shogun Hide-tada. It stated the same terms about Hideyori and his retainers, and added that his mother should not go to Edo, and that if he chose to leave Osaka he should have any province he liked. This was formally sealed with the Shogunal seal and taken back to the castle. Not content with all this, on the twenty-second Itakura Shigemasa and Acha-no-tsubone were sent to the castle and had an interview with Hideyori and his mother, from whom they received a sworn statement "that from now onward Hideyori would not raise any revolt against Ieyasu and Hidetada, that in case of differences of opinion he would at once consult the Shogunate directly, and that in all other matters things should be as before."

A couple of days afterwards Oda Yuraku and Ono Harunaga went to call on Ieyasu at Chausuyama and took the usual presents of silk, etc. He was in a very gracious, almost affectionate, mood, or rather affected to be so, and told them how deeply he had felt the painful necessity of having to oppose in arms such a delightful young man who was also a grandson. And how correspondingly glad he felt, therefore, that he had been able to bring about this peaceable conclusion. Ono had indeed been a most loyal servant to Hideyori, and they admired his valiant defense. The Shogun would be proud to have such retainers himself, and he asked Ono for his upper garment and put it on the shoulders of Honda Kōzuke, who was in attendance, that some of this loyalty might be transferred to him. Harunaga was moved to tears at such condescension, while in the adjoining room Oda Yuraku was expressing his opinion most emphatically that this treaty marked the inaugura-tion of a long era of peace. Making the motions of one engaged in his favorite hobby of ceremonial tea, he said: "And now we shall all be able to spend our time in this delightful occupation."

Ieyasu then left Chausuyama and proceeded to the Nijo castle at Kyoto, leaving Hidetada behind to see to the filling-in of the moats.

He also published an order thanking all the daimyos for their as-sistance, and excusing them from public works for three years.

On the twenty-eighth day he was received in audience by the Em-peror and formally announced the conclusion of the peace.

CHAPTER 35

THE SUMMER CAMPAIGN

WHEN peace was made after the winter campaign of Osaka Date and Todo suggested through Honda Masazumi that since it was not likely that this peace would be lasting, and as the moats of the castle had been thus conveniently filled in, it would be well to make a sudden attack with all our force and overwhelm the fortress without further ado.

There may be some reason in what you say (said Ieyasu), but people who act unjustly and inconsiderately always incur the punishment of Heaven in the end. Quite recently, for instance, we have the examples of Oda Nobunaga who abolished the Shogun Yoshiaki and Takeda Shingen who banished his father Nobutora. Vengeance has fallen on their descendants, and their houses are completely destroyed. I helped Odo Nobuo out of friendship for his father, and opposed Hideyoshi at Nagakude, where the three leaders he relied on were destroyed by my armies. Therefore he sent his mother to me as a hostage and made peace again. And after that I co-operated with him loyally and aided him in his subjugation of the whole Empire. And his son Hideyori I supported too, but Ishida Mitsunari was jealous, and hated me, and plotted with subtle guile to destroy me in the name of Hideyori. But Heaven was indignant at his wickedness, and punished him and his evil associates by overthrowing them all at the battle of Sekigahara. And there were many who clamored that the same punishment should be given to Hideyori too, but I pitied his youth, and not only spared his life but gave him three provinces as his fief and had him advanced to high rank at Court, so great was my good will and benevolence. But so unmindful of all this was he that he started a rebellion against my house, an exceeding wicked thing to do indeed, but since he has now promised to amend his ways and make peace, it is better to leave the matter as it is. But if he should again act unrighteously and stir up a revolt and so provoke the retribution of Heaven, well then it cannot be overlooked. But since peace is now made it is not my will to go back on it.

From this speech one may at any rate define what Ieyasu meant by Heaven. There he does not seem to differ much from his contemporaries in Europe.

It was not long before Ieyasu began to get reports of further activities at Osaka, where the commanders had ordered work to be started on the quiet to clear out the moats and build stockades and other defensive works, while they were also collecting gold and recruiting more Ronin from the provinces. Some people, too were leaving Kyoto because of the rumors that the Osaka forces intended to seize the city, and indeed Furuta Oribe, the great aesthete and tea-master, was put to death with his son and pupils on suspicion of having been concerned in a plot to set fire to the capital and secure possession of the Emperor. Doubtless the Osaka leaders did not believe in the bona fides of the Shogunate and were apprehensive of some further action, and so thought they might as well anticipate it. They probably calculated that they might damage the Tokugawa armies severely if a fight took place in the field, and this held some possibilities. Otherwise they had nothing to hope for. As the fighting proved they were to some extent justified. They therefore concealed their defiant attitude no longer.

Thus provoked, it was only to be expected that Ieyasu would set his armies in motion again without delay, especially as there is every reason to think it was coming about just as he had planned. And so on the fourth day of the fourth month, with Hidetada in supreme command, as befitted the Shogun, he again marched westward. And before long his men were back in their old positions before the castle, which now, in spite of the newly-improvised defenses, was no longer the impregnable place they had formerly found it.

Ieyasu rode in a palanquin, with Honda Masanobu on horseback beside him. Neither of them wore armor, though all the others were in full war panoply. "He wore a white lined garment, with a tea-colored haori and a sedge hat, and sandals on his feet. His armor he had put on an armor-stand beside him, and did not carry a baton. Ishikawa Tadafusa gave him one cut from a green bamboo, and he used that. And when his banner-pole got broken and they wished to replace it, he told them that they could find a bamboo for it anywhere: as long as the banner could be seen it would do."

At the summer campaign Nakarai Yamato, Ieyasu's chief architect, had a small house brought up in pieces to put together at the headquarters at Chausuyama. "Anything as large as that won't be to His Highness's liking, I fancy," said Honda Masazumi, and he consulted Ieyasu, who at once replied, "Nine by twelve will do. I don't want more than six mats." So a six-mat room was quickly set up, and divided into two by a linen curtain. And on the upper three mats Ieyasu lived, while the lower three were used as an audience chamber for the great daimyos who were admitted to his presence.

Hidetada met him at Hirano at about twelve noon. He had been out reconnoitering at Hachio from before dawn. He wore armor with black lacing, and a hood-shaped helmet and a sleeveless haori of feathers, and in his hand he carried a signal flag of white bear's fur. He rode a horse of chestnut color, whose hair stood up more than two inches long. After they had saluted each other, Ieyasu said: "I will go to Chausuyama and do you go to Okayama." But Hidetada demurred. "Round Okayama the roads are bad and the going difficult, so I don't suppose the enemy will attack in that quarter." Ieyasu repeated his injunction, whereupon Hidetada looked sulky and said nothing, so that his father also began to look black. Honda then intervened, and respectfully urged Hidetada to proceed to Okayama. "We must hurry up," added Ieyasu, "It is already about one o'clock, and it is easiest for all to go to their stations of last year." So at last Hidetada assented and went.

Matsudaira Tadanao called for some rice gruel and took several bowls standing, served by a retainer. Then he turned to his men and called out: "Now we have all full bellies, so if we fall we shan't be eligible for the hell of hungry ghosts, but we'll climb right over the mountain of Death and go straight into the Court of the Devil!" And he mounted and set off for Chausuyama.

Ieyasu then issued an order to his army. "Today you are under the command of Hidetada. And this battle is a practical education for Yoshinao and Yorinobu. Don't rush precipitately into action. Leave your horses a cho or two behind, and then go in with your spears."

Just before the battle Ieyasu enticed Ono Harunaga and Hayami Kai-no-kami to his camp to discuss terms of peace, but without success. But when they were seen going back to Osaka afterwards, it was enough to instil some doubt into the minds of their officers and men, so that their spirit was somewhat shaken, and just then Ieyasu launched his attack. "In a battle the defection of a single man may make his side lose heart, as they are correspondingly cheered by an opponent who joins them," observes the commentator.

And though Ieyasu had not been able to detach any of the Western leaders from their allegiance, their plans for the battle were evidently affected not a little by his strokes of diplomacy. They had the intention of sending a force under Akashi round through the city to gain and attack his rear, while Mori Katsunaga, Sanada, Ono, and the rest made a fierce onset on his front, assisted by the dramatic appearance, if all went well, of Hideyori at the head of the troops. But all that eventuated was the frontal attack, though that was serious enough by itself, aided as it was by a rumor of treachery on the Tokugawa side owing to the unexpected movement of Asano's men on the extreme left by the shore, for these suspicions were common to both sides.

Mori Katsunaga broke through the divisions of Honda and Ogasawara in his impetuous rush, and then came rolling on to the troops of Ieyasu behind them. These, under Matsudaira Shigetsuna, Tachibana

Muneshige, Honda Masazumi, and his younger brother Tadazumi, opposed them strongly, and Tadazumi's men for a while made considerable progress, but were then forced to relinquish the ground they had won. Just then the Echizen division wavered and broke, partly as the result of their suspicion that they were betrayed by Asano, who looked like moving over to the enemy. Seeing this, Sanada ordered his men to charge, and the Echizen troops failed to hold them, though they struggled manfully for a while. Ieyasu's men tried to assist them to hold their ground, and Ieyasu himself drew his horse to the side of the road to watch the fight with only one attendant, Oguri Masatada. Seeing how serious matters looked, he sent to his staff to steady their men in ranks behind one another to bring the enemy to a halt by weight of numbers, and it seems that eventually they succeeded. Then the Echizen leaders rallied some of their men and made a counter-attack, and managed to plant their standard on Chausuyama, but Sanada's men resisted strongly still. But now they were tiring, and their leader was wounded and exhausted. So he got off his horse and sat down on his campstool to rest, and while doing so, one Nishio Nizaemon, of the Echizen army, rode at him. "I am Sanada Yukimura, an adversary no doubt quite worthy of you," exclaimed he, "but I am too exhausted to fight any more." And he took off his helmet and bared his head, which the other immediately struck off.

Then Todo and Ii, who led the van of Hidetada's division, seeing their left wing give way before the Westerners, now charged in on the flank of Ono Harunaga, despite the heavy matchlock fire of his men, and advancing attacked Mori Katsunaga's force, who resisted bravely, but since they were unsupported had to give way at last, though not before some of them had set off a land mine and done considerable damage to Todo's troops. Date Masamune, meanwhile, distinguished himself by firing on one Jimbo Sukemochi, of his own side, who was resting after making an attack, excusing himself by telling Ieyasu that his conduct was suspicious, and that he was meditating treachery. He explained that it was his rule to fire on his own men if any of them gave way, and that this applied also to his neighbors in a fight, for so only could he prevent panic spreading to his own troops. Ieyasu seems to have accepted this explanation, but Date's action was severely criticized by the other generals.

The Eastern army now advanced on the castle, but again met strong opposition, for Ono Harunaga, Ono Dōken, and Naito Nagaie hurled their troops at Hidetada's army, and a fierce fight took place in which the result was for some time doubtful, and Hidetada's household troops were severely handled, and many fled in panic. Maeda's force was called on to assist them, but did not hurry to move, complaining that they had not had time to eat their lunch.

Had it not been for the coolness and bravery of Kato Yoshiaki and Kuroda Nagamasa, who rallied the shaken divisions and stopped the panic, the forces of Ieyasu and Hidetada might have been driven from the field altogether. So fierce and rapid was the assault that Ii's two standard-bearers were killed, and Ii Naotaka himself failed to keep his men from giving way, though he strove to do so valiantly, and they reeled back on to the division of Hidetada. Then some sections steadied themselves, and another division of the Tokugawa force threw itself on to the flank of the victorious Osaka men now engaged with Maeda's troops, who had come into action, so that they were eventually forced back.

In Hidetada's division for a while all had been confusion, and the Hatamoto under Doi Oi-no-suke and Sakai Uta-no-kami seem to have lost their formation and fled in all directions. Hidetada went to throw himself personally into the fight, but one of his men seized his bridle and prevented him, hanging on tight in spite of the Shogun's angry commands to desist. Fortunately Honda Masanobu rode up and added his weight to that of the retainer, and assisted to get some order into the ranks. Hidetada was so disgusted with the conduct of his men that he ordered a list to be made of those who had gone to the rear so precipitately, with a view to publishing it when he got back to Edo, but he seems to have been overruled by his father, who doubted the wisdom of such an exposure. But the soldiers expressed their opinion in the sentence: "Fighting Tsushima (Ando), Run-away Oi, and Do-nothing Uta-no-kami."

The Eastern army then surrounded the castle, and Hideyori, who was preparing to go out to lead and inspire his troops, was told that it was too late, for the day was lost. Ieyasu is credited with having arranged for a messenger to be sent to Hideyori, warning him that it was dangerous to leave the castle as treachery was meditated there, and also with corrupting the cook Sara Magosuke, who forthwith set fire to his kitchen so that the flames spread to the other buildings. When the Easterners saw this they pressed on the more fiercely, and penetrated into the enclosure, setting fire to yet other buildings of the castle. Hideyori with his staff and his mother then retreated to the keep, where they eventually committed suicide. According to some accounts this was directly caused by Ii Naotaka and Ando Tsushima directing a cannonade at the keep without asking the permission of Ieyasu, because they feared he might relent and spare them, but others say that orders to fire were given by Ieyasu and Hidetada, while some even state that these two sent a direct order to Hideyori to put an end to himself. Again there is a passage in the *Hagi Bakko Roku* to the effect that Ono Harunaga asked Ieyasu to pardon Hideyori, but he replied that the matter must be decided by the Shogun, and Hidetada refused to spare him. This statement is on the authority of Mori Hidemoto. But there is little likelihood that Hidetada would have been able to give any decision but one in accordance with his father's wishes. Moreover the fact that Ieyasu hunted out Hideyori's small son Kunimatsu, aged eight, and had him beheaded in the Rokujo Kawara execution ground with Tanaka Rokuzaemon, his foster-mother's husband, though for some reason he was kind enough to pardon the foster-mother, was clear proof of his determination to leave none of Hideyoshi's line alive to be a possible menace to the house of Tokugawa in the future. As Tokutomi observes: "Ieyasu was not one to have any sentiment about even blood relationship, since he had put his eldest son to death in order to keep the favor of Nobunaga, while he had deserted his son-in-law Hōjō Ujinao rather than lose the confidence of Hideyoshi. He never spared individuals where the interests of the Empire or of his house, which he considered identical, were in question."

All the contemporary records praise the outstanding bravery and dash of the Western army and its leaders. "Their valor," says the *Satsuma Chronicle,* "has never been surpassed either in ancient or modern times. Sanada Saemon, Kimura Nagato, Goto Matabei, and Suzukida Hayato, these four fell in the struggle after doing mighty deeds. But the leaders of the Shogun's guards fled in panic, and the victory was due only to the good fortune of Ieyasu. When Sanada attacked Ieyasu's men they gave way, and many fled as far as three ri to save their skins. Then at the third onset Sanada was killed. He was without doubt the first warrior in the Empire, and in the ancient histories we hear of none greater."

Hosokawa Tadaoki, also on the Tokugawa side, in his diary of the battle bears similar testimony, and adds the name of Akashi Kamon to the roll of those who fell gloriously, while he observes: "Ono Shume (Harunaga) and Ono Dōken fled the field. They will surely be captured." He comments that Sanada's head was taken by the captain of the Echizen matchlockmen, but since he was wounded and weary it was no great feat. "But some say that Akashi Kamon ran away." Tadaoki, too, remarks on the flight of the Hatamoto. "Few of them did not flee, and they are everywhere laughed at. Some ran as far as Hirano, Kyuhoji, and Iino it seems."

Comparisons naturally suggest themselves between the conduct of the Tokugawa retainers on this occasion and in the fights of the earlier days of Ieyasu, but this was a younger generation, for Mikata-ga-hara was forty years ago. And there was a difference in their spirit, for it was the Osaka men who were fighting with all the valor of desperation, whereas the whole forces of the Empire were mobilized against them, and the campaign could have only one end. These Hatamoto, whose fortunes were now made, could hardly be animated by the fierce ambitious energy of the Mikawa Bushi who fought Takeda and Hideyoshi. They had become less provincial now, and also more luxurious. But as to Ieyasu, Tokutomi well sums up the situation in the words: "He was the same at Osaka at seventy-four as he had been at Mikata-ga-hara at thirty-one. His environment had not altered him one whit. To what he had been and what he had got he held on with a grip of iron. He was indeed a matchless hero, though a sinister one." With this victory the fate of the Empire was definitely decided, for there was now no opposition left. And all remnants of it were very thoroughly and systematically exterminated. Very many of the leaders had already committed suicide, but Chosokabe, former lord of Tosa in Shikoku, and seventy-two others were beheaded and their heads exposed. Ieyasu felt the necessity of getting rid of the Ronins, of which Hideyori's army was largely composed, for they might easily be a menace to the unity of the Empire in the future, since they were ready to fight for anyone who would pay them. And the number of them put summarily out of the way must have been great, for the missionaries describe the heads as being stuck on planks between Kyoto and Fushimi, and say that there were eighteen rows, some with as many as a thousand heads. Murdoch observes that Hideyoshi might have sent them to conquer the Philippines, but Ieyasu had not his unconventional brilliance. He was more typically Japanese, and the average Japanese does not think much about overseas enterprises. Ieyasu must have been pleased to lay hands on the remains of Hideyoshi's hoard in the castle to the amount of about half a million sterling in bullion.

The fate of the wife of Hideyori is an example of the ways of the Bakufu even then. At the fall of Osaka castle, after going to the Tokugawa camp to try and arrange for the life of her husband and his mother to be spared, she went back again to the castle to join them, and as it was now on fire her life was in considerable danger. Whereupon Ieyasu is said to have called out that if anyone would save his granddaughter's life he might have her hand in marriage. One of her ladies had managed to wrap her up in some mattresses and let her drop from the tower, and a certain Lord Sakazaki-Dewa-no-kami Takachika, lord of Tsuwano in Iwami, came forward and received her from the hands of one of his retainers, who caught her. Therefore this lord naturally thought he would obtain her hand, but in this he was disappointed, for the Bakufu had other plans, and it was announced sometime afterwards that she was to marry Honda Nakatsukasa-no-taiyu lord of Himeji, who was to be given an extra 10,000 koku as her dowry. At this Sakazaki became furious, and declaring that he had been purposely slighted, announced his intention of showing his contempt for their lack of faith by taking the lady by force when she proceeded to Himeji. This was reported to the Shogunate and they sent to his family secretly and told them that in order to prevent a breach of the peace it would be well if they persuaded him to commit suicide and arranged for someone to succeed him. The Shogun trusted them to arrange in detail so that such disloyalty be discouraged. They did so arrange by making the truculent lord intoxicated and taking off his head with a halberd, after which they sent it to Edo saying that he had committed suicide. But when some time afterwards the real manner of his death became known, the Bakufu condemned the fief to confiscation for irregular and unfitting behavior in assassinating the lord, and the lady was married to Honda after all.

But she was no very auspicious bride, for he fell ill and died not so long afterwards.

CHAPTER 36

HONAMI KŌ-ETSU

IN the world of art of this time one figure stands alone both for his originality and also for his versatility. This was Honami Kō-etsu. His family were the standard authorities on the connoisseurship of swords, and the first Honami died in 1352 at the age of a hundred, and since it still continues and practices the same calling it can be only of a little less antiquity than some of the lines of swordsmiths themselves. Kō-etsu was also a sword connoisseur and polisher, but that was perhaps the least of his accomplishments. He was reckoned, with Shokado Shōjō and the Kwampaku Konoe Ozan Nobuhiro (or his father Samboin Nobutada), as one of the Three Pens or Finest Calligraphists of his day, while he was not less skilled in painting, lacquer work, pottery, landscape gardening, tea, bronze casting, sculpture, Japanese poetry, and literature generally. He was also famous for his sand pictures and Noh masks. Perhaps he was the most versatile artist in modern Japanese history. He also published books on paper made at his art village, of which he designed the illustrations and binding. He was born in 1558 and died in 1638, aged eighty, and few people can have had a life better spent. Naturally he attracted the attention of Ieyasu, who became his patron, or one of them, for he was intimate with and assisted by the great men of his day, and numbered all the artists and literary men among his friends. He has been called the William Morris of Japan, though perhaps it would be more correct to say that Morris was the English Kō-etsu. The only thing in which they differed was their political ideas, and since those socialistic views held by Morris were only the result of being born in perhaps the most unlovely age the world has ever seen, it is hardly likely he would have had any need for them had he lived in the Japan of Kō-etsu, which was almost certainly the diametrical opposite. Kō-etsu found stimulus in all the beauty, both natural and manmade, which surrounded him, just as he did in the ancient art appreciation of the craftsmen whom he employed, and in the ripe appreciation of the aesthetes his contemporaries. These were not few. There were the two great tea-masters Furuta Oribe Kobori Enshu and Oda Yuraku, the greatest masters after Sen Rikyu, whom he must also have known. Kano Sanraku, and Sotan and Sosetsu, his followers Mitsunobu, Sansetsu, Tannyu, and Doun, all painters of the highest repute. The wealthy merchants Chaya Shirojiro, Suminokura Soan, Sano Soeki, and the Confucian scholar Hayashi Razan. Of the great daimyos he was a friend of Maeda of Kaga and Matsudaira Izu-no-kami Nobutsuna, Doi Toshikatsu, and the two Kyoto Governors, Itakura Katsushige and Shigemune, and the two Konoes, and among the Kuge, Karasumaru Mitsuhiro.

Kō-etsu was always quite well-to-do, for his father received a salary of 200 koku from Maeda, which he inherited, and Ieyasu wished to give him more, but he refused, saying that he had enough. However, in 1615, when he was fifty-eight years old, hearing from Itakura that he was tired of living in the capital, Ieyasu presented him with an estate at Takagamine, a place on the outskirts of Kyoto to the west. The way this came about is thus described:

"When Ieyasu came back after the Osaka campaign he asked Itakura Iga-no-kami how Kō-etsu did. 'Oh, he is still living, but he is tired of doing so at Kyoto on account of people there who differ from him in their views. He has an inclination to go to some more out-of-the-way place,' said Itakura. 'Has he?' observed Ieyasu; 'well, there is a district on the Omi and Tamba road to Kyoto, a dangerous place beset by footpads. That would be a good place for him to go and live. You can give him a plot of land there. Yes, you can give him quite a large piece.'"*

So Kō-etsu went and made his residence beside the stream that runs through it, and after he had done so the place, which had before been quite uninhabited, soon became a flourishing village of craftsmen and littérateurs. And the thieves, not liking such company, ceased to haunt it, as no doubt Ieyasu had intended, wishing as always to kill two birds with one stone.

Having got this land, Kō-etsu proceeded to lay out his own house and garden on a piece of 120 yards frontage, and then allotted the adjacent ground to his family and relations, and to the craftsmen who worked there.

Since Kō-etsu was much interested in Buddhism, he and his family built four small temples in this village. One, the Jōsōji, his heir Kosa built for the Hokke sect, the second was the Myōshuji, the Bodaisho of his mother Myoshu, while the third was the Taikuan or Ko-etsuji, his own place of enlightenment, to which he later retired, and where his tomb still is. (The Ko-etsuji is unchanged, though the rest of the village has naturally altered. But fortunately a plan of it as it was in the days of Kō-etsu has been preserved, showing how the land was allotted, and who lived there.)

---

* Kō-etsu, Gyō-shō-ki.

In the Myōshuji the Sutras were read twice a day by believers who assembled for that purpose, while in the Ko-etsuji the Lotus Sutra was read incessantly for the peace of the Empire and the welfare of the family and ancestors. The other temple was a small cell called Chisoku-an.

Kō-etsu was very pleased with the situation of this village, for it lay to the northwest, which was his lucky direction. The scenery around was exceedingly fine and varied. "On the east is Kamo Hill and Hiei-zan and Nyo-i-ga-take, and on the north Kurama and Kibune. On the south is Hirano and Kitano, with its memories of Sugawara Michizane, while far off through the trees can be seen the waters of the River Yodo by Toba and the boats sailing up and down on it with Otokoyama in the background, and beyond that the famous peaks of Ikoma-ga-take, Kongosan, Yoshino, and Mikasayama. The early morning is especially interesting, when from the sea of white mist that arises the trees project like the masts of a ship, while the gilt roofs of Nijo castle and the pagoda of Kujo seem to float on it. Withal it is only about a mile and a half from the capital." The views must have been finer than most, for it is related that Hidetsugu was especially charmed with them, and brought Rikyu there with him, saying there was nothing equal to it in the whole Empire, so Rikyu made an extemporary tearoom there with bamboo pillars, and made tea, and the site is still preserved.

He seems to have retired to the Taiku-an when about seventy, when he adopted this title as his name.

When he retired he divided all his valuable tea utensils and furniture among his friends and relations, and kept only quite common ones for his own use. When asked why he did this he replied that there must always be some anxiety in using valuable things lest they be broken or attract thieves, but one felt quite easy about what could be replaced at any time. Of course the form of these common things was beautiful, for there has never been any need of ugly utensils. As the commentator observes, "the grace of life lies in quiet simplicity and real taste in the confines of the perfectly natural."

Though Kō-etsu was not involved in the politics of the day, he expressed himself on them very freely, according to the record of a discussion he had with Matsudaira Izu-no-kami at the mansion of Itakura Shigemune. Itakura asked Kō-etsu to give Matsudaira the benefit of his views quite frankly, and he certainly did so. He was a great admirer of Ieyasu, and a severe critic of Hideyoshi. It is not seemly, he said, that a man should rise from the people to rule the Empire in one lifetime. Such a process should take several generations. Otherwise the ruler will be a megalomaniac without any sense of proportion and decency, and liable to trouble the people with such enterprises as the Great Buddha and the Korean Expedition. And it was natural that his house should soon fall as a retribution for his disloyal conduct to the family of his lord. Character is the most important thing, he observes, and farmers and tradesmen have quite a different character and way of life from military men, so that if such become military men, their real character is apt to show itself. From farmers there have arisen many good soldiers and statesmen both in China and in Japan, he considers, but none from tradesmen. These should keep to their account books. They have no capacity to engage in government. Government, he says, should not be too severe, for the people of this Empire are high-spirited, and will commit suicide.

He does not think verse-making to be recommended for warriors, and observes that reading the poems of Li Po and Tu Fu with their praise of wine and drinking is apt to make people inclined to follow their example, which is not good, for they were undesirables, though skilled in poetry. In the same way he does not think rulers need to be learned for learning will never give anyone capacity to rule. If, he says, the erudite Honda Masanobu could bring down Confucius and all the Chinese sages from the heaven where they presumably are to govern this country, they would not be able to accomplish it any better than they could when they were alive, for it is notorious that the ages in which they lived were extremely chaotic.

Kō-etsu also expressed most loyal sentiments toward the Emperor in whose service he was, and the wish that his descendants should not leave and go to Edo, and also lamented that the Court nobility were given such small allowances. He mentions many as having only 30 koku, and thinks that this is not enough to keep them out of mischief, for if they have so little they may take to gambling and careless ways, and consorting with their inferiors, instead of living the proper life of poetry and aesthetics which was all that their seclusion left them.

CHAPTER 37

THE THREE JINNAI OF EDO

THE case of these three rather outstanding characters of the Keicho period (1596–1614) may illustrate how the early Tokugawa Government dealt with the difficulties that naturally came their way in such a time, and the result.

The first Jinnai is immortalized by a bridge called after him in Asakusa, and also by a small shrine not far away. He was, like the other two Jinnai, a highwayman by profession, and a very formidable one, the most efficient of the three it seems. He became a pupil of the great fencing master, Miyamoto Musashi, and was as much at home in the water as he was on land. But as he was given to dissipation he began cutting down people in the streets and taking their purses to supply himself with funds. Which becoming known to Miyamoto Musashi he took him for a walk to the river and suggested that his presence in the city and the world was no longer necessary or desirable. Taking the hint, he jumped into the river, but swam away underneath the water and escaped to take to the road between the two capitals, where he did well, whether as the result of his prayer to a certain deity to make him the greatest thief in the land or owing to his own natural abilities in that direction is as one may be pleased to decide. And whether the authorities would have got him so soon as they did is as uncertain, but fortunately for them he suffered from recurrent fever, and when he was incapacitated by a fit of this complaint they caught him, and not unnaturally condemned him to be crucified. He was not at all dismayed when the sentence came to be carried out at the execution place near the bridge now called after him, but turned to the crowd and called out to them: "I shouldn't have been taken in this disgusting way if it had not been for that ague. If anyone who suffers from that disease will pray to me after death I will heal it, however severe." And with that he got up on the cross and was transfixed. But ever since that time the people of Edo have prayed to him to heal their diseases, and he has done so, or at least they think he has, which is the main thing, so that he is still remembered and revered as Jinnai Sama or Kosaka Sama, and has been of no small profit to the capital of the Tokugawas, little though the authorities of the day foresaw it. And though his life was hardly an unqualified success professionally, he achieved that immortality that many worthier men failed to secure.

The second Jinnai, Tobisawa Jinnai, was also a highwayman who was so unfortunate as to be caught, how is not related, though he was also a great swordsman and as active as a monkey. But he was not put to death but pardoned on condition that he employed his talents on the side of the Government. This he was to do in the not very dignified position of officially licensed chief of the dealers in second-hand clothes, which the magistrate thought would afford him the best opportunity of getting information about thieves and doubtful characters whose ways he was otherwise well qualified to know. And in this business, which was quite lucrative, he would be able to work in harmony with the third Jinnai, who had another kind of net to spread for them. Tobisawa Jinnai's name has also been immortalized, for during the whole of the Tokugawa era the business of second-hand clothes dealing was carried on in the street called after him, and still but little altered into Tomisawa-cho.

The third of the name, Shōji Jinnai, was of somewhat more distinguished origin, for his family had been retainers of Hōjō of Odawara until that lord was dispossessed by Hideyoshi, after which he became a ronin, and as their custom so often was, got his living by lurking on the roads and calling on society to stand and deliver. But Shōji Jinnai fancied himself in the role of a benefactor to society as well, for it seems that he only robbed the evil wealthy and gave some of the results to those he thought especially virtuous, together with an ethical lecture on the probability that virtue would be rewarded in the end. Doing in fact unofficially just what the Tokugawa magistrates did officially. But growing tired of this, he determined to live an even more honest and useful life, so he made a proposal to the authorities in 1613 of an ingenious nature, which they were forced to admit seemed promising. He had observed, he said, that there were various houses in Edo where dancing-girls and courtesans resided, and to which people were accustomed to resort for diversion, and that such places were not as orderly as could be wished. That people were encouraged to stay there as long as they had any money, with the result that many were entirely impoverished.

Also that worthless fellows were apt to kidnap girls or adopt them and sell them to these places. Also, a plea that would make a strong appeal to the Shogunate officials, that unattached samurai who were liable to hatch evil plots and prey on society were in the habit of making them a rendezvous.

Now these were things about which Shōji Jinnai was very competent to give an opinion, for he had himself been one of these unattached samurai, and he was now engaged in keeping one or more of just this kind of establishment. So the City Magistrate, Yonezu Kambei, submitted the proposal for the consideration of Honda Masanobu and Ieyasu. Nothing was done for a while, and it was not till 1618 that permission was given and a piece of land as well. This was about five acres in extent, and situated in what later on became the middle of the business quarter of the city. But at this time it was little more than a reedy marsh, and worth nothing, a haunt of foxes and footpads, so that as usual it was a good bargain for the Bakufu, who hoped to see it put in order for them.

So the Bakufu issued the order for the permission of an amusement quarter subject to the observance of the following rules:

1. That no courtesans be allowed outside this quarter.
2. That no guest be allowed to stay more than twenty-four hours.
3. That with regard to the costumes worn in this quarter, gold and silver embroidery are forbidden and dresses shall be of ordinary dyed materials.
4. That the houses are not to be built in a particularly ornamental style, and that the quarter is to have the same officers and headman as any other in Edo.
5. Information shall be given to the City Magistrate's office about any suspicious character whether Samurai or Citizen, and to this end careful examination of all guests of the quarter shall be made.

The quarter was surrounded by walls, and entrance was only by one gate, at which was stationed a guard of Yōriki from the establishment of the City Magistrate. There was also a notice to the effect that not even a daimyo was to ride through the gate in a palanquin, the only exception being doctors, who might do so. Also that no kind of weapon might be carried in the quarter. They must be left at the guardhouse outside. So by the inauguration of this quarter the Bakufu were able to prepare a very effective trap for bad characters, for if they were not caught when they tried to dispose of some of their spoil in the second-hand clothes shops under the supervision of Tobisawa Jinnai, they were not likely to escape when they went to make merry on the proceeds in the quarter set apart for that purpose under the auspices of Shōji Jinnai. And it was not by any means out of pure benevolence that this worthy had such a regard for the pockets of his guests, but much more likely because he did not wish to kill the goose that would lay more golden eggs for him in the future.

This was one of the matters that his contemporary Akbar also took in hand, for we are informed that "The women of the town were registered and limited to the quarter of the town called Shaitanpur or 'devilsbury,' where their commerce was legalized and taxed. But the seduction of virgins was severely reprobated." What Ieyasu's personal views on the subject were appears from the way he treated it in his own province.

In the Abekawa district of Suruga there was a quarter where a lot of strumpets lived, and as it was near the castle the young soldiers of the garrison used to go there pretty often. Fearing that the foot of idleness would be put into the stirrup of dissipation, the Machi Bugyo Hikosaka Kyubei proposed to move this pleasure quarter two or three ri away. Hearing of this Ieyasu called Kyubei and asked him what would be the result of moving townspeople who had always lived near the castle to a distance. "It would be very bad for their trade for they would lose business," replied the magistrate. "Well, these strumpets are trade, aren't they?" said Ieyasu, "and if you move them all this long distance away the Abekawa people won't be able to get a living. You had better leave them where they are." So they were not disturbed, and the quarter became livelier and more prosperous than ever, and the young samurai went there and spent their money in dissipation so that many of them became hard up and in difficulties.

This, too, soon reached the ears of Ieyasu, and he again sent for the Bugyo, and it was the autumn season. "Of late," he said, "the sound of the dancing and singing of the townspeople has reached me even here in the castle, and it seems very pleasant. I should like to see it as well as hear it, so tell them to come in here and perform. They can come just as they are; they need not have any special dress made for the occasion." So the Bugyo divided the city into three and got together the dancers and their bands and for three nights they came to the castle and performed and were entertained afterwards with rice and red beans and liquor. Then Ieyasu asked, "And what about the dances of the Abekawa people?" "Oh, I didn't invite those strumpets," replied Hikosaka. "But now I am old I don't care so much for the uncouth dances of the men. I would rather see some danced by women," objected Ieyasu. So Hikosaka sent post-haste to the Abekawa quarter and gave orders that the most famous of the performers there should be reported to him and should prepare themselves. So the same evening they presented themselves at the castle, and after Ieyasu had seen them dance he called the best of them up on to the dais and asked their names, after which they retired and were served with cakes in the anteroom. While they were being entertained his confidant Fukuami went and told them on the quiet that as the lord might see fit to summon any of them in the future they were to keep it in mind. But when the young samurai heard of this possibility they were filled with consternation, for they reflected that if their lord called any of these damsels and questioned them there was no knowing what they might not tell him about them. And so thereafter all of those of any standing gave up going to the Abekawa quarter. Thus satisfactorily were the interests of the townsmen and the military alike considered, and in a way that could offend no one.

And incidentally that Ieyasu was no over-strict military martinet with his men is apparent from his leniency on occasions. It seems to have been the habit of his guards at Suruga to go out into the town to see some show like a wrestling-match, leaving one or two only to keep watch. One night he happened to go the rounds himself and found only one man on guard. "Are you a lot of cowards, or a lot of scatter-brains, that you run away like this and leave the place in charge of one man?" he commented. "A pretty useless crew you are!" And they mended their ways without any more ado and played truant no more. Another time he came in suddenly and found the young samurai having a wrestling-match in one of the apartments of the castle sprawled all over the floor, but he was not angry with them. He only told them to reverse the floor-mats if they wanted to take this sort of exercise or Fukuami would rate them if he caught them for damaging the binding of the edges.

CHAPTER 38

LITERARY TASTE OF THE MIKADO AND SHOGUN

ONE of the features of the period of Ieyasu was the interest in literature, mainly due to the intellectual tastes of both Ieyasu himself and the Emperor Go Yozei, though the tendency had existed from the end of the Ashikaga period and perhaps only needed peace to develop it. Asakura and Matsunaga as well as Nobunaga had been patrons of letters, even in that warlike age. It has been suggested that Ieyasu owed this taste to having been brought up in the literary family of the Imagawa, but actually his taste in letters was quite different from theirs. They were given to the Court style of literary activity in Japanese verse, classical Chinese poetry, and the older romances of Court life such as the *Genji* and other *Monogatari,* but for these Ieyasu had little use. It is observed by Shimazu Yoshihisa that when he had to attend such a verse party he got a scholar to write his share for him. What he liked were ethical and historical works, such as the Confucian classics and Chinese history (the *Shi-ki of Ssu Ma chien,* the *Roku-to* and *Sanryaku* or books of strategy and so on), and among Japanese texts the Engishiki and Azuma Kagami. And this, observes Tokutomi, was much to the point, for the life of Ieyasu was no poem. Neither had he any of the artistic taste of Hideyoshi. What he had was an intense craving for information of all sorts, more especially for that kind that he could put to practical use. It was what appealed to the intellect that he liked, and not what appealed to the emotions, with which Ieyasu was not at all liberally supplied. Literature that instructed in duty and how to rule an Empire. In this taste he was followed by his sons Yorinobu of Kishu and Yoshiano of Owari, and especially that great scholar Mitsukuni of Mito, his grandson, as well as his other grandson, Hoshina Masayuki of Aizu, son of Hidetada. Whether he would have been so devoted to history had he been able to foresee that the study of it would lead to the overthrow of his house is another question.

The year before the battle of Sekigahara we find him giving many tens of thousands of Chinese movable types to a scholar, Sanyo Gentetsu, who had been head of the Ashikaga University, and he had met the great Confucian scholar Fujiwara Seikwa in 1594, afterwards attending his lectures at Fushimi, where he was reproved for not coming in ceremonial dress, and took the reproof in good part. In 1601 he had an edition of the Chinese strategical classics printed, and in 1606 one of the Azuma Kagami, the Japanese history of the period of Kamakura, 1180–1266. The original MS. of this work was one that Kuroda Naga-masa had received from his father Jōsui, who had it from the Hojo of Odawara when that place was taken by Hideyoshi. Afterwards in 1613 he ordered Hayashi Razan, the successor of Fujiwara Seikwa, to make an epitome of this work, which he was never tired of perusing during his leisure hours in the intervals of his campaigns. Often he used to discuss the various incidents in the life of Yoritomo, who is the hero of it, with his friends in the evenings at his castle of Shizuoka, and there is no doubt but that he modelled himself to a large extent on Yoritomo. As Ieyasu grew older his interest in these studies became more pro-nounced. After Sekigahara he confiscated the library of Ankokuji Eikei, and gave it to his friends the priests Shotai and Sanyo, and he founded a college at Fushimi and a library at the Fujimitei at Edo.

It was just at this time that the so-called Tei Shu School of Con-fucianism was being introduced into Japan. This was the philosophy or religion associated with the names of Ch'eng and Chu Hi of the Sung period of the eleventh and twelfth centuries. It was a mixture of the original ethic of Confucius with elements taken from Taoism and Buddhism, and thus catered for those who wanted a system of ethics combined with a theory of the Universe and its relation to man. The Universe was produced from the Great Absolute by the action of Yang and Yin, the Positive and Negative principles by Ki or Spirit acting according to Li or Reason, and there was plenty for the teachers to argue about concerning the habits of these elements, very contrary to the views of Confucius, who would never discuss these things. As to the behavior of man, it was to be in accord with natural principles, i.e. the relations of subject to lord and child to parent, and those of junior and senior members of the family, husband and wife, friend and friend: Chū Kō Jin Gi Rei Chi Shin* is the succinct way of expressing all this. Now as this was a family ethic it was always more or less opposed to the ascetic ideal of Buddhism, and so there came to be a natural an-tagonism between these Confucian teachers and the Buddhist priests. But it is very characteristic of Ieyasu that he did not share or support this at all, for he was very anxious to utilize both schools if he could, and he had his Buddhist priest advisers such as Suden and Tenkai, as well as the Confucianists Seikwa and Hayashi; so this extract from his

* Loyalty, Filial Piety, Benevolence, Duty, Etiquette, Knowledge, Truth.

doings is enlightening: "Eighth day of the fifth month 1613 (Ieyasu *aetat* 71), Hino Yuishin, Minase Issai, Asukai Masatsune, Reizei Sammi Tamemitsu, Tsuchi-Mikado Sama-no-suke Hisanobu, and Funabashi Shikibu Shoyu Hidekata came and discussed Chinese philosophy and Buddhism to the accompaniment of crane soup." These guests were all scholars of the Court nobility, and no doubt in such an eclectic atmosphere the discussion would be quite impartial.

Two years after this we find him ordering Suden to have an epitome of the Tripitaka printed, a bird's-eye view of the Buddhist Bible. This was done with copper type, of which he had 89,814, probably brought from Korea, and it was in June 1615, just after the Osaka summer campaign, that he was pleased to inspect the result and then to order a hundred and twenty-five copies to be printed and sealed with the red seal of the Shogun and presented to the temples. However, though Ieyasu liked Buddhism well enough, and used it well, too, it was the Tei Shu School of Confucianism that was to become the official philosophy of the Tokugawa Shogunate, as laid down by Ieyasu and his professorial adviser, Hayashi Nobuatsu, or Doshun or Razan as he was called, just as the political philosophy of that institution was mapped out by him with the assistance of Tenkai and Honda Masanobu. Hayashi was a youthful prodigy who could read the works of the T'ang and Sung poets when he was thirteen, so that he was said to be like the god of wisdom incarnate (Monju no Keshin), and he started lecturing on Confucius when he was twenty-one, becoming a year later the pupil of Fujiwara Seikwa, and a year after that he was summoned to an audience with Ieyasu in the Nijo castle at Kyoto. Here were in attendance the two Buddhist priests, Shodai and Sanyo, and Kiyohara Hidekata, who had objected to his lecturing, and complained to Ieyasu that his teaching was unorthodox, and that he ought to be admonished for lecturing at all, since he was a private person without official standing. Ieyasu proceeded to give them a *viva voce* examination on Chinese history, and Hayashi was the only one who could answer any of the questions (this is his own description of the interview), and so he became a sort of walking dictionary to the Shogunate, and was no doubt employed to draw up much if not all of the legislation.

"How many generations were there from Kobu to Koso? In which book is the incense called Henkonka described? What kind of orchid did Kutsugen fancy?" were the questions that Ieyasu put to these scholars, and though the others had no idea the answers of Hayashi "came quick as an echo."

On another occasion Ieyasu asked the Shinto priest, Bonshun, to read him the part of the *Nihongi* concerning the Mikados Kimmei and

Kōgyoku and he could not, but when Hayashi was called he did it easily. Bonshun explained that he could read the earlier part of this text because it had the Japanese readings in Kana syllabary but that about the Earthly Emperors had none, and so he was at a loss.

Hayashi lived to be seventy-five years old, and was never without a book in his hand, and he established his family as hereditary classical scholars to the Shogunate.[*]

Ieyasu liked learning for its use, it is true, but he seems undoubtedly to have liked it for its own sake too. He was a bibliophile, and liked literary discussions as well as arguments about Buddhist philosophy, and it was one of his greatest pleasures in life to get together several learned priests and start them on a disputation. These were by no means short, for one is said to have lasted from 8 A.M. till 2 P.M. Neither were they at all unprofitable to the participators, for we also read of presents of a hundred koku of rice on one occasion, and a hundred pieces of silver on another, not to speak of robes being given to them afterwards.

Another subject that attracted him was pharmacy, and he would call for both specimens of medicinal herbs as well as books about it.

When he was seventy-three, the year before he died, when he was traveling to Shizuoka in triumph after the fall of the castle of Osaka, he was held up at Minakuchi for three days on account of heavy rain, so he ordered Hayashi Razan to lecture on the *Analects* of Confucius, and whiled away the time with discussions of the excellence of filial piety and loyalty.

And the very last thing he did was to order and superintend the printing of the *Gunsho-jiyo*. This was entrusted to Hayashi and Suden, and they were given the Noh theatre in the San-nomaru at Shizuoka to serve as a printing house. There was not sufficient type, so a Chinese, Rin Go Kan, cast some more for them. He cast thirteen thousand in all. After the collation of the MS. by Naoe Yamashiro-no-kami, the printing was begun about three months after the beginning of the work, which brought it to the seventeenth day of the third month, and unfortunately Ieyasu died on the same day of the fourth month, so he did not see its completion. There still survive the rules that Hayashi and Suden wrote up for the workers:

(a) That work begin at 6 A.M. and end at 6 P.M. After that a rest is allowed.
(b) That loud talking and wrangling is not permitted.

---

[*] The Confucian scholar was, like the physician, conventionally a Buddhist priest, tonsured and using the honorary titles "hoin," "Hogen," etc. It was not actually till 1692 that Hayashi's grandson was enabled to quit this ecclesiastical atmosphere and enter the military caste with the rank of Bangashira and the style Daigaku-no-kami, "Lord of Knowledge." Ever since that time academics have been Government officials. And this change was owing to the efforts of that patron of learning, Tokugawa Mitsukuni, grandson of Ieyasu.

(c) All shall be most diligent. This is not to be overlooked.
(d) No one shall do any work of his own or damage the rooms or the Noh stage in any way.
(e) No one shall be allowed to bring in his friends to look on.

Ieyasu restored to the Ashikaga College the books that Hidetsugu had taken away to the capital, as well as giving a sum of money toward its rebuilding. He also built a college at Fushimi, and gave a number of sets of volumes of Chinese classics to it, appointing Sannyo Gentetsu to be its head. Moreover, he established a temple for this scholar on Higashi-yama, giving it an endowment of 200 koku and presenting it with ten thousand types with which to print copies of the *Jokan Seiyo, Koshi Kago,* and *Buryaku Shichisho.* This is the Enkoji on Higashiyama where these types still are or were kept.

Regretting that so many books had been destroyed in the Onin civil war, he also set himself to collect copies of these if possible, sometimes buying them and sometimes encouraging the Court nobles to present any they might still have. And in this way he procured a large number of valuable texts. He even sent to Shimazu for works on the Luchu Isles, of which the courtiers knew nothing.

Then he started a library in Edo castle in 1602, many of the books for which he got from the old Kanazawa Library, and sent for Kansho, the then head of the Ashikaga Library, to make the catalogue. And in order to obtain copies of ancient MSS. in the possession of the Imperial House and of the courtiers, he got together all the best writers among the priests of the capital and kept them at work all day from six in the morning till eight at night in the Nanzenji temple, with Hayashi and Suden in charge as supervisors. These were chiefly Japanese works, such as the *Kojiki, Nihongi, Nikon Shoki, Zoku Nikon Shoki, Montoku Jitsuroku, Sandai Jitsuroku, Kokushi, Ruiju Kokushi, Ritsurei, Koninskiki, Engi-shiki, Ruiju Sandai-ryaku, Shinsen Seishi-roku, Kogoshui, Shinko Keizu, Honcho Zoku-bunsui, Kwanki Bunshu,* etc., works of which it was said that most people did not even know the names, for they had been stored away untouched for ages. On these texts Ieyasu based much of his legislation and other enactments, and used them for the study of history in the light of which he liked to guide his policy.

He collected, too, a number of the verses of Fujiwara Teika, the compiler of the *Hyakunin Isshu,* which he exhibited to many of the courtiers to their considerable edification. Even the *Gengi Monogatari* was not neglected, though it was not the sort of literature that appealed to him as a rule, for we hear of his having an exposition of parts of it in his tearoom at Shizuoka, and again, the book *Hakakigi* is specified as having been read in the same apartment of the Nijo castle, the ladies-in-waiting being called in to listen on this occasion. He showed a sense of the fitness of things in this, for the atmosphere of the tearoom was not unsuitable for a reading of this elegant work. And he was critical of the text that was used for these readings. On more than one occasion it happened that when Ieyasu put some questions to the stately but not specially profound Court nobles about the ancient poets they replied that it was a mystery not to be lightly discussed, whereupon Hayashi would immediately start a lecture on it, much to their disgust but to the old Shogun's amusement, for he was never disinclined for information. And to this walking commentary of his nothing was sacred.

Even on his hawking expeditions he would spend the evening listening to lectures on the history of the Kamakura period and his favorite hero Yoritomo.

And in order that he might be able to follow any discussion of the ways of foreign countries he had a screen procured with a map of the world on it, and this was set up at Shizuoka, and Goto Shozaburo, the authority on economics, and Hasegawa Sahyoye, former Commissioner at Nagasaki, were summoned so that he might catechize them about it.

"A ruler of the Empire ought to know the Four Books of Confucius," he observed more than once, "and if he cannot be versed in them all he should certainly know *Mencius*. How can one who is ignorant of the way of learning rule the Empire properly? And the only road to this knowledge is through books. So the publication of books is the first principle of good government."

And not only was the Shogun a lover of books and publishing, for so also was the Emperor Go Yozei Tenno. In 1588 he had a work called the *Kinshu-dan* printed with movable wooden type in the manner lately reintroduced from Korea. After this he ordered the publication of the two volumes of the *Jindai-maki* of the Nihon Shoki. In the preface (appendix) he observes that Shinto is the basis of all morality. Confucianism is the branches and leaves and Buddhism is the fruit. These two faiths are the latest offshoots of Shinto, and as such they are profitable in illuminating their origin. Of late there have been many who have studied them, but few, on the contrary, who have devoted themselves to Shinto. Everything has an origin and an after development. Why should we neglect the one and cultivate the other? Living in the Land of the Gods should we neglect the Gods? Reliance on their descendants will ensure the prosperity of the Empire. Their service takes the first place in the government.

There followed the publication of the books of Confucius, the *Great Learning*, the *Chu Yo* or *Universal Standard of Ethics*, the *Analects* and *Mencius,* and afterwards the *Chokonka** and the *Lute Maiden of Po-Chu-i.* This Emperor, it appears, had hoped to be able to make an Imperial progress to Pekin as the result of Hideyoshi's Korean war, and his knowledge of Chinese literature was great. And not less so was his learning in Buddhism. In 1606 he was given the highest title a Buddhist priest could reach, that of Kokushi, Cho-ei-emmyo Kokushi, by Nange Zenji, who proceeded to the palace and heard His Majesty discuss Zen philosophy. Then, too, the Emperor lectured at Court on the Japanese classics, especially the *Ise Monogatari* and *Genji Monogatari,* showing himself deeply versed in all the various commentaries on these books. And though a bibliophile, he was more considerate than such persons sometimes are, for we read that he borrowed a very rare work, the *Shoryaku-in* in manuscript, written by Chisho Daishi, from Myochi-in Osho, and after a month's time returned it with a present of three pieces of silver.

However, although both the Emperor Go-Yozei and his son the Emperor Go-Mizu-no-o had tastes similar to those of the retired Shogun, the relations between them were not so very cordial. Apart from having some sympathy with Hideyori, whose father Hideyoshi had been in high favor at Court, and had been regarded as a Court noble to a large extent while Ieyasu had never been other than a military magnate, the Court may not have been sorry to see the power divided between Toyotomi and Tokugawa.

But the cause of the ill feeling between the Emperor and Ieyasu sprang from a difference of opinion he had with his son when he retired in 1612. He was at this time forty-one, and his son Masahito sixteen. The mother of this son was Chuwamon-in Chika-ko, daughter of the former Kampaku Konoe Sakihisa, or Ryuzan Ko.

When Go-Yozei retired to the "Fairies' Cave"† he took with him all his manuscripts and books and furniture and works of art, and left nothing for the new Emperor. This, of course, the latter resented, and his mother Chuwamon-in complained to the old man of Shizuoka about it, whereupon he, through the Shoshidai Itakura Katsushige, gave orders that all the Imperial properties were to be returned immediately to the palace, excepting only such things as the retired Emperor had acquired in his lifetime as his personal property. Whether it was slander of the Nyogo, as one view has it, it was believed by Ieyasu and acted upon, whereupon the Imperial anger was great. However, as nothing could be done, he had to submit, and after several high Court nobles

---

* Story of the Emperor Hsuan Tsung and the Lady Yang-kuei Fei.
† Palace of the Retired Emperor.

had inspected the Imperial possessions a procession of the ministers and courtiers of various ranks proceeded to the retired Emperor's palace and labelled those that were to be returned, and then bore them solemnly back to the main palace. It was a little excitement for them, no doubt, and they could feel they were really assisting in affairs of State, but from the list of articles given they do not seem very important. Only some screens and cabinets and a statue of Jizo, some leather cases, a hanging lamp, and a few hundred volumes of books of poetry and history.

However, the two Emperors became reconciled not long afterwards, as is attested by the entry in the diary of a Court noble of the time: "Twelfth month, sixteenth day. Fine, with a little snow. Invited to the palace of the retired Emperor, so went. Dengaku was performed. The Lord Hachijo and the Lord Takeuchi were there. The Lord Shirakawa and myself in attendance. Sang Utai and drank many cups of wine, by which latter I was adversely affected. The Empress came and the Emperor, and were offered liquor." But toward Ieyasu, it seems, the Imperial displeasure still continued. However, owing to the efforts of the priest Tenkai, who was a friend of both sides, the matter did not go much further. Tenkai, who was the Chaplain to the Emperor, and by whom he had been ordained, read him and also his son a lecture on their filial duties and this it was, no doubt, that led to their reconciliation, for by it the Dragon Scales were smoothed down.

Shortly before he retired Ieyasu remarked to Honda Masanobu when he came up from Edo to Sumpu on business, "When I was young I had so much fighting to do that I had no time to study, and so I am comparatively unlearned in my old age. Still, there are two sayings of Lao-tze that I have always kept in my mind from my youth, and they are, 'Those who understand how to be content with their lot are always happy,' and 'Recompense enmity with kindness.' The Shogun, of course, unlike me has had plenty of time for reading, and no doubt knows any number of wise sayings of the ancient sages, so there is no need to remind him, but I just tell you this for your own information." Honda was properly impressed, and went back to Edo and reported it to the Shogun, who at once called for an inkstone and wrote the sentences down with his own hand, afterwards telling Suden to write them out in large characters so that he could hang them in his sitting-room and have them always before his eyes. The original writing came into the hands of one Uchida Heizaemon, and when Iemitsu heard of it he sent and had it brought to him and then dressed in ceremonial costume and sat down in front of it and inspected it reverentially, as he was accustomed to do with anything personally connected with his mighty grandfather.

Ieyasu once remarked, "It is because people's minds are not logical and enlightened that the Empire is in disorder. If the country is not properly ruled there will be no end to rebellions. And if anyone wishes to get the knowledge of how to rule it properly he will only find it in books. That is why the publication of books is the beginning of beneficent rule."

A list of his learned friends is significant. First there were the military men, Honda Masanobu and Todo Takatora. Then the ecclesiastics, Son-o of the Zozoji, of the Jodo sect, Hojo-in of the Shingon sect, Nankobo Tenkai of the Tendai sect, Nange Osho, Sanyo Gentetsu, Hokoji Shodai, and Konchi-in Suden of the Zen sect, a very large preponderance. Then there were Shinryu-in Bonshun, the Shinto scholar, and Fujiwara Seikwa, and Hayashi Doshun, who specialized in Confucianism, Hino Yuishin, Nijo Akizane, and Kikutei Harusue, courtiers learned in palace ceremonial, Naka-no-in Michikatsu, Japanese littérateur, and Reizei Tamemitsu, a master of Japanese verse. Finally there came the two foreigners, Jan Joostens the Dutchman, and Will Adams from Gillingham in Kent.

CHAPTER 39

THE HONDAS

OF the many devoted retainers who surrounded Ieyasu and on whom he could rely to carry out his plans none were closer to him than Honda Masanobu and his son Masazumi. Born of a Mikawa samurai family that had served the house of Matsudaira since his grandfather's days, Masanobu had in his youth been in attendance on Ieyasu, to whom his knowledge of falconry would recommend him, until the Monto rebellion broke out. In this he was among those who opposed his lord, and in consequence had to leave his native province, and wandered about the country, eventually taking up his abode in Kaga and becoming one of the leaders of the Monto sect there. So from 1563 till 1582 he led an independent existence, of which not very much is known, no doubt spending a lot of time in his favorite Chinese studies, for he was notable among the Mikawa samurai as a scholar. As that eminent connoisseur Matsunaga Hisahide remarked of him, "I have seen a good many of the Tokugawa retainers, and they are practically all of the simple soldier type. But Masanobu is certainly something different. He's neither too strong nor too weak, neither is he insignificant."

Hideyoshi seems to have recognized his ability too, and wished to attach him to his own suite, but after consultation with Ieyasu, Honda managed to make some excuse and rejoined his former master. It was just before the death of Nobunaga that Ieyasu sent for him, and so he came back to the clan, and before long became the confidential adviser to its chief. For this his wide learning and his extensive knowledge of all parts of the country made him particularly suitable, added to the mentality of the same subtle nature as that of his lord. And this position he was quite content to hold to the end of his life, receiving no more than an income of 20,000 koku, which he was given when Ieyasu became lord of the Eastern provinces, and which he would never allow to be increased.

Slightly older, but having the same astute and calculating temperament as his master, he made an ideal councilor, for he entirely identified himself with his interests and completely suppressed his own individual ones. Never did he aim at wealth or high position, but was quite satisfied to be the trusted servant of his lord, and it is not recorded of him that he once failed him or presumed on his friendship or took advantage of his office in any way. The records of the English factory bear witness to his objection to taking a present of any value, and Spex, the Dutch factor, and Sebastian Vizscaino as well as Saris comment on the same phenomenon, the Spaniard contrasting it with the ways of the mint master, Goto Shozaburo, who received anything gladly, and though his property was worth some six million in gold and silver always wanted more.

So on all critical occasions of his life after Honda joined him we find the two in close consultation, later on shared by his son Masazumi as well; Masazumi nicknamed "Codskin Dono" by the English from his title of Kozuke-no-suke, that of his father being Sado-no-kami, or "Sadda Dono." Before Sekigahara and also before Osaka his advice as to the disposal of Ishida and his suggestions for the filling up of the moats of the latter fortress are good examples of his counsel, though it may be doubted whether Ieyasu himself was in any way lacking where disingenuous tricks were needed. The planning of the city of Edo and arrangement of its gates and moats and escarpments were also drawn up and detailed by Ieyasu and Masanobu in concert.

Then when Hidetada became Shogun the elder Honda was attached to him as secretary, while the younger remained with Ieyasu at Sumpu, and so effective was their co-operation that the often difficult situations that arose at times between the now rather irritable old man and his son were infallibly smoothed over, though Hidetada's even temper and self-control must have assisted not a little. Masazumi's intervention on behalf of Hidetada at Sekigahara placed the future Shogun under an obligation to him too, though that did not save him from disgrace and exile when for some reason he became suspect to the Bakufu. But that was only carrying out Ieyasu's own habit of being "severe to the near and indulgent with the far," and the secretary was treated no worse than the sons.

Unlike Ii and others who showed some discontent when after Sekigahara they only received comparatively modest fiefs, Honda Masanobu always declined further promotion, and is reported to have explained his position thus when Ieyasu pressed him to take a further reward: "I have long been favored by Your Highness, and though I am not rich neither am I poor. Moreover, I have never been capable of any martial deeds as a fighting man, and now I am getting on in years and my usefulness is coming to an end. But in a military State there is always the need of good soldiers, so if the income that would be given to me is used to provide more of them and thus the peace of the Empire is ensured, there is nothing that will make me happier in my old age."

CHAP. XI.
WILL ADAMS BEFORE THE EMPEROR.

In 1600, **William Adams** became the first Englishman to arrive in Japan. He would go on to become an advisor to Ieyasu as well as one of the few Western samurai. In this print, Adams (middle) is shown conferring with Ieyasu (left). (Wikimedia Commons)

The Battle of Sekigahara (1600) was a decisive victory for Ieyasu over a Toyotomi army commanded by Ishida Mitsunari. This battle was the largest fought during the feudal era with over 150,000 warriors facing off. Ieyasu's victory at Sekigahara led to his being appointed Shogun and the establishment of the Tokugawa Shogunate which would rule Japan until 1868. (Wikimedia Commons)

This panoramic print of the city of **Edo** from the 17th century is notable for its detailed view of Edo Castle (top right). When Ieyasu established the Tokugawa Shogunate in 1603, he chose the city of Edo as his capital. Edo Castle would remain the center of power of the Tokugawa Shogunate for the next 265 years. (Wikimedia Commons)

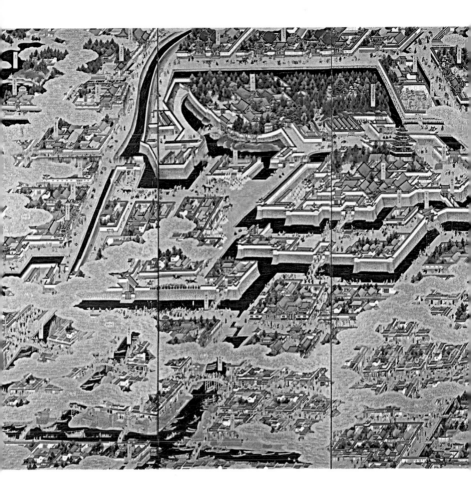

In 1610, Ieyasu ordered a castle to be built on the site of the ruins of a previous fortress in the city of Nagoya. The construction of **Nagoya Castle** was completed 5 years later. The castle was destroyed during the bombing of Nagoya during World War II but was reconstructed in 1959. (Wikimedia Commons)

The Imperial Palace in Tokyo was built on the site of **Edo Castle**, the home of the Tokugawa Clan, which was destroyed by fire in 1873. Pictured here is the Fujimi-yagura (Mt Fuji-view Keep) which lies on the place grounds, one of the few surviving keeps from Edo Castle's inner citadel. (Wikimedia Commons)

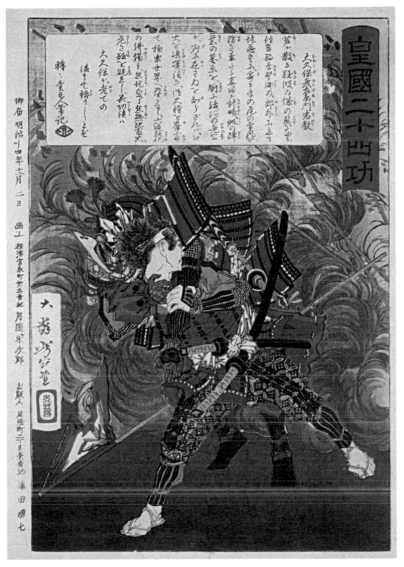

In this print by Tsukioka Yoshitoshi, the warrior **Okubo Tadanori** is shown rescuing Ieyasu on the battlefield at the siege of Osaka Castle (1615–16). In this scene, during a furious attack, Okubo drags Ieyasu to safety as an enormous explosion hits their camp. Okubo was one of Ieyasu's trusted generals and served the Tokugawa clan for many years as an advisor. (Wikimedia Commons)

A portrait of **Tokugawa Ieyasu** by Kanō Tannyū. Ieyasu is shown here presiding as Shogun. After victory at the Battle of Sekigahara (1600), Ieyasu was appointed Shogun in 1603. He would abdicate two years later but effectively held power until his death in 1616. (Wikimedia Commons)

Ieyasu is presented with the severed head of **Kimura Shigenari** during the summer siege of Osaka Castle (1615) in this print by Tsukioka Yoshitoshi. Kimura Shigenari was a general of the Toyotomi clan. (Wikimedia Commons)

The famous **mon (crest) of the Tokugawa clan**. The "triple hollyhock" design is an iconic symbol of the greatest, and last, shogunate. (Shutterstock)

In this detail of a larger 6-piece panel, Osaka Castle keep is shown during the **Summer Siege of Osaka Castle** (1615). Ieyasu laid siege to Osaka Castle during the winter of 1614 through the summer of 1615 in an attempt to put

down the opposition to the Tokugawa Shogunate by the Toyotomi Clan. As a result of the two-part campaign, Ieyasu succeeded in subjugating the Toyotomi Clan and solidified the Tokugawa hold on power. (Wikimedia Commons)

Tokugawa Ieyasu is shown here in his later years as retired Shogun. Although he abdicated in favor of his son, Tokugawa Hidetada, in 1605, Ieyasu was effectively the ruler of Japan until his death in 1616. (Wikimedia Commons)

A life-size wooden statue of **Tokugawa Ieyasu** from the Edo-Tokyo Museum in Tokyo. The statue dates to 1601, after the Battle of Sekigahara. (Wikimedia Commons)

Pictured here is a replica of **armor worn by Tokugawa Ieyasu**. It is an example of *gusoku* design with a lamellar cuirass (breastplate made of armor plates strung together). (Wikimedia Commons)

Tokugawa Ieyasu's hand print displayed at the Kunozan Toshogu in Shizuoka, the first Shinto shrine dedicated to Ieyasu in 1617. (Wikimedia Commons)

Statue of **Tokugawa Ieyasu** at Nikko Toshogu, a Shinto shrine built in 1617 and dedicated to the great Shogun in Nikko, Tochigi Prefecture. Ieyasu is buried on the shrine's grounds. (Shutterstock)

Shiba Toshogu, located in Tokyo's Minato ward, is one of five Shinto shrines where Ieyasu is deified throughout Japan. (Wikimedia Commons)

Statue of **Tokugawa Ieyasu** in Okazaki Park in Okazaki, Aichi Prefecture. Okazaki Castle, where Ieyasu was born, lies on the park grounds. (Wikimedia Commons)

And probably no sentiment could be calculated to please Ieyasu better, as Masanobu was well aware. And again before he died he repeated to Hidetada that he wished his son's income to remain as it was, for it was sufficient if their services were not forgotten and the future of the family assured. Masanobu's relations with Ieyasu and his son are thus described in the *Hankampu:* "He was regarded by Ogosho as a friend and by the Shogun (Hidetada) as a respected elder. He always addressed the former as 'O-Dono,' 'Great Lord,' and the latter as 'Waka-Dono,' 'Young Lord.' In military discussions he was very laconic, giving his opinion in a word or two, and he was clever in allegory." Masanobu had been lamed by a wound when he was young, and that was a good reason why he did not take part in active military work, but he was always by his master's side in the field all the same.

And it was by means of these two "secretaries of a superior order," as they are styled, that Ieyasu carried on his administration, for he had no ministers. His other consultants were his military staff and his friends among the monks and scholars. The only danger might be that he should depend on the Hondas too much or see things through their eyes, but his character was strong enough and his activity sufficiently great to preclude any such likelihood, while the Hondas were far too shrewd to try and monopolize him, for they realized that they would lose influence if they tried it on one so quick to suspicion, and so ready to hear the views of all and sundry. Honda Masanobu was indeed an ideal retainer, but it needed an intelligent lord to make full use of him, and here came in Ieyasu's special capacity for selecting suitable instruments for his work. "For thirty-five years," says Tokutomi, "Honda lived for and slaved for Ieyasu. They had no secrets from each other, and so closely did the secretary keep his master's confidences that the devil himself would have been put to it to find anything out."

And this applied to Masazumi also, for from the age of eighteen he, too, was equally trusted. Oddly enough, he seems to have been addressed by Ieyasu as though he was more respected if Goto Shosaburo's account is to be relied on, for that astute financier remarks, "I wonder why it was that Gongen Sama would say to the elder Honda 'Sado!' Do this or do that (Sado! Aa Itase! Ko se!), while to the son Masazumi it would always be 'Kozuke Dono!' Please do this, or that (Kosuke Dono! Aa mesare! Ko mesare!)."

Thus the equally efficient and assiduous son so assisted his father in conducting administration and diplomacy with the least possible friction that between them they quite monopolized the business of advising Ieyasu and left little room for anyone else, so adept were they in anticipating his wishes and understanding his probable intentions.

And naturally this rapid rise of Honda to such a position of trust was not likely to be regarded with entire acquiescence by the other greater retainers whose place he and his son practically took, for it is very noticeable that for some reason or another several of them like Sakakibara, Ii, and Koriki were more or less eliminated, while Okubo Tadachika, the most influential of all, was deprived of his fief. And these things have been ascribed to the jealousy and slanders of the Hondas.

Particularly in the case of the latter does his uncle, the famous Okubo Hikozaemon, declare that not only was this so, but it was base ingratitude on the part of Honda Masanobu, who had been in his early days a protégé of Tadachika's father Tadayo, who had helped him when he was very poor and was earning a bare living by his knowledge of falconry and who had interceded for him so that he could come back again to his clan. And when Tadayo died he had asked Honda to deal kindly with his son, and declared that if he failed to do so retribution would follow.

And therefore, says Hikozaemon, within three years of Tadachika's fall Honda Masanobu was stricken with the Chinese pox so that one side of his face rotted away and showed his back teeth, and so he died, while not very long afterward his son was deprived of his fief and exiled to Dewa. There may be something in this accusation, for though the direct cause of Okubo's fall seems to have been his connection with his namesake and client Okubo Nagayasu, yet the indirect one may have been Honda, who seems to have been concerned in the disclosures about Nagayasu.

But anyhow Okubo was not so devoted and Ieyasu-centerd as was Honda, for it was one of the complaints against him that he absented himself from attendance when his son died, whereas when a daughter to whom Honda was much attached also died her father carried on his duties exactly as usual. The real reason for the fall of both Okubo and the younger Honda probably was that they both became suspect of lack of whole-hearted co-operation in the plans of the Bakufu and a menace to its complete security than which no accusation was easier to incur or more difficult to refute, and for which no previous merit would normally compensate. High office has always been in Japan a dangerous responsibility, for the individual is not considered but only the system.

[CHAPTER 40]

DEATH OF IEYASU

AFTER the fall of Osaka and the removal of his opponents, Ieyasu went on a hawking tour from Shizuoka to Edo, combining politics with exercise, as was his custom. Ieyasu was as fond of his hawks as Hideyoshi was of his elegant buildings, as the fact of his having ordered a servant to be executed about this time for damaging one of them well illustrates. It may be compared to the crucifixion of the boys by Hideyoshi for scribbling on his gates.

He afterwards returned to Mishima near Odawara and ordered a place of retirement to be built there for him, but after a while he countermanded this order, giving as his reason the burden it would inflict on the daimyos who had to provide the labor so soon after their exertions in the Osaka campaign. Going home again to Shizuoka he was taken ill there after eating rather much of a dish of sea bream cooked in sesame oil as recommended to him by the merchant Chaya Shirojiro. Ieyasu had asked his old friend if there was any new dish he had sampled in Kyoto, and Chaya described this one, which seems to be what afterwards became popular as Tempura. As he had just been presented with some bream he had it cooked in this novel fashion. But though it upset him, it does not seem to have been the cause of his death, which is generally attributed to cancer of the stomach, since the symptoms as described are most consistent with this disease. After this first indisposition he rallied for a while after dosing himself with a pill* in which he had great faith, for he had always taken great care of his health, little need though there had been for doing so, since he had scarcely ever been ill, his only recorded troubles having been a cold and a carbuncle. A frugal diet, the avoidance of any excess, and an active, largely outdoor life added to his well-known capacity for sleep at any time, and a complete absence of nerves had ensured his physical health. However, he had a relapse, and began to get weaker, whereupon it was represented to the Emperor by his friends that it would be a graceful

---

* Among the pills he had compounded was the Manbyo-en, or Pill for a Myriad Ills, and the Hojin-yaku, or Kidney-assisting Pill, No. 8, as he styled it, because he kept it in the eighth drawer of the medicine cabinet he always had by him.

thing to make him Dajodaijin.* The Emperor took the hint, and issued
an edict accordingly, and the commission was brought to him by an
imposing array of Court officials, who were received in great state at
Shizuoka, and after the ceremony, which Ieyasu got up to attend, spite
of his weakness, a Noh performance was given followed by a banquet,
and presents of money to the Emperor, the retired Emperor, and all the
envoys and courtiers. Lower First Court Rank and Dajodaijin, he had
nothing more to attain in this world, though the latter honor was little
but a farewell present for the world to come.

Though so ill he put on his Court dress and received the congratulations of the daimyos, and everything was carried out with the utmost
splendor and dignity. Verses were made as usual, and that composed
by, or rather on behalf of, Ieyasu ran thus:

> In the vernal breeze
> Of Yamato's peaceful land
> Countless cherry trees
> Shall from age to age reveal
> All their charm in perfumed flowers.

During this last illness he received visits from several great lords,
especially from Date Masamune, who had always been a friend of
his, but of whom he was evidently not without his suspicions still,
for Masamune was rather an unfathomable fellow. To him Ieyasu presented a writing by Seisetsu, a Chinese Zen priest of Fuhkien, who had
come to Japan and settled in the Nanzenji. Date put up in a temple
at Shizuoka, and stayed there from the twenty-third day of the second
month till the fourth (or ninth) of the fourth month. Ieyasu died on
the seventeenth.

Looking back some seventeen years to the death of the former lord
of the Empire, Hideyoshi, there was indeed a great difference. For
Hideyoshi had passed away in a state of very great anxiety about the
future of his house, since his only son and heir was a child of six,
and there could be no certainty as to how he would fare. And all the
Regents were wealthy and powerful lords, and little likely to dwell
in harmony for long. Hideyoshi must have been certain that there
would be a struggle for the supreme power, and equally uncertain as
to whether it would continue to abide with his house. Whichever way

---

* That there was a question of some such honor was known to Mr. Cocks on August 22nd, for he notes
in his diary, "Our scrivano of the junk tells me that Ogosho Samme sues to the Dyrio to have the name of
Quambaco, which, it should seeme, is as the names of Ceaser or Augustus amongst the Emperors of Rome,
which is held an honor to all suckceadors. But he denied it till he know Fidaia Same (Hideyori) is dead."
Only he was incorrectly informed about the title.

he looked he could only be anxious, and with very good reason. And Ieyasu was anxious too, but without any particular reason, except that it was his nature to anticipate every possible contingency, however remote. The saying "Asu wa ame, hito wa dorobo to omoe" ("All men are thieves and it will rain tomorrow") was a fairly good summary of his mentality. How very different were his circumstances from those of Hideyoshi. There were no great feudatories left who had any power to oppose his numerous and well-knit family interests, and Hidetada was thirty-eight and had been Shogun twelve years, while his son Iemitsu was a clever and spirited boy of twelve. However, he overlooked nothing. He went over the whole situation with Hidetada, received the Three Lords, Yoshinao, Yorinobu, and Yorifusa, and adjured them to see that they obeyed the Shogun in everything, summoned Todo and Honda, and told them to have adequate forces under arms when his death occurred so that they could immediately strike at any possible rebel. For the peace of the Empire nothing was to be neglected. The peace of the Empire under his family, of course. But, he observed, "the Empire does not belong to any one man; the Empire belongs to the Empire." So no doubt he thought, but like other autocrats he did not at any time think that the Empire knew what was good for it or could carry it out if it did. Those were the things that his family and their advisers were to make it their business to know. And very ably they did so. Ieyasu is credited with telling Hidetada to keep the daimyos in Edo for three years after his death. Hidetada replied that he would prefer to send them home for a year or so, and then summon them again. And if there should be any who did not obey he would march against him and destroy him. This reply pleased Ieyasu immensely.

One cannot say that the prospect of death softened Ieyasu very much. One thing he did was to order the imprisonment of Seikan, the priest who was said to have written the inscription on the bell that so much offended him, or that he alleged did so. He also refused to be reconciled to his son Tadateru, whose behavior at Osaka he had considered dilatory and disrespectful, and would not grant him an interview. Tadateru's mother, Cha-a-notsubone, earnestly begged him to pardon her son, but he was obdurate, merely remarking: "He may be a useful fellow, perhaps, and looks well, but he played the laggard at Osaka and did no fighting at all. Moreover, he put one of the Shogun's retainers to death on the road most arbitrarily. If he acts like this while I am alive, what may he not do after I am gone."

When he was going over the daimyos with Hidetada and discussing them, and they came to Kato Yoshiaki, Ieyasu said: "He has been loyal and sincere in his relations with our house ever since the Taiko's death, and he is a Mikawa man. If he is well treated he will be faithful, but if he takes offence at anything he gets discontented. So take care." "Oh, he is only a small man, anyhow," replied Hidetada, "so there is no need to worry about him." "Not at all, not at all!" retorted Ieyasu. "It never does to overlook people because they are small. In a dance, for instance, a young man may take the lead if he is good and understands rhythm, and under his influence even the seniors may be drawn in and dance to it involuntarily in spite of themselves. It is just the same in the affairs of the Empire. If there is unrest in the air and a man is good enough to be a leader, even though he has no original intention to rebel, he may easily find himself surrounded by a lot of admiring followers he has fascinated and there is the danger. You must be vigilant."

He also interviewed Fukushima Masanori, who was considered to have a partiality for the house of his former lord Hideyoshi, and presenting him with a valuable tea-caddy told him that though Hidetada was very suspicious of him and so had kept him in Edo some time he himself did not think he was in any way disloyal and had insisted on this to the Shogun, so now Masanori had better return to his province and his future relations with the Shogun must depend on how he deported himself. Not unnaturally Masanori was not exactly reassured by this, and his emotions overcame him as he retired from the old man's presence.

The following anecdote may be only of the appropriate type, but it is significant enough. "On the fifteenth (two days before he died) he summoned Suzuki Kyudaiyu Kageharu and gave him the sword Miike Tenda, telling him to go and have it tried on a criminal. He did so, and brought it back, saying that it was a fine blade and cut excellently. Ieyasu then brandished it two or three times vigorously and exclaimed, 'With this sword I will guard and protect my descendants for many ages.' His demeanour was most spirited and impressive." To the very last he was the same energetic and implacable old warrior-statesman. He further ordered Sakakibara Teruhisa, one of the oldest of his retainers, to see that offerings of fish and vegetables were always made before his tomb after his death, and to make a statue of him facing the west to ward off any trouble that might come from that quarter; the only quarter from which he knew it could, and eventually did, come.

"If any trouble starts in the Empire," he said to Hori Tangono-kami, whom he summoned to his deathbed, "do you call Todo Takatora and then Ii Kamon, and they shall stand between the two parties and prevent any collision."

He is said to have called Suden and Tenkai and Honda Masazumi, and told them that when he departed he was to be buried at Kunozan, and that the Buddhist celebration was to be held in the Zōzōji at Edo

while his ancestral tablet was to be placed in the Daijuji in Mikawa.
Then, when the proper time had elapsed a small shrine was to be
erected at Nikko in Shimozuke, where he was to be revered, while
at Kyoto the same services were to be rendered at the Konchiin by
the Nanzenji, to which the Shoshidai and the military men in Kyoto
should go to pay their respects. Then he gave orders about reorganizing
the formation of the troops, directing that in future the archers and
matchlockmen were to be together in the front rank, then the cavalry,
and then the spearmen.

From the fourth day he took little food and grew gradually weaker,
and from the eleventh he took none at all, but only drank a little hot
water.

Quite peacefully he died on the seventeenth day, and before depart-
ing according to custom he made two verses. They may be rendered:

> Whether one passes on or remains behind it is all the same.
> That you can take no one with you is the only difference.
>
> Ah, how pleasant! Two awakenings and one sleep.
> This dream of a fleeting world! The roseate hues of early dawn!

And so we find the simple entry in the diary of Konchiin Suden:
"On the seventeenth day of the fourth month at noon the Great Chancellor of the Empire of the Lower First Court Rank, Minamoto Ieyasu,
passed to another world aged seventy-five. And in the evening of the
same day he was taken to Kunozan."

With little ceremony he was borne at night up this steep hill by the
sea with its splendid views of Miho-no-matsubara and Mount Fuji.
"First went the two city magistrates of Edo, Hikosaka Mitsumasa and
Kuroyanagi Jūgaku, and the chief artificer, Nakai Yamato-no-kami, to
make all ready. Then followed the coffin, borne by Honda Masazumi,
Matsudaira Masatsuna, Itakura Shigemasa, the Shoshidai, and Akimoto
Yasutomo. Doi Toshikatsu attended as representative of the Shogun,
and Naruse Hayato, Ando Naotsugu, and Nakayama Nobuyoshi on
behalf of the three lords Yoshinao, Yorinobu, and Yorifusa. The ecclesiastics Tenkai, Suden, and Bonshun officiated. And there was a
slight drizzle. The coffin was carried up the hill by relays of the lesser
personal attendants. In complete silence they proceeded on their way.
Honda Masazumi walked beside in straw sandals, and whenever the
bearers stopped to rest for a while he would crouch down by the coffin
and say, 'At your service, my lord.' And when they took it up again to
resume the journey he would look up at it and repeat, 'We are all here,
my lord.' Just as though his master were still alive he waited on him."
The loyalty and unselfish devotion that Ieyasu inspired in his retainers

were remarkable, and were to endure far beyond the grave.

His death was rumored abroad months before it took place, for Cocks reports on January 24, 1616: "News was brought to town that the Emperour is dead; but I beleeve rather is a fable and geeven out on purpose to see how the people would take the matter. Once the ould man is subtill." Which needs no comment. He also says: "News is come that wars is like to ensue betwixt the Emperour and his sonne calsa Samme (Tadateru) being backt per his father-in-law Massamone Dono, because he will not give his sonne the fortresse and teretory of Osakay, if it were gotten, as he promised he wold doe." And on March 3rd: "Mr. Eaton advised me that Sade Dono (Honda Masanobu) is dead." Further, on March 31st: "There was reportes given out that the Emperour is dead and that Frushma or Tushma Tay (Fukushima) a great lord or prince in the north is slain per the Emperours people coming from Edo to Miaco: but I esteem this ordenary Japon newes, which prove lyes." And on April 17th: "At the same tyme the King of Crates (Karatsu) came to vizet me, and said it was reported that the Emperour was very sick with a fall he had from his horce in going a hawlking, so that no man might speak with hym. And towards night a cavalero sent me word that it was trew that the Emperour was alive, and had spoken to the King of Firando and two other princes only of purpose to stop the mouthes of those that reported hym to be dead: only it seemed to them that he was not halfe well."

When Ieyasu was buried at Kunozan there immediately started a dispute between Bonshun, Suden, and Tenkai as to what type of Shinto deity he should become. Bonshun, son of Urabe Kanetomo, was the ritualist of the Toyokuni Shrine of Hideyoshi, and an enthusiast for the Yui-itsu Shinto he professed. Suden was of the Zen sect, but he chose to side with Bonshun to oppose the growing influence of Tenkai. So that whereas these two worked to make Ieyasu a pure Shinto deity of the Yui-itsu school, Tenkai maintained that he was really devoted to the Sanno Ichijitsu Shinto of Hieizan and that the more comprehensive title of Gongen should be conferred on him.

After the funeral Hidetada came down from Edo and received those who had been in attendance, and there was a discussion about the posthumous treatment of the late Shogun. Their special claims were then put forward by Suden and Tenkai, the former maintaining that Ieyasu had told him that he wished to sleep at Kunozan and remain or become a Buddha like anyone else, while Tenkai quoted his interview of a later date at which he had intimated his intention of becoming a deity like the late Hideyoshi. This Suden strongly opposed, and got called a venial and worthless worldly priest in return, and perhaps the appellation was not uncalled-for, for Suden, or Konchiin Suden as he is called, was a Zen priest who had also been a warrior, for he fought for Ieyasu at Mikata-ga-hara and took three heads there, as a reward for which he was granted a temple and the crest of three stars for it. He had been employed by Ieyasu since 1608, when he built a temple called Konchiin at Shizuoka, and later he built temples of the same name in the Nanzenji at Kyoto and beside the Zōzōji at Edo. He was employed by Ieyasu to draft his foreign correspondence as well as to supervise religious foundations, so he must have been a man of the world and of affairs.

On this occasion, however, he did not prevail, for though according to one account Honda Masazumi supported him and declared that Tenkai should be banished to some distant island, Hidetada apparently objected and ordered him to accompany him to Edo instead, which gave him an opportunity of putting his case. Hidetada thought that if there was a way of his late father becoming both god and Buddha too, it would be most satisfactory, but admitted that his knowledge of Shinto was slight, and suggested that the Confucianist Hayashi be consulted. Doubtless Shinto was quite to his taste, and so it was decided that he should certainly become a deity. But though Suden was overborne by Tenkai, he was an infinitely adaptable person, and shrewd beyond most of his brethren, so that he kept his place and to a large extent his influence with the authorities right through the period of Hidetada to the early days of Iemitsu, living to 1634, not perhaps as great as he had been under Ieyasu, but still able to avoid the kind of misfortune that overtook Honda Kōzuke. On this occasion, in a letter to the Shoshidai in Kyoto he expressed his opinion that if Ieyasu was to become a deity then it would be well that those who knew the most about the way of the Deities should see to it. It was a matter with which he had little concern.

Another thing that assisted Tenkai was the passing away of the power from the two Hondas, for Honda Masanobu died the next year, 1617, aged seventy-eight, after having been the lifelong companion and adviser of his master, and his son Masazumi, who had been in Shizuoka with Ieyasu while his father had been in Edo with Hidetada, now went to take his place, but he was soon moved thence to Utsunomiya in 1619 and in 1622 exiled to the north, where he died in 1637 aged eighty-one. And already, as soon as Ieyasu died his place was taken by Doi Toshikatsu Oi-no-kami.

The next thing was to find a suitable posthumous name, and from four the title To-sho-dai-gongen was chosen, the others being Nihon-dai-gongen, I-rei-dai, and To-ko-dai: "Dignified spiritual greatness, and

Orient bright greatness." There was a discussion as to whether it would be better to call him *Gongen* or *Daimyojin,* which latter title was favored by the Shinto expert Bonshun,* but opposed by Tenkai because it had been used of Toyokuni Daimyojin, and was not, therefore, of good omen. Asked by Hidetada for a definition of the difference between these two types of deity, the expert Bonshun said it was merely that a Gongen was more definitely Buddhist, and that therefore only vegetarian offerings should be made to him. But it was more distinguished and comprehensive. And Tenkai, of course, got his way. And at the same time the temple of Zōzōji in Edo, Ieyasu's family temple, made a shrine and held services for him for a fortnight under the posthumous name of Ankoku-in-den-tokuren-sha-su-yo-dō-wa-dai-kōji, i.e. Virtuous Lotus Shrine, Revered Belauded Way of Peace, Great Enlightened Recluse in the Hall of Untroubled Empire. (The names Tō-kō-dai-gongen and Nihon Dai-gongen were suggested by the house of Nijo and To-sho-sai-gongen and I-rei-dai-gongen by the Kikutei family. These were then submitted to the Shogun (and Tenkai) for choice.)

Nikko was chosen because according to Tenkai Ieyasu had ordered it in his will. "After my death I am to be buried at Kunozan in Tsuruga, and after a year has elapsed a Divine title is to be sought from the Emperor and I am to be removed to Nikko." (*Reminiscences of Jigen Daishi.*)

So in the new year of the third year of Genna, 1617, the title To-sho-dai-gongen was decreed by the Emperor, and in the third month he was removed from Kuno to Nikko to the shrine that had already been prepared there under the supervision of Todo Takatora and Honda Kozuke since the tenth month of the year before.

The precedent for his removal cited was that of the Great Chancellor Kamatari, and it is thus stated by the eminent littérateur and courtier, Karasu-maru Mitsuhiro, in his pamphlet entitled *The August Removal of the Tosko Gongen:* "Now the removal of the August Presence to Nikko in the third year of Genna (1617) finds its precedent in the transference of the Great Minister Fujiwara Kamatari from Kawamoriyama in Settsu to Tabu-ga-mine at the decision of Joe-Osho. It was because of the meanness of the neighborhood. Tensho Daijin and Yamatohime-no-mikoto, too, have taken up their August Abode on the upper waters of the Isuzugawa, and the God Hachiman of Otokoyama also came thither from Usa in Kyushu. But in this case

---

* There was no difference in rank between the two titles, he said, but Gongen was the title of both the positive and negative Buddhas (In-yo son no Shingo). The Great Chancellor, he urged, should have the title of Daimyojin, for a Daimyojin is one to whom one offers birds and fish. Evidently he did not think the Great Chancellor would care to be a perpetual vegetarian.

the Tōshō Gongen took counsel with the Daisōjō Tenkai while he was
yet living, that so it might be arranged, and was without doubt greatly
rejoiced concerning it.

"The Tōshō Gongen—we speak it with reverence—is the manifestation of the Buddha Yakushi Nyorai, and so he brightens the hundred
and eighteen thousand fields of the Eastern Region." This is the reason
why this title was chosen, for Tōshō means "Illuminating the East."

When Yoshida Kanemitsu, the Chief of the Shinto Ritualists, was
invited by the Court to advise it concerning the deification of Ieyasu,
he gave his views as follows:

"Heaven means ourselves. We call it Ten with regard to its form, and
we call it Tei when we regard it as the ruling power. It is called Kijin
when it works some marvel, and Kan when we think of it as an emotion. Kan is the origin of the Universe, that is Ten, the positive element,
the father and the lord. And so we have the Way of the Gods (Shinto).
Man's virtue lies in not opposing Ten. It lies in cherishing the people,
and we call a man who cherishes and brightens the world like the Sun-
goddess Tensho-daijin a deity.

"Now what hinders us, therefore, from applying these expressions
'virtue' and 'deity' to the lord Ieyasu, seeing the way he has cherished
and nurtured his people? My report is that such a thing is extremely fitting. Now Nikko in Shimozuke is called in poetry Kurogami-
yama, Black-haired Mountain, and the Deity Master of it is the Nikko
Gongen. Now in the roll of deities in the Engishiki it is described as
the shrine of Ni-ko Sanjin, or The Two Rough Mountain Deities, of
the District of Kawachi in Shimozuke, and Ni-ko and Nikko have a
similar sound. And in the Ichi-no-miya-ki, Ni-ko Shin (the two rough
deities) are identified with Koto-shiro-nushi-no-kami (Ebisu), the son
of Onamuji-no-kami (Daikoku), also called Maka-kyara (Maha-kala),
and Susa-no-o-no-mikoto. And it is said that Minamoto Yoritomo built
this shrine, and that it has remained unaltered since his day. But it was
entirely rebuilt to accommodate the Tosho Daigongen."

In the ceremony of removal from Kunozan when the remains were
disinterred Tenkai himself took part and plied the shovel, and a thousand footmen with the great vassals of the late Shogun marched to meet
their lord once again (Honda, Doi, Itakura Matsudaira Masatsuna,
Akimoto Yasutomo, Sakakibara Kirohisa). He was then borne to Nikko
by stages, the place being reached nearly a month later, on the fourth
day of the fourth month.

Arrived at Nikko, the ceremony of handing over the Imperial Edict
of Deity took place. Representatives of the Court Nobles attended
the Envoy, the Minister Ano Saneaki, who formally read the Edict

and handed it to Archbishop Tenkai, who placed it in the shrine after
he had repeated the proper ritual. Afterwards there followed a Shinto
service on the seventeenth at which sacred cars were carried round
in honor of the three Gongen of Nikko. The other two were San-o
Gongen and Madara Gongen, though the popular rumor had it that
they were Tenkai and Todo Takatora, and indeed these two were largely
responsible for the continuance of the spiritual influence of the deified
Shogun which from this time on was to reinforce the temporal power
of his descendants in the flesh.

Todo Takatora was more trusted perhaps than even the Hondas in
Ieyasu's latter years, though he was not a fudai daimyo, and when the
old Shogun was dying it was Takatora who was most in attendance on
him. He is said to have told him that in this life he had indeed been
a loyal servant, but in the next he might not be able to continue thus
since he was of a different sect. So Takatora took the hint, and asked
Tenkai to make him his disciple, which he did, and Takatora was admitted to the Tendai sect and given the rank of Sōzu. He then informed
Ieyasu that he was now ready to be his retainer after death, whereupon
the ex-Shogun was very pleased and declared that Todo and Tenkai
should stand on his right and left hand as tutelary deities of the Tokugawa house. It was really a new type of Tendai that was being created as
the Ieyasu cult, for he himself was of the Jodo sect during his life. And
the center of this influence being situated east of Edo was intended
to counteract any insidious and softening and disintegrating tendencies that might, and certainly after no great period did, emanate from
Kyoto. For two hundred and sixty years To-sho-dai-Gongen remained
the tutelary deity of the ruling powers, and through them of the whole
land until, after the interval of a few decades, his place was taken by
the deity of the Meiji Jingu.

CHAPTER 41

IEYASU'S FAMILY

Mother			
Tsukiyama Dono	Nobuyasu	1558-1578	
	Kame-hime	m. Okudaira Nobumasa	
Nishigori-no-kata	Toku-hime	m. 1. Hojo Ujinao	
		2. Ikeda Terumasa	
O Man-no-kata	Hideyasu	1573-1607	Echizen
Saigo-no-tsubone	Hidetada	1579-1632	
	Tadayoshi	1580-1608	Owari
Shimoyama Dono	Nobuyoshi	1583-1603	Mito
O Take	Furi-hime	m. 1. Gamo Hideyuki	
		2. Asano Nagaaki	
Cha-a-no-tsubone	Tadateru	1593-1683	Echigo
O Kane	Yoshinao	1600-1650	Owari
O Man no kata (II)	Yorinobu	1602-1671	Kii
	Yorifusa	1603-1661	Mito

HIDETADA'S FAMILY

	Sen-hime	m. 1. Toyotomi Hideyori
		2. Honda Tadatoshi
	Daughter	m. Maeda Toshitsune
	Daughter	m. Matsudaira Tadanao
Asai Aeyo(Sōgen-in)	Daughter	m. Kyogoku Tadataka
	Iemitsu	
	Tadanaga	
	Kazu-ko (Tofuku-mon-in)	
		m. Emperor Go-mizu-no-ō
Kamio Shizu	Masayuki (Hoshina)	

IEYASU certainly left behind him a numerous and politically useful family. It has been pointed out that the consorts of Hideyoshi were all ladies of high degree, Yodo being of the families of Oda and Asai, Matsu-no-maru of Kyogoku, Sanjo of Gamo, and Kaga of Maeda, whereas those of Ieyasu were by no means people of any position. His wives were much the same, for one was the daughter of Sekiguchi, and the other the sister of Hideyoshi, and both were political alliances in which he took no personal interest at all, so that his nine sons and three daughters, like himself, hardly had anything at all that could be called family life. He regarded women merely as servants and conveniences.

The eldest son Nobuyasu and a daughter Kame-hime were the children of his wife, the first born when he was eighteen and the second when he was nineteen. This daughter married Okudaira Nobumasa, and seems to have been of a masculine and pugnacious temper, for she assisted her husband at the siege of Nagashino, and after Ieyasu's death had a large part in the overthrow of Honda Masazumi whom she disliked.

Hideyasu, the third child, was the son of O Man, lady-in-waiting to Ieyasu's wife, Tsukiyama Dono, and also a person of no particular family. He proved a fine soldier, and did good service at Sekigahara, commanding the army in the east against Uesugi Kagekatsu, and being rewarded with the fief of Echizen of 750,000 koku. He died at the age of thirty-four. He was a clever but unruly and obstinate character, and cared for nobody, and his preference for the family of Hideyoshi was much resented by his father so that the rumor arose that his death was due to poison administered by him. But this is evidently quite incorrect for he was a very dissipated fellow, and died of collapse following the "Chinese evil," for which three doctors treated him for some time but without success.

After him came Hidetada, born in 1580, and then Tadayoshi in 1581, both the sons of Saigo-no-tsubone,* daughter of Totsuka Gorodaiyu, a country samurai of Mikkawa, adopted by one Saigo and styled O Ai-no-kata. Tadayoshi was a good soldier, too, and did well at Sekigahara, fighting in the van with Ii Naomasa his father-in-law. For this he was rewarded with 570,000 koku in Owari, but died in 1608, aged twenty-eight. How is not stated, but there is a laconic entry to the effect that they did not report his death to Ieyasu when it took place, for he was then very angry owing to the loss of a tea utensil, and that when he did hear he had lost a son as well he did not exhibit any regret, perhaps because he had known that he had been ill for some time.

Then came another daughter, Furi-hime, and her mother was O Take, daughter of Ichikawa Jurozaemon-no-jo-Masanaga, evidently a retainer of the house. She was married first to Gamo Hideyuki and second to Asano Nagaaki, both political marriages, the first arranged by Hideyoshi.

Seventh was Nobuyoshi, son of one Shimoyama Dono, whose parentage seems to be doubtful. He was made lord of several small places, and afterwards elevated to Mito with 25,000 koku. Died 1605, *aet.*

---

* In the year 1605 an endowment of 20 koku was given by Ieyasu to the temple of Ryusenji in Sumpu and its name changed to Hodai-in, this being the posthumous title of his consort, Saigo-no-tsubone, the mother of Hidetada and Tadayoshi.

twenty-one.

Says the *Tokugawa Jikki:*

"Takeda Shingen's daughter had married his Councilor Anayama Baisetsu, and when both of them were dead she became a nun, and was known as Kenseiin. As she was forsaken by the Takeda vassals, who proceeded to attach themselves to one of her husband's sons by another consort, Ieyasu invited her to Edo, and she lived in 'Nun Street,' just outside the Tayasu Gate. And whenever she came to the castle to visit him he used to step down from the dais and greet her most cordially. It was only because she was Shingen's daughter."

If this lady is, as some assert, identical with that Shimoyama Dono who was the mother of Ieyasu's fifth son Nobuyoshi, she would be the only exception to the rule that he chose his consorts from unimportant houses, and yet another example of his preference for widows, and his punctiliousness is understandable though perhaps a little quaint. Anayama Baisetsu it will be remembered was killed by highwaymen shortly after Nobunaga's death in 1582. Nobuyoshi was born in 1583.

Next was Tadateru. His mother was Cha-a-no-tsubone, and her family is unknown, but she is described as the eighth wife and widow of a farmer of Kanaya in Mikawa. Cha-a-no-tsubone's good looks seem to have attracted the attention of the daikan of the district in which she lived, and he trumped up some charge against her husband and had him put to death and took her himself. But she gave him the slip and fled with her three-year old daughter to the castle of Hamamatsu, and appealed to Ieyasu. He investigated the case, punished the daikan, whose taste appealed to him more than his methods apparently, and offered the lady a position in his household. Tadateru rose to be lord of Takada, with 550,000 koku, but incurred his father's ire for his slackness and dilatoriness in the Osaka campaign, and as a result was deprived of his fief and shaved his head and retired and lived in the country in various localities, first in Ise, then in Hida, then in Suwo. He was then twenty-three years old and retirement seems to have suited him so well that he lived thus till the age of ninety-one. He is described as having nothing to his credit but lunacy and length of days.

Yoshinao was the son of O Kame, daughter of a Shinto priest of Iwashimizu Hachiman, who had been married to one Takegoshi Sadawemon, and after his death became lady-in-waiting to Ieyasu. He was fifty-nine when this son was born in 1601. Yoshinao became heir to Tadayoshi at Owari, with 601,000 koku, and founder of this house. Before Yoshinao was born Ieyasu asked O Kame about her family, and was told that her father was a Yamabushi of Iwashimizu, whereupon he observed that there was no need to say any more, but he had better be made a layman immediately and on the quiet. So he grew his hair and was given the name of Shimizu Hachiemon, being made a hatamoto of 3,000 koku and fitted out with the proper number of retainers for his position, a servant, a sandal-bearer, a clothes-box bearer, and a spear-carrier, after which he was introduced by Honda Masazumi, who brought him to the front gate of the castle, from which he was led after a suitable interval into the Hibiscus Chamber, where the other councilors were sitting, where his rank and income were announced by Honda "by reason of his relation to Master Gorota," as he put it, this being the youthful name of the recently born Yoshinao.

Yorinobu came next. His mother was O Man, not the same as the mother of Hidetada, but another of the same name. She was the daughter of one who went by the dignified title of Masaki Sakondaiyu Taira-no-Kunitoki Nyudo Kansai, evidently a military official, and adopted daughter of Kageyama Ujihiro, a retainer of the Hōjō of Odawara. Yorinobu was born in 1604, and his brother, Yorifusa, also son of O Man, in 1605.

When Yorinobu was two he was made lord of Mito, with 250,000 koku. This was increased to 400,000 eventually, and then in 1620 he was moved to Kii with 550,000 and the rank of Gon-Chunagon. The year after his brother Yorifusa, who had been given 100,000 at Shimozuma in Hitachi, took his place and income at Mito. If Ieyasu had any affection for any of his sons it was for these three. He is even described as showing considerable satisfaction when Yoshinao recovered from smallpox. Another entry depicts the old man and Hidetada as interested spectators of a Noh performance at the castle of Shizuoka, in which Yoshinao and Yorinobu took part. Probably their being born too late to have any connection or liking for the family of Hideyoshi was a strong reason for Ieyasu's trusting them.

Other secondary consorts Ieyasu had beside those mentioned above. There was also Nishigori, mother of Toku-hime, daughter of Udono Nagataka, and O Musu-no-kata, whose surname was Mitsui. Ieyasu took her with him to Nagoya during the Korean war, and there she died in labor and her child also. There was, moreover, O Natsu, daughter of Hasegawa Sanjuro, and sister of Hasegawa Gonroku. Again, another, O Roku-no-kata, daughter of Kuroda Nagaharu, became attendant on O Kaji-no-tsubone, and so was favored by Ieyasu. He took her with him on the Osaka campaign. Yet another, O Umc, was given afterward to Honda Masazumi as his wife, and after his exile she became a nun and lived at Shizuoka.

Once Ieyasu took Yoshinao, Yorinobu, and Yorifusa up to the top of the castle keep and when they were all admiring the view asked if any of the three dared to jump down. The two eldest were silent, but Yorifusa said he would if his father would give him anything he wanted. "Well, what do you want?" said Ieyasu. "The Empire," replied Yorifusa. "But," objected his father, "what would be the good of the Empire to you if you had to jump down from here, for you would certainly be smashed to atoms." "Yes, but even so I should have had the imperishable glory of having been Lord of the Empire." This reply pleased the old man immensely. Such a courtier's version of the temptation might well do so seeing that Yorifusa was only about eleven years old. He is also credited with another shrewd reply when Ieyasu asked the three what they would like best that he should give them. "A lot of men," said he. "And what for?" "So that I can get a good knowledge of the Empire." This was the father of the famous Mito Komon Mitsukuni, whose house held the office of Vice-Shogun. But he never married all the same. When he was a young man he is said to have been in waiting on his elder brother Hidetada one day when the Shogun observed that it was time to marry him to someone. "And what house is likely to want a worthless fellow like him for a bridegroom?" asked his wife, the Lady Sogen-in. So irritated was Yorifusa that he persistently declined to receive an official wife.

When Ieyasu's son Tadayoshi died in Edo in 1607 his three chief retainers committed suicide. This displeased his father very much, and he reproved Hidetada because the Edo councilors had not prohibited it and seen the prohibition was enforced. "This custom of 'Junshi,'" he said, "is an old one, it is true, but it isn't a good one. If a retainer is so devoted to his lord as all that he ought to keep himself alive to look after his successor. That's what I call loyalty. Of course there may be exceptional cases where he shows his loyalty by giving his life for his lord, but this useless Junshi is just dying a dog's death. It is culpable carelessness on the part of the lord that he doesn't prohibit it himself." So when a few months afterward his elder son Hideyasu died in his capital in Echizen, the Shogun sent a personal letter to the head of the household forbidding any suicides, and stating that it was an order from Sumpu also.

The Shogun said he thought it likely there might be some suicides following the lord's death, and they must remember that when the head of the house dies it is often difficult to establish the heir and carry on the line, and moreover Kita-no-sho, the capital of Echizen, is an important strategic position in the north country, and essential to the stability of the Empire. Therefore those who wish to show loyalty to their late lord must preserve their lives and protect his heir. On no account must they go to a useless death. If any disobey this order his descendants shall all be disinherited. Actually two of the chief retainers of Hideyasu did commit Junshi before this letter arrived, but the rest were prevented. And because of this strict prohibition there was not a single case of Junshi at the death of either Ieyasu or Hidetada.

When Hideyasu was ill he sent a lady-in-waiting named Tasuke-no-tsubone, who was known to his father, to Suruga to inform him confidentially that his illness was serious and he was not likely to recover. When Ieyasu heard it he was very much surprised, and said: "Hideyasu is my eldest son and a very gallant soldier, who has often done fine deeds in the field, and I didn't mean that he should remain lord of only the one province of Echizen. If he gets better I will give him as a consolation present 250,000 koku in the provinces of Omi and Shimozuke, making his income 1,000,000 koku in all. Do you go back again to Echizen and let him know this. It will cheer him up." And he gave her a written statement to that effect. The lady hurried back, traveling night and day, but had got no farther than Okazaki in Mikawa when she received news of Hideyasu's death. So she went back again to Suruga and sought audience with Ieyasu once more. He was playing Go just then, but when he heard of his son's death he was much affected. The lady took out the document and observing that it was a very valuable paper gave it back to him. "Though she is a woman," commented Ieyasu, as he took it, "she is pretty smart." "Yes," said the samurai of his household when it came to their ears, "these smart women are a damned nuisance." One wonders how far Ieyasu was informed of the course of his son's illness, and what his real feelings were. Certainly he did not grant any increase to Hideyasu's heir, Tadanao, worthy though he was.

Seeing that the trouble in Hideyoshi's household sprang from the existence of two parties which centerd round his wife and the Lady Yodo respectively, Ieyasu was very careful not to bestow any special favor on any one of his own ladies, but to distribute his regard equally among a number and so avoid a repetition of any such calamity in his own house. No doubt this "many ladies and little love" theory suited his nature as well as his policy, but anyhow there were no parties in his family. Still, in his later days the feminine element in his house was not without its power, since it is clear that those who wished to obtain his confidence or keep it sometimes found a short cut to this aim through some of the ladies-in-waiting. Date Masamune, for instance, made presents of money to them (five pieces of gold each to five ladies), and in the Osaka affair Ieyasu used them as go-betweens and spies and for diplomatic purposes generally. And so they naturally obtained power, especially Acha-no-tsubone, formerly wife of Kamio, the retainer of Imagawa, in whose charge Ieyasu had been placed when young, and whose kindness he never forgot, afterwards summoning her to his castle and making her Matron of the Ladies-in-Waiting. In this office she seems to have acquired as much or almost as much influence with him as Honda Masazumi. And in 1621, when Hidetada's daughter became the consort of the Emperor Go-Mizu-no-O, Acha-no-tsubone went with her as an attendant and was raised to the Lower First Court Rank, a great tribute to her ability in statecraft.

Acha-no-tsubone was born in 1555 and died in 1638, aged eighty-three. She became a widow in 1578 and joined Ieyasu, she being twenty-three and he thirty-eight. She was often in the field with Ieyasu. At Nagakude she was present and had a miscarriage. At Osaka she acted as envoy. It is a tribute to her adroitness that she still kept her influence with Hidetada after his father's death in contrast to Honda Masazumi, with whom she worked but who was not so shrewd. She figures with Honda in an incident that rather illustrates this. A certain Sakai Saemon Ietsugu came to bear the New Year congratulations from Edo to Shizuoka, and feeling cold he wore a wadded cap under his black headdress. Unfortunately the head-dress got disarranged and the cap showed, much to the irritation of Ieyasu, who resented the impropriety. Honda scolded him accordingly, saying that it was understandable in an old man but not in a young one, and that he would not wear such a thing in Edo before all the daimyo. But Acha-no-tsubone, who was in waiting also, said that the envoy had caught cold and really was not fit to attend at all, but as he wished to do so she suggested that it would not matter if he wrapped himself up and wore a wadded cap. It was, she thought, less disrespectful than not coming at all. Which explanation quite satisfied Ieyasu.

Still, though Ieyasu used ladies of great capacity like this he could never be said to be used by them. Hidetada, however, was different, and much softer, and seems to have had great respect as well as affection for his wife, Yodo's sister Sogen-in, and though he had one son by Shizu, one of her ladies, he kept it very secret from her and was apparently much in fear of her wrath if she found out, and never received this son, Masayuki, during his lifetime.

Beside receiving presents from the daimyo these ladies were apparently in the habit of lending them money. This came out from a case of fraud in connection with it. They were in the habit of using a Miko or Shrine dancing-girl as a go-between to collect the interest for them, it thus appearing as though they were giving money to the shrine. But when the Miko on one occasion dunned Ikeda Bingo-no-kami for the money and it was handed over in a leather bag by his Yonin as had often happened before, she did not open it but gave a receipt and took it to the moneychanger, and he only found a lot of stones in it. Of course the Yonin knew nothing about it, and the Miko was very indignant at the suspicion falling on her, and the whole thing was revealed. Bingo's wife was apparently the culprit. Ieyasu ordered the City

Magistrate to investigate, and Bingo's reputation suffered somewhat. It is not therefore so remarkable that it is recorded in the fire that occurred in Shizuoka castle in 1608 that the savings of the Court ladies that were destroyed were not small. Acha-no-tsubone 30 pieces, Kame-no-tsubone 1,500, Cha-a-no-tsubone and Man-no-tsubone 500 and 300 respectively, beside that a thief stole 60 pieces of Man-no-tsubone's money in the confusion accompanying the fire. As to this Tokutomi wonders whether Acha-no-tsubone had really saved so much less than the others or whether it was that she was sharp enough to hide it in a safer place.

Next to Acha in sharpness perhaps came O Kaji. She became lady-in-waiting when only thirteen, Ieyasu being then forty-nine. As she had no children she adopted Yorifusa. She was given to Matsudaira Masatsuna, but disliked him and returned after a month. It is she of whom the story is told that when Honda and Okubo and Hiraiwa were discussing before Ieyasu what was the most tasty thing and could not agree, she laughed at them, and when Ieyasu then asked her opinion she said that of course salt was that thing, for without it nothing tasted well, and it was the one thing the people could not dispense with for a day. Her decision was applauded, and then the discussion turned to what was most distasteful, and again they could not agree, and Kaji was asked to arbitrate, and she gave the same answer, for too much salt, she said, was the most unpleasant thing in the world and made anything uneatable. Possibly it was this hint that Ieyasu acted on when he gave orders to the cook that plenty of salt was to be put into the food served to these ladies-in-waiting so that they should not eat too much of it.

The wife of Hidetada was the third daughter of Asai Nagamasa and of the younger sister of Nobunaga. She was six years older than Hidetada, and married him as her third husband when she was twenty-three and he was seventeen. But though she was strongminded enough, she was not later on without a rival in her household, though not in the affections of her husband, but in the matter of the precedence of her sons, for she particularly preferred the younger son Tadanaga to the elder Iemitsu, and wished to arrange matters so that he could succeed to the Shogunate. It was here that she was opposed by another strong-minded lady, Kasuga-no-tsubone, the nurse of Iemitsu, and the most famous woman of her time, who made it her business to champion his cause, and did so very successfully, though Hidetada himself had been persuaded by his wife to support the elevation of the younger. And so in this way there came to be two parties in his household, the Sogen-in party and the Kasuga party. It is perhaps a question whether Hidetada's wife disliked Iemitsu because she disliked his nurse and wished to spite her, or whether she was really fonder of the younger son. But anyhow, Kasuga determined to get her way, and this she did by working through Acha-no-tsubone and Tenkai, who told everything to Ieyasu so that he came down from Shizuoka and paid them a visit. The two sons were then presented to him, and he placed Iemitsu by his side on the dais and gave him a cake with his own hand, after which he picked another one up with the chopsticks and threw it over to Tadanaga, who was seated on the lower bench, saying that it was not proper to treat him in the same way as Iemitsu who was to become Shogun. So that settled the matter, and the result was that Iemitsu came to regard his nurse with more affection than he did his mother, whose preference for Tadanaga only resulted in tragedy for him, since Iemitsu eventually made him commit suicide.

Now this Kasuga-no-tsubone was the daughter of Saito Kurano-suke, a retainer of Akechi Mitsuhide, the slayer of Nobunaga, and was grand-niece of Mitsuhide himself, for her mother was a daughter of Inaba Michiaki, whose wife was Akechi's younger sister. She was chosen as nurse to Iemitsu after a competition, for when Iemitsu was born Itakura Shigekatsu the Shoshidai was ordered to put up a placard in Awataguchi in the capital calling for volunteers for the post, for going to Edo was considered rather an adventure into a barbarous region. She married Inaba Masanari, but was a difficult sort of person, for as she found that her husband had a concubine and a son, she made it her business to find the concubine and stab her to death. This done, she went off to Kyoto, and there noticed the advertisement and presented herself in answer to it. She seems to have been divorced by her husband, or separated herself from him, but this did not cause any particular ill feeling between them, as is evident from her subsequent actions. Having entered the Shogun's household, she was like the proverbial gimlet in a bag: it would not be long before she poked out somewhere. So when, in Hidetada's later days, after his wife was dead and Iemitsu was married to the daughter of the Court Noble Takatsukasa Nobufusa, whom he did not like and of whom he took no notice, Kasuga-no-tsubone became the chief power in the palace, and to her are ascribed the rules that came to govern the procedure in the inner palace and the bronze door that separated it from the middle palace. And not only did she rule the ladies with a rod of iron, and decide who should enter the palace service, but she sometimes invited the younger of the great retainers and ministers of the Shogun to a banquet or reception and gave them advice and told them what she thought of them.

She had a salary of 3,000 koku, and in 1630 she even proceeded to Kyoto, and insisted on being received by the Emperor in audience— quite an extraordinary thing, of which the Court nobility by no means approved. She then became the adopted daughter of the dainagon Sanjo-nishi, and was given Lower Second Court Rank. This visit of hers was a lesson to the Court that even a female retainer of the Shogun could treat it in a high-handed manner if she so desired.

When she got on in years she built herself a temple called the Tentakuji or Rensho-in in Yushima as her place of enlightenment, the latter title being her posthumous name. Her brother was made a hatamoto of 5,000 koku, and she got her former husband, Inaba Masanari, appointed lord of Masaoka with 20,000, while her son Masakatsu was first given 5,000 at Ichioka in Hitachi, and then his father's fief as well on the death of that lord. But before long he was transferred to the castle of Odawara, with 85,000 koku, and made Roju or Member of the Senate, so great was his mother's influence with the Shogun. And this son's son succeeded his father and was entitled Inaba Mino-no-kami Masamori, and also became Roju in 1658.

Now another member of the Senate, Hotta Masatoshi, was an old comrade of Kasuga's husband, both having been fellow retainers of Kobayakawa Hideaki, and had married this husband's daughter, and his son Masamori was also a favorite of Iemitsu.

Now this Hotta's wife was a daughter of Sakai Tadakatsu, the most trusted councilor of Iemitsu. Moreover, as all Iemitsu's councilors had been his youthful boon-companions, they had all grown up with a wholesome respect for Kasuga-no-tsubone. And so it may be said that the influence of this clever old lady lasted right up to the beginning of the rule of Tunayoshi, 1680-1709, for Hotta Masatoshi, his Tairo, was the son of Masamori, and became the old lady's adopted son, and received her 3,000 koku when she died. And it is curious that this Masatoshi was assassinated by Inaba Masayasu, who was a member of the Junior Council, and the son of her husband's younger son Masayoshi, who was also her heir and was appointed chief of the Shoimban.

There is a record of an incident that shows how Kasuga arranged matters. One day Iemitsu told her that he had had a dream in which he said that Kwannon had appeared in a vision to him, and observed that she was very beautiful. "Well," answered Kasuga, "speaking of beautiful people, I have just now in my house a relative, an ex-nun who has come to pay me a visit and she is very beautiful indeed. I may say, remarkably so." "Ah," replied Iemitsu, "I should not be averse to seeing her too." So the relative was brought to the palace and introduced to the Shogun, and found favor in his eyes and eventually rose to be the chief of the ladies-in-waiting. She was besides being good to look on well educated enough to be able to read the Buddhist texts as well as the works of Lao-tze and Chuang-tz to the other ladies. Perhaps this was not so strange seeing that she had been a nun originally. Possibly it also explained the association with Kwannon.

CHAPTER 42

IEYASU'S PERSONAL HABITS AND VIEWS

IEYASU did not care for what he called useless amusements, though he sometimes went to Noh performances and knew how to take part in them, but even there his mind ran on military matters, it would appear, for while at a Noh performance at the Nijo palace he suddenly remarked to Itakura Shigemune, the Governor of Kyoto: "What I was thinking was that it is just about the right time to cut bamboos for the banner poles."

He sometimes killed time by playing at chess and Go, though he never was obsessed by them as were some of the generals.

His only real interest was hawking, and from his early youth to advanced old age he spent all his spare time at it. In fact, he rather overdid it on occasions in the opinion of his advisers, as when his forces were in pursuit of Uesugi Kagekatsu and he was flying his hawks apparently quite oblivious of his military responsibilities. "Now this," said Honda Tadakatsu to him, "is too much." "Not at all," replied Ieyasu. "It's a very good thing for you that I spend my time in this way."

But this love of hawking was not, he often maintained, a mere amusement. "When you go out into the country hawking you learn to understand the military spirit and also the hard life of the lower classes. You exercise your muscles and train your limbs. You have any amount of walking and running and become quite indifferent to heat and cold, and so you are little likely to suffer from any illness. Getting up early in the morning is good for the digestion, and gives one the keenest appetite for breakfast, while after a day at this sport you sleep splendidly at night without any inclination for a bedfellow. This is all very good for the health and superior to the general run of amusements."

Whenever he went hawking he used to take the ladies of the household with him. Those of the highest rank rode in sedans and the rest on horseback, sitting on madder-dyed cushions with wide country-women's hats to cover their faces. Before setting out on one of these expeditions Honda Kozuke-no-suke, who had charge of all the arrangements, said on the quiet to his lord:

"So far the ladies-in-waiting have always gone out on horseback, but now the land is at peace it seems rather indecorous to ride exposed in this fashion. I think it would be better if they all went in sedans."

"There may be some reason in your argument," replied Ieyasu, "but people's conduct differs according to their position. Though it is natural for those of low degree to be informal, yet there are times when they ought to be ceremonious, and similarly important people have to be dignified, but sometimes they should be informal. They should know how to behave according to the circumstances. People ought not always to be the same. Hawking is not only for the purpose of getting a large bag of game. In times of peace like these all classes are apt to grow slack and become enervated so that they cannot act quickly in an emergency. In stag hunting and hawking all must be in training and go on foot and climb up steep places and wade streams and exert themselves to the utmost. It is a good opportunity to note the strong and weak among the retainers, and the hard exercise keeps them all strong and ready for their duties. But though you cannot take women on a campaign, hunting is in some sense a sport, so there is no objection to their joining in, and they too will be rendered more effective in their positions. For just as horsemen have to go on foot at these times, so it is proper that women who sit in sedans should ride on horseback. And that is an example of what I mean by people of high rank being at times informal. And one holding the high office that you do ought to understand all this."

This discourse must have given "Codskin Dono" some food for reflection.

When they went hunting the places for serving meals were arranged beforehand, and they had their meal as soon as they arrived. Or sometimes they would go into the houses of the ordinary people and get them to cook potatoes and other country dishes. It was all very simple and unassuming.

Ieyasu was fond of all kinds of exercise, and was skilled in archery and fencing and horsemanship as a matter of course, but he also excelled at shooting with the matchlock and at swimming. From his early days he regarded it as part of his ordinary day's work to practise with his bow either at a target or at the straw-bale used for improving the style in archery, and fire three shots with a matchlock. Yorinobu, his youngest son but one, who was very much with him when a boy, used often to say that no ordinary man was a match for him at any of these things.

In commending Okudaira Nobumasa for cutting off two enemy heads at the Anegawa battle he said: "You are young and dexterous too, and that is a fine thing. To be a good fighter is not a question of strength but of skill. Who is your fencing master?" Nobumasa replied that he belonged to the Okuyama School of Fencing. "Ah, then you were taught by Kyukasai of your house, no doubt. I took lessons from him when I was young, too, but lately I have not time to practise because I have been too busy with the command of the army. But when I get home again I shall certainly summon him." This Kyukasai was one of the first fencers of the day, and was a relation of Nobumasa, and his school got its name from his having, so it was rumored, received supernatural instruction in the secrets of swordsmanship at the shrine of Okuyama Myōjin in Mikawa.

But though Ieyasu was a good fencer himself he understood its proper place, for when he once interviewed a famous teacher of the art named Hikida Bungo and asked him various questions about it as he was accustomed to do, he afterwards commented: "He has great skill in fencing, no doubt, but he can't discriminate between those who need it and those who don't. A lord of the Empire, for instance, or a daimyo need not cut people down with his own hand, for if he is in a tight place in a fight he can call on his men to do it for him. What he needs first of all is the capacity to judge the capacity of the people he uses." And so when he heard that Hidetada was given to fencing practice he objected that "a general does not need to fight hand to hand. He must know how to avoid taking risks. Leaders should not tire themselves by killing people." And he went on to say that in all the many fights in which he had taken part in the course of his life he had never killed anyone with his own hand. But this was partly owing apparently to the threatened ones making themselves scarce in time.

On the other hand, he once observed that it is a mistake to think that battles can be won by sitting on a camp-stool, baton in hand, and doing nothing but give orders as is the way of many. A commander will not conquer by gazing at his men's backs. In a fight the best thing is to charge with the greatest vigor and boldness, but victory will depend on fortune. When you think you are sure to win you may easily be defeated, and again sometimes you may win when failure seems almost certain. Too much discretion often brings loss.

When he went to battle he did not favor any particular kind of spear. He carried a sword and a spear with a cross-shaped head. When Hidenaga presented him with three hundred suits of light iron armor and a hundred corded two-handed swords (no-dachi), he gave them to the men of Kai to wear. And the day before the battle of the Anegawa Nobunaga brought him a long spear, declaring that the blade was made of an arrow head that had belonged to Chinzei Hachiro Tametomo. "Tokugawa Dono is of the true line of the Genji," he said, "so I have brought this ancient heirloom of that house. With it victory is sure in tomorrow's battle. This is the spear called 'Nagezaya.'"

At the battle of Sekigahara Hosokawa Tadaoki rode up to Ieyasu's headquarters wearing a silver frontlet with the tail of a mountain pheasant mounted in it, and as this blew about in the wind it suggested a stork flying far off in the sky. Ieyasu was much impressed by the device, and exclaimed: "Tadaoki's taste is always quite different." So Hosokawa presented it to him, and he afterwards gave it to Hidetada.

He had the same liking for good omens as anyone else, for he once noticed a war surcoat embroidered with a white sea-gull with its head turned to the left. "Ah," he exclaimed, "that's a returning sea-gull. Crests on armor should always be turned to the right."

He had a banner that was given by Seikyo Shonin, the founder of the Daijuji, to his ancestor Chikatada, on which was the inscription "Renounce this filthy world and attain the Pure Land." This his house had always used, and he had it brought in a box and placed beside his palanquin in the Kyushu campaign and also at Osaka. Beside this he had seven banners eighteen feet long with three black "Aoi" crests on a white ground. In 1566 he much admired the gold fan crest of Makino Yasunari and requested him to let him use it as his horse-insignia. It was mounted on a bearskin. After the campaign against Uesugi Kagekatsu in the fifth year of Keicho, 1600, he used plain banners without any badge, and gave the crested ones to Hidetada. "Ornamental armor is useless," he pronounced, "and so is heavy mail. Ii Hyobu is very strong and wears a heavy suit, but has often been wounded, whereas Honda Nakatsukasa never does and has never got a wound. The best kind is what allows the freest movement." And he recommended the common soldiers to wear a light steel hat. "They can even use it to cook their rice in." It was worn by the men of Kai, but not by those of the Kamigata. It is called the Onogi hat because Onogi Nuidonosuke, lord of Kamiyama in Tamba, was the first to fit out his men with it.

Though renowned for his fine horsemanship, Ieyasu was never rash, and even when a young man he always dismounted and walked when he came to a place where the ground was dangerous for the horse. "That," he once remarked to a retainer, "is according to the teaching of the Otsubo school of horsemanship. One should never ride over dangerous ground. It may not matter for people of rank, who have spare horses led after them, but a man who has to rely on one mount only must spare it as much as possible. People who only think about riding and don't consider the horse will end by damaging its feet. And then it won't be able to carry them properly when they really need it."

This was well illustrated when his army was advancing on Odawara, and Niwa Nagashige, Hasegawa Hidekatsu, and Hori Kyutaro went up to a small eminence by the roadside to see the vanguard pass by. It happened that a group of ordinary retainers gathered just by them, for

said they, "Now we shall be able to get a view of the performance of the
First Horseman on the Sea-road." For below them was a narrow bridge
over a river gorge, and nobody could ride over it; everyone had to
dismount and walk. And Ieyasu dismounted, too, when he came to it,
and had his mount led by several grooms to about fifty yards beyond,
while he himself was carried across by his men. The retainers burst out
laughing with one accord. "So that's the finest riding on the sea-road,
is it?" But the three commanders remarked quietly: "Ah, indeed. We
didn't think he was as good as that. The best riders never take useless
risks. He deserves his title."

His shooting, too, was on the same principle. It is related that once
in Hamamatsu he saw a stork sitting on one of the towers and asked a
retainer how far off it was. "About a hundred to a hundred and twenty
yards," was the reply. "Then the ordinary gun won't carry," he observed,
and told them to bring one specially made by Inatomi Gaiki. Taking
careful aim, he fired and hit it in the body. The retainers then tried to
hold this weapon up and take aim with it, but not one could manage
it, and they wondered at the muscular strength of their lord.

It happened that the stables at Fujimori were damaged, and Kakazume Hayato Masanao asked permission to repair them. "Just repair
the roof where the rain leaks through, and mend the wall where it
has fallen down," he was ordered. "There's no need to do any more."
"Well," said Kakazume, "I saw some of the stables of the daimyos in
Kyoto recently, and they had mosquito nets for use in summer and
quilts to put on the horses in winter. They take every care of their
horses, whereas in our stables we have only a straw curtain hanging
in the doorway. Don't you think we ought to improve things a little?"
"A Bushi's horse is for use and not for show," replied Ieyasu. "Which
kind do you think will do best in awkward places, or gallop faster, or
stand the heat and cold better, mine with their straw curtain or theirs
with their mosquito nets and quilts? We don't want any of these Kyoto
luxuries."

And when he was hunting on Mount Asama in 1612, when he was
over seventy, he hit the mark more often than anyone else, and, shooting
at three white herons one after the other, he brought down two and shot
away the legs of the third. And two years after this at another party his
bag was one stork, three swans, four wild geese, and nine wild ducks.

He was anxious to get the latest thing in artillery if possible, for
when he heard that one Watanabe Saburodaiyu, a retainer of Otomo
of Bungo, had been to China to study fire-arrows and had made some
in Japan, he at once took him into his service, and during the winter
campaign of Osaka Watanabe was in Shizuoka and made these fire-

arrows there. "They are just what we want," commented Ieyasu, and he took him to the summer campaign also. After the war he experimented in smelting iron and copper for Ieyasu. No doubt this interest in fire-arrows was the result of the Japanese experiences in the Korean campaign, where they suffered much from the continental superiority in these things.

Like many other Japanese Ieyasu was fond of swimming, and in the summer months he always went into the river at Okazaki. His retainers accompanied him, for they were all good swimmers, too. This was in his young days, but he kept it up all his life, for when he was just on seventy he went into the Senagawa at a fishing party on that stream. And Iemitsu used to say it was the custom of his grandfather when he swam in the castle moats of Edo.

He once observed to Todo Takatora that there were two things that even the lord of the Empire must always practise, and they were riding and swimming. These were quite indispensable to a man. And there were two other things that ought to be sold—horses and rice. The latter the Empire could not do without for a single day, and horses were to be ridden for the country's use and not neglected.

Ieyasu always used to impress on his men that when warriors went out to battle they should go prepared to die there. Those whose teeth were white should take care that they did not look yellow, and they ought to burn some incense in their hair. At the Osaka summer campaign his retainers all had pieces of incensewood in their clothing, but as they had no incense-burner they were unable to burn it. And when they had armor made he used to say that the body armor and arm-pieces and so on did not matter much, but the helmet ought to be finely wrought, because when a man was killed his helmet was taken by the enemy with the head, so it was important. So when he viewed the head of Kimura Nagato-no-kami-Shigenari he noted that it had been perfumed with incense, for it exuded a sweet scent, and remarked: "That will be a lesson for young men who couldn't burn any." And he admired the way his locks were smoothed and combed back on his head, too. "That's just like Nagato, not to shave away the hair on his forehead. A head looks so much better with the locks left long like this." He then inspected a head taken by Kawano Gonemon Michishige, and this, too, had the hair newly shaved and was nicely perfumed. "Just how a soldier should meet his end," he pronounced, "and whose head is it?" "Naito Kenmotsu's," they told him. "Ah," he replied with a laugh, "he was one of the Mono-gashira in the castle. Quite an unexpected find for a connoisseur to pick up." And after the fight at Takatenjin when the heads were brought to him for inspection there was one of a young person some sixteen or seventeen years old with blackened teeth and beautifully made-up complexion and coiffure, and they could not decide whether it was that of a man or a woman. "Open the eyes," said Ieyasu, "and if the pupils are drawn up right under the lids so that only the white is visible it is a woman, but if you can see the black part it is a man." So they opened the eyes with the "Kogai" of a sword, and as they could see the pupil it was decided that it was a youth. And afterwards this was confirmed, and they learned that it was the head of Makita Tsuruchiyo, the much beloved page of the commander of the castle. And Ieyasu highly commended the tasteful style in which he went out to die, while the retainers were astonished at their lord's acuteness.

"No military man should ever be without a sword, and what is more he ought to be a good judge of them. A man is no good unless he can tell the quality of a blade and whether it belongs to the new or old school." Ieyasu told Todo to be sure and impress this on Hidetada. Actually Hidetada was very expert in both these points. Ieyasu called Honami, and gave him instructions to take particular care of the two blades he most prized among the many he possessed. One was called Sosa and forged by Samonji, and with it Oda Nobunaga killed Imagawa Yoshimoto at Okehazama.* It was two feet six inches long. The other was called Iris and was by Masamune. It was of the same length as the other, and was presented to him by a man of low rank called Nonaka. Honami had to make several spare sheaths for each of these. Ieyasu did not expose the blade when he put them on. He wore the Masamune blade at Sekigahara and the Samonji at Osaka. He also particularly valued the Miike sword. This was the one he ordered Tochiku Kagetada to try on a criminal just before he died, and left orders in his will that it should be kept in his shrine on Kunozan.

There was also another called Honjo Masamune. It had been worn by one Honjo Echizen-no-kami Shigenaga, a retainer of Uesugi Kenshin, but he became poor and had to sell it, and so it came into the possession of Ieyasu. He afterwards gave it to Yorinobu, lord of Kishu, and that house again handed it back to the main family of Tokugawa. It is this sword that is handed to the heir when he succeeds to the Shogunate as a symbol of his office. It is like the sword of the Regalia in the Imperial House.

At Mikawa Makino Haneimon Yasunari showed Ieyasu a sword that a dealer had brought him for sale. He examined it carefully and told

---

* But as related in the description of the battle, it was one Mori Shinsuke who cut off Yoshimoto's head and not Nobunaga. But Yoshimoto was wearing a sword by Samonji.

Yasunari to buy it for him, for he thought it would cut well. He did so and some time afterwards when his lord's swords were tested it turned out as he had predicted, and he reported that it had cut right through the subject into the stand underneath. Ieyasu was highly delighted. When the expert who had tried it came in he said that when he had gone to test it Haneimon had shut his eyes and prayed fervently that the blade would turn out according to his lord's expectations. Ieyasu laughed and replied: "You'd better give it the name 'Closed Eyes,' then." And so it was afterwards called. It is said to be by Hosho Goro Sadayoshi, and has been highly prized ever since.

Once in the Tensho (1573–91) era Ieyasu was hawking when an oil seller got in his way and acted in a rude manner. Handing his sword to Nishio Kozaemon Yoshitsugu, who was in attendance, he told him to cut the fellow down. Yoshitsugu did so, but the man went on walking a few paces before falling divided into two. So the blade was christened "Oil-seller," and much appreciated. It was afterwards presented to Yoshitsugu.

At the fighting at Odawara Makai Hyogo-no-kami Masatsuna took the head of an enemy commander, Suzuki Danjiro, and brought it to Ieyasu at the head inspection, when it was seen to be cut right through the chin and teeth. Ieyasu admired the cut and asked to see the blade. Afterwards he asked to see it again, but was told that the owner had been compelled by circumstances to sell it, so Ieyasu bought it back for two hundred ryo and restored it to him.

Ieyasu liked a sword well polished, for beside having a finer edge it shone well at night. He preferred the sharkskin of the hilt with small rather than large grains, set on a base of oak, and with quite small menuki.

"It has always been the Japanese conviction that the military spirit must be fostered," he once declared, "and for this reason. When peace has relaxed our martial qualities foreign countries have shown an inclination to attack us. And when those countries have similarly become slack we and the Tartars have attacked them—the Empire of the Great Ming, I mean—Hideyoshi's Korean campaign was caused by this unpreparedness. When I was lord of Okazaki I had to be on my guard against the castles of my neighbors, and when I became master of all Mikawa I had to look out for attacks from the neighboring provinces. When I became lord of the eight provinces of the Kwanto I had to keep an eye on all the three regions of the Tokaido, Tosando, and Hokurikudo, and now I am Lord of the Empire I must keep myself well informed on all that foreign countries are doing."

"And speaking of loyalty," he explained, "I am loyal to Heaven by cherishing the loyal retainers of the Matsudaira house, and because of this I have received from Heaven the charge of the Empire of Japan. But if it is ruled improperly Heaven will take it away again. The peace of the realm rests in the mind of the Shogun. The Empire truly belongs to the Empire, the Province to the Province, and the Family to the Family. One must consider the future and make no innovations or new families. And when the Empire is well ruled the military class are obedient. When it is the reverse they are against the authorities. This has always been so, and it is of Heaven.

"And the continuation of peace and security in the realm depends on the kindliness of those who rule it, and this is what is meant by the Way of Benevolence. By making this Benevolence the foundation of everything and putting away all arrogance, it is that the Empire must be governed. Thus a ruler of a Province or of the Empire must found his policy on this principle of compassion, and at the same time he must not forget to prepare for the possibility of rebellion or disorder. This is his first duty, and his second is to consider the prosperity of his own house, to look to the integrity of his conduct, to discern the good or bad points of his councilors and to administer the affairs of his subjects without fear or favor.

"This is the rule that I have inherited from my ancestors. From the days when I only administered part of Mikawa till now when I govern the whole Empire my principle has been the same, though there may be a difference in detail. And every successful lord or administrator has ruled in accordance with the wishes of the people. When Yoritomo took the territory of Fujiwara Hidehira in Mutsu he continued the beneficent government he found there. Some of his proclamations with his seal are even now to be seen there.

"And every administration must work by rules just as a carpenter does. The first rule is to put down extravagance in every grade of society, and very careful inquisition must be made so that it can be extirpated quickly before it spreads, otherwise society will fall into disorder. My first principle has always been to respect Heaven, and Heaven's first principle is to hate extravagance. And if saving and accumulating is for the benefit of the Empire then one must not throw away a single old garment."

In his later days Ieyasu was apt to be short-tempered if anything interfered with his sport. In 1606 two bugyo, Naito Kiyonari and Aoyama Tadanari, were dismissed for negligence in this matter. They had been appointed under Honda Masanobu as Chief Commissioners of the Kwanto district to take charge of all the details of its administration, and their authority was great. Now it happened that Ieyasu was hawking in the provinces of Musashi and Shimosa and the Shogun had sent out orders that birds and animals were not to be caught in any place where his father went hunting. But in spite of this Ieyasu found traps set and birdlime spread where he was hawking, and his countenance grew dark. "Whose doing is this?" he asked, and the farmers said they had the permission of the two bugyo, Naito and Aoyama. "But doesn't the Shogun know about it?" he said, and his anger increased.

When this was reported to Hidetada he was very much perturbed, and at once sent for Acha-no-tsubone and asked her to find out whether the two of them were to be put to death or not. She tried to draw the old man out on the subject, but he said nothing. Then the Shogun sent for Honda Masanobu and asked him to see what he could do, and he replied: "It is because of the filial dutifulness of Your Highness that you have inherited the Empire, so that whatever offends the wishes of your august father cannot be tolerated. Naito and Aoyama have done what is most displeasing to him, and so it goes without saying that they ought to be executed. Still I have an idea and I will go and see how he feels about the matter."

Going in to Ieyasu he said: "That was a very reprehensible thing that happened when Your Highness went hawking. The Shogun has heard about it and is exceedingly angry, and has determined to execute Naito and Aoyama at once. It is perhaps unfortunate for them, and I am old now, and if I had charge of these duties as Commissioner myself I am not certain that something might not happen to displease Your Highness. Still they shall certainly be put to death for it. And now will Your Highness move a little to one side. I wish to put the heads over there." When Ieyasu heard this his mood suddenly changed. "Oh, and is the Shogun so angry with them?" he said, and calling Acha-no-tsubone he told her to hurry off and say that he did not think they need suffer the extreme penalty. The Shogun was extremely pleased to hear it, and at once reprieved the two of them.

This was one of the many occasions when Honda showed himself "a great Professor of Ieyasuology."

Once when Doi Toshikatsu took a month's vacation from his duties in Edo and visited his castle of Furukawa he went round and inspected his domains, and after doing so he called his Karo and observed to them: "In the days of Gongen Sama I have often been with him to the control department of the daikwan and heard him tell those officers that the best thing was to keep the peasants so that they just got a bare living, and were able to pay the taxes. And this he used to tell them every year. When I first came to this fief I went round to inspect it everywhere, and I didn't see a decent house in any of the villages, but now it seems a lot of the farmers have built good houses all over the place. They are living a bit too well, I fancy. The daikwan and koribugyo must be instructed to see that they pay their taxes properly anyhow. I remember reading somewhere...I suppose it must have been the Gongen style of tax-collecting, that seventy odd years ago, if you went to the villages about harvest-time you could see in the house of the daikwan a water-barrel and a wooden horse, and if any peasants were so miserly as to be reluctant to pay their taxes they were put into the one or on to the other and made uncomfortable till they did. Ah, well, I suppose the peasants of today have become so docile and right-minded that nothing of the sort is necessary."

A daikwan, observed Ieyasu, is like the neck of a bottle, more likely than not to be encircled by a cord some day. Those who take this office are like the actors in Kyogen. They wear hats and robes of office, and go out with their attendants Taro and Jiro Kwaja, and really look just like lords. But when their piece is over they become just plain Nani-emon or Nani-bei like anyone else. Yes, a daikwan is just like that. He treats his district as though it were his fief, and the peasants address him as My Lord (Tono-sama) and his wife as My Lady (Oku-sama, Gozensama), and are very respectful indeed. The result is that he begins to live up to the part and behave like a nobleman at home. That means that he spends the taxes entrusted to him and gets behind about one year in three, trusting to make it up somehow in the future. And then when the time for rendering his account comes he is surprised to find how he is involved, and runs round to his relations and friends for help, and has to sell up his property, and even then can't make up the required amount. And that's when he gets the rope round his neck.

When there was a complaint that the falconers and keepers were likely to stir up riots among the farmers by their overbearing manners, Ieyasu only laughed, and replied: "Well, there's no harm in their showing their authority, for then the people will realize that the higher officers above them are much more to be feared, and so they will be properly respectful, and there will be no opposition. The cause of disturbance is letting the farmers have their own way, so the kindest policy toward them is only to curb the arrogant bearing of these falconers and keepers, and also of the daikwans just to the extent that they do not cause positive hardship to the agricultural population." And this always continued to be the Tokugawa policy toward the peasants, treating them like cormorants that have to be dieted to a nicety, for if they are overfed they will be too gorged to hunt, while if they are not given enough they may be too weak to do so. The difference was the tax that the Bakufu exacted the while it took care to safeguard them in their holdings. It suspected any accumulation of capital that would become a means to power just as much among them as among their superiors, the feudal landowners.

Once a certain Jodo priest in Suruga observed that Buddhism was originally the one teaching of Buddha, and had only broken up into a number of sects at a later date, so that it would be better if all devotees studied the same thing and did not learn all sorts of views as propounded by the different sects. "I don't care about my Nembutsu sect at all," he declared. "Yes!" said Ieyasu, "not only Buddhism, but all the arts and crafts are apt to be difficult unless you apply yourself to one principle. Still in these other worldly affairs there is a difference according to one's position in life. If you have nothing to do but consider your own convenience you can apply yourself to attaining Enlightenment through the sect you belong to. But one who is lord of the Empire, for instance, cannot turn his back on society and devote himself exclusively to becoming a Buddha. It is rather his business to desire earnestly that all the people may be given suitable opportunities to become Buddhas. And it is surely a proof of this earnest desire that the rulers have allowed all these sects that have sprung up at various times from ancient days to exist, and so have given their people such a wide choice of the means of salvation through them."

One of the droll things that he did was at the expense of Buddhism, and is rather revealing of his attitude to religion. It is recorded that in the tenth month of 1614, when he was hunting near Toda, he came to a village called Imaizumi, where he found a little rustic Buddhist cell. He asked what the name of it might be, and the monk who lived there replied that it was such an out-of-the-way country place that he had never given it a name. Noticing that there were ten strings of vegetables hanging up to dry under the eaves, he told him to call it "Kansaizan Jurenji," or "Dry-vegetables-mountain Ten-string-temple," and gave it an endowment of 16 koku of rice per annum. The dignified sound of the title and the homely meaning is a good example of that Japanese quip that depends on the varied meanings of Chinese characters having the same sound.

Ieyasu's interest in Buddhism was not confined to one sect, for though his family was Jodo by tradition, and he built and took considerable interest in the Zozoji and Daijuji, he is described as examining and discussing the doctrines of Sodo (Zen), Shingon, and Tendai. This last especially was much expounded to him by the learned and devoted Tenkai, and he ended in receiving adoption into its fold. This did not please the Jodo priests, though it did not affect his position as a member of their sect, for we find the following observation:

"1613.9.2. Genyo Kokushi of the Zozoji visited the castle and discussed Buddhism, but his capacity was not adequate. He reviled the temples of the Tendai sect, and this His Highness did not approve, for he had a great respect for the Tendai sect."

Neither was Shinto neglected altogether. A short time before the above interview it is recorded:

"1613.6.4. His Highness called for Yoshida Shinryu-in Bonshun to come and give an exposition of Shinto, and arranged for this to take place on the sixth day. Shinryu-in presented himself, and was shown into the South Chamber. His Highness however sent to inform him that the time was not suitable, and so Shinryu-in and Konchi-in (Suden) discussed Buddhism."

No doubt after consideration of all the sects Tendai, the most comprehensive of them, seemed most politically useful, and to lend itself best in its combination with Shinto to the building up of the cult of Ieyasu as the tutelary deity of the coming period, which Tenkai set himself so assiduously to consolidate.

There was a sectarian dispute at Sumpu between the Jodo and the Nichiren sects, and they determined to settle it by a public debate. So Ieyasu summoned one of the Nichiren priests and said: "I suppose if you win in the contest tomorrow it will be a serious matter. What do you propose should be done to your beaten opponents?" "I think if their heads were cut off and their sect destroyed there would not be any more of these doctrinal squabbles to trouble Your Highness," was the answer.

Then Ieyasu sent for one of the Jodo priests and asked him the same question, but he said nothing. When further pressed he said that these disputes were caused by too much blind faith in the founders of the sects, and that the side that lost was not to blame so the best thing would be to do nothing. Ieyasu looked irritated. "Why don't you say what you really think," he said, "that's what I want to get at." "Well, I suppose those who lose may be considered to be a disgrace to their sect, so they might be unfrocked." Ieyasu's face cleared. "He seems to be a worthy priest. Take him away and give him something to eat."

Afterwards he asked one of his retainers who he thought would win the next day, and the reply was that he had no idea. "The Jodo will win," said Ieyasu. "I'll tell you why. When the Nichiren priest talked about cutting off his opponents' heads if they lost it shows that his views are rooted in malignant feelings, and have nothing of the benevolence of Buddha about them. The Jodo only suggested unfrocking them, and that is a very suitable penalty for a recluse."

And it fell out just as he had predicted, so that the retainers greatly admired his insight. And after this he prohibited these sectarian contests.

Probably many people have wondered what is the relation of the two great establishments of the East and West Hongwanji that stand so close to each other near the railway station in Kyoto and do not appear to differ from each other either in ritual or in doctrine. In the days of Hideyoshi there was but one sect of Shinshu, with temples called Hongwanji, but Kosa, the head of it, happened to have one son by his first wife named Koju, and another Kosho by his second. At his death Hideyoshi took the second one, who was very beautiful, as his consort, as was his way, and so made her son Kosho Lord Abbot in his father's stead, forcing the elder to go into retirement and become the head of a branch temple, the Shinjo-in. But in his disgust at being thus supplanted Koju sought out Ieyasu before Sekigahara, and offered to stir up the Monto monks of Muro and Omi to make a diversion on his side. Ieyasu declined, since he did not want to be beholden to these turbulent sectaries, as he pointed out to Kuroda Nagamasa when he too suggested it. However, he told Koju he might go to Edo if he did not find things to his liking in Kyoto, and later on he obtained an Imperial Edict appointing him Imperial Abbot (Monzeki), and then had a temple built for him to the east of the main Hongwanji, since known as the Western. Koju was so overjoyed at this that he declared that the benevolence of Amida Buddha could not have been greater, but he was quite mistaken if he thought it was done out of any admiration or affection for him or his, for the fact was that Ieyasu at once perceived an opportunity in this family quarrel to split the Hongwanji into two rival sects, and so weaken it in pursuance of his policy, so ably and persistently carried out after his death by Tenkai, of building up a Tokugawa subsidized Buddhism in the eastern provinces round Edo to counteract the influence of the older type that flourished and intrigued round Kyoto, and had been favored by the house of Toyotomi. One of his retainers once asked Ieyasu whether he did not think that a ruler of the Empire left a great name behind if he did some very remarkable thing as Hideyoshi did when he made the Great Buddha. "Quite likely," he replied. "I daresay the Great Buddha may long keep Hideyoshi's memory green, but personally I prefer to use my resources for the country generally, and leave that to my posterity. That's more profitable than any number of Big Buddhas."

But how little he himself really cared about gods or Buddhas or other supernatural manifestations appears pretty clearly in the following story. One summer at Suruga Ieyasu was sitting with his attendants when the sky suddenly clouded over and there was a heavy thunderstorm. "There is nothing you cannot take precautions against," he said. "For instance, earthquakes are sudden enough, but still by proper construction and so on you can escape their dangers. But lightning is rather a different problem. You never know where it is going to strike, and whether it will come horizontally or vertically, so there is no way of escaping it. What do you recommend?" "It seems to be as Your Hignhess says, there is no way of escaping it." "Oh, well, then I will tell you. Daimyos with their spacious residences, it is unnecessary to say, and those who live in small houses too, if there is a sudden thunderstorm, such as we have had today, must scatter and get as far apart as they can. That is the best precaution, for all the members of the family to separate as widely as may be. If anyone is fated to be struck by lightning it will get him and him only, and there is no help for it. But if the whole family huddles up together in one place for fear of the storm and that place is struck, then the whole house will be destroyed. Last year in the capital there was the case of a man who stayed in his house with all his family in a thunderstorm, and shut the shutters and doors and lighted a fire, and burnt incense and so forth, and the house was struck by lightning, and almost all of them were killed, and those who were not were crippled. Wasn't that awful! Of course people said it was the punishment of Heaven for some offence or other, or that it was the result of the evil Karma of a previous existence, but that is all nonsense. As if lightning were any chooser of persons!" He then called the three Lords of Kii, Owari, and Mito, who happened to be there, and told them not to stay together in one place when there was a heavy thunderstorm.

O-Kaji-no-tsubone once came to Ieyasu and complained that it was very hard on the ladies-in-waiting that he should make them wash his white wadded garments, for it hurt their hands, and sometimes they even bled. Since he had so many garments, would it not be better for him to wear only new ones and not have them washed. "You foolish women don't seem to understand why I do this, so I suppose I must explain." When all the ladies had been sent for he went on: "I consider it my duty first of all to respect the Way of Heaven. And what the Way of Heaven most disapproves of is extravagance. I suppose you consider my possessions here in Suruga considerable?" They admitted that they did. "Yes, well, maybe, and they are by no means all. I have any amount of material as well as bullion in Kyoto, Osaka, and Edo as well. And if I wore new clothes every day it would not strain my resources in the least, I can assure you. But some of this I must give to the people, and some I must keep for my descendants to use when the Empire needs it, so that I cannot afford to waste a single garment." And the ladies were so impressed that they sat listening with their hands clasped together as though before a god or Buddha.

In the ladies' apartments at Suruga castle there were two boxes for tabi (socks). The new pairs were kept in one, and into the other were put those that were soiled. And when this box was full it was brought before Ieyasu, and, putting back a few pairs that were not so particularly bad, he would divide the rest among the lower female attendants. He never ordered any to be thrown away. And he also recommended that the under-girdles of the men be dyed light blue instead of left white. "Ah, His Highness is not unmindful even of our under-girdles!" said these attendants ruefully.

Once a very handsome young man of his entourage at Suruga appeared in a costume much too gay for his position. Ieyasu at once rebuked him. "If those in my household wear things like that it will soon become the fashion outside, and that's how extravagance starts." And he ordered the offender to be gated and fined. "You can't manage the Empire properly without economy," he continued, "for if those at the top are extravagant, taxes mount up and the lower orders are embarrassed, not to speak of the effect it has on military finances. But a lot of people can't understand the meaning of the word thrift, and think it means only omitting to do what you ought to do."

Sorori Bannai, Hideyoshi's famous jester, was once talking to Ieyasu, when he remarked, apropos of something or other: "Ah, yes, people are very much given to celebrating Daikoku as the God of Good Fortune, but I expect few realize why he is so." "Well, why is he so, then?" inquired Ieyasu. "Man can't live without eating, and so Daikoku stands on bales of rice, and even if he could merely live, it wouldn't be very entertaining, so the god carries a bag, and with his left hand he closes the mouth so that the contents shan't escape without good reason, and he has a hammer in the other hand so that when he can't avoid parting with something he can manage to knock out the wherewithal to replace it. Then both summer and winter he keeps his beret well down over his ears so that he is not likely to look above himself and forget his position in life. You must admit he looks the sort of person to make and keep a competence."

"Oh yes, your description is very much to the point. But there's one other quality that Daikoku has beside. It's his most important trade secret. Don't you know what that is?" Bannai considered for a while, and then had to confess that he could not think of any other. "Well, I'll let you into the secret. He keeps his cap on as you say, but when he feels that he has to take it off as a relief, then, I can assure you, he takes it right off and throws it down and looks round both up and down and on all sides. It is so as to prevent anyone meddling with him that he keeps it down over his head as a rule. That's his little secret." Bannai was struck by the shrewdness of this observation, and repeated it to Hideyoshi the next time he was in attendance on him. "Yes," assented the Taiko, "quite so, and there is a living Daikoku walking about too. Didn't you know that?" "I can't say I did," replied Bannai. "Well, it's Tokugawa himself. I wonder you didn't see the likeness."

Hidetada once went to Shizuoka to inquire about his father's health. He stayed there two months. One evening Ieyasu called Acha-no-tsubone and observed: "I fancy the Shogun must be rather lonely all by himself for so long, for he is still young. Now this evening you had better take him a flower with some cakes to cheer him up. By the back gate, you understand, without any ceremony." The flower was eighteen years old, and well qualified to beguile the Shogun's idle hours.

So Acha-no-tsubone informed Hidetada that his father intended to send him an envoy to cheer him up, whereupon Hidetada put on his kamishimo and sat up straight in an attitude of ceremony. Soon there was a knock at the door, and he went and opened it, and then solemnly escorted the damsel who presented herself at it to the dais of the apartment, and bade her take a seat there. He then formally received the cakes she had brought, and knocked his forehead three times on the mats. "And are these indeed presented by my august father?" he inquired solicitously, and on receiving an affirmative answer, he added as he closed the door: "And now that your mission is ended it is well that you convey my respectful thanks to my honored father."

There was nothing to be done but to go and report to Ieyasu, which she did. He laughed. "The Shogun is a very strait-laced and correct fellow, as I have before observed; yes, a bit too correct."

Hidetada was unique in his family, and probably most others, for his monogamous temperament, and his strong-minded consort Asai Aeyo or Sogen-in evidently did not encourage any other attitude. She bore him seven children, and their domesticity was immaculate. Of course with the usual Japanese feeling against complete symmetry in conduct or anything else Hidetada did have one other consort, Kamio Shizu, one of his wife's ladies-in-waiting, and she was the mother of his son Hoshina Masayuki, afterwards Matsudaira Masayuki, lord of Aizu, one of the most distinguished of his house for character, learning, and statesmanship. But Hidetada never dared let his wife know of Masayuki's existence, and it was only after her death that he was able to acknowledge him. It is indeed difficult to figure his father in such a position.

When Ieyasu heard that Hidetada had used some gilt metal mounts on the Wadakura tower of Edo castle he had them all stripped off in one night. And in Suruga castle, too, the Hon-maru had a wooden fence round it, while in the Ni-no-maru, where the chief retainers lived, there were only bamboo fences round their quarters, and when they suggested that this did not look very well, and that they would be glad to replace them by board fences at their own expense, Ieyasu told them to leave them as they were, and so they always remained.

Ieyasu was by no means pleased when someone presented him with a chamber-pot ornamented with gold lacquer. "If such an unclean piece of furniture is to be decorated in this way, what ought to be done with ordinary utensils?" he exclaimed, and told his attendant to take it away and break it.

When people criticized Ieyasu for hoarding gold and silver, he re-marked to Matsudaira Masatsuna that if these metals were collected in the capital it meant that there was little in circulation, and so people valued them the more and prices fell, whereas if there was plenty of them about they rose, and the majority were embarrassed. And when the price of rice rose at Suruga he opened his storehouses and sold his own stock, for when it was cheap he used his revenues to buy it in, and so stabilized the price and prevented speculation. But people misun-derstood his motives and said: "His Highness has gone into business."

When on his way from Edo to Fushimi his train was exceedingly small. He had only two spearmen, one halberdier, one archer, and two clothes-box bearers. Neither did he have a spare mount led before him. In all he had only thirty men with him. But he gave good wages to the retainers of the lower ranks there, and did not require anyone under a thousand koku to keep a horse, neither did he recommend them to have many attendants. Those of no great position were to rent ordinary houses in the town. When Fushimi castle was burnt he did not rebuild the mansion, but had some old timber collected and put up a rough sort of residence. This amused the people of Kyoto, who regarded it as just another example of his parsimony.

On his return journey to Edo, too, he might have had about a hundred horsemen with him. They rode a little behind, singing and beating time with their fans. And when they drank sake they did so out of the ladles with which they watered their horses, or right out of the kegs. And if there was a tippler among them they would ride round and round him offering him a drink. They always rode in this informal way when Naruse Hayato commanded the escort.

In the third month of Keicho 9 (1605) Ieyasu arrived at Fushimi on his way to Kyoto, and all the lords in the capital went out to Otsu to meet him. It was raining hard, so they stood about here and there under trees to get some shelter, and Ieyasu passed by quite unobserved with a small train of two spearmen, one halberdier, two hasami-bako, twelve footmen, and ten horsemen. His sedan was all covered in to keep out the wet. They all thought it was Honda Kōzuke-no-suke Masazumi preceding his master, but later it dawned on them that it was

Ieyasu himself, whereat they hurried off and met him at the entrance of Fushimi town. There he stopped and thanked them for their courtesy in coming to inquire after his health.

When he went to stay in the Nijo palace that was built for the Shogun in Kyoto, Honda Masazumi asked what fare he would like provided. "The ordinary soldiers' rations," was the reply. "Three sho of hulled rice, ten pieces of dried bonito, a salted bream, and a little pickled radish will do."

Itozaka Bokusai relates that when he was in attendance Ieyasu gave him a piece of ginseng out of a jar. In order to receive it with proper ceremony he took a piece of the Hosho paper that he saw on the sideboard of the room to put it on, but Ieyasu at once stopped him. "That is for writing letters to daimyos and such people. It must not be used for ordinary purposes. I give you ginseng because it is a medicine that will keep you healthy, but a sheet of Hosho paper is another matter. It is very expensive. Take off your haori." So Bokusai took off his haori and received it on that, and put back the sheet of paper again. He used to say that in all his years of service he was never so put out as on this occasion.

Ieyasu was very temperate in eating and drinking, and expressed his views accordingly. He was once somewhat indisposed at Sumpu, but soon got well again. When the doctors came to feel his pulse he said, "I know I am better, for I have some appetite." "Ah, that is most important. We are very pleased to hear that, my lord, for you know the maxim, 'Food is man's life!' " "Yes, I have heard that," replied Ieyasu, "but I should like to ask your considered opinion about it. Milk is the food of a newly born child, but the parents have to take great care that it has the right amount, neither too much nor too little. Don't you think the main thing is the proper regulation of what you eat and drink?" "That is very true," replied the physicians. "We have not really understood the meaning of the saying till now." "Sake," he said on another occasion, "may stimulate the spirits, but people often start quarrelling when they take too much at celebrations or other times. It is better to be moderate. When on campaign or out hawking, if a man who normally abstains has a cup or two he will be exhilarated and feel comfortable. Still, to see anyone sipping from a little cup at a banquet looks rather mean, while a hard drinker swigging it out of a tea-cup fills us with admiration."

The outstanding feature of Ieyasu's character was his selfcontrol in word as well as in deed. So well had he disciplined himself in the part he considered it necessary to play that it became a second nature, and he is described by one critic as one who played a part all his days and taught his son to do the same. Hosokawa Tadaoki once told Iemitsu how when Hideyoshi had boasted in full court that he had never been beaten in battle, Ieyasu at once burst out, "Have you forgotten Komaki? One should be accurate in military matters!" to the great dismay of all the other nobles, who stood aghast at his want of *finesse*. But to their relief Hideyoshi said nothing, but just left the room. When he reappeared soon after he made no reference to the incident, and was quite affable. The explanation was that Hideyoshi had only said it to test Ieyasu, of whom he never could be quite certain, but Ieyasu was quite equal to the occasion, and answered according to his role of a plain blunt soldier. Had he dissembled or returned a diplomatic answer Hideyoshi's suspicion would have been confirmed. No doubt some remained, but Ieyasu was far too wary to provide any occasion for disagreement, and their amity remained unbroken.

Ieyasu was certainly not overburdened with emotions, and his exemplar Yoritomo is generally credited with more. It is claimed that he shed tears more readily and often, whatever that may be worth, but those who lived in the twelfth century make the impression of having been more sympathetic than those of the sixteenth, no doubt because they had not been so long subjected to a military régime. The one recorded case of Ieyasu being moved to tears was when he took leave of Torii Mototada, who had been his friend and retainer ever since he was seven years old, whom he knew would never leave his post alive. On women he wasted no emotion, and but little on his children. Though it was not pleasant for him to have to put his eldest son to death, yet he showed no particular feeling when he referred to him later on at Sekigahara, when he remarked, "I am an old man now, and yet I get no rest. If my eldest son had been here now things would have been easier." A purely practical observation. Irritation or displeasure he now and then exhibited, for there was nothing reprehensible in that. Fear or apprehension never, for he does not seem to have known the meaning of them.

He is described as an ordinary personality developed to an extraordinary degree. About the exploits of Nobunaga there was always something striking and unexpected, but Ieyasu on the contrary never went in for any specially original or spectacular actions. He did just what most people would do, or expect to see done. Hideyoshi sometimes did original and sometimes commonplace things, so that nobody knew quite what to expect of him. So that on the whole Ieyasu was understood and trusted more than the other two, and this confidence he inspired made success less difficult for him. It by no means follows that he was any more trustworthy than they. But he had a great capacity for making people think he was when he wasn't. He could act the turncoat whenever he thought it expedient. He went over from Imagawa to

Oda, from Oda to Hojo, and from Hojo to Toyotomi, and eventually he deserted the house of Toyotomi and rose over its ruins. But he could always make it seem the obvious and really right and proper thing to do, both to himself and to everyone else. As his countrymen often say of the English, he was always able to persuade others that his interest was the public interest and for the good of humanity. He was rather conservative by nature, but by no means incapable of changing his standpoint, and exceedingly supple and adaptable. His habit was invariably to conserve his energy and his resources until he saw his opportunity, when he would dash in and grasp it with the concentrated force and speed of one of his favorite falcons.

Only at the end of his life did he make any exception to his unhurrying manner of waiting for the plums to fall into his mouth, though they never fell without a good deal of prearrangement. But until this time he acted as though confident of outliving the majority. And here, too, he left nothing to chance, for he always looked well after his health, studied the medicine of his day, and never omitted to keep by him his carefully numbered pill-box.

He was a great believer in the gospel of might. Might that seemed like right perhaps, if that was desirable. For he saw very clearly that without strength and power no stable government or peace was possible, and that these depended on armies and money to equip them and build strong places from which to dominate the strategic points of the country, and also on confidence that would lead the great lords to throw in their lot with his family and save him the trouble and expense of conquering them. This last quality he must have been most desirous of acquiring because it cost him so little. And he was much better equipped to acquire it than either Nobunaga or Hideyoshi, because he was so much more like the average man, and not apparently such an obvious superman as they had been.

Even his personal appearance facilitated his favorite attitude of seeming to be deceived while himself deceiving others, for this is how he impressed his contemporaries, "No one cuts such an odd figure as the lord Tokugawa. He has such a fat belly that he can't tie his own girdle. So he gets his ladies-in-waiting to do it for him. He is the very picture of a good-hearted and openhanded nobleman." Generally speaking, he was perhaps "that unaffected, undetected nobleman," but not by everyone, for when some of Hideyoshi's retainers were making merry at his expense at the Daigo Flower-viewing, they drew the remark from their lord, "Well, Ieyasu has three accomplishments in which none can equal him. One is strategy, the second is shrewdness, and the third is getting hold of money. These are not things to laugh at." And again in a Noh performance, Hideyoshi and Oda Nobuo and Oda Yuraku all took part and acquitted themselves very well, especially Nobuo, whose "Tatsuta" brought down the house. Then Ieyasu essayed the part of the young and handsome Yoshitsune in *Benkei in the Ship,* but his corpulence and incapacity to keep in time with the music made the piece quite a caricature, and everyone laughed immoderately. Afterwards Hideyoshi commented: "Yes, Nobuo is good enough at Noh, but he has lost all his territories. I don't see much credit in that. The lord Tokugawa doesn't care much about these parlour tricks, but the country possesses no greater soldier. People who neglect great things for small are not very wise."

But this feigned simplicity did not deceive everyone, for while he was dancing this Noh Kuroda Nagamasa, Ishida Asano, and Shimazu were looking on, and one remarked, "Look at that old badger making a fool of himself to diddle the Taiko! And what a fine soldier he is! That's a dangerous fellow." "Yes," said Gamo Ujisato, "he can act the fool when it doesn't matter, but be sharp enough when it does."

And though he took full advantage of his ungainly figure it was like him to cover up the disability it implied almost instinctively, for it is related how, when Todo Takatora came to see him one morning shortly after his victory at Osaka and found him wearing an ordinary hakama and haori, he asked him why he was not in armor, and Ieyasu replied, "Well, now that that youth Hideyori is defeated there is no need to wear it." But when Takatora had retired he turned to Matsudaira Masatsuna, who was in attendance, and observed: "Takatora is a Kyoto man, and so I didn't give him the real reason. The fact is that now I am old and have a fat belly, I can't mount and dismount my horse with armor on."

Yet Todo Takatora was one of his most trusted friends. He treated him like one of his house retainers, and discussed all manner of things with him, and especially in his latter years liked nothing better than to sit chatting with him. But Todo's sight became very bad as he got older, and he excused himself, for he was afraid of embarrassing Ieyasu in some way. But Ieyasu told Doi Toshikatsu to tell him that now he was old he liked to talk over old times with Takatora, and would be very bored if he did not come. His bad sight did not matter. He could come right up to the ante-room of his apartment in his palanquin—a very special privilege—and also he would have any sharp turns in the corridors made straight so that it would be easier for him to find his way. Takatora was very touched by this consideration and resumed his visits.

Another glimpse of Ieyasu in his old age that is very revealing is one of him making tea for another old friend, Date Masamune. Not noticing that the lid of the kettle was very hot, he went to take it off when a jet of steam came out and he involuntarily drew back, whereupon Masamune in the unceremonious way for which he was noted burst out laughing. But Ieyasu quietly took the scalding lid in his hand and kept it there with the remark, "It would take more than steam to make me drop anything."

"If you want to tell lies that will be believed, don't tell the truth that won't," was one of his maxims. He was always consistent in what he said and did, and it is not related of him that he ever cultivated eloquence. "His handwriting was bad and his words few." Ieyasu was the real strong, silent man, though he did not at all fancy himself in that role, for he took part in the ordinary diversions of the time, and made no impression of being reserved beyond the ordinary.

When Hideyoshi announced his intention of visiting him once, Honda and Sakakibara suggested that he ought to entertain him in some uncommon way, but Ieyasu replied that he thought not, for he did not wish to seem to compete with him in cleverness. It was much wiser to appear just an ordinary honest fellow without any tricks.

Even his well-known parsimony was not quite what it seemed, for though he was penny-wise in such devices as seeing that his pages reversed the floor-mats before a wrestling match so that they should not be damaged, and telling his cook not to spare the salt in the pickled radishes when he saw that his ladies-in-waiting were likely to eat less of them, yet he never grudged money when there was any profit in spending it, as in the case of the large sum he gave to Hosokawa. He is described as the master of money, as he was of love, for he understood the power of these things, and used them only where most effective.

Tokutomi suggests that Ieyasu may have been somewhat of a neurotic by nature, seeing that there had been several members of his family who were afflicted with rather savage tempers and also short lives. His father died young of disease. It is true, but his mother lived to be seventy. He was born when his mother was fifteen and his father seventeen, and after his mother was divorced she married again and had seven other children, which does not suggest much defect in her constitution. This rather wild temperament showed itself in more than one of his sons, and possibly to some extent in his grandson Iemitsu, while his grandson Tsunayoshi was certainly less normal than many. But in this they did not differ perhaps from most families, and especially the pugnacious ones that were likely to be the survivors in such an age, so that to call it bad temper or pugnacity would seem to be rather nearer the mark than neurasthenia. One is inclined to a judgment similar to that pronounced on Hideyoshi's likeness to a monkey, that if Ieyasu was neurotic then everybody must be neurotic.

An alleged example of this neurasthenic temper is an incident that took place at the battle of Sekigahara. "A certain Nonomura pushed his horse against Ieyasu, who immediately flew into a rage, drew his sword, and made a cut at him. The blow missed, and Nonomura slipped away, but so irritated was Ieyasu that he slashed off the pennon of Monna Chosaburo, one of his pages, just where it stuck in the holder, though without harming him. He did not really mean to hit him, but only did it to relieve his feelings."

He was fearless both morally and physically. "On the battlefield he seemed like a War-god. At first he would direct his men with his baton quietly enough, but when the battle got fierce he would hammer on the pommel of his saddle with his fist, shouting out 'Kakare! Kakare! At them! At them!', till the blood flowed, and though after the fight he would put some ointment on it, he would be sure to do the same thing again before it healed, and in the end the middle joints of his fingers got calloused and stiff, and in his old age he found it difficult to bend them." As, according to his own statement, he took part in nearly ninety fights during his career this is understandable. And his observation that a general does not win by contemplating the backs of his men's necks is in accordance with his own practice. But that he was not regarded as merely a hard-fighting leader is testified to by the criticism that he was a general heard to be pusillanimous but seen to be fearless. This because he never underrated any opponent, and avoided hostilities as long as possible, so that he could have plenty of time to take every precaution and get all information to make victory as certain as possible, though, like all great leaders, he declared it to be the one thing of which no one could be absolutely certain.

CHAPTER 43

TOKUGAWA LEGISLATION

THE legislation that kept Japan in order for some two hundred and sixty years without any revolt or disorder was neither very bulky nor particularly original. It carried on the former codes of Yoritomo and the amendments of Hideyoshi, and did not contain very much that was new, though what there was of this kind was very significant and effective. And it was entirely directed to the purpose of keeping the Tokugawa family in a position of complete and unassailable domination in the Empire. If the Imperial House or the feudal or Court nobles had seemed to have any power of interference or veto before, it entirely disappeared now. The short series of legislative enactments issued by Ieyasu and Hidetada thus consisted of, in the first place, the terms of the oath to be taken by all the daimyos, and secondly of the laws to be observed by the Imperial House and Court nobles, and by the feudal nobles and samurai.

The oath for the daimyos imposed in 1611 ran as follows:

Since the laws of the generations of the Shogunate established by Yoritomo the General of the Right at Kamakura are in our own interest we will strictly obey all their ordinances.

Should there be any who disobey these laws or who differ from the expressed views of the Shogun they shall not be allowed any refuge in any of our provinces.

Should any of the samurai, our retainers, or their subordinates be guilty of rebellion or homicide and the matter be reported to us, we shall none of us take such a person into our service.

If any of us disobey any of these articles, after a proper inquiry has been held into the facts, he shall be liable to be dealt with strictly according to the law.

Next followed the *Buke Sho-hatto* or laws for the military families. This set of regulations, together with the Kuge Shohatto or laws for the Court nobles, was promulgated at Fushimi by Hidetada in the year 1615 in the month of August, after the summer campaign of Osaka. Ieyasu was at this time in the Nijo castle in Kyoto, so it was a suitable opportunity to impress on the feudal and Court nobles a sense of their future responsibilities. As usual the pill was to some extent gilded, for Hidetada invited the daimyos to a Noh performance, in the middle of which a banquet was served to them, but before the beginning of this entertainment, early in the morning, they had to listen to the reading of this set of regulations by Konchi-in Suden at the instance of Honda Masanobu. They had, therefore, a mixture of admonition and diversion that ought to have given them plenty of food for thought.

The articles of the code are thirteen in number:

1. The way of letters and arms, of archery and horsemanship must be cultivated with all the heart and mind.

    First letters and then arms was the rule of those of old. Neither must be neglected. Archery and horsemanship are essential for the Military Houses. Militarism may be an ill-omened expression, but it is an unavoidable necessity. In times of order we cannot forget disorder; how, then, can we relax our military training?

2. Drinking parties and amusements must be kept within proper limits. In the observation of this article strict moderation must be insisted on. Devotion to women and gambling is the primary cause of loss of one's fief.

3. Law breakers shall not be allowed refuge in any fief. Law is the foundation of etiquette and social order. Law may be contrary to reason, but reason is no excuse for breaking the law. So those who break it will not be excused.

4. Feudal lords both greater and lesser and other feudatories shall expel from their fiefs any retainer in their service who shall be guilty of rebellion or homicide.

    Savage and unruly retainers are edged tools for overthrowing the Empire and deadly weapons for destroying the common people. How can they be tolerated?

5. From henceforth there is to be no intercourse with the people of other fiefs outside one's own province.

    The customs of the various fiefs are commonly different. Revealing the secrets of one's own fief to another or reporting the secrets of another fief to one's own is a sign of a desire to curry favor.

6. Even when castles are repaired the matter must be reported to the authorities. Much more must all new construction be stopped. A castle with a wall more than 100 chi (10 feet by 30 feet), i.e. 1,000 feet, is harmful to a fief. High walls and deep moats are the cause of great upheavals when they belong to others.

7. If any innovations are attempted or factions started in a neighboring fief, the fact is to be reported to the authorities without delay.

    People are always forming parties, but few ever come to anything. Still there is disobedience to lords and fathers, and strife between neighboring villages on this account. If the ancient precepts are not respected there will probably be restless scheming.

8. Marriages must not be privately arranged.

    Marriage is the harmonious combination of the male and female principle. It must not be lightly undertaken. It is written in the *Book of Changes:* "Not being enemies they can arrange marriage and should make known their wish, for when they become enemies they lose the opportunity." A good thing must be hastened. Also in the *Odes* it is written: "Men and women should act correctly and marry at the right time. Then there will be no widowers in the country. But to form parties through marriage, that is the source of nefarious plots.

9. Concerning the manner of the daimyos coming up to render service. In the *Shoku Nihongi* it is written: Except when on public service, no one is to assemble his clan within the capital or go about attended by more than twenty horsemen. So it is not permitted to lead about a large force of retainers. Lords below a million koku and above two hundred thousand must not exceed twenty horsemen. For those above a hundred thousand the number is to be in proportion. But when on public service his forces are to be according to his means.

10. There must be no confusion about the materials used for costume. There must be a clear distinction between lord and vassal, superior and inferior. White figured material, white wadded silk coats, purple lined garments, garments with purple lining, wadded silk coats (of nerinuki) without crests may not be worn casually without permission. Of late ordinary retainers and soldiers have taken to wearing costumes of figured material and brocade, a thing quite contrary to ancient rule and very objectionable.

11. The common herd are not to ride in palanquins.

There are some who have had the right to ride in palanquins from ancient times, and there are others who have received permission afterwards. But lately ordinary retainers and soldiers have been riding in them. This is flagrant insolence. Henceforth only lords of provinces at least and distinguished members of their families are to be allowed to ride thus without permission. Beside these high retainers, doctors, and astrologers, persons over sixty years old and sick people may be given permission to ride. If ordinary retainers and soldiers ride it will be considered the fault of their lords. But these rules do not apply to Court Nobles, Imperial Abbots, and priests.

12. The samurai of all the fiefs are to practise economy.

The wealthy are apt to be ostentatious and so the poor ashamed of their inequality. This is a common weakness. Nothing is more reprehensible. It must be strictly repressed.

13. Lords of provinces must select men of ability for official positions under them.

The art of government lies in obtaining the right men. There must be clear discrimination between merit and demerit and accurate distribution of praise and blame. If there are capable men in a fief it is sure to be prosperous. But if there are none it is as sure to be ruined. This is the clear admonition of the ancient sages.

The above regulations must be observed.

Keicho 20. 7th month. 1615.

These rules were for the control of the military class, who in their turn controlled the whole country, and they are fairly drastic in their meaning, and in practice the most harmless ones, such as the exhortation to economy and the prohibition of immoderate revelling, were very often made the pretext for severe measures by the Bakufu against a daimyo, against whom they had a black mark because he seemed likely to become in some way a menace to them. It was easy to make such a one retire from the headship of his fief, or confine him to his house, or diminish his revenue, or order him to exchange with another feudatory, or even deprive him altogether. A charge of luxury or levity was quite enough. Even a platitude was useful to the Shogunate. Tokutomi calls this set of regulations "a velvet bag full of gunpowder."

Not less strictly were the rules to be observed by the Emperor and Court nobility. Here there was a very decided difference between the outlook of Ieyasu and Hideyoshi and his predecessors. Hideyoshi had considered himself as one of the Court nobles, and regarded the Imperial Family just as they did. He was head of the Military Government, but also as one of the Court nobles he looked on the Emperor as his chief, and there was not in his mind any particular distinction between the two positions. But Ieyasu held quite a different view. He regarded himself as a military administrator only, and the Court and military nobles as two entirely separate groups, the former to be completely subordinated to the latter. And it was to this end that his regulations for the Court were directed. Henceforth it could do nothing without the consent of the Shogunate, and was to restrict itself to ceremony and aesthetics. And even these things were to be done according to rules laid down by Edo. This was only another example of his all-embracing forethought. He had determined that the military class, under his family, should be the ruling power, and he took every care to ensure that no person or institution should be able to interfere with it. Henceforth the Court was short-circuited for a couple of centuries, though with its functions unimpaired and its emoluments to some extent increased and ensured. Under the circumstances it is difficult to see what other course would have been compatible with the security of the Empire. For if the Court nobles had had any opportunity for intriguing with some of the powerful daimyo civil war might have broken out again. And of this the Empire had certainly had enough. Only by some such methods could the land be kept in order to develop quite a unique culture, and eventually to be able to adapt itself to the circumstances of the Restoration and take its place as equal to the greatest of modern powers. And at that time the Emperor was able to emerge from his seclusion and become the head of the nation once again.

As to the emoluments of the Court, Ieyasu allowed the Imperial Family a stipend of ten thousand koku, which was not so large, but was three thousand more than Hideyoshi had provided. This did not include such donations as the ten thousand koku dowry which Hidetada's daughter took with her when she became the consort of the Emperor Go-Mizu-no-o, or the rebuilding of the palaces, which was one of the expensive privileges conferred on the daimyos by the Shogun.

Ieyasu is reported to have said: "Court nobles are like gold and silver, while the military nobles are like iron and copper. Gold and silver are certainly precious, but they are not as useful as iron and copper. From these useful metals are made the farmer's implements, the artisan's tools, the weapons of the soldier, and the needle of the housewife. Gold and silver are quite decorative, it is true, but too much attachment to them leads to trouble. Warriors must not neglect the sword for the purse."

The first set of laws for the Court nobles was issued in 1613 and consisted of five articles. It is probable that the opportunity for such legislation was first furnished by the Emperor Go-Yozei himself, when in 1609 he complained to Ieyasu of the misbehavior of some of the Court nobles and Court ladies, and Ieyasu disciplined them accordingly. The affair is thus related by the Tokugawa Jikki:

"When it was reported that several young Court nobles, including Kazan-in, Asukai, and Inokuma, with the dentist Kaneyasu Bitchu-no-kami, had enticed several of the ladies-in-waiting of the Inner Court to an entertainment, at which there had been dancing and unseemly and inebriate merriment, the said Bitchuno-kami was arrested and examined. On a detailed account being sent to the Court, the Emperor's anger was extreme, and he bade the Shoshidai Itakura Katsushige punish the offenders with the greatest severity." This Imperial Order Katsushige sent to Suruga to Ieyasu for consideration, and it was from there forwarded to Edo for the opinion of the Shogun, after which the following advice was sent through Katsushige: "From ancient times disturbances at Court have been by no means a rarity, and of the penalties inflicted in connection with them there have been various kinds. In the present case, if the Court would treat it with exceptional benevolence and a broad-minded generosity no doubt in future people will feel ashamed of themselves and refrain from disorderly conduct." This advice seemed good to the Emperor, and in consequence the death penalty was remitted, and the Court ladies were only banished to the Isles of Izu, while Kazan-in was sent to Tsugaru, Asukai to Oki, two others to Io-ga-shima, and so on, but in the case of Inokuma and Bitchu-no-kami, who were responsible officials, the latter in charge of one of the gates, it was considered inadvisable to be lenient, so they were both executed. The Shogunate was naturally not slow to improve on such an occasion. The laws were as follows:

1. The various houses of Court Nobles shall be ordered to apply themselves to their studies with all diligence, both by day and night.

    (It is unnecessary to say that these were unpractical studies. Only the year before Ieyasu had forbidden the Court Nobles to go hawking and recommended them to keep to their proper business.)

2. If any of them, whether old or young, transgress the law, he will certainly be banished. The term of years is to be in accordance with the degree of guilt.

3. Guard duty must be performed by all both young and old, and not neglected. Beside this they are to be ordered to be in waiting at such times as are specified in the Court Rules, and to maintain the proper dignity and etiquette required of them.

4. It is strictly forbidden to them to go strolling about the streets and lanes of the city, whether by night or day, in places where they have no business.

5. Except at public entertainments they are not to indulge in improper competitive games at their will, and also they are not to keep in their households worthless young samurai or the like. Those who do these things will be banished as stated in the former article.

The articles above are hereby laid down. When the five regent families or the denso, who are the liaison officers of the Shogun at Court, shall report any breach of them, the matter shall be dealt with by the military authorities.

Then two years after this, when he had issued the laws for the daimyos, Ieyasu and Hidetada summoned the representatives of the Court nobles to the Nijo castle.* The seventeen articles were then read out by Hirohashi Kanekatsu. Lords Nijo and Kikutei listened, and Suden and Sanjo Saneeda and the other Court nobles were in waiting. When it was finished these two latter declared that it was very remarkable and complete, which was not strange, seeing that in all probability they had quite a share in its composition. The laws were as follows:

---

* "Of the Court noble families first came the five Regent families from which the Kambaku might be chosen, Konoe, Takatsukasa, Kujo, Nijo, and Ichijo.

Officials called denso, whose business it was to transmit all communications between the Mikado and the Shogunate, were appointed from the Court nobles. Normally they reported to the Shoshidai, the Shogunate Governor of Kyoto, and he from the Shogun to them, but in special cases an Imperial envoy would go up to Edo or a messenger come from the Shogun to Kyoto. There were also Giso or administrators of the Imperial Household who were of the rank of dainagon, also nominated by the Shogun. These Denso and Giso were selected from the families that ranked next after the five Regent families: they were Kuga, Sanjo, Saionji, Imadegawa (now called Kikutei), Tokudaiji, Kazanin, Oi-no-Mikado, Hirohata, Daigo, Naka-no-in, Saga, Sanjo-Nishi, Hino, Karasu-Maru, Yanagihara, Hirohashi, Hashimoto, Shimizudani, Yotsutsuji, Nishi-no-Doin, Ogimachi, Okura, and Nakayama. Except through these officers no approach could be made to the Imperial Court.

1. As to the arts and accomplishments of the Emperor. First of all comes
   the study of letters. Without study one cannot know the Way of the
   Ancients, nor can such an one maintain the peace of the Empire, as the
   Jo-kwan Seiyo clearly states. Though the Kampyo Ikai shows a want
   of knowledge of the classics and histories, the *Gunsho Seiyo* should be
   carefully studied. Japanese poetry has been cultivated by the Emperors
   ever since the days of Kōkō Tenno, and though it may be merely a
   superfluous embroidery of language, yet it is an ancient custom of
   our country, and should not therefore be neglected. The *Kinpi-sho* or
   private records of the Imperial Family should be the subject of special
   study. (In being limited to the contemplation of flowers, birds, snow,
   wind, and moon, the Emperor shared the fate of all from whose minds
   the Bakufu wished to banish political ideas.)
2. Princes of the Blood rank below the Three Great Ministers (San-Kō),
   i.e. Dajo-daijin, Sa-daijin, U-daijin. And the reason is that the U-daijin
   Fuhito had precedence over Toneri Shinno (659–720). And the rank of
   Dajo-daijin was conferred on Toneri Shinno and Nakano Shinno after
   their death, and that of U-daijin on Hozumi Shinno. All these were
   Princes of the Blood of the First Rank, yet their promotion to Daijin
   followed this rank. Can there be any doubt that they were below the
   Three Ministers? After the Princes of the Blood come former Great
   Ministers. While they hold the office of Minister they are to rank above
   the Princes, but after they retire from it they come after them. After
   that come all the other Princes of the Blood. But the Crown Prince is
   an exception. When former Ministers or Kampaku hold office a second
   time they are to rank with the Five Regent Families.

     (It seems to have been on occasions of Court festivals, poetry parties,
   and such like that these questions of precedence arose. They can hardly
   have been very important for nothing depended on these Ministers.
   Still the Shogun settled them.)
3. Ministers of the Pure Flowery Families (Tokudaiji, Kwazan-in, Oi-no-
   mikado, Sanjo, Saionji, Kikutei, Kuga, and afterwards Hirohata and
   Daigo) when they resign office shall rank after the ordinary Imperial
   Princes.
4. Even members of the Five Regent Families, if they lack ability, shall not
   be appointed to the offices of Regent and Minister. Much more shall
   this apply to any other families.
5. Men of ability, even though they be advanced in years, shall not resign
   the offices of Regent and Minister. And even if they do resign they shall
   be appointed again.

     (It must be understood that the Shogunate was the sole judge of
   ability to fill such offices.)

6. Adopted sons may maintain the family in an unbroken line. But they must be of the same surname.* Females cannot maintain the succession. It has never been permitted of old, nor will it be now.

7. Members of military families holding Court rank and office shall be quite apart from Court Nobles holding the same office. That is to say, such military men shall not go near the Court or have anything to do with it. Their office shall be purely honorary.

8. The names of year-periods shall be chosen from among those of the Chinese Empire that are suitably auspicious. However, if it be done with mature knowledge of custom and example, then former Japanese precedent may be followed.

9. Concerning the Ceremonial Robes of the Emperor, Retired Emperor, and Courtiers.

10. Concerning the promotion of the various families of Court Nobles. The old established customs of the respective families are to be followed. But scholarship, knowledge of ancient customs, and skill in verse are to be encouraged. Besides these promotions may be made, even over the heads of superiors, for specially meritorious service. Shimotsu-michi-no-mabi (Kibi-no-mabi)† was only a courtier of the lower eighth rank, but yet he rose to be Udaijin. This was very right and proper. Meritorious diligence in learning should never be overlooked.

11. With regard to orders given by the Kampaku, the Denso, and the Bugyo, any courtier who disobeys them, whether of the higher or lower rank, will be banished.

12. The degree of guilt in any such breach is to be assessed according to the code of the era Daiho.

13. Lord Abbots of the Regent Families shall rank after Lord Abbots of the Imperial House. This is in accordance with members of Regent Families' rank after Princes of the Blood when they have retired from the office of Great Minister, though they take precedence of them while holding such office. And except sons of the Emperor, the rank of Prince of the Blood shall not be conferred on any Lord Abbot. The position of the consort of a Lord Abbot depends on her own rank. Princes of the Blood who become ecclesiastics should be few. There is no justification for the existence of as many as there are nowadays. With the exception of Lord Abbots of the Imperial Family and of the Regent Families all other Lord Abbots shall be only Honorary Lord Abbots.

    (There had been cases of Lord Abbots from the Regent Families obtaining the rank of Jun-san-ko or treatment equal to the Three Dowagers, and thus taking rank before Princes of the Blood, and this it was desired to prevent in future.)

14. As to Sojo of the three ranks (Dai-sojo, Sho-sojo, Gon-sojo), Lord

---

* This would prevent any member of the Imperial Family becoming Minister, for they have no surname.
† 693–775. He spent twenty years in China, and introduced embroidery biwa and Go to Japan.

Abbots (Monzeki), and Abbots, promotions shall be made according to ancient precedent. Commoners if of extraordinary ability may be appointed, but their rank shall be only honorary.

This, however, does not apply to tutors to the Imperial Family or Great Ministers.

15. Lord Abbots may be promoted to Sozu (Dai-sho and Sho-sozu) or Hoin. Abbots may of course be given the rank of Sozu (Dai-Sho-Gon-sozu), Risshi, Hoin, and Hogen in accordance with ancient precedent. Only commoners, after being recommended by their own temple, must be selected according to ability.

16. Concerning the conferring of purple robes on the incumbents of temples. In former days this was seldom done, but lately there have been cases of improper appointments by Imperial permission. This interference with seniority and bringing ecclesiastical rank into contempt is most reprehensible. In future only those who are of distinguished ability and well advanced in learning and seniority shall be dignified by this appointment.

17. As to the title of Shonin (His Eminence). It shall be conferred on ecclesiastics of wide learning who are chosen by their own temples. And the title shall be conferred by Imperial permission with the distinction of Real and Vice Eminence. The superior title of Sho-shonin is only to be conferred on such distinguished ecclesiastics as have been Buddhist priests for twenty years, while those who have not completed this term shall receive the lower rank. If anyone agitates and strives to get this title improperly he shall be sent into exile.

Besides these general enactments about the priesthood, Ieyasu published several sets of rules for the various sects. Tokutomi remarks that no military ruler showed as much interest in religion as Ieyasu, except possibly Ashikaga Takauji, but in his case what he was interested in was his own salvation, whereas Ieyasu regarded religion as one of the instruments of government, though this is not to say he had no taste for it for its own sake, to some extent at least, for he was a Jodo believer, and was very fond of listening to discussions of Buddhist philosophy.

Judicial sentences, he considered, should be quick and severe. Like fire blazing up, and not like water flowing quietly. Because when people see a fierce fire they keep away from it and so are not burned, whereas with quietly flowing water they cannot tell whether it is deep or not, and so often get drowned. So one must always be firm and severe at first, and only relax afterwards, for so people will go in fear of the law and not break it and incur punishment. But if one appear indulgent at first and then adopt severe measures afterwards, it will result in a far greater number of executions than was ever anticipated.

He did not believe in sentencing to death lords of over 10,000 koku income. It was better to send them into exile. In criticizing the politics of his day he blamed Imagawa Yoshimoto for entrusting all his government to the Rinzai Zen monk Sessai to the exclusion of his House councilors. For when Sessai died everything fell into confusion.

Then also it did not do to have councilors with a greater income than their lord, as was the case with Chiba Kunitane in the Kwanto, for he could not keep them in order.

Again Ashikaga Yoshimasa, Takeda Katsuyori, and Saito Yoshitatsu were examples of rulers who departed from their ancestral custom and started a new system of government. This resulted in the loss of their domains. In all matters to forsake the ancestral law is to court disaster. So Ieyasu always paid the greatest reverence to his ancestors, and never altered their enactments unless it was absolutely unavoidable. And this not only in his own fiefs, but in those that he acquired, for he did not change Shingen's laws when he took over Kai. The only thing he altered was the taxation, by lightening it, and so naturally the people welcomed him. So, too, with Hojo's provinces, when he moved into the Kwanto. He made no drastic alterations, and so everyone remained quiet. This he did in accordance with the ancient saying that good government consists in keeping the goodwill of the governed.

After Sekigahara he lost no time in summoning Hosokawa Fujitaka, who was living in retirement on Higashiyama at Kyoto, for consultation about the administration, for the Hosokawa family had long held the office of Kwanryo to the Ashikaga Shogunate, and so knew all the details of their government. And this Fujitaka was a great scholar as well as a famous poet, and had compiled a work on the Muromachi laws in three volumes. He also sent for Honda Mimasaka-no-kami Nobutomi, who had served under the Ashikaga Shoguns Yoshiteru and Yoshiaki, and afterwards under Nobunaga, and made him Sosha or liaison officer between his Government and the Court. Soga Mataemon and Ninagawa Chikamasa were also taken into his service, so that he might profit by their knowledge of the proper etiquette and procedure in which they had been experts to the late Shogunate.

He sent into exile some members of the Fuju-fuse, a branch sect of Nichiren-shu, because they had refused to perform some ecclesiastical function owing to conscientious objections, on the ground that this contempt of the law and want of proper respect for the Government was a bad example to other clerics.

Not even reason, much less conscience, if it be so called, was any excuse for transgressing the laws of the Bakufu. And all clerics had to understand that they were only allowed to exist on sufferance. At the same time he would not tolerate daimyos interfering with these ecclesiastics. One Hori Kenmotsu Naotsugu was accused of arbitrary behavior, and brought before the judges, and Ieyasu sat and listened unseen behind the sliding doors. When it was alleged that he had provoked a controversy between the Jodo and Nichiren priests and decided it himself and condemned ten of the former to death, Ieyasu flung open the shoji and confronted the accused with a wrathful countenance, demanding to know by what authority he had decided the question. "By that of a learned man," replied Kenmotsu. "Religious controversy is against the law," retorted Ieyasu hotly. "And it is intolerable that anyone should break it in this flagrant manner, not to speak of deciding these matters arbitrarily and putting people to death. I don't need to hear any more." And he shut the shoji and left the chamber. Kenmotsu was sent into exile and deprived of his fief, while even his younger brother, who was acquitted of any fault, and who gave evidence against him, was shorn of 20,000 koku of his income of 50,000.

CHAPTER 44

THE LEGACY OF IEYASU

THE legacy of Ieyasu or private instructions to his successors in the Sho-gunate, embodying his views as to how best the government should be carried on by them, is a document that exists in several recensions, and has obviously been supplemented at a later period to include develop-ments up to the middle of the seventeenth century or beyond, since it mentions institutions that had not come into being at the death of the Divine Lord, but only developed in the days of Iemitsu and Ietsuna. This fact has cast some discredit on it, but it seems, however, that a large part of it quite succinctly represents the principles and intentions of the founder of the Edo Shogunate as to how it was to be carried on, formulated no doubt not without the assistance of his confidants, the Hondas, Hayashi, Suden, and Tenkai. And since this latter, with Kasuga no Tsubone, lived right on into the period of the third Shogun Iemitsu, the pair of them being then generally credited with being the neces-sary "elder statesmen" whose advice was always taken, and since also Tenkai maintained that he was in communication by means of inspired dreams with the Divine Ieyasu, as did also on more than one occasion his grandson Iemitsu, these would be quite capable of redacting the legacy in any way that might be profitable to the family. This document therefore hardly differs in principle from other religious and ethical in-structions that purport to emanate from some great one, and to control an institution that he launched. It corresponds to the house laws of the other clan chiefs, and in many cases contains identical material, the product of experience in administering clans and military rule that had been gathered in the course of the preceding centuries since Yoritomo. And since the Tokugawas administered the country exactly like a feudal clan and at their own expense, it would hardly be otherwise.

Several translations have been made of this text, one appended to Murdoch's *History of Japan,* and another very complete and scholarly version by Gubbins with various readings of the different editions in the *Transactions of the Japan Society in London.* This may be consulted by those who wish to study the complete text. The translation here given is an independent one made of that part of it that may well be the product of Ieyasu's day, merely omitting what is obviously later.

Its strongly rationalist and nationalist flavor is most characteristic of him, as is the reinforcing of the dicta by an appropriate Confucian quotation, where the subject admits of it. Buddhist influence is conspicuously lacking, and this philosophy is in fact repudiated as nonnational, though it may sometimes be useful. In these apothegms the various facets of the author's character seem to stand out definitely and entertainingly. Sometimes he is purely didactic and rather conservative, while at others he exhibits his very shrewd insight into human nature and his rational plans for taking suitable advantage of it. Again, he will strike the note of benevolence, and even go so far as to stand up in the pulpit and proclaim himself a model of single-minded altruism and loving-kindness that merit the admiration and imitation of posterity. And since he can hardly have been lacking in a sense of proportion, he may well have stepped down again with a grin.

That very much of what Ieyasu embodied in his various maxims was part of the feudal wisdom of the day is evident from a perusal of similar rules and advices given by the other lords for the guidance of their descendants and clan officers. A good example is the Admonition of Kuroda Jōsui, part of which runs thus:

Fear the retribution of your lord more than that of Heaven, and that of your retainers and peasants more than that of your lord. You can avert the retribution of God by prayer and that of your lord by excuses, but if you incur the enmity of your retainers and tenants you are likely to lose your province, for neither prayer nor apology will avert it. You must remember that ruling a province is no easy matter. You cannot behave like a private individual, for in government there is no privacy. You must order your conduct and behavior correctly so that it may be an example to those under you. Even your personal fancies must be carefully regulated because what a lord likes becomes the fashion for his retainers and peasants.

As the ancients have observed, the arts of war and letters are indispensable like the two wheels of a cart, and certainly literary culture is to be practised in times of peace as well as in those of war and disturbance. But it is most essential not to forget war in times of peace and culture in the days of strife. If a commander forgets his profession in peace the art of war will suffer and his retainers become incapable so that they will lose interest in and neglect their duties, so that even their weapons will deteriorate and become unfit for use. Then when an emergency arises what can they do? They cannot act promptly without preparation, but will be irresolute and confused. It is like starting to dig a well when you need a reservoir.

One born in a military family must never neglect his profession, though he shows that he does not understand it if he overlooks culture in times of strife. For then his laws will be defective, and crime and punishment will increase in his fief. Because such a lord shows no benevolence toward his retainers and tenants they will resent him, for martial prestige alone without justice and benevolence will not command. A commander of this type may win a victory or two, but he will certainly lose in the end.

And culture does not mean merely reading a lot of books and making Chinese poems, and knowing all about what happened in the past, and cultivating a fine handwriting. It means a proper outlook on affairs and knowing how to investigate accurately and devise accordingly, being logical and not making mistakes, being able to judge with discrimination and reward and punish without fear or favor, at the same time preserving a sympathetic temper.

Moreover, the military art of a general must not only consist in a devotion to the technical side of it and putting on an air of swagger and bluster. He must know how to put down any disorder, be ever vigilant, and keep his men well trained. Therefore he must punish and reward the right persons, keeping up their warlike spirit, and taking care nothing is neglected even when there is no sign of trouble. To think only of personal prowess is what is called animal courage, the quality of the lowest kind of fighter perhaps, but not at all suited to a general. At the same time, since it is the business of soldiers to be skilled in handling sword, bow, and spear, if one has never practised these arts oneself it will not be easy to stimulate others to do so. So you must show them what you can do in this way sometimes, while never forgetting your real function, just as you must do some intellectual work to encourage those under you to do the same. Certainly without this combination of military and literary pursuits you cannot govern a province.

When one remembers that Jōsui was one of the most prominent Christian converts, these sentiments are the more interesting.

THE LEGACY OF TOKUGAWA IEYASU

The duty of the lord of a province is to give peace and security to the people, and does not consist in shedding lustre on his ancestors, and working for the prosperity of his descendants. The supreme excellence of T'ang of the Yin dynasty and Wu of the Chou dynasty lay in making this their first principle.* There must be no slighting of the Imperial Dignity or confusing the order of Heaven and Earth, Lord and Subject.

---

* T'ang of Yin and Wu of Chou were the founders of these two Chinese dynasties.

The civil and military principles both proceed from Benevolence. However many books and plans there may be the principle is the same. Know therefore that herein lies the way of ruling and administering the Empire.

The Empire does not belong to the Empire, neither does it belong to one man. The thing to be studied most deeply is how to act with Benevolence.

Benevolence is within you. You have the Nine Classics and the Four Books. Let their precepts be in your mind always. This realm is a land of Divine Valor clearly manifest, but in letters we are inferior to foreigners. Let colleges be established therefore, and in this sphere also let us show the capacity of our country.

If the lord is not filled with compassion for his people and the people are not mindful of the care of their lord, even though the government is not a bad one, yet rebellions will naturally follow. But if the lords love Benevolence, then there will be no enemies in the Empire.

If Benevolence abides in the Empire there is no distinction between domestic and foreign or noble and commoner, for the sun and moon shine on the clean and unclean alike. The Sage established the law on this principle, and according to it there are fixed and immutable rules applying to the degree of intimacy, rank, the three allegiances, and the eight rules. If one man is supreme in the Empire then all warriors are his retainers, but he does not make retainers of the whole people. There is the distinction of Outside Families and our own Family, Outside Lords (Tozama) and House Retainers (Hatamoto). Outside houses are those that are temporarily powerful. Family vassals or Fudai are those bound to us by lineage and history, whose ancestors did loyal service to our house as is clear to all by their records. Since their fidelity and affection exceeds that of the Outside houses, these others must not be displeased at this preference, resting as it does on such a basis.

In employing men and recognizing ability, if the Fudai are overlooked and the Tozama elevated there will be inward rage and outward regret, and loyal retainers will naturally be lost. One thing is quite certain, men are not all saints and sages. This fact it is well to bear very much in mind.

All feudatories, whether Fudai or Tozama, are to have their fiefs changed after a certain number of years, for if they stay long in one place and get used to their positions these lords will lose their fidelity and become covetous and self-willed, and eventually oppress their subjects.[*] This changing of fiefs shall be according to the conduct of these lords.

If there be no direct heir to the Shogunate, then the question of succession must be settled by a conference of the veteran houses of Ii, Honda, Sakai, Sakakibara, and others, after careful consideration.

Should anyone break the laws I have laid down, even if he be a son or heir, he shall not succeed. The Chief Senator (Tairo) and Senators (Roshin) shall then hold a consultation and shall choose a suitable person from among the branch families of our house (Kamon) and make him head of the family.

The right use of a sword is that it should subdue the barbarians while lying gleaming in its scabbard. If it leaves its sheath it cannot be said to be used rightly. Similarly the right use of military power is that it should conquer the enemy while concealed in the breast. To take the field with an army is to be found wanting in the real knowledge of it. Those who hold the office of Shogun are to be particularly clear on this point.

A warrior who does not understand the Way of the Warrior and the samurai who does not know the principles of the samurai can only be called a stupid or petty general, by no means a good one. One may excel in the art of war and in strategy, but it must be understood that this is not enough for a Shogun.

If your defenses are according to my instructions traitors will not be able to spy them out. But even so, if another family plans to overthrow this Empire the attempt will only be made when those who uphold it are given up to drink and dissipation. It is inevitable that those who are incapacitated by these things should be deprived of office and commit suicide.

In ordinary matters, if one does not disobey these instructions of mine, even if he is far from being a sage, he will commit no great fault.

---

[*] The territories of lords of provinces are not to be held in perpetuity, and the fiefs of lesser lords are not to be continued for many generations. Every year these feudatories must be considered, and some of them moved elsewhere, for if they are allowed to remain in possession for long they will become recalcitrant and oppress the people.

From my youth I have not valued silver or gold or treasures. Virtue only I have treasured. And now I have thus attained this office. If we always consider without ceasing the golden words that declare that it is by learning that emolument comes, we can always attain our purpose.

The strong manly ones in life are those who understand the meaning of the word Patience. Patience means restraining one's inclinations. There are seven emotions, joy, anger, anxiety, love, grief, fear, and hate, and if a man does not give way to these he can be called patient. I am not as strong as I might be, but I have long known and practised patience. And if my descendants wish to be as I am, beside the Five Relations and the Nine Classics, they must study Patience.

When the Empire is at peace do not forget the possibility of war, and take counsel with the Fudai vassals that the military arts be not allowed to deteriorate. And be temperate in your habits.

The sword is the soul of the warrior. If any forget or lose it he will not be excused.

Archery, musketry, fencing, and the use of spear and halberd are the accomplishments demanded of a samurai, but the whole art of the warrior does not consist in such minor attainments; how much less does the equipment of one who commands an army. He must try to imitate the character of the Minister I Yin and the Councilor Lu Chang.*

The descendants of those retainers who were loyal to our ancestors, except they become traitors to our house, must never have their fiefs confiscated, even if their conduct is not good.†

If fellows of the lower orders go beyond what is proper toward samurai, or if any sub-feudatory samurai is remiss toward a direct retainer, there is no objection to cutting such a one down.

There shall be no striving for precedence among samurai. They shall take their places according to their office. Neither must there be any

---

* I Yin, Minister of the Founder of the Yin dynasty. He refused office five times, and banished the heir-apparent for misconduct. He overthrew the tyrant Kieh Kuei.

Lu Chang. Usually called Tai Kung (Japanese: Tai Ko Bo), Minister of Wu Wang of Chou, whom he assisted to overthrow the despot Chou Sin.

† All the fudai, both great and small, are retainers who have proved their loyalty by the endurance of every kind of hardship in my service. Even if their descendants behave badly, unless they are traitors they shall not have their fiefs confiscated.

competition among those of equal importance, for then precedence shall be decided according to income, or priority of appointment, or age. Let them only strive to be first to give place to others. But old people should act as old people.

In all the military works it is written: To train samurai to be loyal separate them when young, or treat them according to their character. But it is no use to train them according to any fixed plan, they must be educated by benevolence. If the superior loves benevolence then the inferior will love his duty.

Authority to subdue the whole Empire was granted by Imperial Edict to the Shogun, and he was appointed Lord High Constable (Sotsui-Hoshi). The orders that the Shogun issues to the country are its law. Nevertheless every province and district has its particular customs, and it is difficult, for example, to enforce the customs of the Eastern Provinces in the Western, or those of the North in the South, so that these customs must be left as of old and not interfered with.

In country districts of the distant provinces the farmers are of equal standing, but in every village and locality there are some who are distinguished by ancient lineage. They are the same as ordinary farmers and yet not the same. These ancient families shall be chosen to hold office. Those in a low position shall not be exalted over their betters. This is the great principle of the Empire. Orders to this effect shall be given not only to Tozama and Fudai Daimyos, but also to Lords of Provinces (Kokushi) and Lords of Fiefs (Ryoshu), as well as to District Commissioners (Daikwan).

In accordance with ancient precedent, a Court of Judgment is to be established, and there, in the light of these articles I have drawn up and without regarding the high or repressing the low, justice is to be done openly to all.

Now the officials who administer justice in this court are the pillars of the government of the country. Their character shall be carefully considered, and they shall be chosen and appointed after consultation with the veteran councilors. This will be no easy task.

Should the Bugyo or Headmen take bribes and pervert justice they are criminals. Such crime is equal to treason, and the death penalty shall not be spared.

The law may upset reason, but reason may never upset the law. Therefore the sage first studies the people's way of reasoning, and then establishes the law and determines the method of government. And if he does not publish it people may go astray. In short, the law may be used to confound reason, but reason must certainly not be used to overthrow the law.

Nagasaki in Hizen is the port at which foreign shipping arrives. It shall be administered by one of the most trusted retainers chosen from the fudai vassals. The great lords of the neighboring territories shall also be instructed to furnish guards, that our military might may be demonstrated to all countries. It is strictly forbidden that any of these ships shall enter any other port but Nagasaki.

The entertainment tendered to foreigners who come to pay their respects shall be as heretofore. It shall not be rough or scanty. It shall brilliantly reveal the Imperial Benevolence and Divine Might.

Beside the Four Classes there are Eta, Beggars, Blindmen, and Blindwomen, people one does not mention, but to whom the means of living must be given and kindness must be shown. Know that from ancient days benevolent rule began with this.

Strumpets, dancing-girls, sodomites, and street walkers are people who will certainly be found in castle towns and prosperous places, and though they are the cause of bad conduct in many, yet if they are strictly prohibited very great evils will be continually arising. Gambling, disorderly drinking, and dissipation will be regarded as serious offences.

Singing and recitation are the origin of music and began with the ancient sages. Changes in the Five Elements must result in sound. The sages investigated these and made musical instruments, and therefore softened the character of the people. Instrumental music flourished greatly in the Middle Ages, so the military class by patronizing it can dispel melancholy, celebrate auspicious occasions, and tranquillize the people.

Bugaku is of various kinds.* There is the music of the Emperor, and that of the great lords. There are also different varieties for samurai and officials, and for the lower classes. It must be performed by each class within the prescribed bounds.

---

* Bugaku, the classical music and dances used at Court and the Noh.

Confucianism and Shinto and Buddhism are different systems, but are no more than direction in the way of virtue and punishment of evil. According to this view, their sects may be adopted and their principles followed. They must not be hindered, but disputes among them must be strictly prohibited. It is evident from past history that such have been a misfortune to the Empire.

Temples and shrines and Yambushi and so on are idle parasites, but from old times have been a feature of the Empire. If they wrangle about precedence and position, and have to be suppressed they will again be a source of trouble to the country. Regulations must be made for them, and they should be summoned to the Court and their affairs settled there. But in the matter of the temples and shrines where the Emperor worships nothing must be done arbitrarily.

Good and bad luck, fortune and misfortune are to be left to Heaven and natural law. They are not things that can be got by praying, or worked by some cunning device.

Since one person differs from another in disposition, when men are appointed to offices this should be tested, and their tendencies observed and their ability estimated, so that the office may be well filled. A saw cannot do the work of a gimlet, and a hammer cannot take the place of a knife, and men are just like this. There is a use for both sharp and blunt at the right time, and if this is not well apprehended the relation of lord and vassal will become disturbed. This article is to be considered carefully.

Generally people of bad character have some good point, just as those of good character have some bad one, and you must choose the good and leave the bad, or get rid of the evil without sacrificing the good. For it must be understood that there is no waste material in this realm to be lightly cast away.

Lords of provinces both great and small and lords of fiefs and officials both in and outside Edo shall hold official stipend, and rank only if they conduct themselves properly. If he offend, the greatest feudatory or official, even if he be a relation of our house (Kamon), shall be punished. So in their persons shall they the better guard the Shogun's office.

The great Tozama lords of provinces have no part in the house laws and ancestral instructions of my family. But if they transgress the code of the samurai, which is the great bond of society, and oppress the people, even though they do not rebel, they shall be deprived of their territory as an example to others. That is the duty of the Shogun.

The first,* fifteenth, and twenty-eighth days of the month are days of ceremony. The beginning and end of the year, the five festivals, auspicious commemorations, and the first hog-day of the tenth month are occasions when with suitable purification respectful homage must be paid to the Emperor, and after that on the other hand the congratulations of vassals are to be accepted. Such ceremonies are to be carried out as laid down in our instructions. If indisposed, then the Tairo or one of the Roju shall officiate instead so that the proper observance be not omitted.

At Momijiyama in the western castle are enshrined the spirits of the warrior chiefs of the Minamoto clan from Prince Sadazumi, sixth son of the Emperor Seiwa, and it is the principal Tutelary Shrine of the castle. Future generations must revere it, and never omit to celebrate the customary festivals.

I was born of the family of Matsudaira of the province of Mikawa, of the lineage of the Seiwa Genji, but on account of the enmity of a neighboring province I had for long to suffer hardships among the common people. But now, I am happy to say, encompassed by the grace of Providence I have restored the ancestral lines of Serata, Nitta, and Tokugawa, and from henceforth the successive generations of my family are to use these four names. This is in accordance with the saying (of Confucius):

Pay all respect to your parents, and follow the customs of your ancestors.

The basis of knowledge as to how to govern the Empire is in the teachings of the Sage, and one who wishes to understand the Way of the Warrior without entering on these is as one who thinks to get fish from trees or fire from water. You must avoid such extremely improper and foolish conduct.

Diviners, male and female, wandering priests and mendicants, blind women and blind men, beggars, outcasts, and all such nonproducers have their traditional rulers. But if they dispute among themselves, or forget their proper place and break the law, there must be no neglect to punish them.

---

* When the Feudal Lords came to call on the Shogun.

The distinction between wife and concubine is on the principle of lord and vassal. The Emperor has twelve consorts, the great lords may have eight, high officials five, and ordinary samurai two. Below these are the common people. Thus have the ancient sages specified in the *Li Chi*,* and it has always been the rule. But fools ignorant of this treat their wife with less respect than a favorite concubine, and so confuse the great principle. This has always been the cause of the fall of castles and the ruin of countries. Is it not well to be warned? And know too that those who give way to these inclinations are no loyal samurai.

The business of a husband is to protect the family outside, while that of the wife is to look after it at home. That is the order of the world. Should the wife, on the contrary, be the one to guard the house the husband loses his function, and it is a sure sign that the house will be destroyed. It is the disorder of the crowing hen. All samurai should beware of it. Its existence will assist you to judge people.

When I was young I desired nothing but to subdue hostile provinces and take vengeance on the enemies of my father's house. But since I discovered the teaching of Yuyo that helping the people and thus tranquillizing the country is the Law of Nature, I have undeviatingly followed it until now.† Let my descendants continue my policy. If they reject it they are no posterity of mine. For be very certain that the people are the foundation of the country.

That man and woman should cohabit is the great principle of mankind. None shall remain single after the age of sixteen. The offices of a matchmaker shall be secured, and the marriage ceremony duly performed. But those of the same family shall not marry. Such alliances shall only be made after investigation of the pedigree and heredity of the parties. That there should be a succession of descendants is the first law of nature for man, and a cause of rejoicing to ancestors. Let this be published that none may forget it.

From of old the relations of lord and vassal have been compared to water and fish, and it will not be difficult for it to continue thus. If the golden rule that what one does not like oneself is not to be done to others be not forgotten, the inferior will be influenced by this good

---

* *Li Chi*. Book of Ceremonies.

† Yuyo. This reference is obscure. Ieyasu is said to have awakened to his responsibilities as the result of the admonition of the priest Kanyo, abbot of the Daijuji, whither he had fled for refuge after the battle of Okehazama. He was about eighteen years old then.

example, and not only vassals but the whole Empire will become docile as water.

Both our own family and all others receive their bodily existence from this Land of the Gods, and if we should prefer such foreign doctrines as those of Confucianism, Buddhism, and Taoism, and adopt them in their entirety, it would be to desert our own master and serve an outsider. Would not this be to deny the origin of our own existence? In these matters we should clearly and calmly deliberate what is best to retain and what to reject. And further, the practice of delusions and spells should not necessarily be entirely banned, though it should not be definitely accepted.

When military authority goes beyond bounds there is not necessarily extravagance and luxury, but there is a tendency to think lightly of the Throne and hold it less in awe. Of this there have been many examples in the past. If we thus neglect the source and origin of this Land of the Gods and let selfish desires overflow, our offence will not be a light one, and the punishment of Heaven will follow.

With regard to the Three Chief Families of Nagoya,* Wakayama, and Mito, and the fifteen related houses (Kamon), who come next to them, the eldest son shall inherit, and the second and third sons shall not receive incomes from these fiefs. They shall make alliances with influential and wealthy families and enter them as adopted sons, and these families shall be allied with our family and shall rank next after the Kamon. But they shall not be treated as equal to the Eighteen Families.

People who neglect their occupations and indulge in gambling and disorderly drinking are cheating the daylight. Still this can hardly be called a criminal offence. But if there is looseness in these matters the lower classes will imitate it, and their families may be ruined and their lives spoiled. If the teacher does not teach them ignorance is his fault, but if he teaches and is not followed then the fault lies with his pupils. Therefore punishment should be according to the circumstances.

When a lord of a province or of a castle who has a large revenue commits a fault against the Empire unintentionally, or disagrees with the Government, it is not necessary to punish him. But when the affair

---

* The three families from which the Shogun was selected failing an heir in the main families. The Kamon or families of the lineage were those descended from the other sons of Ieyasu. Their name was Matsudaira.

is one that cannot entirely be overlooked, some large undertaking that is beyond his means should be imposed on him as a fine.

The Supreme Sovereign of the Empire looks on the people as children under his protecting care, and my family to which the administration of his realm is committed should exhibit this attitude even more. This is what is called Benevolence. Benevolence includes the Five Relationships, and the distinction of superior and inferior. In accordance with it I make a difference in intimacy between the Fudai and the Tozama Daimyos. That is government according to the natural way of the world. It is not favoritism or prejudice or self-interest. It must not be polluted either by tongue or pen. And as to the degree of this intimacy with retainers, whether deep or the reverse, you must know how to maintain a deep reserve.

Since I have held this office of Shogun I have drawn up these many statutes, both amplifying and curtailing the ancient regulations of the Minamoto house. But with a view to transmitting and not to creating, for they are no new laws decreed at my will. Thus I have drawn them up in this form as an exemplar. They may not always hit the mark exactly, but they will not be far out. In all things administration is not so much a matter of detail as of understanding past history. I have no time to add more.

APPENDICES

REGULATIONS FOR THE PEASANTS UNDER IEMITSU

JUST how the Bakufu regulated the life of the country people in accordance with the principles approved by Ieyasu can be seen by a set of rules for them issued under Iemitsu, his grandson, in 1642. Their object was to ensure the maintenance of capacity to pay the taxes and to emphasize the distinction between the ranks of society.

They are as follows:

Both in the Shogun's domains as well as in others no tobacco is to be grown on cultivable land. It is forbidden to put a blanket on the packsaddle when riding it.

During this present year sake must not be made in the country districts. An exception may be made in the case of a town on a high road. And such a town is the only place where it may be sold. It must not be sold to peasants in the country. Anyone found selling it to them will have all his sake-brewing gear confiscated.

During this present year spaghetti and vermicelli and buckwheat-vermicelli, as well as the rice and bean-jam cake called Manju, must not be sold. This year, too, bean curd must not be manufactured. With regard to the cultivation of the fields this year, the greatest care must be taken, and the Commissioners must insist on this fact being understood by every village in their jurisdiction.

This year matters are particularly urgent. But peasants are not to be overworked in useless ways. And to those who do not appreciate working for the Government a bill had better be given and the affair settled thus. Things must be arranged so that the peasants are not unduly harassed.

As to the peasants' food. They must eat mixed grain. They certainly must not eat much rice. This must be made quite clear to them.

Collecting any kind of subscription and the selling of relishes are forbidden in villages.

As heretofore the law allows only a Shoya or Headman to wear coarse silk or pongee, and the ordinary farmer linen and cotton. But in addition no cravats are to be worn.

Should there be any worthless farmers who don't cultivate their land properly, and so fail to pay their tax, they shall be deprived of their holdings.

Should any farmer be single-handed or in difficulties, then the rest of he village shall come to his assistance and help him with his tillage so that he may be able to pay his taxes.

Expenditure on religious festivals and Buddhism shall be in accordance with one's position.

Any combination of persons, for whatever purpose, shall be unlawful.

Money spent on houses must be in proportion to the means of the owner, and no conspicuous buildings may be erected.

No traveller shall lodge even for a night in any place other than a public inn unless information be first given to the headman, the guild chief, and other members of the guild of the persons concerned.

And no innkeeper shall receive anyone of suspicious character.

No farmer or shoya may dye any of his clothes red or pink. Moreover, whatever be the colors he must not dye them in patterns.

Peasants must not go to the towns and drink sake immoderately.

Farmers must build houses strictly in accordance with their means, but townsmen may build what the Jito (land-steward) or Daikwan (District Commissioner) see fit to allow.

No subscription lists for any purpose shall be circulated in the villages before taxes are paid.

People who come from elsewhere and do not engage in cultivating the land shall not be allowed in any village.

If farmers who are well-to-do can buy land they may become more wealthy still, while those who sell it will naturally become less so; therefore it is forbidden that land be sold for all time.

The Daikwan must encourage the poor and unsuccessful farmers to work harder, and if necessary loan them foodstuffs and so help them to produce.

As for those who are guilty of small delinquencies, the penalties imposed shall be repairing the riverbanks, planting trees and bamboos, and doing other repairs to constructions for the benefit of their locality. Serious offences shall be punished with imprisonment or death.

Inspectors will be sent round the villages so that Daikwans who are negligent are likely to have their defects discovered, and had better see to it that they do their duty with diligence.

When water is sprinkled in the streets care must be taken that it is not sprinkled on the passers-by.

SHINTO AND BUDDHISM IN THE EIGHTEENTH CENTURY

An illuminating discussion of the relations between Buddhist teaching and Shinto and their bearing on the problems of the ordinary man is one found in a popular didactic work entitled *The Bag of Information for Citizens,* published rather over a hundred years after the death of Ieyasu in the days of Yoshimune the philosopher Shogun, by some considered the greatest of his successors, dated 1742. It runs thus:

"A man asked a certain scholar, 'Do you think it is well to assume the existence of such places as Heaven or Hell or not?' 'I think it may be better to assume it,' was the answer, 'for when you come to consider the matter, townspeople and those below them in station are liable to bad impulses, and even if a saint were to appear on earth he would hardly be able to instruct such a numerous crowd in the right way. The thing is to correct these people, not to instruct them. This degenerate age is full of people with evil desires, liable to pride and ostentation, so it is better to let them think there is a Hell waiting for them.'

"When of old Prince Shotoku brought the Buddhist philosophy into our country, was it not to discipline the people with fear of the future and so maintain order in the realm and assist the Shinto cult? And in his famous Constitution, too, he spoke of Buddhism as an alien supporter of the Imperial Way. And the Imperial Way is nothing but Shinto or the Way of the Deities.

"Anyhow, if we give definite instruction about the future, which is actually quite unknowable, the stupid farmers and tradespeople will naturally be inspired with fear. And if this fear is always maintained among the population generally it will be the foundation of keeping peace and order in the Empire. That is why I should like to be able to think there are a lot of people who believe Heaven and Hell really exist.

"Unfortunately, however, the clergy nowadays vie with one another in preaching a lot of sophisticated highbrow stuff to these peasants and tradesmen, and tell them there is no Heaven and Hell, so that even the women and children have come to regard these places as no more than a joke, and I imagine almost nobody believes in them. This does not seem to be in accordance with Shotoku Taishi's views of supporting the Monarchical Principle, and we are told in the *Taiheiki* and elsewhere that in degenerate times many hindrances to this principle are likely to appear.

"Still, it is quite clear that even tradesmen and farmers, if they are a bit educated, have no reason to do unethical things even if they don't believe in Heaven and Hell or to worry themselves much if they do. And the prospect of leading an easy existence in Heaven won't make much appeal to them, so it really does not matter whether they believe in it or not.

"There is a story about a samurai who was dying, and to whose bed a monk came and said, 'You have done good service in this life, and so without question you will go to Paradise, so set your mind at ease.'

" 'And what kind of place is Paradise?' said the samurai.

" 'It is a land where there is neither heat nor cold, and where food and drink can be got for the asking, a place of nothing but comfort and happiness.' 'Hm,' returned the samurai, 'that kind of place is very suitable for Court nobles, ladies-in-waiting, women, children, and invalids, but I was born in a warrior family accustomed to brave the rain and the cold and to sleep on the ground with my head on a stone. Thus I have lived all my days so that I could render loyal service to my lord and destroy his enemies, and now I have come to die do you think I can change my nature? A beastly sort of place, I consider your Paradise.'

"There was also a merchant who asked a monk whether when a man dies he is born again in another state. The monk told him he had no doubt of it. 'Well, then, when I die how shall I be reborn?' asked the merchant. 'It is true you don't seem to know much about Buddhism,' replied the monk, 'but you have been honest and charitable in your life so you may well be reborn as the greatest kind of merchant or else as a member of the military class.'

" 'That is a very unpleasant outlook,' observed the other, 'for with the amount of property I now have and the number of relatives I possess and the anxiety as to whether my descendants will maintain our prosperity in the future I have enough to worry me as it is, so whatever should I do if I had twice as much to look after? As to being reborn a samurai that would be much worse. Always busy thinking how he can serve his lord, forever fussing about his honor and reputation, and only good at striking dignified attitudes. What a life! I had sooner be a mere wardsman. It is indeed sad to think that this kind of rebirth is what you are liable to get for living a virtuous life. It is the sort of kindness that is deadly.' So you see the prospect of Heaven and Hell is not likely to influence people like this. Samurai and wardsmen are quite different. According to many, it is better to be reborn a stork and live a thousand years than to be like Akechi Mitsuhide and be Shogun for only three days."

THE CEREMONY OF INVESTITURE OF THE SHOGUN. FROM THE TOKUGAWA JIKKI

ON the second day of the twelfth month of 1603 the appointment of Ieyasu to the office of Shogun was announced and a Military Council was held in the palace. The Senior Courtier was the Dainagon Hirohashi Kanekatsu, and the Commissioner the Sachuben Karasu-Maru Mitsuhiro, while the Secretary was Ogawa-Bojo Toshiaki. When the Council was ended the Saisho Kajuji proceeded to Fushimi castle as Imperial Envoy. The Envoy and the Commissioner and the courtiers of highest rank rode in carriages, and the secretaries and lower officials in sedans. All wore full Court dress. Those of the highest rank alighted from their carriages in front of the inner porch of the castle, while the rest got down at the third gate.

Then after his body had been fortified by Tsuchi-Mikado Hisazumi, Chief of the Court Astrologers, Ieyasu proceeded to the southern hall of the castle precisely at noon, clad in a hitatare of scarlet, while all the high military officials who attended on him also wore hitatare and the lower samurai their mantles of ceremony. He was received by the Imperial Envoy, and the courtiers tendered their congratulations to him on his appointment.

Then the Senior Courtier, the Commissioner, and the Secretaries proceeded to the middle dais while the Herald, Nakahara Shokuzen, went out into the courtyard, and standing at the foot of the front steps made obeisance, and striking his clappers twice, made proclamation of the appointment, and after another obeisance retired.

Then the two courtiers, Hirohashi and Kajuji, took their seats to the right and left of the second hall on the upper dais, while the Commissioner and the Secretaries sat on the right and left sides of the third hall. Meanwhile, Mibu Kwammu Takaaki was stationed in waiting at the wide verandah, and the Vice-Envoy, Sakon-no-Shogen Nakahara Noritada, brought the Edict of Appointment as Sei-i Tai Shogun in a casket from the narrow verandah and handed it to him, whereupon he in turn brought it and delivered it to Ozawa Shosho Motoyasu, who laid it at the left hand of Ieyasu's seat. He then took away the casket and retired with it to an inner apartment, where Nagai Ukon-daiyu Naokatsu received it, placed two bags of gold dust in it, and returned it to Motoyasu. He took it to Mibu, who made an obeisance and retired with it.

Then the Edict of Appointment as Clan Chief of the Minamoto was brought forward in the same way by Oshikoji Daigeki Morau, received by

Motoyasu, and laid before the Shogun. The casket that contained this was also given back to Motoyasu and taken by him into the inner chamber, where Nagai put into it one bag of gold dust, which was returned by Motoyasu to Oshikoji, who received it with an obeisance and retired in his turn.

Then the Edict of Appointment as Uji Choja was presented by Mibu and that of appointment to be Udaijin by Oshikoji. Then followed the Imperial Permission to ride in an ox-carriage, also presented by Daigeki, and then the Privilege of a Special Guard of Honor and of the Baton of Supreme Command. After this came the patent of the office of Lord Warden of the Imperial Academies of Junna and Shogaku. And on each occasion the casket containing these documents was borne into the castle and a bag of gold dust placed in it.

The Commissioner and the Secretaries then retired. Motoyasu then proclaimed that the Envoy and the Senior Courtier would present the certificate of the pedigree of the Official Sword. This was then brought in by the Secretaries and lower officers, who took up their position in the third hall of the castle and did obeisance in the wide verandah, as did also the officials of lower rank. Then Daigeki brought the Sword into the third hall and made obeisance in the wide verandah outside. The officials did not present the Sword, but made obeisance in the wide verandah and proceeded to retire.

Then Ukondaiyu Nagakatsu and Nishio Tango-no-kami Tadanaga presented 100 ryo of gold to the Senior Courtier, Hirohashi Kenekatsu, with a horse and gold-mounted saddle with the Shogun's crest, while to the Commissioner Mitsuhiro was given 50 ryo of gold and a horse and saddle, after which the Shogun retired. To all the other lesser officials who had attended a present of 500 hiki of money each was made.

Now, though this important office of Barbarian-quelling General had its beginning with the Imperial Prince, Yamato-take-no-mikoto, yet Bunya-no-Wadamaro, Saka-no-ue no Tamura Maro and others were all summoned to the Imperial Palace to receive their appointments. The sending of an Imperial Envoy to the Bakufu to confer the commission there began with the Udaisho Yoritomo of Kamakura. In his case the Envoy was received at the shrine of Hachiman at Tsurugaoka by his three great vassals, Miura Yoshizumi, Hiki Yoshikazu, and Wada Munezane, with ten retainers in full armor, and they received the Edict of Appointment, and from them it was accepted by the Shogun in the western corridor of his mansion.

This, then, was the origin of the ceremony, and it was so continued by the Ashikaga house, except that during the rule of the first three Shoguns of this family, Takauji, Yoshinori, and Yoshimitsu, there was civil war, so that there was no time to consider etiquette or ceremony until the time of Yoshimochi, the fourth of the line. And again in the Onin period of civil war (1467–9), the Shogunate was in complete disorder, and no investiture could be held. So that this investiture of Ieyasu was a restoration of what had been interrupted, and a revival of what had been practically discontinued. And the proceedings of the Kamakura and Muromachi periods were reviewed and revised to make the ceremony suitable for the present generation. Neither was this first ceremony repeated unaltered, but was improved with each succeeding generation until it reached its final form in the early eighteenth century.

After the ceremony the Envoy and other Court officials were entertained at a banquet at which Gien, the Imperial Abbot of the Daigo Sambo-in Monastery, officiated. This also was according to the precedent of the Muromachi period.

THE MAXIMS OF IEYASU

Man's life is like going a long journey under a heavy burden: one must not hurry.

If you regard discomfort as a normal condition you are not likely to be troubled by want.

When ambition arises in your mind consider the days of your adversity.

Patience is the foundation of security and long life: consider anger as an enemy.

He who only knows victory and doesn't know defeat will fare badly.

Blame yourself: don't blame others.

The insufficient is better than the superfluous.

THE TOKUGAWA SHOGUNS

(Figures in brackets are Age at Accession, Duration of Office, and Age at Death)

	Father.	Mother.	Wife.	Posthumous Title.	Mausoleum.	Born.	Succeeded.	Retired.	Died.
1. IEYASU	Matsudaira Hirotada	Daughter of Mizuno Tadamasa (Denzuin)	Sister of Toyotomi Hideyoshi (Nammeiin)	Tōshōgu	Nikko	1542	1603 (61)	1605 (2)	1616 (74)
2. HIDETADA	Ieyasu	Daughter of Mizuno Tadamoto* (Hōdaiin)	Daughter of Asai Nagamasa (Sōgenin)	Daitokuin	Shiba	1579	1605 (26)	1623 (18)	1632 (53)
3. IEMITSU	Hidetada	Sōgenin	Daughter of Takatsukasa	Taiyuin	Nikko	1604	1623 (19)	(28)	1654 (47)
4. IETSUNA	Iemitsu	Sister of Masuyama Masatoshi	Sister of Prince Fushimi Sadakiyo	Genyuin	Ueno	1641	1651 (10)	(29)	1680 (39)
5. TSUNAYOSHI	Iemitsu	Daughter of Honjo Munemasa (Keishōin)	Daughter of Takatsukasa Nobufusa	Jokenin	Ueno	1646	1680 (34)	(29)	1709 (63)
6. IENOBU	Tsunashige Lord of Kofu	Daughter of Tanaka Toshimichi (Chōshōin)	Daughter of Konoe Motohiro	Bunshōin	Shiba	1662	1709 (47)	(3)	1712 (50)
7. IETSUGU	Ienobu	Sister of Katsuta Norinari (Gekkōin)	Imperial Princess Kichiko, daughter of Emp. Reigen (Jōrinin)	Yushōin	Shiba	1709	1712 (3)	(3)	1716 (7)

						Born			Died
8. YOSHIMUNE	Mitsusada Lord of Kii	Daughter of Kose Toshikiyo	Daughter of Prince Fushimi Sadanori	Yutokuin	Ueno	1684	1716 (32)	1745 (29)	1751 (67)
9. IESHIGE	Yoshimune	Daughter of Okubo Tadanao	Daughter of Prince Fushimi Kuninaga	Junshinin	Shiba	1711	1745 (34)	1760 (15)	1761 (50)
10. IEHARU	Ieshige	Daughter of Umedani Michieda	Daughter of Prince Kanin	Shimmeiin	Ueno	1737	1760 (23)	(23)	1686 (50)
11. IENARI	Hitotsubashi Harunari	Daughter of Iwamoto Masatoshi	Daughter of Konoe Tsunehiro	Bunkyōin	Ueno	1773	1786 (13)	1837 (51)	1841 (68)
12. IEYOSHI	Ienari	Daughter of Osada Masakatsu	Daughter of Prince Arisugawa	Shintokuin	Shiba	1793	1837 (44)	(17)	1853 (60)
13. IESADA	Ieyoshi	Daughter of Atobe Masayoshi	(1) Daughter of Takatsukasa Masamichi (2) Daughter of Ichijo Tadayoshi (3) Daughter of Shimazu Nariyoshi	Onkyōin	Ueno	1824	1853 (29)	(5)	1858 (34)
14. IEMOCHI	Nariyuki Lord of Kii	Daughter of Matsudaira Roku-oemon	Imperial Princess Tomoko	Shotokuin	Shiba	1846	1858 (12)	(8)	1866 (20)
15. YOSHINOBU	Nariaki Lord of Mito	Daughter of Prince Arisugawa	?	?		1837*	1866 (29)	1868 (2)	1903 (76)

* So the *Japanese Biographical Dictionary*.

BIBLIOGRAPHY

Azuchi Momoyama Jidai Shiron. Essays on the Azuchi and Momoyama Periods. Japan Historical and Geographical Society.

Bungaku ni arawaretaru Waga Kokumin Shiso. The National Ideals as revealed in our Literature. Tsuda Sokichi.

Chado Bidan. Kumata Ijo.

The Japanese Tea Ceremony: Cha-no-yu. Sadler, A. L.

Dai Nihon Jimmei Jisho. Biographical Dictionary of Japan.

Dai Nihon Zenshi. History of Japan. Omori Kingoro.

De Reis van Mahu en De Cordes door de straat van Magalhaes. Wieder, F. C.

Edo Jidai Shiron. Essays on the Edo Period. Japan Historical and Geographical Society.

Edo Kaikō Roku. Antiquities of Edo. Kumata Ijo.

Hankampu. History of the Feudal Clans. Arai Hakuseki.

History of Japan. Murdoch, J.

History of the Japanese People. Brinkley, F.

Honami Ko-etsu. Ko-etsu Society.

Ishida Mitsunari. Oike Yoshio.

Ishida Mitsunari. Watanabe Yosuke.

Japan. A Short Cultural History. Sansom, G. B.

Kinsei Nihon Kokuminshi. History of the Japanese People in Modern Times. Tokutomi Sōhō.

Kokushi Dai Jiten. Dictionary of Japanese History.

Kuroda Josui. Count Kaneko.

Kuroda Josui. Fukumoto Makoto.

Mikawa Fudoki. Annals of Mikawa.

Nihon Joseishi. History of Japanese Women.

Nihon Minkashi. History of the Japanese Dwelling House. Fujita, M.

O-Edo. The City of Edo. Edo Research Society.

Taikoki. Annals of Hideyoshi.

Takeda Shingen. Ichinohe Ōgai.

Tokugawa Ieyasu. Dōmeki Chiren.

Tokugawa Ieyasu. Yamaji Aizan.

Tokugawa Jidai Tsushi. History of the Tokugawa Era. Ibara Gi.

Tokugawa Jikki. Annals of the Tokugawa House.

Tokugawa Sambyakunenshi. Record of the Three Centuries of the Tokugawas. Nagata Genjiro.

Tōshōkō Den. Life of Ieyasu. Nakamura Toshiya.

Transactions of the Asiatic Society of Japan.

Transactions of the Japan Society of London.

Uesugi Kenshin. Naito Ryu-ū.

INDEX